ENTREPRENEUR'S LAUNCHPAD
Basics to Brilliance

NEW AGE ENTREPRENEURSHIP

NEP 2020 Aligned

Dr Poornima Charantimath

ISBN 979-8-89610-357-8

This Book is Lovingly Dedicated to My Family

My Husband, Manoj; Son, Amit; Daughter-in-law, Chandana

Granddaughter, Nayonika

Contents

Foreword

In the vast canvas of global economies, businesses are the vital strands that bind creativity, advancement, and expansion. The path from a fledgling idea to a thriving organization is nothing short of amazing in the constantly changing business world. The road to entrepreneurship is paved with creativity, perseverance, and a clear vision. **"Entrepreneur's Launchpad: Basics to Brilliance",** is more than just a book; it's a beacon of wisdom for would-be business owners, providing the skills and information needed to turn dreams into reality. It is a call to action and a guide for starting from scratch and creating long-lasting, significant businesses.

This book serves as a beacon of insight, illuminating the diverse facets of entrepreneurship—from the initial spark of an idea to the intricate details of building and sustaining a successful business. It embraces the spirit of creativity and the necessity of strategic planning, encouraging readers to dream big while grounding their visions in pragmatic steps.

As you explore the pages, you will discover the collective knowledge of seasoned business owners, influential people, and sector specialists. Their success, encounters, and activities are interwoven into a complex fabric that provides motivation and useful advice. The **"Entrepreneur's Launchpad"** gives you the necessary skills and mindset to handle the opportunities and challenges of the entrepreneurial world, regardless of whether you're just starting or looking to improve your existing business.

You will learn as you go along that starting an enterprise is about more than just building a company; it's also about influencing futures, promoting economic growth, and leaving a lasting impression. This book inspires you to have great dreams, take deliberate action, and face obstacles head-on. Being an entrepreneur is not a solo endeavour. It is a team effort that benefits greatly from cooperation, coaching, and a caring environment. This book encourages the feeling of community by giving potential business owners a forum to interact, share knowledge, and develop as a group.

I encourage you to embark on this adventure with an open mind and a strong will. As you travel the thrilling journey of entrepreneurship, let **"Entrepreneur's Launchpad"**, be your guide, mentor, and inspiration. I hope it gives you the courage, tenacity, and vision to start your business.

My congratulations go out to **Dr. Poornima M. Charantimath**, author of "Entrepreneur's Launchpad"! Her outstanding accomplishments demonstrate her commitment, wisdom, and enthusiasm for entrepreneurship.

Her work enables people to realize their ambitions and paves the way to successful entrepreneurship. Many readers will surely be greatly impacted by the breadth of your expertise, helpful suggestions, and real-world examples.

Wishing you continued success and recognition for this outstanding contribution to the world of business literature.

Raman Gujral
Director,
Department of Projects-Corporate.
Regional Director, Southern Regional Office, Bengaluru
Entrepreneurship Development Institute of India (EDII)
Southern Regional Office, Richmond Town, Bengaluru, Karnataka
560025
Email: srob@ediindia.org

Recommendations

"The book **'Entrepreneur's Launchpad: Basics to Brilliance'** is an essential guide for developing an entrepreneurial mindset. It effectively blends theory with practical applications to help individuals thrive in a Volatile, Uncertain, Complex, and Ambiguous (VUCA) world, influenced by Industry 5.0 and the United Nations' Sustainable Development Goals (SDGs). Focusing on experiential learning and innovative tools, this book empowers professionals across various fields to harness their creativity, innovation, and emotional intelligence. It is a roadmap for career planning, startup creation, and advancing sustainable development. Placement and Entrepreneurship Development (ED) cells in Higher Education Institutions (HEIs) will find this book particularly valuable for enhancing employability and promoting entrepreneurial initiatives among students. I highly recommend this book."

Dr. N A Charantimath
Chartered Accountant
Chairman, KES's IEMS B-School, Hubballi, Karnataka, India

"There are many books on entrepreneurship, but *'Entrepreneur's Launchpad: Basics to Brilliance'*, stands out for its practical insights. **Dr. Poornima** shares her extensive experience in a do-it-yourself format with case studies, activities, and a self-study approach. This comprehensive guide addresses modern needs, especially in technology and AI. I highly recommend it as a 'must-read and apply' for aspiring and early-stage entrepreneurs."

Dr Mita Dixit
Director & Family Business Advisor. Equations Advisors Pvt., Ltd.
Mumbai, Maharashtra, India

"The book titled *Entrepreneur's Launchpad: Basics to Brilliance*, clearly focuses on experiential learning and addresses the need for Entrepreneurship Development Programs (EDPs) of incubation centres housed in higher education institutions' distinguishing it as a unique resource. It doesn't merely provide theoretical knowledge but equips learners with tools to practice and refine their entrepreneurial skills. The six-chapter framework logically builds a learner's journey, covering mindset, skills, and practical implementation. The mapped outcomes are well-defined, measurable, and aligned with Bloom's taxonomy".

Dr M G Anantha Prasad
CEO, Atal Incubation Centre, Jyothy Institute of Technology Foundation
Bangalore, India

"We live in a dynamic world, and with the emergence of advanced technologies, the nature of our jobs is changing. It is essential to evaluate the entrepreneur within us. The book *Entrepreneur's Launch pad: Basics to Brilliance* is a valuable resource that will help you understand the fundamentals and guide you in thriving during challenging times."

Ramchandra Prabhu Salgaonkar
Managing Partner, Amaze Warriors Consulting, Austria.
Adjunct Faculty, Goa Institute of Management, Goa, India

"I highly recommend *Entrepreneur's Launchpad: Basics to Brilliance*, as a must-read for aspiring entrepreneurs and leaders. This insightful and practical guide empowers readers with the tools, mindset, creativity, and innovation essential to navigate the challenges of entrepreneurship in a dynamic world. A transformative resource for personal and professional growth!"

Prof. Bholanath Dutta
Founder & President: *MTC Global*
Chairman, Global Entrepreneurs Grid (GEG), Bangalore, India

Preface

The ability to cultivate an entrepreneurial mindset is a universal necessity. Students across all academic disciplines, potential entrepreneurs, startups, professionals, and aspiring to enhance their innovative and leadership capabilities benefit immensely from embracing an entrepreneurial mindset. Whether your ambitions lie in future employment, self-employment, or entrepreneurship, the curriculum designed in **"Entrepreneur's Launchpad: Basics to Brilliance"**, offers a powerful toolkit for navigating new-age leadership.

We live in a world defined by Volatility, Uncertainty, Complexity, and Ambiguity (VUCA), where Industry 5.0 and the Sustainable Development Goals (SDGs) established by the United Nations have reshaped how we learn, work, and contribute to society. A leader with an entrepreneurial mindset is pivotal to driving creative problem-solving, fostering innovation, addressing global challenges, and advancing economic, social, and environmental sustainability.

In this landscape, there has never been a more pressing need for entrepreneurial thinking. Government agencies, Non-Governmental Organisations (NGOs), Higher Education Institutions (HEIs), Incubation centers, and Business accelerators are at the forefront of this transformation, reshaping educational experiences to create meaningful impacts in their local ecosystems and society at large. This book is a testament to that effort, serving as a guide for individuals seeking to achieve sustainable development through entrepreneurial action.

Uniqueness of the Book

"Entrepreneur's Launchpad: Basics to Brilliance", is the culmination of extensive research and insights aimed at addressing the evolving needs of education and training. Comprising six thoughtfully crafted chapters—Entrepreneurial Mindset, Emotional Intelligence, Creativity, Innovation, Business Plan, and Building and Growing a Startup. This book offers a practical and comprehensive approach to developing entrepreneurial skills through real-life scenarios, integrating contextual applications for immediate relevance.

The book greatly enhances employability skills by focusing on the development of an entrepreneurial mindset, emotional intelligence, creativity, and innovation—competencies that are highly valued in various industries. Its practical approach includes activities and experiential learning that help students cultivate problem-solving abilities, critical thinking, logical reasoning, and business acumen. These skills are essential for success in dynamic job markets.

Salient Features

- **Global Growth Mindset:** Develop a growth mindset with a global perspective.
- **Entrepreneurial Competencies**: Develop essential skills for success in dynamic environments.
- **SWOT and KASH Models**: A structured approach to achieving career goals.
- **Emotional Intelligence**: Harness your potential to lead effectively.
- **Creativity and Innovation**: Empowerment to discover and seize business opportunities through creativity and innovation.
- **Startup Foundations:** Craft a lean business canvas model, business plan, and strategies for growth.

Pedagogical Tools: Learning objectives, Key takeaways, Key terms, Quizzes, Exercises, Activities, Situation analysis, Simulation Games, Role

Plays, Self-study boxes, AI tools, Projects, Case studies, Self-assessment questions, and References.

Course Outcomes

Upon completing this book, readers will be able to:

a. Utilize entrepreneurial skills and apply the effectuation principles to seize opportunities while minimizing risks in entrepreneurial ventures.
b. Formulate career goals using SWOT and the KASH model.
c. Develop emotional intelligence for leadership.
d. Apply creative problem-solving and innovation tools to tackle challenges and identify opportunities.
e. Create and implement a business plan for a startup and develop strategies to grow your project.

This workbook is your launchpad to endless possibilities. Whether you are a student, an aspiring entrepreneur, a startup, or a professional, this book is a valuable resource for fostering talent and innovation. So, open your mind, embrace curiosity, and take the first step toward creating a brighter, more sustainable future!

Chapter 1

Entrepreneurial Mindset

Ratan Tata: Leader with Integrity and Compassion

Ratan Tata (28th Dec 1937- 8th Oct 2024) was an Indian industrialist, philanthropist, and former chairman of Tata Sons, the holding company of the Tata Group. His tenure was a remarkable example of visionary leadership and strategic transformation, leaving an indelible mark on the global business landscape.

A member of the prominent Tata family, he was educated at Cornell University. He completed the Advanced Management Programme at Harvard Business School in 1975. He worked in various Tata Group businesses. He became chairman of Tata Industries and later succeeded his uncle, J.R.D. Tata, as chairman of the Tata Group in 1991.

Tata aggressively expanded the conglomerate, focusing on globalizing its businesses. In 2000, the group acquired Tetley Tea for $431.3 million, and in 2004, it purchased the truck-manufacturing operations of Daewoo Motors for $102 million. In 2007, Tata Steel completed the biggest corporate takeover by an Indian company by acquiring Corus Group for $11.3 billion.

In 2008, Tata Motors purchased Jaguar and Land Rover from Ford for $2.3 billion, the largest acquisition by an Indian automotive firm. The following year, Tata Motors launched the Tata Nano, a tiny, affordable car aimed at middle- and lower-income consumers in India and abroad. Ratan Tata retired as chairman of the Tata Group in 2012, briefly served as interim chairman in 2016, and then retired again in 2017.

Established in 1919 by Ratan Tata, the trust works towards the well-being of the underprivileged in various sectors. Ratan Tata was the Chairman of the Sir Ratan Tata Trust and Allied Trusts, and the Sir Dorabji Tata Trust and the Allied Trusts. He was the Chairman of the Council of Management of the Tata Institute of Fundamental Research. He also served on the board of trustees of Cornell University and the University of Southern California.

In 2000, Ratan Tata received the Padma Bhushan, one of India's most distinguished civilian awards. Mr. Ratan N Tata, Chairman of Tata Trusts, has been conferred with the prestigious KISS Humanitarian Award 2021, in recognition of his unwavering commitment to philanthropic activities. He has also received honorary doctorates from several universities in India and overseas. Ratan Tata is remembered as a business titan and compassionate leader who left a legacy and lasting impact on the lives of millions.

Learning Objectives

1. Discuss the Significance of a Global Mindset for 21st Century
2. Differentiate Fixed Mindset and Growth Mindset and identify the Importance of Growth Mindset
3. Identify the Importance of an Entrepreneurial Mindset for a Sustainable Future.
4. Assess your Entrepreneurial Competencies, Choose Entrepreneurship as a Career and Demonstrate Effectuation

5. Plan Personnel Finance
6. Apply the SWOT Framework and KASH Box to Formulate SMART Goals
7. Use AI Tools for Career Planning and Progression

"Your mind is a powerful thing. When you fill it with positive thoughts, your life will start to change".

Introduction

Leadership is crucial as it provides vision, direction, and motivation, driving individuals and teams toward common goals. It is characterized by a focus on growth, resilience, and the ability to inspire and influence others towards achieving common goals. It involves a commitment to continuous learning, self-awareness, and the ability to adapt to changing circumstances. Leaders with this mindset prioritize ethical behavior, effective communication, and the development of their team members. They view challenges as opportunities for growth, maintain a positive and proactive attitude, and strive to create a collaborative and supportive environment. Ultimately, a leadership mindset is about fostering a vision, empowering others, and driving collective success.

Industry 5.0 and 21st Century Skills

Industry 4.0, also known as the Fourth Industrial Revolution, represents the digitalization of manufacturing. Meanwhile, 21st century skills refer to the skills relevant to this era and are closely associated with Education 4.0, which aims to prepare students for the demands of Industry 4.0. While companies and industries are still amid Industry 4.0, the next industrial revolution, Industry 5.0, is already underway. Industry 5.0, therefore, marks a shift towards a more collaborative, responsible, and human-focused industrial paradigm, addressing not only technological advancements but also the social and environmental impacts of production.

The concept of Industry 5.0 represents the next evolutionary phase in industrial development, expanding upon the principles of Industry 4.0 by embracing a more human-centered and sustainable approach. While Industry 4.0 prioritizes intelligent automation, digitalization, and interconnectedness facilitated by technologies such as AI, IoT, and big data, Industry 5.0 places emphasis on fostering collaboration between humans and machines to establish more tailored, efficient, and environmentally conscious production systems. Industry 5.0 involves the integration of robots and intelligent machines working alongside individuals, with a focus on enhanced resilience and sustainability objectives. While Industry 4.0 revolves around technologies like the Internet of Things and big data, Industry 5.0 aims to reintegrate human, environmental, and social considerations into the framework.

Industry 5.0 in education involves the collaboration between technology, educators, and students to improve the efficiency and effectiveness of teaching and learning. These technologies have the potential to transform the way students learn and teachers teach, shaping the vision for the future of education known as Education 5.0. This concept aims to use new technologies and teaching methods to prepare students for the challenges. Industry 5.0 is changing how we work, live, play, and learn. It brings the principles of Industry 4.0 a step further into automation, connected devices, AI systems, robotics, and human-machine collaboration.

The driving factor of Industry 4.0 was the digitalization of information, which allowed people to access and share data in new ways. Industry 5.0 is the next step in this evolution, where we see an exponential increase in connectivity between people, machines, and data that unlocks previously untapped value.

Education 5.0 is an emerging concept that parallels the evolution of industrial revolutions, aligning educational practices with the needs of Industry 5.0. It envisions an education system that is human-centric, technology-enhanced, sustainable, and future-ready, aimed at producing learners who are adaptable, innovative, and socially responsible. The workforce of Industry 5.0 is expected to possess a unique blend of technical skills, creativity, problem-solving abilities, and adaptability. Continuous learning and upskilling will be essential.

21st Century skills are essential for success in today's Industry. They go beyond traditional academic knowledge and focus on preparing individuals for lifelong learning and success in a complex, ever-changing world. These skills are critical for navigating the globalized economy, technological advancements, and complex social environments. They foster adaptability and prepare people to face emerging challenges and seize new opportunities in the workforce and society. Here are 21st century skills:

1. **Critical Thinking** – The ability to analyze, evaluate, and form judgments logically and rationally.
2. **Creativity** – The capacity to generate new ideas, think outside the box, and innovate.
3. **Collaboration** – Working effectively with others, contributing to a team, and cooperating across diverse groups.
4. **Communication** – The ability to express ideas clearly and effectively, both verbally and in writing, as well as active listening.
5. **Curiosity** – A strong desire to learn, explore, and ask questions to deepen understanding.
6. **Cultural Awareness** – Understanding and respecting different cultures, perspectives, and global diversity.
7. **Computational Thinking** – Approaching problems in a structured and logical way, often used in technology and programming.
8. **Citizenship (Global/Local)** – Being an informed, responsible, and active member of society, including awareness of social, environmental, and political issues.
9. **Character** – Personal qualities like integrity, resilience, and ethical behavior in various situations.
10. **Cyber Literacy** – Knowledge and skills related to safe, responsible, and ethical use of technology and the internet.

A Journey to Skill Country: A Traveler's Tale

As the sun rose over the horizon, illuminating the vibrant landscapes of Skill Country, a traveler named Maya embarked on a quest to explore the ten essential 21st-century skills. With her backpack filled with curiosity and excitement, she was ready to immerse herself in a world where these skills were not just taught but lived.

Day 1: Creativity in the Artisan Village: Maya's first stop was the artisan village, where creativity thrived. She met skilled artisans crafting stunning pieces of art from recycled materials. Inspired, Maya joined a workshop where she experimented with different mediums, blending traditional techniques with modern ideas. She discovered that creativity was not just about making art, but also about thinking outside the box to solve problems.

Day 2: Critical Thinking at the Innovation Hub: Maya then visited the innovation hub, which was bustling with critical thinkers brainstorming solutions for global challenges. While there, she took part in a debate about climate change. This experience sharpened her critical thinking skills as she evaluated different perspectives and formulated well-reasoned arguments. Maya learned that asking the right questions was just as important as finding the answers.

Day 3: Collaboration in the Community Garden: In the community garden, Maya encountered diverse groups working together to grow sustainable crops. She joined a team that was tasked with planning the layout of the garden. Through collaboration, they learned to respect different viewpoints and leverage each member's strengths. Maya realized that teamwork was essential for achieving shared goals.

Day 4: Communication at the Storytellers' Camp: Maya traveled to the storyteller's camp, where she engaged with master storytellers from different cultures. They shared tales that transcended borders and connected hearts. Maya participated in a workshop that honed her verbal and non-verbal communication skills. She left the camp with the understanding that effective communication is about more than just words; it's about connecting with people.

Day 5: Curiosity at the Explorers' Academy: The Explorers' Academy was a sanctuary for inquisitive minds. Maya set out on a treasure hunt, decoding clues that led her to historical artifacts. Each discovery ignited her curiosity and love for learning. She discovered that nurturing a sense of wonder fosters innovation and personal growth.

Day 6: Cultural Awareness at the Global Village: In the global village, Maya took part in cultural exchange programs, where she learned about various traditions and values. Engaging with people from diverse backgrounds broadened her worldview. Maya realized that cultural awareness nurtures empathy and strengthens communities.

Day 7: Computational Thinking in the Tech Lab: During her time at the Tech Lab, Maya learned about computational thinking, coding, and robotics. She worked with her peers to develop a simple game, learning to break down complex problems into smaller, manageable parts. This experience gave her the skills to navigate the digital world with confidence.

Day 8: Citizenship in the Civic Center: Maya's visit to the civic center was an enlightening experience. She gained valuable knowledge about civic responsibility and community service during her time there. Volunteering at a local shelter for a clean-up drive provided her with a deeper understanding of the significance of active citizenship. She also learned about the Sustainable Development Goals (SDGs). This experience made Maya appreciate the importance of contributing positively to society and advocating for change as a responsible citizen.

Day 9: Character at the Resilience Retreat: At the Resilience Retreat, Maya participated in activities for pooling resources for the shortage of water in drought-affected areas that challenged her to step outside her comfort zone. She learned the value of integrity, perseverance, and empathy. These experiences reinforced her character, teaching her that true strength lies in facing challenges with a positive attitude.

Day 10: Cyber Literacy in the Digital Sphere: Maya's final destination was the digital sphere, where she explored the importance of cybersecurity and digital ethics. Workshops on safe online practices and critical evaluation of information sources enhanced her cyber literacy. She left with the understanding that being digitally literate is crucial in today's interconnected world.

Takeaways from the Journey

As Maya concluded her journey through skill country, she reflected on the ten skills she had acquired. Each skill is interlinked, forming a holistic framework for personal and professional development. Maya realized that in the 21st century, success hinges not only on academic knowledge but also on the following essential skills.

1. **Creativity** fosters innovation.
2. **Critical Thinking** enables informed decisions.
3. **Collaboration** drives collective success.
4. **Communication** builds bridges across cultures.
5. **Curiosity** ignites lifelong learning.
6. **Cultural Awareness** promotes empathy.
7. **Computational Thinking** empowers problem-solving in a digital age.
8. **Citizenship** encourages community engagement.
9. **Character** instills resilience and integrity.
10. **Cyber Literacy** safeguards against digital risks.

Maya returned home not just as a traveler but as an empowered individual ready to make a meaningful impact in her community and beyond, armed with the skills needed to thrive in the 21st century.

Global Mindset

The core of our thoughts, emotions, and consciousness is the mind. The term "mindset" describes a person's pre-existing attitudes, convictions, and conceptual framework. Their perception, actions, and reactions to different circumstances or obstacles that influence their decisions are shaped by their mindset.

Global Mindset is the ability to absorb information, traditions, and cultural norms from around the world and be able to conceptualize how to make an impact in all environments. A global mindset describes the ability to appreciate and learn different traditions and cultures worldwide, and to create ideas to impact all environments positively. A global mindset is important as it enhances customer service and encourages cultural awareness. Cultivating a global mindset enables businesses and leaders to operate effectively in multinational contexts, allowing them to identify opportunities, mitigate cross-cultural risks, and build resilient international relationships. It's often seen as a key asset in competitive, globalized industries.

Fixed Mindset Vs Growth Mindset

There are two main mindsets we can navigate life with fixed and growth. Having a growth mindset is essential for success. The psychologist Carol Dweck popularized the ideas of fixed mindset and growth mindset in her book (2006) "Mindset: The New Psychology of Success." A fixed mindset is the idea that intelligence and talent are unchanging characteristics, which makes people avoid criticism and difficulties and give up easily when things don't go their way.

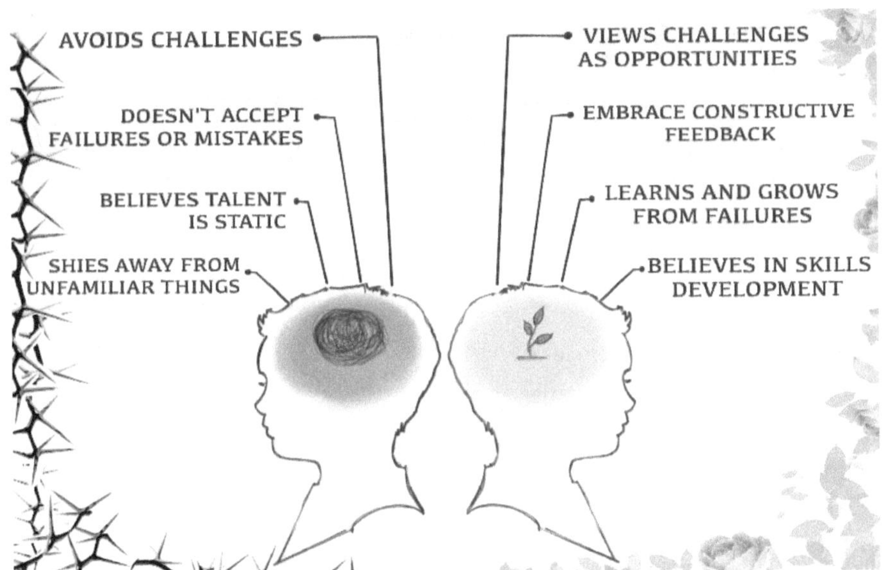

Figure 1.1. Fixed Mindset vs Growth Mindset

The idea that aptitude and intelligence can be developed via hard work and perseverance is known as a growth mindset. In pursuing their objectives, people with a growth mindset can confront obstacles, ask for feedback, take preventative and remedial action, and ultimately strive for continual progress. A growth mindset can help one achieve more success and advancement in personal and professional efforts. Success is not about being the best, but rather being the best version of yourself. **Figure 1.1** shows the difference between a Fixed mindset and a Growth mindset.

Table 1.1 provides the difference between a fixed mindset and a growth mindset based on various parameters. A **fixed mindset** believes that traits like intelligence or talent are innate and unchangeable. This mindset often avoids challenges, fears failure, and views effort as pointless if one isn't naturally good at something. A **growth mindset** believes that abilities can be developed through effort, learning, and persistence. Those with this mindset embrace challenges, learn from feedback, and see failure as part of the learning process. This differentiation can help in understanding how a mindset affects one's approach to learning, challenges, and personal development. Work on **Exercise 1.1** to assess your mindset.

Table 1.1. Fixed Mindset vs. Growth Mindset

Parameter	Fixed Mindset	Growth Mindset
View of Intelligence	Intelligence is static and unchangeable.	Intelligence can be developed through effort and learning.
Attitude Towards Challenges	Avoids challenges to avoid failure.	Embraces challenges as opportunities for growth.
Response to Obstacles	Gives up easily when faced with difficulties.	Persists through obstacles, seeing them as part of the learning process.
Effort	Believes effort is fruitless if you're not naturally talented.	Believes effort is essential for improvement and mastery.
Reaction to Criticism	Takes feedback personally and feels threatened by criticism.	Welcomes feedback as a tool for learning and growth.

Parameter	Fixed Mindset	Growth Mindset
View of Failure	Sees failure as a reflection of their inherent ability.	Sees failure as a learning opportunity and a step towards success.
Reaction to Others' Success	Feels threatened or envious of others' success.	Finds inspiration in others' success and learns from it.
Belief in Change	Believes abilities and talents are fixed.	Believes abilities and skills can be developed over time.
Risk-Taking	Avoids taking risks to prevent failure or embarrassment.	Is willing to take risks and try new things for the sake of learning.
Self-Perception	Defines self-worth based on validation and outcomes.	Defines self-worth based on personal growth and effort

Entrepreneurial Mindset

An **Entrepreneurial Mindset** refers to a set of attitudes, skills, and behaviors that enable individuals to identify opportunities, overcome challenges, and take action to create value—whether in business, personal ventures, or within an organization (intrapreneurship). It is characterized by adaptability, creativity, resilience, and a proactive approach to problem-solving.

In today's fast-paced and ever-changing world, the **Entrepreneurial Mindset** has emerged as a vital attribute not only for business founders but for anyone navigating complex, dynamic environments. This mindset is characterized by an approach to thinking, problem-solving, and action that allows individuals to embrace uncertainty, recognize opportunities, and take calculated risks to bring about innovative solutions and value.

Entrepreneurial Competencies

Entrepreneurial competencies are the distinct set of attributes that individuals possess to effectively initiate, manage, and grow in their careers and professions. Acquiring these competencies enables you to navigate the complexities of your professional journey, identify opportunities, overcome challenges, and ultimately succeed in your career and profession. Work on

Exercise 1.2 to assess your entrepreneurial competencies. The following are the top ten entrepreneurial competencies.

1. **Opportunity Recognition and Problem Solving:** The ability to identify and capitalize on promising opportunities with empathy to understand the environment, market needs, gaps, and trends through critical thinking is crucial for problem-solving and decision-making.

2. **Creativity and Innovation:** The capacity to think creatively, generate new ideas, and innovate to develop unique products, services, or business models.

3. **Leadership and Team building:** Leadership skills to build trust, inspire, and motivate team members, envision long-term goals, formulate strategic plans, and make the right decisions, that align with the overall vision of the organization.

4. **Risk Management:** Skill in assessing and managing risks associated with a professional journey, including financial risks, market risks, and operational risks.

5. **Endurance:** The ability to persevere in the face of challenges, setbacks, and failures, and to bounce back with renewed energy and determination.

6. **Adaptability and Flexibility:** The capacity to adapt to changing environments, market conditions, customer preferences, and technological changes, and to pivot strategies as needed.

7. **Networking and Relationship Building:** Effective networking abilities to build and nurture strong and sustainable relationships with stakeholders such as customers, investors, mentors, and partners.

8. **Communication and Persuasion:** Excellent and effective communication skills to articulate ideas, negotiate deals, pitch to investors, and build rapport with stakeholders.

9. **Goal Setting and Self-motivation:** The inner drive and determination that individuals possess to set, achieve goals, and overcome obstacles. This is also called **achievement motivation**.

Identify what you want to achieve. Make sure your goals are Specific, Measurable, Achievable, Relevant and Time-bound (SMART). The ability to stay focused, persistent, proactive, and self-motivated in pursuing one's goals without relying solely on external factors or rewards.

10. **Passion:** It is the intense enthusiasm, interest, and emotional connection that individuals feel towards a particular activity, pursuit, or goal. It is the driving force behind one's actions, inspiring dedication, creativity, and perseverance in the pursuit of their passions. Passion fuels self-motivation, propelling individuals to invest their time, energy, and effort wholeheartedly into activities that they find deeply meaningful, purposeful, and rewarding.

Ayesha's Journey Through the Ten I's of Entrepreneurship

In a Vibrant University, there was a youth named Ayesha. She had always been curious about solving problems around her, and one day, she noticed an opportunity—a problem that everyone seemed to overlook. The streets were constantly littered with waste, and although the government had introduced waste management systems, they were inefficient.

Insightfulness – (Opportunity Recognition and Problem-Solving)

Ayesha saw this as an opportunity. She believed that technology could offer a solution. Recognizing the gap in the existing system, she began researching ways to create a smart waste management solution that could track waste levels, optimize collection routes, and promote recycling. Her goal was to make her city cleaner and more efficient.

Inventiveness – (Creativity and Innovation)

While others had tried different approaches, Ayesha's innovation was unique. She designed smart bins with built-in sensors that could monitor the amount of waste and send real-time data to waste management centers. These centers would use AI to predict when and where waste collection was needed most, reducing the number of unnecessary pickups and lowering costs.

Inspiration – (Leadership and Team Building)

Realizing that she couldn't do this alone, Ayesha built a team of experts—a software engineer, a logistics specialist, and an environmental scientist. She led with a vision that inspired them, emphasizing collaboration and open communication. Together, they worked tirelessly to turn her idea into a reality.

Insurance – (Risk Management)

But the road was not smooth. Investors were skeptical, the market was unpredictable, and there were regulatory hurdles. Ayesha knew that launching this new product came with risks—financial and operational. However, she managed these risks by creating a detailed business plan and building strategic partnerships with local authorities and environmental organizations.

Indomitable – (Endurance, Adaptability, and Flexibility)

The initial prototype didn't perform as expected. The sensors were unreliable, and technical glitches slowed down the project. But Ayesha didn't give up. She endured long nights and constant revisions, adapting the design based on customer feedback and testing. Flexibility became her ally as she shifted focus from immediate profits to perfecting the product's functionality.

Interconnection – (Networking and Relationship Building)

Ayesha understood that building a business wasn't just about the product—it was also about people. She and her team networked extensively, attending conferences, connecting with potential clients, and forming alliances with government bodies. These relationships later become key to the expansion of her project.

Influence – (Communication and Persuasion)

She had to pitch her idea to various stakeholders, including investors, city officials, and waste management companies. Her ability to communicate her vision clearly and persuasively was crucial. She used real-world examples, statistics, and compelling stories to convey the urgency of the problem her solution addressed.

Intentionally – (Goal Setting and Self-Motivation)

Ayesha set short-term and long-term goals for herself and her team. She kept them motivated with small victories, celebrating milestones like securing initial funding or completing a pilot project. Self-motivation kept her moving forward, even when challenges seemed overwhelming.

Ignition – (Passion)

What fueled Ayesha's journey was her passion. She wasn't just driven by profit but by the desire to create a cleaner and greener world. Her passion was contagious, inspiring her team to give their best and her investors to believe in her vision. Ayesha's smart waste management system became a success. Cities across the country adopted it, and it revolutionized the way waste was managed.

Box 1.1. Transformational Leadership

Transformational leadership involves inspiring and motivating followers to achieve extraordinary results by appealing to their purpose and values. This style of leadership mainly focuses on team building to create positive change within organizations. Transformational leaders have been shown to significantly enhance team performance, and increase people engagement and satisfaction. They foster a culture of innovation and continuous improvement within organizations.

The **Leadership Quotient (LQ),** is a measure of an individual's leadership performance. It encompasses a combination of traits, skills, and behaviors that determine one's ability to lead and influence others. Leadership Quotient provides a framework for assessing and developing leadership competencies, including fostering team-building efforts. Leaders with higher LQ are better equipped to understand and address the needs and dynamics of their team members.

Team building refers to the process of bringing together a group of individuals to form a cohesive and high-performing team. It involves activities and strategies aimed at improving communication, collaboration, trust, synergy, and mutual understanding among team members.

Transformational leadership often acts as a catalyst for effective team building. Leaders who exhibit transformational qualities such as vision, charisma, and empowerment are more likely to inspire trust and collaboration among team members.

Effective team building reinforces the principles of transformational leadership by creating a conducive environment where team members are aligned with the organization's vision, purpose and empowered to contribute their ideas and talents, and supported in their growth and development.

Transformational leadership, Leadership Quotient, and team building are interconnected and are essential for driving organizational success. Effective leaders who exhibit transformational qualities and possess a higher Leadership Quotient can leverage team-building strategies to create high-performing teams that are capable of achieving extraordinary results.

Here are some transformational leaders from around the world: Nelson Mandela (South Africa), Mahatma Gandhi (India), Abdul Kalam (India), Martin Luther King Jr. (United States), Steve Jobs (United States), Elon Mask (United States), Aung San Suu Kyi (Myanmar), Winston Churchill (United Kingdom), Angela Merkel (Germany), Mother Teresa (India), Margaret Thatcher (United Kingdom), Deng Xiaoping (China).

Note: Work on Exercise 1.3. to assess your leadership qualities

Entrepreneurship as a Career

Entrepreneurship as a career path offers individuals the opportunity to pursue their passions, create innovative solutions, and have a significant positive impact on society. Entrepreneurs have the opportunity to make a meaningful difference in the world, by solving pressing societal problems, fulfilling unmet needs of society, creating jobs, and or fostering environmental sustainability. To become an entrepreneur, one must develop the right entrepreneurial mindset, skills, competencies, and knowledge.

Historically entrepreneurs have altered the direction of national economies, industries, and markets. Entrepreneurship contributes to national income and increase in Gross Domestic Product (GDP) through job creation, value creation, and wealth creation and serves as a bridge between innovation and the marketplace. Entrepreneurship is the process of developing, organizing, and running an enterprise using resources to create value for profit under any of its uncertainties.

The term **Entrepreneurship** was coined by the French economist and philosopher Jean-Baptiste Say. The term entrepreneur is derived from the French word "entreprendre," which means "to undertake" or "to embark on a venture." Joseph Alois Schumpeter is regarded as the father of entrepreneurship. He introduced the concept of entrepreneurship.

Etymologically, the word "**entrepreneur**" was derived from the Sanskrit words "anthah" (or "inner") and "prerna" (or "motivation"). In other words, entrepreneurs are those who have passion and are self-motivated. The word entrepreneur is derived from the Sanskrit word "Antara Prerana" meaning "intrinsic motivation".

An **entrepreneur** is a person who starts, organizes, and manages an enterprise using resources and creates value to make a profit. They are typically associated with creating new companies, products, or services, and make decisions, take significant financial risks in pursuit of their goals.

Enterprise: An enterprise is a term in the commercial world used to describe a project or venture undertaken for gain. The enterprise is the basic unit of economic organization. It transacts with another unit in the economy, it produces a product/service worth more than the resources used. Here are some points to consider when discussing entrepreneurship as a career:

- **Freedom and Independence**: One of the most appealing aspects of entrepreneurship is the freedom to be your boss. Entrepreneurs make their own decisions, set their schedules, and pursue projects they are passionate about.

- **Opportunity for Innovation**: Entrepreneurship allows individuals to identify gaps in the market and develop innovative solutions to address them. This can lead to the creation of new products, processes, services, and business models that disrupt industries and drive positive change in society.

- **Potential for Financial Rewards**: While entrepreneurship comes with risks, it also offers the potential for significant financial rewards. Successful entrepreneurs have the opportunity to build profitable, scalable, and sustainable businesses that generate substantial profits, value, and wealth.

- **Learning and Growth**: Entrepreneurship is a journey that involves continuous learning, development, and personal growth. Entrepreneurs are constantly faced with new challenges and opportunities, which provide valuable learning experiences and opportunities for skill development.

- **Impact and Fulfillment**: Many entrepreneurs are driven by a desire to make a positive impact on the world. Whether it's solving a pressing societal problem, creating jobs in society, or supporting environmental sustainability, entrepreneurship offers a better opportunity to pursue meaningful purpose and create positive change.

- **Challenges and Uncertainty**: It's important to acknowledge that entrepreneurship also comes with its share of challenges and uncertainties. Building a successful business requires commitment, resilience, and the ability to navigate obstacles such as funding constraints, market competition, and regulatory hurdles.

- **Lifestyle Considerations**: Entrepreneurship can also have implications for lifestyle, including long working hours, financial instability in the early stages, and the need to balance work and personal life effectively.
- **Support Systems**: Building a successful business often requires support from friends, mentors, advisors, investors, and a strong network of peers. Access to resources and support networks can significantly bring success in an entrepreneur's journey.

Myths of Entrepreneurship

1. Entrepreneurs are born not made
2. All you need is money to be an entrepreneur
3. All you need is luck to be an entrepreneur
4. Entrepreneurs are overnight successes
5. You need a groundbreaking idea
6. Entrepreneurship guarantees wealth
7. Entrepreneurs fit an ideal profile
8. Having no boss is a great fun
9. My best friend will be a great business partner
10. A great idea is the only ingredient in a recipe for business

Sustainable Development Goals

In today's ever-changing world, Environmental, Social, and Governance (ESG) considerations have become pivotal in shaping sustainable practices for organizations. ESG represents a transformative shift in how organizations approach sustainability and societal impact. By embracing ESG principles, organizations contribute to a more sustainable and equitable future. Each small gesture, whether it is adopting sustainable practices, promoting social equality, or demonstrating responsible governance, plays a vital role in driving positive change. By raising awareness and inspiring action, we can collectively create a better world.

New-age leadership characterized by innovation, risk-taking, collaboration, and impact orientation, can be a powerful force for advancing the

Sustainable Development Goals (SDGs). By harnessing the entrepreneurial spirit, individuals and organizations can drive meaningful progress toward a more sustainable, equitable, and prosperous future for all. Leadership is seen as the panacea for sustainable development. Leaders can play a key role in contributing to Agenda 2030 and SDGs by building resilient infrastructure, promoting inclusive and sustainable industrialization, and fostering innovation.

The Sustainable Development Goals are the blueprint to achieve a better and more sustainable future for all. The Sustainable Development Goals (SDGs), also known as the Global Goals, are a set of 17 interconnected goals adopted by all United Nations Member States, including India, in 2015 as part of the 2030 Agenda for Sustainable Development. The SDGs are aligned with the five SDG pillars of people, profit, planet, peace, and partnership. These goals furnished in **Figure 1.2** aim to address the world's most pressing challenges and promote sustainable development in three dimensions: Environment, Social, and Governance.

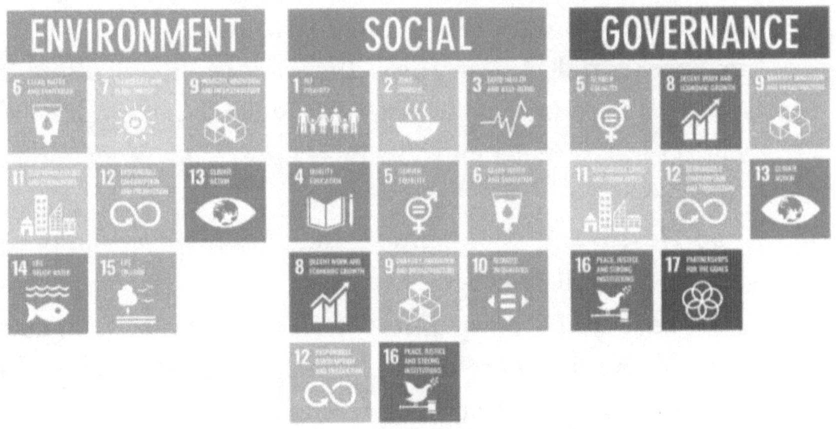

Figure 1.2. Sustainable Development Goals
Source: Courtesy United Nations

Achieving these goals requires an entrepreneurial mindset to collaborate with governments, the private sector, civil society, and individuals. The 17 Sustainable Development Goals (SDGs) established by the United Nations aim to address global challenges and promote a sustainable future. Entrepreneurship is a vital driver for achieving the SDGs. By creating innovative solutions and fostering inclusive growth, entrepreneurs can play a significant role in addressing global challenges and building a sustainable future. Each goal presents unique opportunities for entrepreneurs to contribute to a more equitable and sustainable world. Each goal presents opportunities for entrepreneurship to contribute positively to society and the environment. Here is a brief overview of each goal and how entrepreneurship aligns with each of the 17 SDGs :

1. **No Poverty**: Eradicate extreme poverty for everyone, everywhere, currently measured as people living on less than $1.90 a day.

2. **Entrepreneurial Opportunity:** Microfinance, social enterprises, and inclusive business models can provide economic opportunities for low-income communities, helping lift people out of poverty.

3. **Zero Hunger**: End hunger, achieve food security and improved nutrition, and promote sustainable agriculture.

   Entrepreneurial Opportunity: Innovations in agriculture, such as vertical farming and agri-tech solutions, can improve food security and sustainability by increasing food production and reducing waste.

4. **Good Health and Well-being**: Ensure healthy lives and promote well-being for all at all ages.

   Entrepreneurial Opportunity: Health tech startups can develop affordable healthcare solutions, telemedicine, and wellness apps to improve access to healthcare services and promote well-being.

5. **Quality Education**: Ensure inclusive and equitable quality education and promote lifelong learning opportunities for all.

   Entrepreneurial Opportunity: EdTech companies can create accessible learning platforms, online courses, and skill development programs that cater to diverse learning needs and improve educational outcomes.

6. **Gender Equality**: Achieve gender equality and empower all women and girls.

   Entrepreneurial Opportunity: Businesses focusing on empowering women through training, access to finance, and mentorship can enhance gender equality in the workplace and promote women's leadership.

7. **Clean Water and Sanitation**: Ensure availability and sustainable management of water and sanitation for all.

   Entrepreneurial Opportunity: Water purification technologies and sustainable sanitation solutions can address water scarcity and improve sanitation facilities, particularly in underserved communities.

8. **Affordable and Clean Energy**: Ensure access to affordable, reliable, sustainable, and modern energy for all.

   Entrepreneurial Opportunity: Renewable energy startups can develop solar, wind, and other sustainable energy solutions, making clean energy accessible and affordable to all.

9. **Decent Work and Economic Growth**: Promote sustained, inclusive, and sustainable economic growth, full and productive employment, and decent work for all.

   Entrepreneurial Opportunity: By creating new businesses and jobs, entrepreneurs can stimulate economic growth and promote fair labor practices, contributing to decent work opportunities.

10. **Industry, Innovation, and Infrastructure**: Build resilient infrastructure, promote inclusive and sustainable industrialization, and foster innovation.

    Entrepreneurial Opportunity: Innovative startups can drive technological advancements and create resilient infrastructure, enhancing industry productivity and sustainability.

11. **Reduced Inequality**: Reduce inequality within and among countries.

    Entrepreneurial Opportunity: Social enterprises and inclusive businesses can create opportunities for marginalized groups, helping to reduce economic and social inequalities.

12. **Sustainable Cities and Communities**: Make cities and human settlements inclusive, safe, resilient, and sustainable.

    Entrepreneurial Opportunity: Urban planning and smart city innovations can enhance the sustainability of urban environments, improving public transport, waste management, and green spaces.

13. **Responsible Consumption and Production**: Ensure sustainable consumption and production patterns.

    Entrepreneurial Opportunity: Businesses focused on circular economy models can promote sustainable practices, reducing waste and encouraging responsible consumption.

14. **Climate Action**: Take urgent action to combat climate change and its impacts.

    Entrepreneurial Opportunity: Green technology companies can develop solutions that mitigate climate change impacts, such as carbon capture, renewable energy, and sustainable agriculture.

15. **Life Below Water**: Conserve and sustainably use the oceans, seas, and marine resources for sustainable development.

    Entrepreneurial Opportunity: Enterprises focused on marine conservation and sustainable fisheries can protect ocean ecosystems and promote responsible use of marine resources.

16. **Life on Land**: Protect, restore, and promote sustainable use of terrestrial ecosystems, manage forests sustainably, combat desertification, and halt and reverse land degradation and biodiversity loss.

    Entrepreneurial Opportunity: Eco-friendly businesses can promote biodiversity conservation, reforestation, and sustainable land management practices, contributing to healthy ecosystems.

17. **Peace, Justice, and Strong Institutions**: Promote peaceful and inclusive societies for sustainable development, provide access to justice for all, and build effective, accountable, and inclusive institutions at all levels.

    Entrepreneurial Opportunity: Startups focused on transparency, civic engagement, and legal tech can enhance accountability and empower communities to participate in governance.

18. **Partnerships for the Goals**: Strengthen the means of implementation and revitalize the global partnership for sustainable development.

    Entrepreneurial Opportunity: Collaborative ventures among businesses, NGOs, and governments can amplify efforts toward achieving the SDGs through shared resources, knowledge, and expertise.

Effectuation

Do what you want from what you have

This concept was introduced by Dr. Saras Sarasvathy, a professor at the University of Virginia's Darden School of Business. Effectuation is a way of thinking and decision-making framework that is based on the idea that entrepreneurs create their future by taking action and making things happen. It is a way of thinking that is focused on creating opportunities and solving problems by using the available resources, rather than making predictions and trying to plan for the future.

Using causal reasoning, one begins with a specific goal and a given set of means for achieving it. Using effectual reasoning, one starts with only a set of available means and the process of deploying them, and goals gradually emerge. Effectuation is an idea with a sense of purpose and a desire to change and improve the state of the world. It brings improvement in the standard of living of individuals by enabling the creation of new ideas, processes, products, markets, services, and firms. The entrepreneurial mindset and effectuation form a powerful synergy, empowering entrepreneurs to navigate challenges, and complexity, capitalize on emergent opportunities, and drive sustainable success in dynamic environments.

Entrepreneurial thinking (effectual) is characterized by creativity, innovation, and a growth mindset, while managerial thinking (causal) is more focused on strategic planning and efficient resource allocation. **Figure 1.3** depicts Managerial thinking vs. Entrepreneurial thinking.

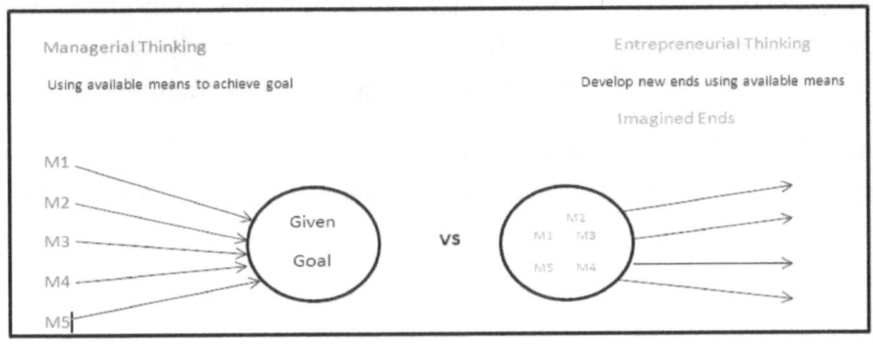

Figure 1.3. Managerial Thinking vs. Entrepreneurial Thinking.

Effectuation is particularly relevant in contexts of high uncertainty, such as in emerging economies or markets, where traditional planning approaches may be less effective. It emphasizes action, learning, and adaptability, enabling people to navigate the uncertainties, and complexities of starting and growing a venture more effectively. Key principles of effectuation include:

Means-driven (Bird in hand): Effectuation is an entrepreneurial mindset and starts with the means, already have. Such as skills, knowledge, and networks, and then seek to create opportunities based on available resources. Effectuation is not mainly concerned with predicting the future or waiting for the perfect conditions to start a project or venture.

Affordable Loss (Focus on Downside): Instead of focusing on potential gains, effectual thinkers consider what they can afford to lose. This mindset allows to take calculated risks without risking everything. Failure is viewed as a natural part of the entrepreneurial process and learn from mistakes rather than being paralyzed by fear of failure.

Leveraging contingencies (Lemonade): Effectual thinkers are adept at recognizing and capitalizing on unexpected events, turning them into opportunities. They are flexible and open to changing their plans based on the feedback they receive from the market and other stakeholders.

Co-creation of opportunities (Crazy Quilt): Effectual thinkers involve stakeholders in the creation of their projects or ventures. They engage with potential customers, partners, and investors to iteratively develop their ideas and implementation rather than relying solely on their vision.

Controlled Pilot Experiments (Control vs Prediction): Rather than committing to large-scale investments, effectual thinkers conduct pilot experiments to test their ideas, models, beliefs, and assumptions. This allows them to validate their concepts, and models, learn from real-world feedback, and adjust plans accordingly.

Example: Flipkart

Flipkart is one of India's most successful e-commerce companies, founded by Sachin Bansal and Binny Bansal in the year 2007. Their journey embodies the principles of effectual entrepreneurship:

1. **Means-driven:** Sachin Bansal and Binny Bansal, who were former Amazon employees, leveraged their expertise in e-commerce and their understanding of the Indian market to kickstart their new venture. The founders started Flipkart with available and limited resources. They began by selling books online, utilizing their savings and the modest investments they received from family and friends.

2. **Affordable Loss:** Rather than waiting for perfect conditions or seeking large investment support, the Bansals took calculated risks and focused on what they could afford to lose. They started with a pilot project, testing the market with a limited selection of products, and gradually expanded as they gained traction. This approach allowed them to mitigate potential losses while learning and adapting to the evolving needs of their market.

3. **Leveraging contingencies:** Flipkart identified the unique challenges and opportunities in the Indian market, such as infrastructure limitations and diverse consumer preferences. Instead of viewing these as obstacles, they embraced them as opportunities for innovation. For example, Flipkart introduced cash-on-delivery as a payment option, in the beginning, to address concerns about online transactions to build trust among Indian consumers.

4. **Co-creation of opportunities:** Flipkart actively engaged with stakeholders to co-create value. They invested in creating a user-friendly platform, implementing features based on user feedback, and partnering with sellers to expand their product offerings. By involving stakeholders in the development process, Flipkart was able to tailor its services to the specific needs of the Indian market, gaining a competitive advantage.

5. **Controlled pilot experiments:** Rather than scaling up rapidly, Flipkart conducted controlled pilot experiments to test new ideas and features. For instance, they experimented with different delivery models and logistics solutions to optimize efficiency and

customer satisfaction. This iterative approach allowed Flipkart to fine-tune its operations, adapt, and scale up sustainably, avoiding high risks and expensive mistakes.

Flipkart's success story exemplifies how effectual entrepreneurship principles can drive innovation, resilience, and growth in the Indian context, enabling startups to navigate challenges and exploit opportunities in a rapidly evolving market.

Box 1.2. Power of Passion

"Do not sprint after success, but rather strive with passion to secure something great".

The power of passion is an incredible force that drives individuals to achieve their goals, overcome challenges, and make a meaningful impact on the world around them. When someone is passionate about something, whether it's a hobby, a career, or a cause, they are more likely to put in the effort, time, and dedication required to excel in that area.

Passion ignites enthusiasm, fuels perseverance, and fosters resilience. It gives people a sense of purpose and direction, motivating them to push through obstacles and setbacks. When faced with difficulties, passionate individuals are more likely to find creative solutions and adapt to changing circumstances, turning challenges into opportunities for growth.

Moreover, passion is contagious. When people are passionate about what they do, they inspire and influence others around them. Their enthusiasm can spark curiosity, drive innovation, and build communities of like-minded individuals who share similar interests and goals. Here are five brief examples illustrating the power of passion:

Entrepreneurship: Ratan Tata's passion for innovation drove the growth and success of the Tata Group, one of India's largest conglomerates. Steve Jobs' passion for innovation led to the creation of revolutionary products like the iPhone. Elon Musk has revolutionized multiple industries by advancing electric vehicles, space exploration, and renewable energy through his companies Tesla, SpaceX, and SolarCity, while also promoting futuristic projects like Neuralink and the Hyperloop.

Sports: Sachin Tendulkar's love for cricket made him one of the greatest batsmen in the history of the sport. Serena Williams' love for tennis propelled her to become one of the greatest players in history.

Science: Dr. APJ Abdul Kalam's passion for aerospace engineering led him to play a pivotal role in India's missile and space programs. Dr Jane Goodall's passion for wildlife conservation led to groundbreaking research on chimpanzees.

Arts: Rabindranath Tagore's passion for literature and music made him the first non-European to win the Nobel Prize in Literature for his poetic work, Gitanjali. Vincent van Gogh's passion for painting produced iconic works like "Starry Night."

Social Activism: Mahatma Gandhi's passion for non-violence and independence inspired India's freedom struggle and influenced civil rights movements worldwide. Malala Yousafzai's passion for education inspired a global movement advocating for girls' rights to education.

In essence, the power of passion is transformative. It empowers individuals to pursue their dreams with unwavering determination, make a positive difference in the world, and live a fulfilling and meaningful life. So, whether you're passionate about art, science, technology, or any other pursuit, harnessing your passion can lead to incredible achievements and a life filled with purpose and joy.

Plan Personal Finance

Personal finance is all about managing your money wisely to achieve your financial goals. It involves Income, budgeting and spending, saving, investing, debt management, and protection for the future. Personal finance is about making informed decisions to optimize your financial well-being and achieve your life goals. It requires discipline, planning, and ongoing attention to ensure financial stability and security. Here are some key aspects:

1. **Income:** Income refers to a source of cash inflow that an individual receives and uses to support themselves and their family. It is a starting point of the personnel financial planning process. The common sources of income are salaries, bonuses, hourly wages, interests, pensions, and dividends.

2. **Budgeting and Spending:** Creating a budget helps you understand your income, expenses, and where your money is going. It enables you to allocate funds effectively toward your priorities. Spending includes all types of expenses an individual incurs related to buying goods and services, All expenses fall into two categories cash and credit. The common sources of spending are rent, food, education fees, entertainment, travel, taxes, and credit card payments. Managing expenses is as important as generating income. If expenses are greater than income, the individual has a deficit.

3. **Saving:** It refers to excess cash that is retained for future spending. Saving for short-term goals like education, and vacations and long-term goals like retirement is essential. Common forms of savings include physical cash, savings bank accounts, and money market securities.

4. **Investing:** It is the most complicated area of personal finance and most people seek professional advice. It relates to the purchase of assets that are expected to generate a positive rate of return. Investing allows your money to grow over time. It's important to diversify your investments across different asset classes like stocks,

mutual funds, bonds, real estate, commodities, private companies, and others based on your risk tolerance and financial goals.

5. **Debt Management:** Managing debt is essential to avoid high-interest payments and maintain a healthy financial situation. Strategies include paying off high-interest debt first, consolidating debts, and negotiating with creditors.

6. **Protection:** Personal protection refers to a wide range of products that can be used to guard against an unforeseen and adverse event. Common protection products include insurance retirement and estate planning.

7. **Retirement and Estate Planning:** This involves estimating your future expenses and income sources, such as pensions, social security, and investments. Starting early and contributing regularly to retirement accounts like 401(k)s and IRAs can help build a comfortable retirement nest egg. Estate planning involves creating a plan for how your assets will be managed and distributed after your death. This may include drafting a will, establishing trusts, and designating beneficiaries for accounts and insurance policies.

8. **Insurance:** Having appropriate insurance coverage, such as health insurance, life insurance, and property insurance, protects you and your family from financial risks in case of unexpected events.

Tips for Personal Finance

- ✓ Create a budget
- ✓ Save first, spend later, and save early
- ✓ Track your spending
- ✓ Set financial goals
- ✓ Start investing early
- ✓ Monitor the fluctuations in the BSE and NSE indices
- ✓ Monitor gold prices and the rupee-dollar exchange rate
- ✓ Manage debt wisely such as education loan
- ✓ Consider investing in a Systematic Investment Plan (SIP) of a Mutual Fund as a means to build a corpus over time.

- ✓ Plan for major expenses
- ✓ Build an emergency fund
- ✓ Review your insurance coverage
- ✓ Continuously educate yourself

SWOT Analysis for Personal and Professional Growth

SWOT is an acronym for Strengths, Weaknesses, Opportunities, and Threats. The SWOT analysis technique is credited to **Albert Humphrey,** who led a convention at Stanford University in the 1960s and 1970s using data from Fortune 500 companies. SWOT analysis is a strategic planning method used to evaluate the Strengths, Weaknesses, Opportunities, and Threats involved in a career planning, project, or business venture. It involves specifying the objective and identifying the internal and external factors that are favourable and unfavourable to achieve that objective.

A SWOT analysis with a focus on **personal and professional development** can help you assess your strengths, weaknesses, opportunities, and threats to better understand how to achieve your growth goals. It provides a structured way to reflect on your capabilities, challenges, and the external factors influencing your journey. Strategic planning, guided by the SWOT analysis, ensures that your goals are aligned with your strengths and opportunities while addressing weaknesses and mitigating potential threats. Applying this tool to career planning enables individuals to assess their current status, identify areas for improvement (weakness), leverage strengths, capitalize on opportunities, and navigate potential threats and how to mitigate them.

The Four Elements of SWOT

i. **Strengths**: Internal factors such as competitive advantages of individual, team, or business.

ii. **Weaknesses**: Internal factors (Inherent disadvantages) or liabilities of individual, team, or business.

   iii. **Opportunities**: External factors that give the individual, team, or business a chance to succeed.

   iv. **Threats**: External factors that could prevent the individual, team, or business from succeeding.

Strengths: Begin the SWOT analysis by evaluating your strengths, which encompass your core competencies, skills, and inherent talents. Consider your educational background, certifications, and relevant work experience. Identify what sets you apart—personal traits, soft skills, or technical proficiencies. These strengths form the foundation of your career advantage and can be instrumental in achieving your goals.

For instance, if you possess strong leadership skills, excellent communication abilities, or a particular technical proficiency, these can be considered strengths. Acknowledging and leveraging these strengths can help in career positioning and decision-making.

Weaknesses: Every individual has areas where improvement is possible. Identify your weaknesses objectively, focusing on skills or knowledge gaps that may be hindering your professional progress. Consider personal traits or habits that might be impeding your success, such as procrastination or difficulty managing time effectively.

By acknowledging weaknesses, you set the stage for personal development. This might involve acquiring new skills, seeking additional education or training, or addressing personal habits that may be counterproductive. The goal is to transform weaknesses into opportunities for growth and improvement.

Opportunities: Opportunities are external factors that you can harness to advance your career. This includes potential career paths, industries, or roles that align with your interests, strengths, and goals. Be aware of emerging trends in your field and consider how you can position yourself to take advantage of these opportunities. Leverage your strengths to pursue opportunities aligned with your career objectives. If networking is a strength, actively engage in professional networks to explore new opportunities and collaborations.

Networking events, mentorship programs, and professional development opportunities are avenues to explore. Identify courses, certifications, or workshops that could enhance your skills and make you more competitive in your chosen field. Recognizing and capitalizing on opportunities can propel your career forward and open up new possibilities.

Threats: Anticipating and managing potential threats is crucial for effective career planning. Threats can be external factors that may impact your job security or hinder your career advancement. Changes in the industry, economic downturns, or technological disruptions are examples of threats that may need consideration.

Identifying threats allows you to proactively address them, whether through additional training, seeking mentorship, or developing contingency plans. Being aware of potential threats positions you to navigate challenges effectively and sustain your career growth. The various benefits of SWOT analysis are furnished below:

- **Decision-Making Tool:** The SWOT analysis is a valuable decision-making tool, particularly when faced with pivotal career choices. Whether considering a job change, pursuing further education, or embarking on an entrepreneurial venture, the analysis provides a structured approach for evaluating options and making informed decisions.

- **Personal Development and Continuous Learning:** Personal development is an ongoing process, and the SWOT analysis guides continuous improvement. By acknowledging weaknesses and actively working to address them, you enhance your overall employability and professional value. Continuous learning is a key component of personal development. Identify opportunities for skill enhancement, stay informed about industry trends, and invest in professional development.

- **Career Planning and Professional Growth:** career landscapes are dynamic, and changes can occur unexpectedly. Regularly revisiting your SWOT analysis allows you to adapt your career strategy to evolving circumstances. This adaptability ensures that your career plan remains relevant and effective in the face of changing industry trends, economic shifts, or professional growth.

- **Seeking Input and Collaboration:** While the SWOT analysis provides valuable self-reflection, seeking input from others enhances its effectiveness. Engage with mentors, colleagues, or career counselors to gain external perspectives on your strengths, weaknesses, opportunities, and threats. Collaborative input can offer valuable insights, identify blind spots, and provide guidance on areas for improvement.

By systematically evaluating strengths, weaknesses, opportunities, and threats periodically, individuals gain a holistic view of their professional selves. This structured approach informs strategic planning, and decision-making, fostering adaptability, and continuous personal development, and helps in goal setting.

How to do a SWOT Analysis?

Doing a SWOT analysis involves a structured process of gathering information and evaluating both internal and external positive and negative factors.

1. Define the objectives of the SWOT analysis
2. Gather information on internal (Strengths and Weaknesses) and external (Opportunities and Threats) factors
3. Create the 4-quadrant matrix and list three to five items in each quadrant
4. Analyze each item and prioritize the most important factors in each quadrant
5. Develop goals to leverage strengths and opportunities, and mitigate weaknesses and threats
6. Set actionable steps with specific timelines and responsible parties

7. Regularly track progress
8. Learn from successes and failures to refine the goals in the future.

Example: SWOT analysis for a student interested in web design

Strengths

- **Creativity and Design Skills:** The student has a natural interest in creative design and is skilled in using graphic design software.
- **Passion for Web Design:** The student is genuinely enthusiastic about web design and stays updated with the latest design trends and technologies.
- **Portfolio of Projects**: The student has already completed several web design projects, showcasing a range of design styles and concepts.
- **Quick Learner**: The student has a proven ability to quickly grasp new concepts and tools, making them adaptable to evolving technologies.
- **Good Communication Skills:** Effective communication skills help the student understand and convey client requirements and collaborate with team members.

Weaknesses

- **Limited Coding Knowledge**: The student's proficiency in coding languages like HTML, CSS, and JavaScript is relatively basic, which may limit the complexity of designs.
- **Time Management**: Balancing academic commitments, projects, and personal life is a challenge, leading to occasional project delays.
- **Lack of Professional Experience:** The student has yet to gain professional experience, which could impact their ability to understand and meet client expectations.
- **Limited Networking:** The student hasn't actively engaged in networking opportunities within the web design industry.

- **Critique Handling:** The student struggles with receiving and implementing feedback, which could hinder growth and development.

Opportunities

- **Online Learning Resources:** Taking advantage of online courses can help students improve their coding skills and expand their design repertoire.
- **Internship or Freelance Opportunities:** Gaining hands-on experience through internships or freelance projects can provide valuable real-world exposure.
- **Industry Events and Workshops**: Participating in workshops, conferences, and design meetings can facilitate networking and learning from industry experts.
- **Building a Strong Portfolio:** The student can continue building a diverse portfolio by undertaking personal projects and collaborations.
- **Collaboration with Developers:** Partnering with skilled developers can help bridge the student's coding knowledge gap and produce more complex designs.

Threats

- **Rapid Technological Changes:** The web design field evolves quickly, and failure to keep up with new tools and techniques could lead to obsolescence.
- **Competition:** The web design industry is competitive, with many talented designers vying for limited opportunities.
- **Client Expectations**: Clients often have high expectations; failing to meet these could result in negative feedback and a tarnished reputation.
- **Scope Creep:** Poorly defined project scopes and changes in client requirements could lead to project delays and dissatisfaction.

- **Economic Factors:** Economic downturns could lead to reduced demand for web design services as businesses cut discretionary spending.

The SWOT analysis of a student interested in web design is furnished in **Figure 1.4.** It suggests setting goals for taking online coding courses, seeking internships or freelance projects, participating in industry events, practicing effective feedback reception, and staying updated with the latest design trends. Regularly reviewing and revising this SWOT analysis can guide the student's ongoing development in the web design industry.

INTERNAL FACTORS	
Strengths (+)	**Weaknesses (-)**
1. Creativity and Design Skills 2. Passion for Web Design 3. Portfolio of Projects 4. Quick Learner 5. Good Communication Skills	1. Limited Coding Knowledge 2. Time Management 3. Lack of Professional Experience 4. Limited Networking 5. Feedback handling
EXTERNAL FACTORS	
Opportunities (+)	**Threats (-)**
1. Online Learning Resources 2. Internship of Freelance opportunities 3. Industry Events 4. Building a Strong Portfolio 5. Collaboration with Developers	1. Accelerated Technological Shifts 2. Competition 3. Client Expectations 4. Scope Creep 5. Economic Factors

Figure 1.4. SWOT Analysis

SWOT Scenarios and Outcomes

Here are a few scenarios and the questions you should ask once you've completed your SWOT analysis:

1. **Scenario**: Few strengths, many weaknesses
   What are things I can do to overcome my weaknesses or enhance my strengths?
2. **Scenario:** Few opportunities, many threats
   Is this a viable business opportunity? Are there just too many players to make this business entry worthwhile?
3. **Scenario**: Many strengths, many weaknesses, many opportunities, many threats

Perhaps the scenario is too broad. Could you narrow the market to better capitalize on your strength and in the meantime face less competition?

4. **Scenario:** Many strengths, few weaknesses, many opportunities, few threats

   The perfect storm. Is your analysis correct, do you have the dominance to destroy this market?

Work on ACTIVITY 1.1. Understanding Your Potential - Comprehensive SWOT Analysis for Career Planning and Goal Setting

Goal Setting

Once you have conducted a thorough SWOT analysis, use the insights gained to formulate a strategic plan and goal-setting process. If a weakness is identified, set specific goals to address and overcome it. For example, if the analysis reveals a gap in a particular skill set, establish a goal to acquire that skill through relevant training or education.

Setting goals is a fundamental aspect of personal and professional development. Effective goal setting provides direction, motivation, and a clear roadmap for achieving desired outcomes. Here are five simplified steps to set well-defined goals.:

1. Define Your Goal

Identify what you want to achieve. Make sure your goal is specific and clearly defined. Ask yourself what you want to accomplish and why it's important to you.

2. Make it SMARTER

Use the SMARTER criteria to define and refine your goal:

- **Specific:** State exactly what you want to achieve.
- **Measurable:** Define criteria for tracking progress and determining success.
- **Achievable:** Ensure the goal is realistic and attainable.

- **Relevant:** Ensure the goal aligns with your values, aspirations, and long-term objectives.
- **Time-bound:** Set a deadline for achieving the goal to create a sense of urgency.
- **Evaluate:** Monitor and track progress periodically
- **Review:** Making adjustments as needed to maximize chances of outcome

3. Break it Down:

- Divide your goal into smaller, manageable tasks or milestones.
- Breaking down larger goals into smaller steps makes them easier to tackle.

4. Develop an Action Plan:

- Determine the specific actions you need to take to reach each milestone.
- Create a timeline and allocate resources to each task.

5. Monitor and Adjust:

- Regularly track your progress toward each milestone.
- Adjust your action plan as needed based on feedback and changing circumstances.
- Celebrate your achievements along the way to stay motivated.

Example

Objective: Secure a summer internship by the end of the semester in the field of marketing to gain hands-on experience and expand my professional network in the technology industry. With this objective defined, we can now create a SMART goal to support it.

SMART Goal

Specific: Apply for and secure a summer internship in the marketing department of a reputable technology firm.

Measurable: Submit applications to at least 10 internship positions at leading technology firms listed on industry job boards and company career pages by the end of January.

Achievable: Enhance my resume by completing a Google Analytics certification course and attending a marketing workshop to develop valuable skills and showcase initiative to potential employers by the end of February.

Relevant: This internship aligns with my long-term career goal of becoming a digital marketing specialist in the technology sector, leveraging passion for marketing and interest in technological innovation.

Time-bound: Secure an internship offer from one of top-choice companies by the end of March, allowing sufficient time for preparation and arrangements before joining

Evaluated: Monitor and track application progress weekly, to ensure timely completion of applications and qualifications enhancement.

Reviewed: Making adjustments as needed to maximize chances of securing an internship offer by the end of April.

This refined SMARTER goal provides even more specificity, ensuring the student targets top-tier companies in their desired industry. It also emphasizes measurable actions, achievable steps to enhance qualifications, clear relevance to their career aspirations, and a specific deadline for securing the internship offer. **Work on Activity 1.2. Goal Setting**

<u>Box 1.3. Time Management</u>

Good time management skill enables you to work smarter and avoid stress. The Urgent Important Matrix is a powerful time management tool to help you to manage time more effectively. This matrix is also known as the **Eisenhower Matrix**, which helps prioritize tasks based on their level of importance and urgency. It divides tasks into four quadrants according to how urgent and important they are. The quadrants help you to understand where your time goes and be more productive with the time you have.

QUADRANT 1 **Urgent and Important** **Tasks you will do Immediately (CRISES)**	**I M P O R T A N T**	QUADRANT 2 **Not Urgent but Important** **Tasks you will schedule to do later (GOALS AND PLANNING)**
URGENT		NOT URGENT
QUADRANT 3 **Urgent but Not Important** **Tasks you will ask somebody to do (INTERRUPTIONS)**	**NOT I M P O R T A N T**	QUADRANT 4 **Not Important nor Urgent** **Tasks you will eliminate (DISTRACTIONS)**

By categorizing tasks into these quadrants, you can focus your time and energy on what truly matters, thereby improving productivity, reducing stress, and achieving goals. The tasks in Quadrant 1 need immediate attention, complete them now. The focus is to spend more time in Quadrant 2, where activities contribute to long-term goals and success. While minimizing time spent in Quadrants 3 and 4, where activities are less impactful or even unproductive. **Work on Activity 1.3. TIME MANAGEMENT**

Tips for Time Management

- ✓ Develop a Routine
- ✓ Set Clear Priorities
- ✓ Avoid Procrastination
- ✓ Focus on Single Taking
- ✓ Create a Sense of Urgency
- ✓ Practice the Law of Forced Efficiency
- ✓ Plan Your Day in Advance
- ✓ Keep Learning and Improving
- ✓ Delegate Whenever Possible
- ✓ Breakdown Tasks into Smaller Steps
- ✓ Tackle the Most Important Task First

KASH Box

KASH is an acronym for Knowledge, Attitude, Skill, and Habit. The KASH Box is a performance coaching tool introduced by **David Herdlinger** to illustrate that poor performance is not just a lack of knowledge and skills. The students learn in an environment that is experiential, fun, enjoyable, and highly conducive to adult learning. The academic development is driven through a Competency framework, the four pillars of which are Knowledge- Attitude- Skill-Habit (KASH model).

Before you understand the concept of KASH Box understand the human brain. The human brain is divided into symmetrical left and right hemispheres. Each hemisphere is in charge of the opposite side of the body. Your right brain controls your left hand and the right hemisphere also takes in sensory input from your left side and vice versa. The left side of the brain is cognitive and refers to the mental processes of acquiring and processing information, such as perception, memory, and reasoning. It is responsible for logical, analytical, linear, verbal, factual, sequential, and language. The right part of the brain is responsible for behavioral, and emotional responses, creativity, and intuition as shown in **Figure 1.5**. In reality, both sides work together, and stronger skills result from the two hemispheres working well together.

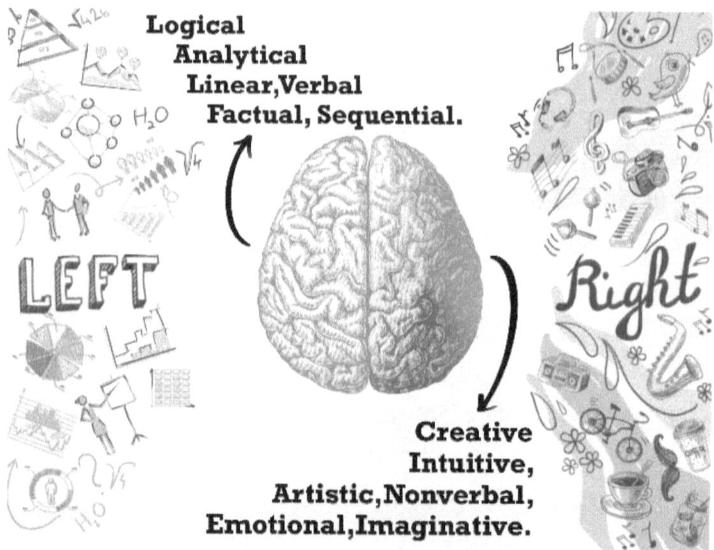

Figure 1.5. Left Brain Vs Right Brain

Left Hemisphere:

- **Language processing:** The left hemisphere is dominant for language functions in most individuals. It's primarily responsible for speech production, language comprehension, verbal, reading, and writing.

- **Logical Reasoning and analytical thinking:** It's often associated with factual information, logical reasoning, mathematical abilities, and analytical thinking.

- **Sequential processing:** This hemisphere tends to process quantitative and qualitative information in a sequential and organized manner.

Right Hemisphere:

- **Visual-spatial processing:** The right hemisphere is intuitive and more specialized in processing visual and spatial information. It helps in tasks such as recognizing faces, understanding spatial relationships, non-verbal communication, and interpreting maps.

- **Creativity and imagination:** The right hemisphere is often associated with creativity, imagination, and artistic abilities.
- **Emotional processing:** It plays a significant role in recognizing and expressing emotions, as well as understanding the emotional content of others' expressions.

Using both hemispheres of the brain effectively involves engaging in activities that stimulate and integrate functions associated with both sides. Here are some strategies to help you utilize both hemispheres:

1. **Cross-lateral movements:** Take part in exercises that require you to cross your body's midline, including cross-crawls, which include contacting your opposite knee with your hand while crawling, or marching while doing so. These exercises can facilitate better coordination and information integration between the hemispheres.

2. **Bilateral activities:** Practice tasks that call for hand-eye coordination or bilateral body coordination. Sports like badminton or tennis, typing, sketching, and playing musical instruments can all aid in synchronizing the activity of the two hemispheres.

3. **Brain training exercises:** Numerous games and brain-training activities aim to concurrently activate both hemispheres. Games such as scrabble and chess are examples of strategic board games, as well as crosswords, puzzles, and memory tests.

4. **Learning new skills:** Take up new hobbies like gardening, woodworking, or language study to enhance your cognitive abilities. You can also stretch your mind by learning to play an instrument. Acquiring novel activities has the potential to activate both hemispheres and foster neuroplasticity.

5. **Mindfulness and meditation:** Through the promotion of awareness of both internal and external experiences, practices such as mindfulness meditation can aid in the integration of the functioning of both hemispheres. Enhancements in focus, emotional control, and cognitive flexibility may result from this.

6. **Balanced thinking:** Make a conscious effort to strike a balance between left-hemisphere analytical and right-hemisphere creative thinking. Encourage yourself to tackle issues from several angles, fusing creative thinking with reasoned analysis.

7. **Physical exercise:** Frequent exercise has been demonstrated to improve hemispheric integration as well as general brain health and function. Cycling, dance, yoga, aerobic activity, and gymnastics are a few exercises that might enhance cerebral blood flow and foster neuronal connectivity.

By incorporating these strategies into your daily routine, you can enhance the integration and coordination of both hemispheres of your brain, leading to improved cognitive abilities, creativity, and overall brain function.

Figure 1.6 is a KASH Box, which is a performance coaching tool to highlight the fact that subpar performance is caused by negative attitudes and bad habits in addition to a lack of knowledge and skills. Performance attributes are separated into four different categories by the K.A.S.H. box. A framework for evaluating knowledge, attitude, skills, and habits is called the KASH box. As indicated in **Table 1.2,** Knowledge is information and expertise; Attitude is attitudes and beliefs; Skills are practical abilities; and Habits are behavioral patterns.

The success of an individual depends not only on the Knowledge and Skills that come from the left side of the brain but also on Attitudes and Habits that come from the right side of the brain which reflect the soft aspects of the personality. The knowledge/skill gap is overcome by training. The deficiency in attitude/habit, which is a performance gap is bridged by coaching and mentoring as shown in **Table 1.3.**

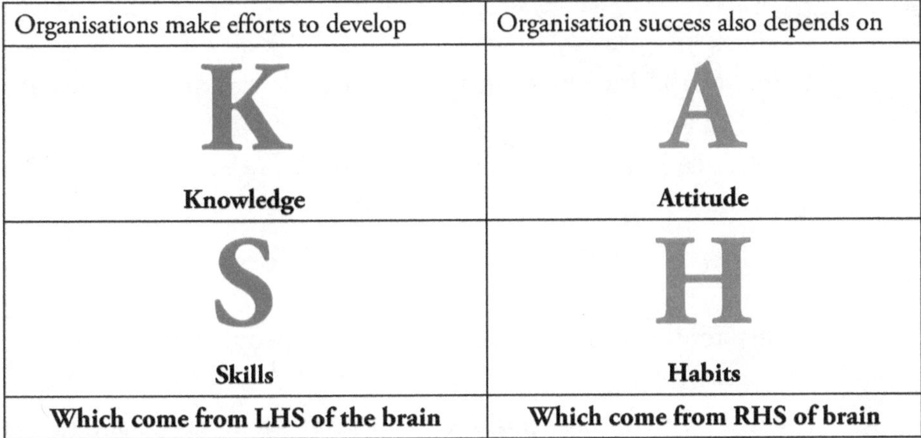

Figure 1.6. KASH Box

Table 1.2 KASH Description

KASH	Description
Knowledge	Condition of being aware of Facts or Concepts
Attitudes	Feelings, emotions, beliefs or values
Skills	Ability to perform tasks or activities measured in time and precision
Habits	Behavior pattern that is repeatedly and consistently done without effort

Table 1.3. KASH Gap

Issue or Deficiency	Gap	Solution
Knowledge or Skill	Knowledge or Skill Gap	Training
Attitude or Habit	Performance Gap	Coaching and Mentoring

The KASH box emphasizes an individual's holistic development, covering not just the acquisition of knowledge and abilities but also the development of positive attitudes and habits that foster success over the long term. People can successfully create and accomplish their goals while promoting ongoing personal development by concentrating on all four components. An alternate method for creating goals is the "KASH box," which focuses on four essential components: knowledge, attitudes, skills, and habits. An explanation of each part is provided below:

Knowledge

- Refers to the information, facts, and understanding required to achieve a goal.
- Involves learning and acquiring relevant knowledge related to the goal.

Attitudes

- Refers to the mindset, beliefs, and perspectives that influence behavior and actions.
- Involves cultivating positive attitudes such as perseverance, optimism, and resilience to overcome challenges.

Skills

- Refers to the abilities and competencies needed to perform tasks and achieve objectives.
- Involves developing and honing specific skills relevant to the goal, such as communication, problem-solving, or technical skills.

Habits

- Refers to the behaviors and routines that contribute to consistent progress and success.
- Involves establishing positive habits and routines that support goal achievement, such as time management, self-discipline, and goal tracking.

Example: Let's apply the KASH box to a specific scenario

Scenario: Ashok wants to improve his public speaking skills to become a more effective communicator in his professional career.

Knowledge:

- **Acquiring Knowledge**: Ashok can start by understanding effective public speaking techniques, attending effective public speaker sessions, studying famous speeches, and understanding the principles of effective communication.

- **Learning Resources**: He can enroll in public speaking courses, attend workshops or seminars, and read books on public speaking and communication.

Attitudes:

- **Positive Mindset:** Ashok needs to cultivate a positive attitude towards public speaking, believing in his ability to improve and overcome any challenges.
- **Resilience:** He should embrace setbacks and failures as opportunities for growth, maintaining a resilient attitude in the face of difficulties.
- **Confidence**: Building self-confidence is crucial for effective public speaking. Ashok can practice positive self-talk and visualize successful speaking engagements to boost his confidence.

Skills:

- **Presentation Skills**: Ashok can focus on developing skills such as structuring speeches, using visual aids effectively, and engaging the audience.
- **Verbal and Nonverbal Communication**: He can work on his tone of voice, postures, gestures, voice modulation, body language, and eye contact to convey confidence and credibility.
- **Handling Q&A Sessions**: Practicing impromptu speaking and learning strategies for handling audience questions can enhance Ashok's speaking skills.

Habits:

- **Regular Practice**: Ashok should establish a habit of regular practice to improve his public speaking skills. He can set aside time each week for practicing speeches, presentations, or even speaking in front of a mirror.
- **Seeking Feedback:** Developing a habit of seeking feedback from peers, mentors, or public speaking coaches can provide valuable insights for improvement.

- **Continuous Learning**: Ashok should make it a habit to stay updated on new public speaking techniques, attend workshops or seminars, and seek opportunities for further skill development.

By applying the KASH box to his goal of improving public speaking skills, Ashok can systematically address each element - knowledge, attitudes, skills, and habits - to enhance his effectiveness as a communicator and achieve his professional objectives.

Etiquettes

Etiquette refers to the respectful, polite behavior that guides our interactions in various settings, helping to create harmony and positive impressions. Here are ten important etiquettes that foster respect, understanding, and positive relationships:

1. **Greeting Etiquette:** Always greet others politely with a smile or handshake, maintaining eye contact to show respect and friendliness.
2. **Listening Etiquette:** Give full attention to the speaker, avoid interrupting, and respond thoughtfully to show genuine interest in what they are saying.
3. **Dining Etiquette**: Follow proper table manners—wait until everyone is served before eating, use utensils properly, and chew with your mouth closed.
4. **Punctuality:** Arrive on time for appointments, meetings, and gatherings, showing respect for others' time.
5. **Digital Etiquette:** Be courteous in online interactions, use respectful language, and avoid oversharing or inappropriate posts on social media.
6. **Respect for Personal Space:** Maintain a comfortable distance in conversations, respecting physical boundaries in both personal and professional settings.
7. **Thank-You Etiquette**: Express gratitude verbally or in writing after receiving assistance, gifts, or kind gestures to acknowledge the effort.

8. **RSVP Etiquette**: Respond to invitations promptly and only commit if you genuinely plan to attend, helping hosts plan appropriately.

9. **Dress Code Adherence**: Respect the dress code for events, workplaces, or cultural settings, demonstrating respect for the occasion and context.

10. **Politeness and Courtesy**: Use "please," "thank you," and "excuse me" regularly, showing kindness and consideration for others in every interaction.

Box 1.4 The Art of Networking

Successful professional networking and relationship-building can be essential for career advancement. Developing new connections and strengthening current ones are the goals of networking. You can increase the size of your professional network and create new avenues for growth. Here are some networking and relationship-building tips.

- **Define Your Goals**: Before you start networking, clarify the objectives of networking and identify what you want to achieve. It may be finding an internship, looking for a job, seeking mentorship, building a team, or expanding your knowledge base.

- **Positive Attitude:** Developing a positive attitude makes you more approachable and likable to others. A positive attitude facilitates networking and collaboration opportunities. It enables to building of strong relationships and fosters connections.

- **Attend Events**: Participate in professional networking events, conferences, seminars, workshops, and industry exhibitions. These are excellent venues for networking with industry experts, idea sharing, and connection building.

- **Make use of Social Media:** Professional Facebook groups, LinkedIn, Twitter, and other sites can be great places to network. Post thought-provoking articles, participate in dialogues, and establish connections with industry experts who have similar interests or work in your field.

- **Communicate Clearly and Make Eye Contact on Purpose**: Don't be afraid to get in touch with organizations and experts whose work you find inspiring or whose values coincide with your own. Write brief, tailored messages outlining your qualifications and why you would like to connect. Show consideration for their time. To learn about their hobbies, be sure to listen actively to them making eye contact and speaking clearly.

- **Create Relationships That Will Benefit Both Parties:** Networking is a two-way conversation. Provide value to the people you connect with by sending them links to insightful articles or connecting them to someone who could expand their network. Establishing a partnership that benefits both parties builds relationships and trust.

- **Attend Work-related Social activities**: Try to make it to activities such as professional organization meetings, youth festivals, cultural events, competitions, and team-building exercises. These casual environments present chances to socialize.

- **Join Associations or Professional Groups:** Participating in associations or professional groups in your industry can help you grow professionally by offering learning, networking, and career growth opportunities. Participate actively in these communities to establish deep relationships.

- **Follow-up and Maintain Relationships:** Exchange mobile numbers with people you meet at events or make online, and don't forget to follow up. Thank them for their time and let them know that you would like to stay in touch with them in an email or whatsApp message. By sending updates on your career accomplishments, sharing thought-provoking articles, or just dropping by to see how they're doing, you may stay in regular contact with your network.

Enterprise AI for Career Planning and Progression

Technology plays a crucial role in education and employment. In today's competitive job market, AI can help students recognize and enhance their skills, making them stand out during a job interview. The same applies to educators who can use AI to teach and instruct students more efficiently. Enterprise AI is revolutionizing education, offering students a pathway to a successful career as given below:

1. **Personalized Learning Journeys**: Enterprise AI tailors learning experiences to individual needs. In India, platforms like Unacademy, and Swayam leverage AI algorithms to create personalised study plans, ensuring that no student is left behind.

2. **Skill Enhancement and Upskilling**: AI identifies skill gaps and recommends relevant courses. For instance, Coursera uses AI to suggest courses based on a student's career aspirations and existing skills,

3. **Job Matching and Career Guidance**: Enterprise AI analyses job markets, predicts trends, and matches students with suitable career paths. LinkedIn and Naukari.com employ AI algorithms to recommend job openings based on a candidate profile. These platforms empower students to make informed decisions about their careers.

4. **Automating Administrate Tasks**: AI streamlines administrative processes, allowing educational institutions to focus on academic rigor from attendance management to grading, AI reduces manual workload.

5. **Industry Specific Requirements:** AI provides real-time insights into industry demands. For instance, Turing.com analyzes job postings to identify emerging skills. Students can align their studies with these trends, ensuring relevance in the job market.

6. **Gather on Company Information:** By engaging with a chatbot, students can get quick and easy intel to assess the employee experience at different firms—going beyond the corporate

boilerplates they'd find through search, and without having to scour various sites for employee reviews for internship and placement.

7. **Work with the AI to unpack keywords in job descriptions**: To help students prepare for their mock interviews, have them choose a few keywords or skills highlighted in real job descriptions at the companies they're interested in. Make sure they ask the AI to tell them more about how companies generally assess applicants for those specific traits.

8. **Get guidance from the AI on how to answer potential interview questions:** Many recruiters are using AI to source interview questions, so it makes sense for your students to use AI to better prepare, too. For instance, students can ask AI what kind of interview questions are most common, how to best answer them, what mistakes to avoid, and what a hiring manager would typically try to assess.

9. **Partner with the AI to hold a mock interview:** Generative AI tools such as ChatGPT and perplexity, are particularly good at facilitating mock interviews, simulating a company's hiring manager, and providing honest, critical feedback on how students can improve their answers to typical and not-so-typical questions. These tools can also reverse roles and show students how a good interviewer might answer the questions managers (i.e., the students) pose.

10. **Foster Creativity and Innovation**: AI is not meant to replace human creativity but to augment it. AI-powered tools can assist students with brainstorming ideas, generating creative content, and exploring innovative solutions to problems. This fosters a culture of innovation and prepares students to thrive in the dynamic job market. Some of the popular

AI tools for career planning and progression are furnished in **Table 1.4** and **Table 1.5** provides AI Tools used to prepare for Job Interviews. These tools can be selected based on the specific area of interview preparation you want to focus on, such as communication skills, job-specific questions, or video interview performance.

Table 1.4. AI Tools for Content Creation

Sl. No	Name of AI Tool	Application
1	Jasper	Blog Post Writing
2	Copy	Social Media Copywriting
3	Surfer SEO	SEO Writing
4	Canva	Image Generation
5	InVideo	Video Content Creation
6	Synthesis	Avatar Video Creation
7	Murf	Text-to-Voice Generation
8	Descript	Audio and Video Editing
9	HubSpot	AI-powered Content Strategy
10	ChatGPT	Content Ideation and Writing
11	Gemini	Multimodal AI Reasoning
12	Chatbot	Gather on Company Culture
13	Perplexity	Resume building, Mock Interview
14	Grammarly	Writing Partner

Source: Complied from various sources

Table 1.5. AI Tools to Prepare for Job Interview

AI Tool	Purpose	Key Features	How It Works
Interview Warmup (Google)	Practice answering job-specific questions	Feedback on word usage, role-specific questions	Respond to questions; AI analyzes language and key terms
Prepper	Realistic mock interviews	Job-specific questions, response analytics	Record answers; AI assesses clarity, conciseness, performance
Yoodli	Improve communication and public speaking skills	Feedback on filler words, pacing, clarity, and speech patterns	Analyze speech patterns for verbal improvements

AI Tool	Purpose	Key Features	How It Works
Mock-AI (VMock)	Simulated interviews with detailed feedback	Evaluates content, tone, delivery	Simulates interviews, provides AI-based feedback
Hiration	Mock interviews and overall job preparation	Role-specific questions, feedback on confidence and communication	Analyze recorded answers with AI
HireVue	AI-driven practice for video interviews	Feedback on verbal and non-verbal cues, body language, and tone	Record responses, AI analyzes body language and tone
Big Interview	Comprehensive interview preparation tool	Custom interview tracks, industry-specific questions, AI feedback	Record answers, AI evaluates speaking skills and content
LinkedIn Interview Preparation	AI-based feedback for interview answers	Sample questions, feedback on responses, expert tips	Record or type answers; AI provides feedback
Otter.ai	Analyze verbal responses through transcription	Speech-to-text analysis, identify filler words and unclear phrasing	Transcribe answers to analyze language patterns
InterviewBuddy	Real-time mock interviews with coaching	Personalized feedback on body language, communication, and response quality	Simulate interviews; AI provides real-time performance feedback

Source: Complied from various sources

LinkedIn: It is a professional networking platform designed to help individuals and businesses connect, build relationships, and grow their professional networks. Launched in 2003, LinkedIn allows users to create a profile showcasing their skills, experiences, and accomplishments, making it one of the most popular tools for job searching, recruiting, and professional development.

Key Features of LinkedIn:

1. **Profile Creation:**

   - Users can create a detailed professional profile, including work experience, education, skills, certifications, and achievements.
   - It acts as an online resume and portfolio for showcasing expertise.

2. **Networking:**

   - LinkedIn allows users to connect with colleagues, business partners, potential employers, and industry professionals. You can send invitations to people to join your network and expand your professional relationships.

3. **Job Searching and Recruitment:**

   - LinkedIn has an extensive job board where users can search for jobs, apply directly, and follow companies of interest.
   - Recruiters use LinkedIn to find potential candidates by searching profiles that match job requirements.

4. **Groups and Communities:**

   - LinkedIn offers the opportunity to join industry-specific groups where professionals can discuss topics, share information, and network with others in similar fields.

5. **Content Sharing and Publishing:**

   - Users can post updates, share articles, and engage with others' content by liking, commenting, or sharing posts.
   - LinkedIn also allows users to publish long-form content (articles) to share their expertise, opinions, or insights on various topics.

6. **Learning and Development:**

   - LinkedIn Learning offers courses on various professional skills, such as leadership, digital marketing, coding, and more, to help users improve their competencies and advance their careers.

7. **Endorsements and Recommendations:**

   - Your connections can endorse the skills you've listed on your profile or write recommendations, adding credibility and trust to your profile.

8. **Company Pages:**

   - Companies can create their profiles, post updates, share insights, and list job openings. This helps businesses establish a presence and attract potential employees or clients.

Who Uses LinkedIn?

- **Job Seekers:** To search for jobs, network with potential employers, and build an online presence.
- **Recruiters and Employers:** To find suitable candidates, post job openings, and showcase company culture.
- **Entrepreneurs and Business Owners:** To connect with clients, partners, and investors, and to promote their business.
- **Professionals:** To stay updated on industry trends, expand their network, and share insights or knowledge.
- **Students and Graduates:** To build a professional presence and connect with potential employers early in their careers.

Why LinkedIn is Important?

- **Visibility:** Helps individuals and businesses establish a professional online presence.
- **Networking:** Facilitates connections with industry leaders, mentors, colleagues, and potential clients.

- **Job Opportunities:** Provides access to job postings and networking opportunities that can lead to career advancements.
- **Knowledge Sharing:** Offers a platform for exchanging ideas, learning, and growing professionally through interaction with others in the same industry.

Key Takeaways

✓ Mindset refers to a person's set of beliefs and attitudes that shape their perception and response to the world.

✓ A global mindset is the ability to perceive, interpret, and respond to the world with a broadened perspective that values diversity, adaptability, and intercultural awareness.

✓ There are two main types: fixed mindset, where abilities are seen as static, and growth mindset, where abilities can be developed through effort and learning. Cultivating a growth mindset leads to greater resilience, motivation, and success.

✓ An entrepreneurial mindset is a set of attitudes, behaviors, and skills that enable individuals to identify opportunities, embrace challenges, and take initiative in creating value.

✓ Entrepreneurial competencies refer to the specific skills, knowledge, and abilities that enable individuals to effectively identify opportunities, launch ventures, and succeed in personal and professional development.

✓ An entrepreneurial mindset is not limited to starting a business but can also be applied in various contexts, including personal development and achieving SDGs.

✓ To become an entrepreneur, one must develop the right entrepreneurial mindset, skills, competencies, and knowledge.

✓ Effectuation is a decision-making framework introduced by Saras Sarasvathy, particularly useful in uncertain and dynamic environments where traditional planning and prediction may be less effective.

✓ Personal finance is all about managing your money wisely to achieve your financial goals. It involves Income, budgeting and

✓ spending, saving, investing, debt management, and protection for the future.

✓ SWOT analysis is a planning tool used to assess the Strengths, Weaknesses, Opportunities, and Threats used in translating goals into actions.

✓ Goal setting is essential for continuous personal and professional development. The SMART framework is used for setting well-defined goals.

✓ KASH stands for Knowledge, Attitude, Skills, and Habits. The KASH box is a framework used to analyze and evaluate various aspects of the holistic development of an individual, team, or venture.

✓ Good etiquette helps foster positive, harmonious relationships and can create favorable impressions across various aspects of life.

✓ Professional Facebook groups, LinkedIn, Twitter, and other sites can be great places to network. Post thought-provoking articles, participate in dialogues, and establish connections with industry experts who have similar interests or work in your field.

✓ Enterprise AI is now revolutionizing education, offering students a pathway to carve out successful careers.

✓ LinkedIn is often considered a critical tool for professional development and career success.

Key Terms

AI Tools, Career Planning, and Progression, Education 4.0, Education 5.0, Effectuation, Entrepreneurship, Enterprise AI, Entrepreneurial Competencies, Entrepreneurial Mindset, Etiquettes, Fixed Mindset, Global Mindset, Goal Setting, Group Discussion, Growth Mindset, Industry 4.0, Industry 5.0, KASH Box, Leadership, LinkedIn, Managerial Thinking, Personal Finance, Sustainable Development Goals (SDGs), SWOT Analysis, Time Management, Transformational Leadership, Twenty-First Century Skills.

Quiz – Multiple Choice Questions

1. Why is an entrepreneurial mindset considered important in today's economy?

    a. It fosters innovation and drives economic growth.

    b. It encourages dependency on traditional employment structures.

    c. It limits opportunities for individuals to pursue their passions.

    d. None of the above

2. Which competency involves the ability to identify and seize opportunities for innovation and growth?

    a. Creativity

    b. Risk-taking

    c. Adaptability

    d. Leadership

3. Which competency involves the ability to bounce back from setbacks and failures?

    a. Endurance

    b. Creativity

    c. Decision-making

    d. Risk-taking

4. Which of the following statements best describes a characteristic of a growth mindset?

    a. Believing that abilities are fixed and cannot be changed.

    b. Embracing challenges and seeing failure as an opportunity for growth.

    c. Avoiding risks and challenges to maintain comfort.

    d. Feeling threatened by the success of others.

5. **Which Sustainable Development Goal (SDG) focuses on ensuring access to clean water and sanitation for all?**

    a. SDG 2
    b. SDG 3
    c. SDG 6
    d. SDG 9

6. **Which principle is associated with the entrepreneurial decision-making framework of effectuation?**

    a. The Butterfly Effect
    b. The Domino Principle
    c. The Bird-in-Hand Principle
    d. The Hindsight Bias

7. **In SWOT analysis, which component focuses on identifying internal factors that may hinder or limit success?**

    a. Strengths
    b. Weaknesses
    c. Opportunities
    d. Threats

8. **Which component of the KASH Box focuses on the concepts possessed by an individual?**

    a. Knowledge
    b. Attitudes
    c. Skills
    d. Habit

9. **What does the "S" represent in SWOT analysis?**

    a. Strategies
    b. Strengths
    c. Solutions
    d. Scenarios

10. Which of the following is a characteristic of a well-defined goal?

    a. Vague and ambiguous

    b. Unrealistic and unattainable

    c. Specific and measurable

    d. Specific, measurable, achievable, realistic and timebound

11. Which of the following is considered a liquid asset?

    a. Real estate

    b. Stocks

    c. Jewelry

    d. Savings account

12. What is the primary purpose of a budget?

    a. To restrict spending

    b. To track income only

    c. To allocate resources effectively

    d. To maximize debt

13. Which AI tool is suitable for blog post writing

    a. Jasper.ai

    b. Copy.ai

    c. Surfer SEO

    d. Canva

14. Which AI tool is effective for image generation

    a. Canva

    b. InVideo

    c. Synthesis

    d. Murf

15. Which AI tool is suitable for content ideation and writing

    a.   Murf

    b.   Descript

    c.   HubSpot

    d.   ChatGPT

16. Which of the following is a key feature of Industry 4.0 in education??

    a.   Focus on rote learning and memorization

    b.   Integration of advanced technologies like AI and IoT in classrooms

    c.   Limited access to digital resources

    d.   Emphasis on traditional manufacturing skills

17. Which of the following is an important characteristic of academic leadership?

    a.   Maintaining a strictly theoretical approach to research

    b.   Focus on publishing research in prestigious journals

    c.   Collaborating with industry for applied research and innovation

    d.   Avoiding any commercialization of research findings

18. What is the most important factor to ensure a successful group discussion?

    a.   Speaking the most during the discussion

    b.   Actively listening to others and contributing constructively

    c.   Disagreeing with all opinions to stand out

    d.   Waiting for the moderator to guide every step of the conversation

19. Which of the following is a common mistake to avoid during a group discussion?

    a.   Encouraging others to share their thoughts

    b.   Respectfully acknowledging differing opinions

    c.   Dominating the conversation without allowing others to speak

    d.   Summarizing key points at the end of the discussion

20. How do group discussions facilitate critical thinking among participants?

    a. By allowing individuals to express their opinions without any feedback

    b. By promoting the evaluation of diverse perspectives and ideas

    c. By focusing solely on reaching a consensus at all costs

    d. By encouraging participants to avoid challenging each other's views

Answers:

1. a) It fosters innovation and drives economic growth
2. a) Creativity
3. a) Endurance
4. b) Embracing challenges and seeing failure as an opportunity for growth.
5. c) SDG 6
6. c) The Bird-in-Hand Principle
7. b) Weakness
8. a) Knowledge
9. b) Strengths
10. d) Specific, measurable, achievable, realistic and timebound
11. d) Savings account
12. c) To allocate resources effectively
13. a) Jasper.ai
14. a) Canva
15. d) ChatGPT
16. b) Integration of advanced technologies like AI and IoT in classrooms
17. c) Collaborating with industry for applied research and innovation
18. b) Actively listening to others and contributing constructively
19. c) Dominating the conversation without allowing others to speak
20. b) By promoting the evaluation of diverse perspectives and ideas

Exercise 1.1

<u>Assess Whether You have a Fixed Mindset or a Growth Mindset</u>

To assess whether you have a fixed mindset or a growth mindset, this questionnaire consists of **statements** based on **ten parameters of mindset**. After responding to each statement, compare your responses with the explanations at the end to see which mindset you align with more.

1. View of Intelligence

> A. Intelligence is something you're born with and cannot change much.
> B. Intelligence can be developed with time and effort.

2. Attitude Towards Challenges

> A. I tend to avoid challenges to minimize the risk of failure.
> B. I embrace challenges because they help me grow.

3. Response to Obstacles

> A. When faced with an obstacle, I often give up easily.
> B. Obstacles are part of learning, and I persist through them.

4. Effort

> A. Putting in effort feels like a sign of inadequacy.
> B. Effort is a necessary part of growth and improvement.

5. Reaction to Criticism

> A. I take criticism personally and feel threatened by it.
> B. Criticism is a valuable tool for learning and improving.

6. View of Failure

> A. Failure defines me and reflects my lack of ability.
> B. Failure is an opportunity to learn and adjust.

7. Reaction to Others' Success

A. I feel threatened by the success of others.

B. I find inspiration in others' success and seek to learn from it.

8. Belief in Change

A. People can't change their basic qualities.

B. People can grow and develop with effort over time.

9. Risk-Taking

A. I avoid risks to protect my sense of competence.

B. I take calculated risks because they are necessary for learning.

10. Self-perception

A. I often feel like I need to prove myself.

B. I focus on learning rather than proving my worth.

Answer Key

If you resonated with more A statements, you lean towards a Fixed Mindset.

If you resonated with more **B** statements, you lean towards a **Growth Mindset**.

Exercise 1.2

Assess Your Entrepreneurial Competencies

The self-assessment will help you identify your strengths and weaknesses of entrepreneurial competencies and take the necessary corrective measures. For each of the following statements, select the number on the scale that corresponds with your answer. Remember there are no right or wrong answers, so be as honest as you can.

Scale: 1=Not at all   2=Disagree   3=Neither agree nor disagree
4=Agree   5=Strongly agree

	Statements	1	2	3	4	5
1	When faced with challenges or problems, I view them as opportunities for growth, innovation, or improvement.					
2	I can understand the needs, desires, and pain points of others, and I actively seek ways to address those needs with compassion and empathy.					
3	I often find myself exploring unconventional ideas, thinking outside the box, and seeking innovative solutions to problems or tasks."					
4	In a complex situation, I tend to rely upon my intuition and instinct to help make a decision					
5	I enjoy building and working in teams where we can combine our skills to achieve our goals effectively					
6	I believe in building trust through actions, by consistently demonstrating integrity, reliability, and accountability					
7	I believe in taking calculated risks, and carefully evaluating potential outcomes and opportunities for growth before making decisions					
8	I'm willing to take well-considered risks to achieve my goals.					
9	I persevere through challenges and setbacks, staying resilient even when faced with adversity.					
10	I thrive in situations that require endurance, focus, and motivation until I reach successful outcomes					
11	I easily adjust to changing circumstances and embrace new situations with an open mind.					
12	I embrace uncertainty as an opportunity for growth, quickly adapting to unexpected changes with resilience and creativity.					

13	I actively seek out opportunities to expand my network and build meaningful connections with others.					
14	I leverage my network effectively to access resources, gather information, and create mutually beneficial opportunities					
15	I effectively convey ideas and information to others, adapting my communication style to suit different audiences					
16	I actively listen to others' perspectives and concerns, fostering constructive dialogue and collaboration.					
17	I maintain a positive attitude and stay focused on my objectives, even in the face of obstacles.					
18	I am internally driven to pursue my goals, finding fulfillment and satisfaction in the process of learning, growing, and achieving.					
19	I approach my goals with unwavering enthusiasm and energy, driven by a genuine love					
20	I find joy and fulfillment in immersing myself fully in activities that align with my interests, leading to a sense of purpose					

Scoring: Add up the score for each statement and take a look at the final score to understand your profile.

A score between **40 to 59** indicates **Low Entrepreneurial Capability**. You may lack the competencies provided in this chapter. Identify weak areas and develop goals and action plans to overcome them.

A score between **60 and 79** indicates a **Medium Entrepreneurial Capability**. You need to identify certain areas of weakness which may act as barriers to achieving your goals.

A score of **80 and above** indicates a **High Entrepreneurial Capability**. It shows you have a firm belief in your capabilities and a powerful drive to achieve your goals. You can take risks, and bounce back from setbacks, the ability to solve problems will stand you in good stead as you plan your venture.

Entrepreneurial Profile: You can draw your profile using MS Excel. Please follow the instructions given below.

- **Opportunity Identification:** Add the scores of Questions 1 and 2
- **Creativity and Innovation:** Add the scores of Questions 3 and 4
- **Leadership and Team building:** Add the scores of Questions 5 and 6
- **Risk Management:** Add the scores of Questions 7 and 8
- **Endurance:** Add the scores of Questions 9 and 10
- **Adaptability and Flexibility:** Add the scores of Questions 11 and 12
- **Networking and Relationship building:** Add the scores of Questions 13 and 14
- **Communication and Persuasion:** Add the scores of Questions 15 and 16
- **Goal Setting and Motivation:** Add the scores of Questions 17 and 18
- Passion: Add the scores of Questions 19 and 20

Draw a chart by plotting competencies along the Y-axis and Scores of each competency along the X-axis. You will know your stronger and weaker competencies. Set goals and prepare an action plan to work on at least 3 weaker competencies.

Exercise 1.3

Assess Your Leadership Quotient

Instructions: Work through the leadership quotient self-assessment, which asks you to assess yourself on a scale of 1 to 10. Where 1 is the least and 10 is the highest. Think about each quality carefully and try to be as honest as possible with yourself.

Sl. No	Trait	Description	Rating
1	Inspiration	Find a cause or purpose and inspire others to work	
2	Integrity	Demonstrate honesty, transparency, and ethical behavior, earning the trust of others	
3	Adaptable	Adapt to changing circumstances	

4	Innovation	Embrace innovation, and navigate ambiguity with resilience and flexibility.	
5	Decision	Take initiative and be able to make decisions	
6	Impact	Take responsibility for making a positive impact on the task	
7	Influence	Ability to affect the behavior of others in a particular direction	
8	Empathetic	Understand the needs, feelings, and perspectives of others	
9	Communication	Effective communication skills	
10	Team building	Ability to build the team, collaborate, and work towards a goal	

Scoring

Low: Less than 50: Need to work on acquiring leadership traits

Moderate: 51-70: Good beginning identify those traits with lower scores and work on them

High: 71 and above Strong leadership quality.

Activity 1.1

Comprehensive SWOT Analysis for Career Planning

Introduction: Identifying your strengths, weaknesses, opportunities, and threats is an important part of self-improvement. By evaluating the areas where you excel, as well as the areas you need to work on, you can gain a better understanding of yourself and set goals for growth. Self-awareness is the key to unlocking your full potential. When you understand your SWOT, you can make better decisions, set realistic goals, and work towards achieving them. This activity represents a projective technique to understand your potential.

If you're thinking about starting a business, identifying your SWOT isn't just an exercise to make you feel good (or bad) about yourself. It's a process that will allow you to understand how you can be most effective at what you do, and where you'll need to improve if you want to be successful.

Objectives

A SWOT analysis is a strategic planning tool used to identify the Strengths, Weaknesses, Opportunities, and Threats related to a particular situation or decision. When applied to students' career planning and goal setting, it can help them gain clarity about their current situation and make informed decisions about their future. A SWOT matrix is a framework for analyzing your strengths and weaknesses as well as the opportunities and threats that you face. This helps you focus on your strengths, minimize your weaknesses, take the greatest possible advantage of opportunities available to you, and address threats.

Instructions

- Clarify your strengths and weaknesses and list them (at least five) in the order.
- Identify the opportunities that are available to you, as well as the threats you're exposed to and list them (at least five) in the order.
- Use your SWOT Analysis as the starting point for a solid career and life plan and goal setting.

Strengths:

1. Academic achievements: Strong grades, honors, awards, etc.
2. Skills and talents: Abilities in specific subjects, extracurricular activities, leadership skills, etc.
3. Personal qualities: Determination, resilience, creativity, etc.
4. Support network: Family, friends, mentors, teachers, etc., who can offer guidance and support.
5. Resources: Access to educational resources, libraries, online courses, etc.

Weaknesses:

1. Lack of experience: Limited work experience or internship opportunities.
2. Skill gaps: Areas where improvement is needed, such as communication skills, technical skills, etc.

3. Time management: Struggles with balancing academic workload, extracurricular activities, and personal life.
4. Limited network: Few connections within desired industries or professions.
5. Financial constraints: Limited resources for further education or professional development.

Opportunities:

1. Networking events: Opportunities to meet professionals in desired fields through workshops, conferences, career fairs, etc.
2. Internships and volunteer work: Gaining hands-on experience in relevant industries or roles.
3. Educational programs: Scholarships, grants, and other opportunities for further education or skill development.
4. Industry trends: Identifying growing sectors or emerging career paths.
5. Mentorship: Finding mentors who can provide guidance and support in career development.

Threats:

1. Economic factors: Job market fluctuations, economic downturns, etc.
2. Technological advancements: Automation, AI, and other technologies disrupting traditional job roles.
3. Competition: High competition for jobs, scholarships, and other opportunities.
4. Changing industries: Industries becoming obsolete or facing significant changes.
5. Geographic constraints: Limited job opportunities in a specific location or region.

By conducting a SWOT analysis, students can develop a better understanding of their strengths and weaknesses, identify growth opportunities, and prepare for potential challenges in their career planning and goal-setting process. This analysis can serve as a foundation for creating action plans and making informed decisions about education, internships, networking, and other career-related activities.

SWOT MATRIX TEMPLATE

Internal Factors	
Strengths (+)	**Weakness (–)**
1.	1.
2.	2.
3.	3.
4.	4.
5.	5.
External Factors	
Opportunities (+)	**Threats (–)**
1.	1.
2.	2.
3.	3.
4.	4.
5.	5.

Activity 1.2

Goal Setting

Based on your SWOT analysis Set one SMART goal using the following template under each category. Based on SWOT analysis and goal setting write a story about yourself and what you want to be five years from now.

Goals	Specific	Measurable	Achievable	Relevant	Time-bound
Personal Growth					
Professional Growth					
Health					
Financial Growth					
Family and Friends					
Hobbies					

Activity 1.3

Time Management

Objective: To provide students with essential time management skills for academic success and personal well-being.

Materials Needed: Presentation slides, Whiteboard, or flip chart, Markers, Timer, or stopwatch

Introduction: Welcome students and introduce the importance of time management.

Understanding Priority setting: Explain the concept of prioritization and its role in effective time management. Introduce the Eisenhower Matrix and its four quadrants. Provide examples of tasks for each quadrant.

Prioritization Exercise: Divide students into small groups. Provide scenarios for students to categorize into the Eisenhower Matrix quadrants. Facilitate group discussion on task prioritization.

Time Management Strategies: Present practical time management strategies, such as goal-setting, creating to-do lists, and using calendars.

Application and Reflection: Have students reflect on their current time management habits and identify areas for improvement. Facilitate students to develop a personalized time management plan.

Q&A and Wrap-up: Address any questions or concerns from students.

Summarize key takeaways and encourage students to implement the strategies learned. This activity provides students with a concise overview of time management principles and practical strategies for immediate application. It emphasizes active participation and reflection to empower students to take control of their time and productivity.

Activity 1.4

<u>Story of Me: Personal Branding - The Puzzle Pieces of My Life</u>

Objective: Personal branding is the process of defining and promoting what you stand for as an individual. Your brand is a culmination of the experiences, skills, and values that differentiate you. To introduce yourself in a unique, thoughtful way by sharing key aspects of your life, personality, and interests using symbolic "puzzle pieces" that represent different areas of who you are.

Materials (for a group setting):

- Pre-cut blank puzzle pieces (made of paper or cardboard) or a digital template for virtual settings.
- Markers, pens, or colors (for in-person).
- For virtual settings: a shared document or slide where participants can add text or images.

Steps:

1. **Prepare Your Puzzle:**
    Choose 5-6 key aspects of your life that define who you are. These aspects will represent the "puzzle pieces" of your identity. For example:

    a. **Personal Background:** Where you're from, cultural influences, your family background, and educational qualification.
    b. **Values:** The core beliefs or principles that guide your life.
    c. **Skills and Talents:** Your strengths and weaknesses. What you excel at, professionally or personally.
    d. **Passions/Interests:** Hobbies, things that excite you, or what you love doing in your free time.
    e. **Milestones:** Significant moments in your life that have shaped who you are today.
    f. **Aspirations:** Where you see yourself heading in the future, your dreams or career goals.

2. **Fill in the Puzzle Pieces:** Each puzzle piece should reflect one of the aspects above. On each piece, either:

   - Write a short sentence or keyword that encapsulates that part of your life.
   - Draw a simple image or symbol to represent that aspect (for visual creativity).
   - For virtual settings: Use digital images, icons, or text in a shared slide or document.

3. **Put the Puzzle Together:**

   - Now that you've created your puzzle pieces, think of how they come together to form the "whole picture" of who you are.
   - Present your puzzle in order (chronologically, by importance, or in a creative sequence).
   - As you introduce each piece, explain why it is important to you and how it connects to the next piece. This forms the narrative of your story, making the introduction more cohesive and meaningful.

4. **Sharing the Final Picture:**

   - In a group setting: Lay your pieces on the table or hold them up one by one, sharing the meaning behind each.
   - In a virtual setting: Share your screen or upload your digital puzzle, talking through each piece as you go.

Example:

1. **Personal Background:** Born in a small town, having a bachelor's degree in commerce, from an agricultural family, details of your siblings, were raised with diverse cultural influences
2. **Values:** "Empathy and innovation guide everything I do."
3. **Skills and Talents:** "Great with numbers, passionate about solving problems creatively." Need to improve communication skills and overcome stage fear.

4. **Passions/Interests**: "Love exploring nature and practicing photography."
5. **Milestones:** "Started my own business last year, a huge leap forward."
6. **Aspirations:** "Dream of working internationally, promoting sustainability."

Reflection Questions (for deeper engagement):

- What was the most important puzzle piece, and why?
- How do all these pieces connect to shape the person you are today?
- Which piece represents where you're heading in the future?

Wrap-Up:

This activity gives a complete picture of yourself beyond simple facts, allowing your audience to see the experiences, values, and aspirations that make you who you are. It's both creative and personal, allowing you to share what matters most to you.

Activity 1.5

Group Discussion to Enhance Critical Thinking

Objective: Group discussions are a dynamic way of exchanging ideas, exploring different perspectives, and engaging in collective problem-solving. They are commonly used in educational, professional, and assessment settings to encourage collaboration and test critical thinking. Here's a guide on how to design and participate in an effective group discussion.

What is a Group Discussion (GD)?

A group discussion involves a group of people (typically 5–10) discussing a particular topic or problem for a set period (usually 20-30 minutes). The objective is to share opinions, discuss various perspectives, and sometimes come to a consensus on the issue at hand.

Key Elements of a Group Discussion

1. Topic or Problem: The central point of discussion, which could be a current issue, case study, abstract idea, or business problem.
2. Participants: Individuals contributing to the discussion with their insights, ideas, and arguments.
3. Moderator (optional): A facilitator who may guide the discussion, ask questions, and ensure that everyone gets a chance to speak.
4. Conclusion: Ideally, a summary or conclusion is drawn based on the points discussed.

Topics For Group Discussion: Factual, Controversial, Abstract, Case Study

Steps to Conduct a Successful Group Discussion

1. Select a Topic:

- Choose a topic relevant to the group's objectives or goals.
- Ensure it is open-ended enough to allow diverse perspectives and deep engagement.

2. Introduction by the Moderator (Optional):

- Briefly introduce the topic and rules.
- Set expectations for respectful and constructive communication.
- Define the time limit for the discussion.

3. Initial Opinions (2-3 minutes):

- Each participant is allowed to share their initial thoughts or a brief opening statement about the topic.
- This sets the stage for further debate and discussion.

4. Discussion (10–25 minutes):

- Open the floor for interaction, debate, and elaboration on the points made.

- Encourage active listening, building on others' points, and providing evidence or examples to support arguments.
- Ensure that quieter participants are also encouraged to contribute.

5. Summarization (5 minutes):

- In the final phase, either the moderator or one of the participants summarizes the key points discussed.
- If appropriate, the group should try to reach a conclusion, consensus, or action plan based on the discussion.

Tips for Participants in a Group Discussion

1. Preparation:

- Research the topic if provided in advance. Have a few key points, statistics, or examples to back up your ideas.
- Be ready to think critically and express your opinions clearly.

2. Communication:

- Be clear and concise: Express your points succinctly. Avoid long-winded explanations.
- Listen actively: Engage with others' ideas, build on them, or counter them respectfully.
- Stay calm and composed: Even in a debate, keep your tone professional. Don't interrupt others.

3. Collaboration:

- Work towards fostering a discussion, not dominating it. Encourage quieter participants by asking for their views.
- Look for common ground and areas of agreement, especially in case of conflicts.

4. Body Language:

- Maintain eye contact and exhibit positive body language to show engagement.

- Avoid negative non-verbal cues like crossing your arms or looking disinterested.

Common Mistakes to Avoid in a Group Discussion

- Interrupting Others: Cutting someone off can be perceived as disrespectful and may create a negative impression.
- Over-Dominating: Speaking too much without giving others a chance can derail the discussion and limit collaboration.
- Off-Topic Statements: Stay focused on the topic to ensure that the discussion remains relevant and productive.
- Being Passive: Not contributing enough or merely agreeing with others without adding value may reflect poorly on your involvement.

Activity 1.6

How to Excel in Interviews Using AI

Objective: Our students are entering an ever-more-cutthroat job market, in which the competition not only includes highly qualified candidates with in-demand hard and soft skills but also applicants who are using AI to finesse their resumes and cover letters and excel at their interviews.

Follow the following four steps to research potential employers, hold mock interviews, don't accept a mismatched job offer, and find a job that aligns with personal preferences, values, interests, and dispositions.

Step 1: Research Potential Employers

As an example, here's what you get when you ask an AI tool such as Chat GPT-4 about the culture at a large global technology company (this is a lightly edited excerpt of my interaction with this tool):

Prompt: What kind of culture should I expect if I join Company Ozone?

Response: At Company Ozone, we prioritize recognition, empowerment, teamwork, empathy, the evolution of performance management, internal mobility, continuous feedback, and talent development.

Prompt: What are the downsides/negatives of Company Ozone's culture?

Response: Lack of diversity and inclusion.

Step 2: Work with the AI to Unpack Keywords in Job Descriptions

If you want to help your students prepare for mock interviews, suggest they select keywords or skills from job descriptions of companies they're interested in, and then ask the AI how companies evaluate candidates for those qualities.

For example, if your students are applying for a position that necessitates strong business development skills, they can use the following prompt:

Prompt: Name the top three personality traits, values, and skills associated with people who are great at business development.

Response: Personality traits: relationship building, strategic thinking, adaptability. Values: integrity, persistence, collaboration. Skills: communication skills, analytical skills, project management.

Remember to focus on adaptability and communication skills when answering interview questions about overcoming challenges and accomplishments.

Step 3: Get Guidance from the AI to Answer Potential Interview Questions

Students can use AI to learn about commonly asked interview questions, the best ways to answer them, common mistakes to avoid, and evaluation criteria. AI can personalize the output with details about the student's background, education, experience, skills, and job specifics. Here are some general prompts and example answers for students to use.

Prompt: What are some of the most common questions asked in job interviews?

Response: Tell me about yourself; why do you want to work in this company; what are your greatest strengths and weaknesses; tell me about a challenging situation and how you handled it; where do you see yourself in five years?

Prompt: How should I answer the dreaded question about what my greatest weakness is?

Response: Identify a genuine weakness that is honest and relevant for the job, but not a critical job requirement. Show self-awareness, explaining how you became aware of it. Discuss actions taken to address it, including personal training and learning initiatives to mitigate it. Highlight progress and results, and end on a positive note.

"One of my greatest weaknesses has been my public speaking skills. I realized this during a presentation in the project viva voce examination when I noticed I was feeling anxious and struggled to convey my ideas effectively. To address this, I enrolled in a public speaking course and joined a local Toastmasters club. Over time, I've seen significant improvement in my confidence and ability to engage an audience."

Prompt: What are some examples of bad behavioral etiquette to avoid in job interviews?

Response: Arriving late, inappropriate attire, lack of preparation, interrupting the interviewers, not making eye contact, showing nervousness, neglecting the question, and bringing up sensitive topics.

4. Partner with the AI to Hold a Mock Interview

Here are some sample prompts students can use to begin a mock interview exercise:

Imagine I'm a job candidate answering the below question during an interview. I will provide some answers and you can tell me what job interviewers are likely to think, and what I can do to improve.

I'm applying for an interview for the role of management trainee. Pretend you are the interviewer and ask typical questions in this context.

Follow-up questions could include:

Tell me what you think of my answers and how I can improve them.

Tell me how you would answer these questions if you were a top candidate.

Let's repeat this with other questions/answers.

Here's a sample exchange with ChatGPT so you can see how a mock interview may play out for your students.

Prompt: Imagine I'm a job candidate answering the below question during an interview. I will provide some answers and you can tell me what job interviewers are likely to think, and what I can do to improve.

Response: Do you enjoy working with others?

Prompt: Sometimes. It's easier when they agree with me and share my values. However, when they think differently, I tend to find them somewhat obnoxious, so I prefer to work alone.

Response: Here's what interviewers might think and how you can improve your answer:

    a.   Lack of Teamwork
    b.   Closed Mindedness
    c.   Negative Attitude

"Collaboration leads to innovative solutions and a richer work environment. I value diversity in thought and open communication to find common ground. Working as a team allows us to achieve more than we could individually."

Situation 1.1

Rohit's Dilemma: Entrepreneurship - A Challenge or an Opportunity

Rohit is an environmental science graduate who is eager to have a positive impact on the world and is passionate about sustainability. He's thinking about his alternatives for the future and can't decide between launching his own sustainable focused company or going after a standard position in the environmental field.

Challenge Perspective:

Rohit views entrepreneurship as a formidable undertaking from one perspective. He understands the dangers involved in managing regulatory obstacles, building a brand, and recruiting customers in addition to securing money. He is concerned about his lack of experience in areas such as marketing, finance, and management because he is a novice to the corporate world. Rohit is aware that creating a profitable company involves perseverance, commitment, and a readiness to experience setbacks and disappointments along the road. Being an entrepreneur comes with a lot of uncertainty, therefore he questions his readiness for such a challenging endeavor.

Opportunity Perspective:

However, Rohit sees entrepreneurship as a fantastic opportunity. He sees it as an opportunity to make his love of sustainability into a worthwhile endeavor that fits with his principles and objectives. Rohit thinks he can directly and physically address environmental challenges and bring about positive change in his community by launching his own business. The idea of being in charge, setting his direction, and starting from zero to create something that embodies his values and vision excites him. For Rohit, becoming an entrepreneur is an opportunity to express his creativity, innovate, and grow personally. It also gives him the chance to meet new people, work with like-minded people, and change the world.

What is your suggestion to Rohit?

Learning

From this situation, Rohit understands that being an entrepreneur presents both opportunities and challenges. Risks and uncertainties notwithstanding, it's a chance for him to follow his passions, fulfill his aspirations, and make a lasting impression. Rohit thinks he can have a successful and meaningful job that changes the world if he embraces the chances and challenges that come with being an entrepreneur.

Simulation Game 1.1

Decision-Making

Title: Entrepreneurship vs. Employment

This simulation game revolves around the choice between pursuing entrepreneurship as a career path or working as an employee.

Background:

You are a recent graduate with a degree in business administration. You have two opportunities: starting your business venture or accepting a job offer at a well-established company.

Options:

Entrepreneurship: Start your business venture, taking on the challenges and risks of entrepreneurship. This option offers autonomy, freedom, creativity, and the potential for high rewards, but also involves uncertainty, financial risk, and working long hours.

Employment: Accept a job offer at a reputable company, providing stability, benefits, and opportunities for career growth. This option offers a steady income, structured work environment, and potential for professional development, but may limit freedom, autonomy, and creativity.

Potential Consequences:

Option 1 (Entrepreneurship): Potential for financial success and personal fulfillment but also risk of failure, financial loss, and stress.

Option 2 (Employment): Stability, benefits, and career advancement opportunities but the potential for limited creativity, autonomy, and entrepreneurial fulfillment.

Decision-Making Exercise:

Individual Reflection:

- Present participants with the entrepreneurship vs. employment dilemma.
- Instruct participants to individually reflect on their career aspirations, personal values, and risk tolerance.
- Encourage participants to consider their long-term goals, passion for entrepreneurship, and willingness to embrace uncertainty.

Decision and Justification:

- Have participants choose one of the two options—entrepreneurship or employment—based on their personal preferences and career aspirations.
- Instruct participants to justify their decision, explaining why they believe their chosen option aligns with their values, goals, and circumstances.

Group Discussion:

- Divide participants into small groups based on their chosen options.
- Instruct groups to discuss the advantages, disadvantages, and potential consequences of their chosen option.
- Encourage groups to share personal experiences, insights, and perspectives related to entrepreneurship and employment.

Debate and Exploration:

- Facilitate a debate and exploration of the different viewpoints and perspectives among the groups.
- Encourage participants to challenge each other's assumptions, explore alternative viewpoints, and consider the potential trade-offs of entrepreneurship vs. employment.

Reflection and Debrief:

- Lead a reflective discussion on the decision-making exercise
- What factors influenced participants' decisions?
- How did participants weigh the trade-offs between entrepreneurship and employment?
- What insights can be gained from exploring the potential consequences of each option?

Application to Real Life:

- Discuss strategies for making career decisions and navigating the opportunities and challenges of entrepreneurship and employment.
- Encourage participants to reflect on how they can apply the insights gained from the exercise to their own career paths and decision-making processes.
- Through this simulation exercise, participants gain practical experience in making decisions about their career paths and aspirations. They explore different factors influencing the choice between entrepreneurship and employment, such as risk tolerance, passion, and long-term goals, fostering critical thinking skills and self-awareness essential for navigating career decisions in the real world.

Simulation Game 1.2

Tower Together: The Team Building Challenge

Objective: To build team, effective communication, and problem-solving skills within the team through a tower-building simulation game.

Game Overview: Five teams (4 to 6 members) are assigned the task of constructing the tallest and most structurally sound tower with aesthetic value using limited materials. The game emphasizes collaboration, creativity, and strategic planning as teams work together to design and build their towers within a specified time frame.

Game Elements

1. **Materials:** Provide teams with a set of materials such as paper cups, cardboard, tape, straws, and other common office supplies to construct their towers. Each team receives the same materials to ensure fairness.

2. **Constraints:** Introduce constraints such as time limits, budget restrictions, or specific design requirements to challenge teams and encourage creative problem-solving.

3. **Team Roles:** Assign roles within each team, such as project manager, architect, builder, and quality control inspector, to ensure effective coordination and division of tasks.

4. **Planning Phase:** Allow teams a designated planning phase to brainstorm ideas, develop a construction plan, and allocate responsibilities among team members.

5. **Construction Phase:** Teams begin building their towers based on their plans, utilizing their creativity and teamwork to assemble the structure.

6. **Testing Phase:** After the construction phase, each team presents their tower to the group. The towers are tested for stability by placing weights on top to simulate real-world conditions.

7. **Scoring Criteria:** Establish scoring criteria based on factors such as height, stability, aesthetics, planning, and teamwork. Encourage teams to focus not only on building the tallest tower but also on demonstrating effective teamwork and problem-solving skills.

8. **Reflection and Feedback:** Facilitate a debriefing session after the game to allow teams to reflect on their performance, share insights, and provide feedback to one another. Discuss lessons learned and identify areas for improvement.

Benefits:

- Promotes teamwork and collaboration as teams work together towards a common goal.

- Encourages identifying the talent of each team member such as creative thinking, communication, attitude, critical thinking, and problem-solving skills.
- Enhances communication and coordination among team members.
- Builds trust and camaraderie within the team.
- Provides a hands-on and engaging learning experience for participants.

Scoring:

Criteria	Planning	Height	Stability	Aesthetic	Teamwork	Total
Score	20	20	20	20	20	100
Team A						
Team B						
Team C						
Team D						
Team E						

Note: Adjust the difficulty level and complexity of the game based on the size of the teams, available resources, and desired learning outcomes. Encourage a supportive and inclusive environment where all team members have the opportunity to contribute and participate.

Role Play 1.1

The Importance of Communication

Role play set in the Career Guidance Cell on a college campus, demonstrating the **importance of communication for career development.**

Setting: The Career Guidance Cell of a college campus where students are seeking advice and guidance for their career paths to the career advisor.

In this role play, the career advisor along with college students effectively demonstrates how communication skills such as networking, active listening, and presentation can significantly impact career development, all within the setting of the Career Guidance Cell on the college campus.

Character 1: Vinayak - The Career Advisor

Character 2: James - The Proactive Communicator

Character 3: Maya - The Active Listener

Character 4: Ashwini - The Networking Enthusiast

Character 5: Sarah - The Presentation Expert

Vinayak: (Speaking to the students assembled in the Career Guidance Cell) Good morning to all of you! We're going to talk about how important communication is to the development of your career. First, let's examine how having strong communication skills might affect your career path.

James: Hello, Vinayak I've been actively using my communication abilities to improve my chances of getting a job. I've been successful in securing informative interviews and even job shadowing chances in my target field through aggressive networking and tailored outreach emails.

Maya: (Acknowledging with a nod) Well done, James. Active listening is equally vital, I've discovered. I've learned a lot about various businesses and career choices by actively participating in talks at networking events and informational interviews. I've been able to make better judgments regarding my professional path because to this.

Ashwini: (Entering the dialogue) For me, networking has also changed the game. I've grown my professional network and made valuable connections with professionals in the sector by going to employment fairs, alumni networking events, and professional workshops. In order to leave a lasting impression, effective verbal and nonverbal communication has been essential.

Sarah: (Wanting to impart) Having strong presentation abilities has helped me greatly in my work. Being able to articulate my ideas convincingly and effectively has helped me stand out from the competition, whether I'm pitching for an internship or presenting a concept to a panel of business experts.

Vinayak: As you can see, success in the cutthroat job market of today requires strong communication abilities. Developing your abilities in networking, active listening, and professional presentation will surely lead to great job prospects. Apart from what you've previously described, could each of you tell me what other elements make up effective communication?

James: Clarity and Vocabulary. Your message must be precise and succinct. Make use of clear, concise language; stay away from jargon and excessively complicated terminology. Get right to the point while making sure that all pertinent details are successfully communicated. Being concise makes it easier to keep your audience's interest and avoid confusion. Make sure the people in your audience can understand what you're saying.

Maya: Numerous clues can be revealed through gestures, facial expressions, and body language. Make sure your body language supports your message, keep eye contact, and make suitable facial expressions. Nonverbal clues have the power to improve or worsen your conversation.

Ashwini: Communicating with confidence gives your message credibility and trustworthiness. Maintain a straight back, exude confidence through your tone of voice, and speak with assurance. Respect your audience by paying close attention to what they have to say, taking into account their points of view, and not talking over or interrupting them. Open communication and healthy relationships are promoted by respectful communication.

Sarah: Adjust your communication style to fit various contexts and target audiences. Adapt your strategy, language, and tone to the situation and the tastes of your audience. Your conversation will be more effective if you are flexible.

Vinayak: (Supporting the collective) I appreciate everyone sharing their stories. Practice active listening by paying attention to the speaker, responding appropriately, deferring judgment, providing feedback, be careful about your body language. and practicing empathy. Clarity, vocabulary, concision, confidence, gesture, posture, body language, active listening, tone, timing, purpose, cultural sensitivity, and constructive criticism are the essential elements of effective communication.

Project 1.1

<u>Demonstrate Entrepreneurial Mindset in Achieving Sustainable Development Goals</u>

This is a project on **Sustainable Development Goal 13: Climate Action,** featuring college students. This project is designed for college students to **brainstorm** and demonstrate effective leadership, team building, communication, decision-making, and a commitment to addressing **SDG 13: Climate Action within their campus and community through their extension activity.**

Character 1: Arun - The Enthusiastic Leader

Character 2: Maya - The Researcher and Analyst

Character 3: Lakshmi - The Communicator and Liaison

Character 4: Priya - The Creative Innovator

Character 5: Ryan - The Decision-Making Facilitator

Setting: A college campus where a group of students is involved in the brainstorming session for an extension activity focused on **SDG 13: Climate Action**.

Arun: (Taking the lead with enthusiasm) Hello, everyone! Thanks for joining. Today, we're diving into SDG 13: Climate Action. Let's brainstorm ways we can contribute to combating climate change within our campus and community.

Maya: (Analytical and research-oriented) Before we start brainstorming, let's gather data on our campus's carbon footprint and examine local climate change impacts. Understanding the situation will guide us in formulating effective solutions.

Lakshmi: (Facilitating communication) I suggest we reach out to campus sustainability groups, environmental organizations, and local government agencies to gather insights and identify ongoing initiatives related to climate action. Collaboration will amplify our efforts.

Priya: (Injecting creativity) As we research, let's think outside the box. We could organize eco-friendly events, develop posters to promote eco-friendly activities, implement recycling and composting programs, or advocate for sustainable transportation using bicycle on the campus.

Ryan: (Focusing on decision-making) Once we have a list of potential ideas, let's assess their feasibility, impact, and scalability. We'll need to prioritize initiatives that can make a tangible difference while engaging our campus and community.

Arun: (Synthesizing ideas) Great suggestions, everyone. Let's divide into teams to conduct research, reach out to stakeholders, brainstorm ideas, and assess feasibility. Maya, could you lead the research team? Lakshmi, can you coordinate our communications efforts? Priya, I'd like you to head the brainstorming sessions. And Ryan, please oversee the decision-making process. You can form your subgroups for designated tasks.

(They break into smaller teams and begin their respective tasks. After a designated time, they reconvene.)

Maya: (Presenting research findings) Our team discovered that our campus emits a significant amount of greenhouse gases, primarily from energy consumption and transportation. Additionally, local climate impacts include more frequent heatwaves and extreme weather events.

Lakshmi: (Sharing insights from outreach) Through our conversations with campus sustainability groups and local organizations, we identified initiatives like energy efficiency campaigns, tree planting projects, and advocacy for renewable energy policies.

Priya: (Presenting creative ideas) Building on that, we brainstormed ideas like hosting a sustainability fair, launching a campus-wide carbon footprint reduction challenge, and creating art installations to raise awareness about climate change.

Ryan: (Facilitating decision-making) Based on our criteria, let's prioritize initiatives that can reduce our campus's carbon footprint, raise awareness about climate change, and mobilize our campus community to take action. We'll need to allocate resources accordingly and establish timelines for implementation.

Arun: (Making decisions) Thank you, everyone, for your hard work, commitment and dedication. Let's move forward with initiatives focused on energy efficiency campaigns, tree planting projects, and hosting a sustainability fair. We'll form project teams to execute each idea and continue collaborating with our campus and community partners to maximize our impact.

The team used AI tools and developed a video for building awareness of SDGs among the various stakeholders. The team also developed an action plan and implemented the project on the campus within three months.

Note: Similarly, Projects may be developed for remaining SDGs for other groups

Quick Case 1.1

<u>Airbnb Demonstrating Principles of Effectuation</u>

Introduction

Airbnb's entrepreneurial journey is a classic example of **effectuation**, a theory developed by Dr. Saras Sarasvathy, which explains how entrepreneurs make decisions and act in conditions of uncertainty. Instead of setting out with a clear vision or comprehensive plan, effectuation emphasizes starting with the resources at hand and adjusting the business model as opportunities and constraints evolve. Airbnb's founders, **Brian Chesky, Joe Gebbia, and Nathan Blecharczyk**, demonstrated effectuation principles throughout their entrepreneurial journey.

1. Bird-in-Hand Principle (Start with What You Have)

When Chesky and Gebbia faced financial challenges, they didn't start with a grand plan. Instead, they used what they had—their San Francisco apartment—and offered air mattresses for rent during a design conference. This modest beginning led to the creation of Airbnb. By leveraging the limited resources they had at the moment, they were able to test an idea and gauge interest, a classic application of the bird-in-hand principle.

2. Affordable Loss Principle (Focus on Downside)

Airbnb's founders embraced the idea of **affordable loss** by experimenting with the platform despite numerous early setbacks, including failed attempts to secure funding. They didn't invest large sums but rather used small, manageable resources (e.g., a basic website and personal effort) to test the market. They were willing to face failure but ensured that the cost of failure was bearable.

3. Crazy-Quilt Principle (Forming Partnerships)

In the early days, Airbnb formed partnerships with early adopters (hosts) and investors to build the platform. By collaborating with stakeholders who believed in their vision, Airbnb co-created a business that leveraged its partners' resources and networks. This principle allowed Airbnb to scale without having to control every aspect of its expansion directly.

4. Lemonade Principle (Leverage Surprises)

Airbnb's founders turned unexpected challenges into opportunities. For example, they initially struggled to gain traction, but they used setbacks as learning opportunities. By listening to feedback and improving their platform, particularly in areas like trust, safety, and ease of use, they turned failures into successes.

5. Pilot-in-the-Plane Principle (Control vs Prediction)

The founders believed that the future wasn't something to be predicted but something they could shape. They didn't wait for the right moment or perfect conditions but acted on the opportunities as they came, shaping Airbnb's future based on the evolving market.

Conclusion

Airbnb's success can be seen as a manifestation of **effectuation principles**—they started with limited resources, embraced uncertainty, formed strategic partnerships, and adapted to challenges. Their journey highlights the power of effectual thinking in creating and scaling a globally disruptive business from humble beginnings.

Case Questions:

1. How did Airbnb use the "affordable loss" principle to mitigate the risks in its early days?
2. In what ways did Airbnb's founders apply the "bird-in-hand" principle to leverage their limited resources?
3. How did forming partnerships (crazy-quilt principle) contribute to Airbnb's growth?
4. How can Airbnb continue to use effectuation principles to remain innovative in a competitive industry?

Discussion Questions

1. Why is an entrepreneurial mindset essential for success in today's VUCA world?
2. How can individuals develop and improve their entrepreneurial competencies?
3. What role do creativity and innovation play in a growth mindset, and how can they be fostered?
4. Differentiate between an entrepreneur and a salaried Person.
5. How to develop networking and relationship-building skills to enhance entrepreneurial competencies?
6. What are the main advantages and challenges of pursuing entrepreneurship as a career?
7. Describe a goal using the KASH model that focuses solely on developing new skills to excel in your chosen career field.

8. In conducting a SWOT analysis for your project, which internal and external factors do you identify as posing significant threats to its success?

9. How does effectuation impact entrepreneurial decision-making? what are some practical examples of how entrepreneurs apply this principle in their ventures?

10. Create a SMART goal for improving your grades in a specific subject this semester.

11. How can educational institutions better prepare students with the skills and mindset needed for leadership?

12. How can entrepreneurship be aligned with the Sustainable Development Goals to drive positive social and environmental impact?

13. What are the key components of a personal financial plan, and why is it important to have one?

14. What are the differences between saving and investing? Provide examples of each.

15. Identify various enterprise AI tools for career planning and progression.

16. How does academic leadership contribute to bridging the gap between theoretical knowledge and real-world applications?

References

1. Chinchure Aranvind (2021), New Age Organisation, Notion Press Media Private Limited.

2. Clark, D. (2017). Entrepreneurial You: Monetize Your Expertise, Create Multiple Income Streams, and Thrive. Harvard Business Review Press.

3. Drucker, P. F. (1985). Innovation and entrepreneurship: Practice and principles. Harper & Row.

4. Dweck, C. S. (2006). Mindset: The new psychology of success. Random House.

5. Humphrey, A. (2005). SWOT Analysis: A Practical Guide to Analyzing Your Strengths and Weaknesses, Opportunities and Threats. American Management Association.

6. Hisrich, R. D., Peters, M. P., & Shepherd, D. A. (2017). Entrepreneurship (10th ed.). McGraw-Hill Education.

7. Jadin, L., & Jones, S. (2023). The Twin Thieves: How Great Leaders Build Great Teams. Morgan James Publishing.

8. Joshi, A. (2020). Artificial Intelligence: A Guide to Intelligent Enterprise. Wiley.

9. Kuratko, D. F., & Hodgetts, R. M. (2017). Entrepreneurship: Theory, process, practice (10th ed.). Cengage Learning.

10. McClelland, D. C. (1961). The achieving society. D. Van Nostrand.

11. McGrath, R. G., & MacMillan, I. C. (2019). Entrepreneurial Mindset: How to Think Like an Entrepreneur. Harvard Business Review Press.

12. Northouse, P. G. (2021). Leadership: Theory and Practice (9th ed.). Sage Publications.

13. Sarasvathy, S. D. (2001). Causation and effectuation: Toward a theoretical shift from economic inevitability to entrepreneurial contingency. Academy of Management Review, 26(2), 243-263.

14. Sarasvathy, S. D. (2008). Effectuation: Elements of entrepreneurial expertise. Edward Elgar Publishing

15. Smith, J. A. (2020). Personal Development Strategies: Enhancing Knowledge, Attitudes, Skills, and Habits. Acme Publishing.

16. Smith, E., & Patel, D. (2022). Implementing AI in Higher Education: Strategies and Best Practices. Academic Press.

17. Stern, C. (2023). The Emotionally Strong Leader: An Inside-Out Journey to Transformational Leadership. Lioncrest Publishing.

18. United Nations. (2015). Transforming our world: The 2030 Agenda for Sustainable Development. United Nations.

<u>WORKSHEETS</u>

Chapter 2

Emotional Intelligence

MS Dhoni: Leading With Emotional Intelligence

Mahendra Singh Dhoni, fondly known as MS Dhoni, is one of the most iconic figures in Indian cricket history, and his journey is filled with instances that exemplify emotional intelligence (EI). He handled the team and his calmness, the things that he does behind the scenes like building a relationship with each person are a demonstration of empathy and social skills.

One notable example of Dhoni's EI is his leadership during the 2011 ICC Cricket World Cup final. India was playing against Sri Lanka in the final match, and the pressure was immense as the entire nation had high expectations. When India found itself in a challenging situation, with early wickets falling, Dhoni demonstrated remarkable composure and confidence.

Instead of panicking or succumbing to the pressure, Dhoni remained calm and focused. He understood the importance of leading by example, both on and off the field. With his strategic thinking and emotional intelligence, he promoted a sense of confidence and unity within the team.

Dhoni's decision to promote himself up the batting order in the final by self-awareness was a masterstroke of emotional intelligence. It showed his understanding of the situation and his ability to take calculated risks for the greater good of the team. His innings of 91 not outplayed a crucial role in India's victory, and he sealed the match with a six, etching his name in cricketing history.

Dhoni's leadership style was characterized by his ability to connect with his teammates on a personal level. He knew how to motivate and inspire them, instilling belief and confidence even in the most challenging circumstances. His calm demeanor and unwavering confidence had a positive impact on the team's morale, making them believe that they could achieve greatness together.

Off the field, Dhoni's humility and grace further highlight his emotional intelligence. Despite his immense success and fame, he remained grounded and approachable, earning the respect and admiration of fans and fellow cricketers alike. In essence, Mahendra Singh Dhoni's story is a testament to the power of emotional intelligence in leadership and sports. His ability to stay composed under pressure, make strategic decisions, and connect with his teammates on a deeper level contributed significantly to India's success on the cricket field, making him a true legend of the game.

Learning Objectives

1. Understand the Concepts and Types of Emotions
2. Identify the Importance and the Components of Emotional Intelligence
3. Develop Intrapersonal and Interpersonal Relationships
4. Apply Emotional Intelligence in Leadership, Teamwork and Conflict Resolution

5. Identify the Importance of Mental Health, Manage Stress and Emotional well-being

"The Hope of a Nation Lies in the Education of Youth"

Introduction

Emotion is the feelings we experience in response to different situations. Emotions are reactions that human beings experience in response to events or situations. The type of emotion a person experiences is determined by the circumstance that triggers the emotion. For instance, a person experiences joy when they receive good news and fear when they are threatened.

Emotions have a strong influence on our daily lives. We make decisions based on whether we are happy, angry, sad, bored, or frustrated. We also choose activities and hobbies based on the emotions they incite. Understanding emotions can help us navigate life with greater ease and stability.

Six Basic Emotions

Paul Ekman is a renowned psychologist known for his groundbreaking work on emotions and facial expressions. He proposed that six basic emotions as shown in **Figure 2.1** are universally expressed and recognized across different cultures:

1. **Happiness:** Happiness is characterized by feelings of joy, love, acceptance, pleasure, relief, contentment, satisfaction, and delight. It is typically expressed through smiles, laughter, pride, and upbeat body language. Research has supported the indisputable fact that happiness can play a role in both physical and mental health, that is psychological. Happiness was associated with an assortment of results, including increased longevity and increased satisfaction. Unhappiness happens to be associated with many bad wellness results. Stress, anxiety, depression, and loneliness, are connected to things such as lowered immunity, increased inflammation, and decreased life expectancy.

Coping with happiness involves embracing positive emotions, maintaining balance, and practicing gratitude to sustain well- being without becoming complacent or overly reliant on external factors for happiness.

2. **Sadness**: Sadness involves feelings of sorrow, grief, and disappointment. It is often expressed through tears, frowns, and slumped posture. Prolonged sadness may lead to depression. Sadness is an emotion marked by feelings of sorrow or disappointment, often triggered by loss or unmet expectations. It can lead to reduced energy, social withdrawal, and changes in appetite or sleep.

    Coping strategies include seeking support, engaging in comforting activities, and practicing self-care.

3. **Fear**: Fear is an emotional response to perceived threats or danger. It triggers the body's fight-or-flight response and is expressed through wide eyes, raised eyebrows, and tense facial muscles. It may lead to phobia and panic. Fear could be the emotional reaction to a threat that is immediate. We can also produce an effect similar to common threats and our thoughts about potential hazards, which is precisely what we generally think of as anxiety. Personal anxiety, as an example, involves a fear that is anticipated in situations.

    Coping with fear involves understanding its source, practicing calming techniques like deep breathing and mindfulness, and gradually facing fears with support to build resilience.

4. **Anger:** Anger is an intense emotional state characterized by feelings of frustration, irritation, and hostility. It is expressed through clenched fists, furrowed brows, and a flushed or tense facial expression. It may lead to hatred and violence. Unchecked anger makes it difficult to make choices that can be rational and can have an effect on your physical health. Anger is connected to the coronary heart and diabetes. It's additionally been related to behaviors that pose health dangers such as aggressive driving,

alcohol consumption, and smoking cigarettes. While anger is often regarded as a low emotion, it can occasionally be considered a great thing. It may be constructive in helping explain your preferences in a relationship.

Coping with anger involves recognizing triggers, practicing relaxation techniques such as deep breathing or counting to ten, expressing feelings constructively, and seeking solutions to the underlying issues causing the anger.

5. **Surprise:** Surprise occurs when something unexpected happens. It is characterized by widened eyes, raised eyebrows, and an open mouth. It may lead to shock, wonder, and astonishment. Surprise makes us pause and pay attention when something unexpected happens. It can lead to quick changes in emotions and behaviors as we try to understand and adapt to the new situation. Plus, surprising events such as unpleasant and pleasant surprises, stick in our memory better, helping us learn and react differently in the future.

   Coping with surprise involves pausing to process the unexpected event, staying curious to understand it, adapting to the new situation, and using the experience as a learning opportunity.

6. **Disgust:** Disgust is a visceral reaction to offensive or unpleasant stimuli. It is expressed through wrinkled noses, raised upper lips, and narrowed eyes. It may lead to aversion, guilt, embarrassment, and shame. This feeling of disgust can originate from several things, including a flavor that is an unpleasant sight or scent. Researchers believe that disgust develops as a protective response to potentially harmful or toxic food.3

   Coping with disgust involves recognizing the source of the feeling, setting boundaries to avoid the trigger when possible, reframing negative thoughts, and practicing self-care to manage and reduce the intensity of the emotion.

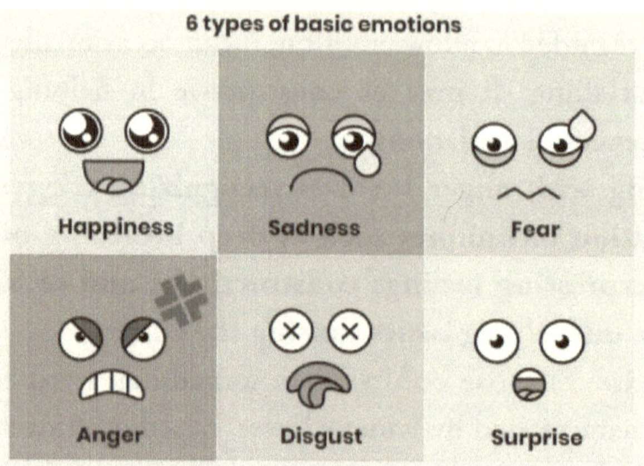

Figure 2.1 Six Basic Emotions

Emotional Resilience: Asha's Journey Through Life's Highs and Lows

Asha had experienced one of the most emotionally intense days of her life. Her day took unexpected turns, evoking six basic emotions in ways she never anticipated. What made it truly transformative was how she learned to cope with the range of emotions she experienced.

Happiness: The day began with pure happiness. Asha, brimming with joy, assisted her sister Maya in getting ready for the wedding. As the ceremony unfolded, she felt overwhelmed with happiness for Maya's future. To fully appreciate this joy, Asha made a conscious effort to stay present in the moment. She captured mental snapshots of her sister's radiant smile and the family's laughter. Asha understood that embracing happiness fully when it came would help her create cherished memories to draw strength from during difficult times. She often reminded herself: *Live in the moment, cherish the present.*

Coping mechanism: Practicing gratitude and mindfulness to enhance her happiness, making her feel grounded and appreciative.

Sadness: As the wedding drew to a close, a wave of sadness washed over Asha. The thought of Maya leaving for another city left her heart heavy. Instead of pushing the sadness away, Asha found a quiet corner to process her feelings. She allowed herself to cry, knowing that sadness was a natural response to change and loss. Later, she talked to Maya about how much she would miss her, which brought them closer.

Coping mechanism: Acknowledging her sadness instead of avoiding it and expressing it through conversation helped her accept the inevitable changes with more ease.

Fear: That night, Asha was driving home when her car broke down on a desolate road. Fear gripped her as her mind spiraled into worst-case scenarios. She felt her heart race, her palms grow sweaty, and her mind fog with panic. However, Asha reminded herself to take deep breaths. She focused on what she could control—checking her phone for help, locking the doors, and staying inside the car until help arrived. Breathing exercises helped her calm down, and she repeated to herself: *I can get through this.*

Coping mechanism: Grounding herself with deep breathing and focusing on what was within her control in the present situation helped her manage fear.

Disgust: While trying to relax in the car, Asha caught a whiff of something foul. Searching the backseat, she discovered an old, rotting sandwich left behind by a cousin earlier that day. The smell was revolting. Her first reaction was to scrunch up her nose in disgust. Instead of letting it overwhelm her, she decided to handle it calmly. She carefully removed the offending item, wrapped it up, and threw it out of the car. After, she aired the car out and used a spare air freshener from her glove compartment.

Coping mechanism: Asha swiftly tackled the issue instead of letting her disgust hold her back, and in doing so, she regained her peace of mind.

Anger: Asha waited for roadside assistance for over an hour with no response. Each passing minute fueled her frustration. She slammed the steering wheel in anger, venting her annoyance at the situation. After a few deep breaths, she realized that anger wasn't helping her. So, instead of lashing out further, she reached for her phone again, contacted the company, and expressed her concerns calmly. Venting her frustration through assertive communication made her feel heard.

Coping mechanism: Asha gave herself space to release her anger but then took constructive action by calmly expressing her dissatisfaction, ensuring that her feelings led to positive results rather than further escalation.

SurpriseJust as Asha was about to lose hope, Maya and her husband appeared on the road. They had taken a different route and saw her car. Asha was stunned, filled with surprise. What were the chances they would pass by at that exact moment? Rather than letting the surprise overwhelm her, Asha embraced it. She welcomed them with a laugh, realizing that life often throws in moments of unexpected help when we least expect it.

Coping mechanism: Asha learned to embrace surprise with a sense of openness and gratitude, understanding that not all surprises are bad. She leaned into the unexpected and allowed herself to feel relieved.

By the end of the day, Asha realized that although she couldn't control everything that happened to her, she could control how she responded. Each emotion – whether joy or sadness, fear or anger, surprise or disgust – was part of life. By learning to cope with them effectively, she could navigate through life's ups and downs with greater resilience.

The Impact of Emotions

Emotions exert a profound influence on behavior, health, learning, and achievement. Recognizing and understanding the role of emotions can lead to more effective strategies for managing them and harnessing their power to promote well-being and success. Emotions play a significant role in shaping human behavior, impacting health, learning, and achievement in various ways:

Behavior: Emotions influence how individuals perceive and respond to their environment. For example, someone feeling happy might be more inclined to engage in social activities or take risks, while someone experiencing fear might seek safety or avoid certain situations. Emotions can also affect decision-making processes, leading individuals to make choices based on their emotional state rather than rational considerations.

Health: Emotions have a profound impact on physical health. Chronic stress, for instance, can weaken the immune system and increase the risk of various health problems such as heart disease, obesity, and depression. Conversely, positive emotions like joy and contentment can boost the immune system, lower blood pressure, and promote overall well-being. The field of psychoneuroimmunology explores the intricate connections between emotions, the brain, and the immune system.

Learning: Emotions significantly influence the learning process. Emotionally charged events are often better remembered due to the amygdala's involvement in encoding emotional experiences. Additionally, emotions can affect attention, motivation, and cognitive processes, all of which are essential for effective learning. Positive emotions such as curiosity and interest can enhance learning by promoting engagement and persistence, while negative emotions like anxiety and frustration can hinder learning by impairing concentration and memory.

Achievement: Emotions play a crucial role in determining individuals' achievement and success in various domains, including academic, professional, and personal endeavors. Positive emotions such as enthusiasm and confidence can fuel motivation and persistence, leading to higher levels of achievement. On the other hand, negative emotions such as self-doubt and fear of failure can undermine performance and inhibit goal attainment. Emotional intelligence, the ability to recognize, understand, and manage one's own emotions and those of others, is increasingly recognized as a critical factor in achieving success and fulfillment in life.

The Three Minds: Emotional Mind, Rational Mind, And Wise Mind

The concept of the three minds, associated with Dialectical Behavior Therapy (DBT), developed by Marsha M. Linehan, focuses on the integration of emotional and rational aspects of thinking to achieve wise decision-making and effective behavior. DBT helps individuals develop and strengthen their wise minds by learning to recognize and regulate their emotions, cultivate mindfulness and self-awareness, and enhance their problem-solving and decision-making skills. By integrating emotional and rational aspects of thinking, individuals can achieve greater balance, resilience, and well-being in their lives.

The **Emotional Mind** is used when feelings control an individual's thoughts and behaviors. They may act impulsively and give little consideration to the consequences. An emotional mindset is a state of mind in which emotions and feelings are more dominant than logical thought and reasoning. An example of an emotional mindset is when a person makes a decision solely based on their emotions and feelings rather than a logical analysis of the situation. For instance, if a person buys an expensive item because they feel happy and excited, even though they know they cannot afford it, they are operating from an emotional mindset. In this case, their emotions are the driving force behind their decision, rather than practical considerations such as their budget or financial responsibilities.

A **Rational Mind**, also known as the reasonable mind, guides us into thinking over a situation clearly without feelings getting in the way. For instance, if a person is considering buying a new car, they may research different models, compare prices, evaluate their budget, and weigh the pros and cons of each option before making a decision. They might also talk to experts or ask trusted sources for advice to make sure they are making an informed decision. In this case, the person uses their rational mind to evaluate the decision based on facts and practical considerations rather than being swayed by emotions or impulsive desires that affect their decision.

Although using your rational mind can lead to accurate and correct decisions, it may not always lead to making wise choices. Therefore, it's important to know how to tap into your wise mind. A **"wise mind"** is a mental state in which a person integrates their rational and emotional minds to make decisions based on logic, intuition, and values. A wise mind is considered a balance between the two states of mind, where a person can use their logical reasoning and emotional responses to make decisions and solve problems effectively. It gets more interesting when one can use both their rational and emotional minds in sync. In short, the wise mind is where the emotional and rational minds overlap.

An example of a wise mind is when people combine their emotional and rational minds to make decisions grounded in logic and aligned with their values, beliefs, and intuition. For instance, if a person is considering a job offer, they may use their rational mind to evaluate the salary, benefits, and job requirements, but they may also tap into their emotional mind to consider how the job aligns with their passions, career goals, and personal values. They may also listen to their intuition or gut feelings to make the right decision. In this case, the person is using their wise mind to make a logical and authentic decision to their values and beliefs. **Figure 2.2** gives the three minds.

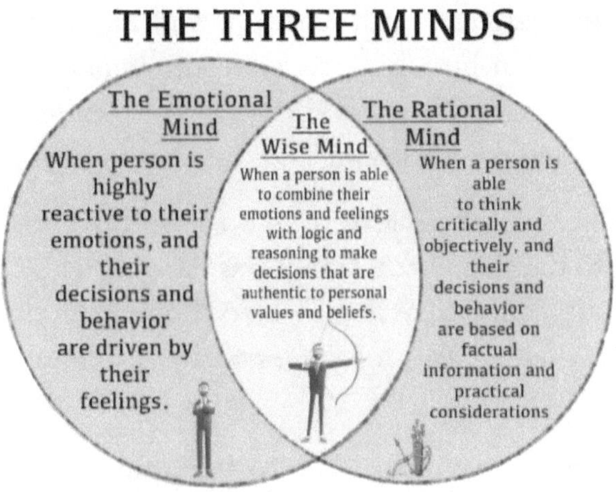

THE THREE MINDS

Figure 2.2. The Three Minds

Finding Balance: The Journey of Emotional Mind, Rational Mind, and Wise Mind

Once upon a time, in a Garden University nestled between mountains and rivers, lived three students: Emotional, Rational, and Wise. Each of them had a unique way of seeing the world, and together they made an unlikely yet inseparable trio.

Emotional was vibrant and impulsive. She felt everything deeply, whether it was joy, sorrow, anger, or love. She wore her heart on her sleeve, and her feelings often took her on wild emotional journeys. When someone complimented her, she floated on clouds, but a single harsh word could send her crashing down. The emotional mind's life was full of intensity, like a flame burning brightly—sometimes too brightly.

Rational on the other hand, was the complete opposite. He was analytical, logical, and always thinking things through. He relied on facts, data, and reasoning, often detaching himself from emotions to make decisions. A rational belief that every problem has a solution if you just think about it hard enough. He loved structure, order, and clarity, often finding Emotional Mind's impulsiveness overwhelming.

Wise, the quietest but most balanced of the three, Wise was the one who could sit still and listen to both emotions and logic. He saw the value in Emotional's passion but also recognized the importance of Rational's calm, level-headedness. Wise was not swayed by extremes; instead, he knew that life required both feeling and thinking in harmony.

One day, the three friends decided to go on a short trek to a nearby forest. As they set off to the forest, **Emotional** was bursting with excitement. She danced along the path, marveling at every flower, cloud, and bird they passed. "Look at that sky! Isn't it just *breathtaking*?" she exclaimed, twirling in circles.

But soon, **Rational** interrupted. "Yes, it's beautiful, but we need to focus on the route. We'll never make it to the target if we stop every few minutes. We should calculate how fast we need to walk to get there by sunset."

Emotional rolled her eyes. "You always think about plans and numbers! Sometimes, you just have to feel life, not analyze it."

Wise chuckled softly but said nothing.

As they continued their journey, the weather suddenly shifted, and dark clouds rolled in. Soon, rain began to pour down. **Emotional** felt her mood plummet instantly. "This is terrible!" she cried, looking up at the sky. "Why does it always rain when I'm having fun? Everything is ruined!"

Rational stayed calm. "It's just rain. No need to panic. We need to find shelter or else we'll catch a cold."

But **Emotional** was too lost in her sadness to think practically. She sat down under a tree, refusing to move. "What's the point? Everything is ruined anyway."

Sighing, **Rational** searched for the best way to proceed. He pulled out a map and calculated how far they were from a nearby inn. "If we head east, we can reach the inn in 20 minutes. We'll be dry, and we can wait out the storm there."

Wise, who had been observing quietly, spoke up. "**Emotional**, it's okay to feel disappointed about the rain. It's natural to feel upset when things don't go as planned. But the **Rationale** is also right. We can feel disappointed *and* still take steps to make things better."

Emotional looked up at **Wise**, her eyes filled with frustration but also understanding. She sighed and nodded. "I guess you're right. I'm just so upset that the fun had to end."

Wise smiled gently. "The fun doesn't have to end. It's just taking a new form. Let's make our way to the inn together."

Reluctantly, **Emotional** stood up, and the three friends continued their journey.

At the inn, they sat by the fire, drying off from the rain. As they waited for the storm to pass, they talked about their journey.

Rational spoke first. "You know, **Emotional**, you may feel things too strongly sometimes, but your excitement for life does add color to our days."

Emotional smiled. "And you keep us safe and on track with your plans and logic. I don't always show it, but I appreciate that."

They both turned to **Wise**, who had been quietly sipping tea. "And you, **Wise**," **Emotional** said, "you help us find balance. You remind me that it's okay to feel, but not to be overwhelmed by feelings."

Rational nodded in agreement. "And you help me see that not everything can be solved with logic alone. Sometimes, we must listen to what's happening in our hearts."

Wise smiled, feeling the warmth of their friendship. "That's what makes us strong together. We each bring something unique, and when we listen to each other, we find balance."

As the storm cleared and the sun shined again, the three friends set off toward the forest to trek again. This time, they walked in harmony—The **Emotional** enjoying the beauty of the world, the **Rational** keeping track of their progress, and the **Wise** ensuring that they moved forward with both heart and mind aligned.

Their journey wasn't perfect, but together, they made it better. And that's what mattered most.

Emotional Intelligence (EI) and Its Significance

Emotional Intelligence (EI), assessed by Emotional Quotient (EQ), refers to the ability to recognize, understand, and manage one's own emotions and recognize, understand, and influence the emotions of others. It encompasses a range of skills and competencies related to emotional awareness, empathy, self-regulation, social skills, and relationship management.

The concept of emotional intelligence has its roots in various psychological theories and research. However, it gained widespread attention and popularity in the early 1990s, largely due to the work of psychologists Peter Salovey and John D. Mayer.

Salovey and Mayer introduced the term "emotional intelligence" in a landmark article published in 1990. They defined emotional intelligence as "the ability to monitor one's own and others' feelings and emotions, to discriminate among them, and to use this information to guide one's thinking and actions."

Building upon this initial conceptualization, psychologist and science journalist Daniel Goleman further popularized the concept of emotional intelligence with his bestselling book, "Emotional Intelligence: Why It Can Matter More Than IQ," published in 1995. Goleman proposed that emotional intelligence plays a critical role in personal and professional success, often outweighing cognitive intelligence (IQ) in determining life outcomes.

Since then, research on emotional intelligence has expanded across various disciplines, including psychology, neuroscience, education, business, and leadership. Numerous studies have highlighted the importance of emotional intelligence in areas such as interpersonal relationships, leadership effectiveness, workplace performance, mental health, and overall well-being.

Today, emotional intelligence is recognized as a key factor in personal development, social interaction, and success in various domains of life. It is often considered a fundamental skill that can be cultivated and enhanced through self-awareness, practice, and learning. As society continues to place greater emphasis on emotional intelligence, its implications for education, parenting, healthcare, and organizational development are increasingly being recognized and integrated into various aspects of life and work.

Application of Emotional Intelligence

Emotional intelligence is a key determinant of success and fulfillment in both personal and professional life. By cultivating self-awareness, self-regulation, self-motivation, empathy, and social skills. Individuals can enhance their emotional intelligence and unlock their full potential for growth, resilience, and meaningful connections with others. Emotional intelligence (EI) plays a crucial role in influencing various aspects of behavior, decision-making, and relationships. Here's why EI is significant in both realms:

Leadership Effectiveness: In the professional realm, EI is particularly critical for effective leadership. Leaders with high emotional intelligence can inspire and motivate their teams, create a positive work environment, and foster collaboration and innovation. They can also navigate complex organizational dynamics and lead with empathy and authenticity. High emotional intelligence fosters better communication, empathy, and understanding in personal and professional relationships. Emotional intelligence enables individuals to make more rational and informed decisions by considering both emotional and logical factors.

Stress Management: Individuals with strong emotional intelligence can effectively manage stress, adapt to change, and maintain resilience in challenging situations.

Personal Well-being: Emotional intelligence is associated with greater overall well-being, including lower levels of anxiety, depression, and interpersonal conflict.

Adaptability and Resilience: EI enables individuals to adapt to change, cope with stress, and bounce back from setbacks. In today's fast-paced and uncertain world, the ability to remain flexible, resilient, and optimistic is invaluable for personal and professional success.

Conflict Resolution: EI facilitates constructive conflict resolution by promoting understanding, empathy, and collaboration. Individuals with high emotional intelligence can navigate conflicts calmly, listen to others' perspectives, and find mutually beneficial solutions, leading to more harmonious relationships and productive outcomes.

Box 2.1. Daniel Goleman: Mastering Emotional Intelligence

Daniel Goleman's life story is a testament to the transformative power of emotional intelligence. As a young psychologist, Goleman was fascinated by the interplay between emotions and human behavior. However, it wasn't until later in his career that he stumbled upon the concept that would define his legacy.

In the late 1980s, Goleman came across the work of two psychologists, John Mayer and Peter Salovey, who proposed emotional intelligence as a critical factor in personal and professional success. Building upon their research, Goleman began to delve deeper into the subject, conducting his studies and synthesizing insights from various disciplines, including psychology, neuroscience, and sociology.

Daniel Goleman played a pivotal role in bringing the concept of emotional intelligence to a broader audience. In 1995, Goleman published his groundbreaking book, *"Emotional Intelligence: Why it can matter more than IQ,"* which catapulted him to international acclaim. In the book, Goleman argued that emotional intelligence—the ability to recognize, understand, and manage one's own emotions and those of others—was a more accurate predictor of success than traditional measures of intelligence, such as IQ.

Drawing on compelling research and real-life examples, Goleman demonstrated how emotional intelligence influences every aspect of our lives, from relationships and careers to physical and mental well-being. He emphasized the importance of skills like empathy, self-awareness, and social competence in navigating the complexities of the modern world.

Goleman's book sparked a global conversation about the role of emotions in human behavior and reshaped the way we think about intelligence and success. It became a bestseller, translated into dozens of languages, and inspired countless individuals to cultivate their emotional intelligence skills.

Throughout his career, Goleman has continued to advocate for the importance of emotional intelligence in education, leadership, and organizational development. His work has had a profound impact on fields ranging from business and education to healthcare and parenting, leaving a lasting legacy as one of the foremost authorities on the subject.

Daniel Goleman exemplifies how a deep understanding of emotional intelligence can not only transform individual lives but also shape our collective understanding of human nature and behavior.

EI - Theoretical Framework

Several theoretical frameworks have been proposed to conceptualize and measure emotional intelligence. Two prominent models are Daniel Goleman's model and Mayer and Salovey's model. Here's an overview of each:

Daniel Goleman's Model

Daniel Goleman's model suggests that emotional intelligence is critical for personal and professional success. Daniel Goleman's model of emotional intelligence, outlined in his book "Emotional Intelligence: Why It Can Matter More Than IQ," emphasizes the following five key components as shown in Figure 2.3.

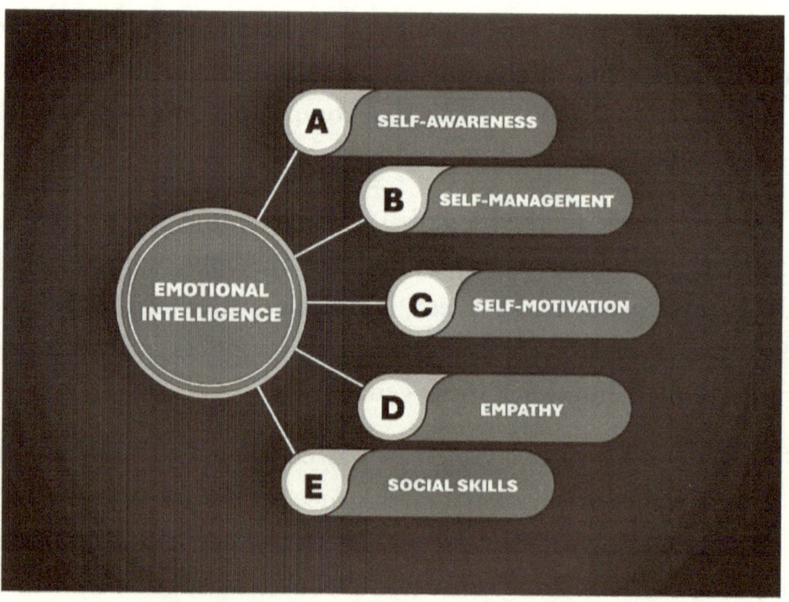

Figure 2.3 Daniel Goleman's Model on Emotional Intelligence
Source: Goleman, 1995, p. 25

a. Self-Awareness: The ability to recognize and understand one's own emotions, including strengths, weaknesses, values, and motivations. Self-awareness is all about recognizing a feeling as it happens, is the key to emotional intelligence. People with great certainty about their feelings are better pilots of their lives. They have a clear sense of how they feel about personal and professional decisions. Emotional Self-awareness is all about:

- Improvement in recognizing and managing one's own emotions
- Able to understand the causes of feelings
- Recognising the difference between feelings and actions.

b. Managing Emotions/Self-Regulation: The ability to manage and regulate one's emotions, impulses, and reactions effectively, even in challenging situations. People who are poor in this ability are constantly battling feelings of distress, while those who are good in it bounce back far more quickly from life's setbacks and upsets. Managing Emotions is all about:

- Better frustration tolerance and anger management
- Fewer verbal tolerance and fights
- Able to express anger appropriately, without fighting
- Fewer suspensions and expulsions
- Less aggressive or self-destructive behavior
- More positive feelings about self, family and workplace
- Better at handling stress
- Less loneliness and social anxiety

c. Self-motivation: Self-motivated people are resilient and driven by an inner ambition rather than being influenced by outside forces, such as money or prestige. People who have this skill tend to be more highly productive, responsible, and high achievers in whatever they undertake. They have the drive to pursue goals with energy, persistence, and optimism, even in the face of setbacks or obstacles. Self-motivation is harnessing emotions productively:

- Being responsible
- Able to focus on the task at hand and pay attention
- Less impulsive and more self-control
- Achievement motivation

d. Empathy: It is the ability to build on self-awareness and self-regulation and is a fundamental people skill. An empathetic person is better at listening to others and compassionately connecting with other people on an emotional level. The empathetic person understands other needs and wants, helping them respond genuinely to other people's concerns. The ability to empathize and understand the emotions, perspectives, and needs of others, fosters better interpersonal relationships. Empathy deals with:

- Better able to take another person's perspective
- Improved empathy and sensitivity to other's feelings
- Better at listening to others

e. Social Skills: People with social skills can communicate effectively, resolve conflicts, be assertive, and build trust with other people. They are good at handling relationships. These are the abilities that enable them to develop popularity, leadership, and interpersonal skills. This is all about relationship management and is related to the skill of managing emotions in others. Being able to handle emotions in relationships and being able to influence and inspire others are essential foundation skills for successful teamwork and leadership. Social skills are all about handling relationships:

- Increased ability to analyze and understand relationships
- Better at resolving conflicts and negotiating disagreements
- Better at solving problems in relationships
- More assertive and skilled at communicating
- Friendly and involved with peers, popular and outgoing
- More sought out by peers
- Concerned and considerate
- Harmonious in groups
- Sharing, caring, cooperative, helpful and compassionate
- Democratic in dealing with others

Mayer and Salovey's Model

The model provides a comprehensive framework for understanding the various facets of emotional intelligence, from basic emotional awareness to higher-level emotional management and interpersonal skills. Peter Salovey and John D. Mayer introduced the concept of emotional intelligence and proposed a model consisting of four branches: Perceiving Emotions, Using Emotions, Understanding Emotions, and Managing Emotions.

Both Goleman's model and Mayer and Salovey's model highlight the importance of emotional intelligence in personal and professional life, emphasizing its role in self-awareness, self-regulation, empathy, social skills, and relationship management. These theoretical frameworks have influenced research, assessment tools, and interventions aimed at enhancing emotional intelligence and promoting individual well-being and success.

Box 2.2. IQ vs EQ

IQ (Intelligence Quotient) and EQ (Emotional Quotient) are two different measures that assess different aspects of human abilities, capabilities, and characteristics. Both are important for success and well-being. Striking a balance between intellectual and emotional intelligence can lead to a more harmonious, fulfilling, and successful life. The difference between IQ and EQ is given below.

IQ vs EQ

Aspect	IQ	EQ
Definition	A measure of cognitive intelligence	A measure of Emotional Intelligence
Abilities	Logical reasoning, quantitative skills, learning languages, memory, problem-solving, decision-making, and processing speed.	Self-awareness, self-regulation, self-motivation, empathy, social skills
Success in workplace	Academic and professional	Leadership, team building, interpersonal, networking, collaboration, people skills
Acquisition	Innate ability	Learned and developed ability
Development	Training	Mentoring and Coaching

Measurement	Stanford-Binet Intelligence Scales, and Woodcock-Johnson Tests of Cognitive Abilities,	Mayer-Salovey-Caruso Emotional Intelligence Test (MSCEIT) and Dr. Daniel Goleman Leadership tool kit

In education, more weightage is given to IQ to attain higher scores and grades. Research has shown that IQ is just like the tip of the iceberg, whereas EQ is bigger and hidden inside the base. IQ determines 20-25% of career success, whereas EQ determines 75-80%.

The Emotional Competence Framework

The Emotional Competence framework comprises Personal Competence and Social Competence. It is furnished in Table 2.1.

Table 2.1. Emotional Competence Framework

PERSONAL COMPETENCE determines how we manage ourselves.
Self-awareness: Knowing one's internal states, preferences, resources, and intuitions • **Emotional awareness:** Recognising one's emotions and their effects • **Self-assessment:** Knowing one's strengths and limitations • **Self-confidence:** A strong sense of one's capabilities and self-worth
Managing Emotions (Self-Regulation): Managing one's internal states, impulses, and resources • **Self-control:** Keeping negative emotions and impulses in check • **Trustworthiness:** Maintaining standards of values, honesty and integrity • **Conscientiousness:** Taking responsibility for personal action and performance • **Adaptability:** Flexibility in handling change • **Innovation:** Being comfortable with novel ideas, approaches, and new information

Self-Motivation: Emotional tendencies that guide or facilitate reaching goals

- **Achievement motivation:** Striving to improve or meet a standard of excellence
- **Commitment:** Aligning with the goals of the group or organisation
- **Initiative:** Readiness to act on opportunities
- **Optimism**: Persistence in pursuing goals despite obstacles and setbacks

2. SOCIAL COMPETENCE determines how we handle relationships

Empathy: Awareness of others feelings, needs and concerns

- **Understanding others:** Sensing others' feelings and perspectives, and taking an active interest in their concerns
- **Developing others:** Sensing others' development needs and holstering their abilities
- **Service orientation:** Anticipating, recognising, and meeting customers' needs
- **Leveraging diversity**: Cultivating opportunities through different kinds of people
- **Political awareness:** Reading a group's emotional currents and power relationships

Social Skills: Positive interpersonal skills (people skills)

- **Influence:** Exercise effective tactics for persuasion
- **Communication**: Active listening and sending appropriate messages
- **Conflict management**: Negotiating and resolving disagreements
- **Leadership:** Inspiring and guiding individuals and groups
- **Change catalyst:** Initiating or managing change
- **Building bonds**: Nurturing relationships
- **Collaboration and cooperation**: Working with others towards shared goals
- **Team capabilities:** Building a team and creating synergy in pursuing collective goals

Source: Daniel Goleman, "Emotional Intelligence" Bloomsbury, 2013

Developing Emotional Intelligence

1. **Self-reflection**: Self-reflection is a powerful tool for personal growth and development. It involves examining your thoughts, feelings, and actions to gain insight into yourself and your life. Take time to reflect on your own emotions, reactions, and behaviors, and consider how they impact yourself and others.

2. **Practice mindfulness:** Mindfulness is the practice of being fully present and engaged in the moment, without judgment or distraction. It involves paying attention to your thoughts, feelings, bodily sensations, and the surrounding environment with openness and curiosity. Mindfulness techniques can help increase self-awareness, regulate emotions, and improve focus and attention.

3. **Seek feedback:** Ask for feedback from trusted friends, family members, or colleagues to gain insights into your emotional strengths and areas for improvement. By seeking feedback thoughtfully and proactively, you can gain valuable insights, accelerate your growth, and achieve your goals more effectively.

4. **Develop empathy**: Developing empathy is a fundamental aspect of emotional intelligence and can greatly enhance your relationships, communication skills, and overall well-being. Practice active listening, perspective-taking, and putting yourself in others' shoes to enhance your ability to understand and empathize with their emotions.

5. **Build social skills:** Building social skills is essential for forming and maintaining positive relationships, whether in personal or professional settings. Work on communication, conflict resolution, and collaboration skills to strengthen your interpersonal relationships and navigate social situations effectively. Like any skill, social skills improve with practice. Put yourself in social situations regularly, whether it's attending social gatherings, joining clubs or groups with shared interests, or participating in

networking events. The more you practice interacting with others, the more confident and skilled you'll become.

IQ-EQ Fusion for Success

Combining IQ (Intelligence Quotient) and EQ (Emotional Quotient) can be a powerful approach to achieving success in various aspects of life. Here's how you can fuse the two for success:

1. Self-awareness:

- **IQ**: Understand your strengths, weaknesses, and areas for improvement.
- **EQ**: Recognize and understand your emotions, triggers, and how they influence your thoughts and behaviors.
- **Fusion**: Use your intellectual abilities to analyze and understand your emotional responses, helping you make more informed decisions.

2. Emotional Regulation:

- **IQ**: Develop problem-solving skills to address challenges and find solutions.
- **EQ**: Manage and regulate your emotions to maintain composure and resilience in stressful situations.
- **Fusion**: Combine your analytical skills with emotional awareness to address problems rationally while managing your emotional reactions effectively.

3. Empathy:

- **IQ**: Understand the perspectives and feelings of others through cognitive understanding.
- **EQ**: Feel and connect with others' emotions, fostering deeper relationships and understanding.
- **Fusion**: Utilize your cognitive understanding to empathize with others genuinely, enhancing communication and building stronger relationships.

4. Communication:

- **IQ**: Articulate ideas, logically, and persuasively.
- **EQ**: Listen actively, understand non-verbal cues, and communicate with empathy.
- **Fusion**: Combine logical reasoning with emotional intelligence to communicate effectively, fostering mutual understanding and collaboration.

5. Decision Making:

- **IQ**: Analyze information, weigh pros and cons, and make logical decisions.
- **EQ**: Trust your intuition, consider emotional implications, and make decisions aligned with your values.
- **Fusion**: Integrate analytical thinking with emotional insights to make balanced and well-rounded decisions.

6. Relationship Building:

- **IQ**: Collaborate effectively, contribute to teamwork, and understand group dynamics.
- **EQ**: Build trust, show empathy, and connect with others on an emotional level.
- **Fusion**: Leverage your intellectual and emotional skills to build meaningful relationships, foster teamwork, and create a positive and supportive environment.

7. Adaptability:

- **IQ**: Learn new skills, adapt to changes, and innovate.
- **EQ**: Embrace change, remain flexible, and manage uncertainty with resilience.
- **Fusion**: Combine your intellectual curiosity with emotional flexibility to adapt to new situations, learn from experiences, and grow personally and professionally.

By integrating both IQ and EQ, you can develop a holistic approach to success that combines cognitive abilities with emotional intelligence. This fusion allows you to navigate challenges effectively, build strong relationships, make informed decisions, and achieve your goals with resilience and adaptability.

Building Bridges: The Power of IQ and EQ Together

Once upon a time, in Bright School, there were two students, **IQ** and **EQ**, who were known for their unique strengths. Although they were the same age and attended the same classes, they approached life and learning in completely different ways.

IQ was brilliant. He excelled in every subject, from mathematics to science, history to literature. He had an incredible ability to solve problems, memorize facts, and think logically. IQ could solve complex equations faster than anyone in the class, and teachers often praised him for his sharp intellect. He loved challenging puzzles and difficult problems that required analytical thinking. His report cards were always filled with top grades.

On the other hand, **EQ** wasn't as academically exceptional as **IQ**, but she had a different kind of brilliance. **EQ** had an incredible ability to understand people. She could sense when her classmates were upset, and she always knew just what to say to make them feel better. When there was a group project, **EQ** made sure everyone felt included and worked together harmoniously. She was empathetic, a great listener, and always helped solve conflicts between students with her calm and understanding nature.

One day, a big competition was announced at the school—a team challenge that required both intelligence and teamwork. The winning team would get a scholarship to a prestigious summer camp, and students were excited. **IQ** was confident that his intellect would carry the team to victory. "All we need is to get all the answers right, and we'll win for sure!" he boasted.

EQ, however, had a different approach. "It's not just about getting the answers right. We need to work well together as a team," she said. "If we don't communicate and support each other, we might struggle, even if we know the answers."

IQ shrugged, thinking teamwork wouldn't be a big issue as long as they had the smartest students.

The day of the competition arrived. **IQ** and **EQ** were placed on the same team, along with three other students. The first few rounds were based on academic questions—math problems, science trivia, and historical facts. As expected, **IQ** led the team with his quick and accurate answers. The team was in the lead, and **IQ** was sure they would win easily.

But then came the final challenge: a problem-solving task that required the entire team to work together to build a bridge using only limited materials. It wasn't just about knowledge; it was about creativity, communication, and teamwork. The other teams immediately began discussing plans and dividing tasks, but **IQ** was impatient. "Let's just start building. I've already figured out how to make the strongest bridge," he declared, taking control without listening to anyone else.

As **IQ** rushed to assemble the bridge, the other team members felt confused and left out. **EQ** noticed the growing tension. "Wait," she said gently, "we need to talk through this first. Everyone should share their ideas."

IQ sighed. "We don't have time for that. I know the solution."

EQ shook her head. "The best solutions come when everyone is heard. If we don't work together, the bridge might fail."

Seeing that the team was frustrated, **EQ** stepped in and encouraged everyone to share their thoughts. One teammate suggested a new design that could balance weight more effectively, while another pointed out how they could use fewer materials by building a triangular structure. **EQ** made sure that everyone had a voice, and the group began to work together, feeling more connected and motivated.

At first, **IQ** was reluctant to listen, but as the structure started taking shape, he realized that his teammates' input was making the bridge stronger and more stable. **EQ** guided the team through the process, making sure no one was left behind and that everyone's contributions were valued.

When the time was up, the judges tested each team's bridge. To everyone's surprise, many of the other teams' bridges collapsed under the weight. But **IQ** and **EQ**'s team's bridge held strong—it was a combination of intelligence, creativity, and collaboration. They had won the competition, not just because of **IQ**'s knowledge, but because **EQ** had brought the team together, encouraging communication and cooperation.

As they accepted the trophy, **IQ** turned to **EQ**. "I thought being smart was all that mattered," he admitted, "but I see now that understanding people and working together is just as important. Without you, we wouldn't have been able to build that bridge."

EQ smiled. "And without your problem-solving skills, we wouldn't have known where to start. We needed both our strengths."

From that day on, **IQ** and **EQ** became close friends. **IQ** began to appreciate the importance of emotional intelligence—knowing how to understand and work with others. **EQ** also realized the value of logical thinking and knowledge. They made a perfect team, complementing each other in every way, and soon became the most respected students in the school—not just for their intellect or empathy, but for their ability to blend both in everything they did.

Learning: True success comes when intelligence (IQ) and emotional understanding (EQ) work hand in hand.

<u>Box 2.3. The Power of Positive Thinking</u>

The power of positive thinking refers to the belief that maintaining a positive mindset can lead to better outcomes in various aspects of life, including health, relationships, career, and personal fulfillment.

It is important to note that the power of positive thinking is not about denying reality or ignoring problems. Instead, it's about cultivating a constructive mindset that enables individuals to approach life's challenges with optimism, resilience, and determination. Integrating positive thinking into one's life often involves practices such as gratitude journaling, mindfulness meditation, and cognitive restructuring to challenge negative thought patterns.

The concept gained popularity through the work of Norman Vincent Peale, particularly his book "The Power of Positive Thinking," published in 1952. Here are some key principles and benefits associated with the power of positive thinking:

- **Optimism:** Positive thinking fosters optimism, which can help individuals see challenges as opportunities for growth rather than insurmountable obstacles.
- **Resilience:** A positive mindset can enhance resilience, enabling individuals to bounce back more quickly from setbacks and adversity.
- **Improved Health:** Research suggests that maintaining a positive outlook can have tangible benefits for physical health, including a stronger immune system, lower levels of stress hormones, and better cardiovascular health.
- **Enhanced Relationships:** Positivity tends to be attractive, leading to better interpersonal relationships and greater social support networks.
- **Increased Motivation:** When individuals believe in themselves and their abilities, they are more likely to pursue their goals with enthusiasm and persistence.
- **Better Problem-Solving:** Positive thinking can facilitate creative problem-solving by broadening individuals' perspectives and helping them approach challenges with a constructive mindset.

> • **Reduced Stress**: Focusing on positive thoughts can help reduce stress levels and promote a sense of calm and well-being.

Note: Watch YouTube at https://www.youtube.com/watch?v=HwLK9dBQn0g on the power of positivity. A motivational video for positive thinking.

The Turning Point: Rahul's Journey with Positive Thinking

Rahul was a student at Green Valley University who was struggling with his studies. He had always been an average student, but college seemed to overwhelm him. Every time he faced a difficult assignment or exam, negative thoughts flooded his mind—"I'm not smart enough," "I'll never succeed," or "I'm wasting my time here."

While sitting alone in the campus library one day, he overheard a conversation between two professors. One of them was explaining the concept of **positive thinking** to the other. "The power of positive thinking is incredible," the professor said. "When we believe in ourselves, we open up possibilities we never imagined. It's not just about thinking everything will be perfect, but about building resilience and confidence."

Intrigued, Rahul decided to give it a try. Instead of approaching his studies with dread, he began replacing his negative thoughts with positive affirmations. "I can figure this out," "I am capable of learning and growing," he told himself before each challenge. He also started visualizing himself succeeding—acing his exams, giving great presentations, and enjoying his time at the university.

At first, it wasn't easy, and he still struggled. But over time, Rahul noticed a change. When he faced tough problems, instead of giving up, he persisted. With a clearer, more positive mindset, he became more open to asking for help and trying new approaches. His grades began improving, and soon, his self-confidence grew.

At the end of the semester, Rahul's academic performance had transformed. More importantly, he felt happier and more motivated than ever. His friends started noticing the change and asked how he did it.

Rahul simply smiled and said, «It is amazing what you can achieve when you believe in yourself. The power of positive thinking can make all the difference"

Learning: From then on, he shared his story with others, inspiring his peers to cultivate a positive mindset. In the end, it wasn't just his grades that improved—it was his outlook on life, making his university experience more fulfilling than he ever imagined.

Stress Management and Emotional Well-Being

Stress management refers to a variety of techniques and strategies aimed at reducing, coping with, or preventing the negative effects of stress on mental, emotional, and physical well-being. Given the prevalence of stress in modern life, effective stress management is crucial for maintaining overall health and quality of life.

Effective stress management involves a combination of self-awareness, lifestyle changes, coping strategies, and social support to build resilience and enhance overall well-being in the face of stressors. Here are some key components of stress management:

Identifying stressors: Recognizing the sources of stress in your life is the first step in managing it effectively. Stressors can be external (e.g., work demands, financial pressures, relationship conflicts) or internal (e.g., perfectionism, negative self-talk).

Healthy lifestyle habits: Adopting a healthy lifestyle can help mitigate the impact of stress. This includes regular exercise, adequate sleep, a nutritious diet, and avoiding excessive caffeine, alcohol, and other substances.

Time management: Poor time management can contribute to feelings of overwhelm and stress. Learning to prioritize tasks, set realistic goals, and delegate, when necessary, can help you better manage your workload and schedule.

Relaxation techniques: Practicing relaxation techniques such as deep breathing, progressive muscle relaxation, meditation, and mindfulness can help calm the mind and body, reducing the physiological symptoms of stress.

Social support: Maintaining strong social connections and seeking support from friends, family, or support groups can provide emotional support and perspective during stressful times.

Setting boundaries: Learning to set boundaries and say no to unrealistic demands can help prevent burnout and overwhelm.

Cognitive restructuring: Identifying and challenging negative thought patterns and replacing them with more balanced and realistic thinking can help reduce stress and improve resilience.

Seeking professional help: If stress becomes overwhelming or chronic, it may be helpful to seek support from a mental health professional, such as a therapist or counselor, who can provide personalized strategies and support.

Engaging in enjoyable activities: Making time for hobbies, interests, and activities that bring joy and fulfillment can help counteract the negative effects of stress and promote overall well-being.

Mindful awareness: Cultivating present-moment awareness through mindfulness practices can help individuals better cope with stress by increasing their ability to respond to challenging situations with clarity and equanimity.

Emotional Well-Being refers to the state of being in good mental and emotional health, characterized by a positive sense of self, the ability to cope with life's challenges, resilience in the face of adversity, and the capacity to form and maintain healthy relationships. Achieving and maintaining emotional well-being is essential for overall happiness, fulfillment, and quality of life. Here are some key components and strategies for promoting emotional well-being:

Self-awareness: Developing self-awareness involves understanding one's thoughts, feelings, strengths, weaknesses, and values. This awareness allows individuals to recognize and manage their emotions more effectively.

Emotional regulation: Learning to regulate emotions involves the ability to recognize and manage feelings in healthy ways. Techniques such as deep breathing, mindfulness, and cognitive reframing can help individuals regulate their emotions and respond more adaptively to stressors.

Healthy coping mechanisms: Cultivating healthy coping mechanisms, such as engaging in physical activity, practicing relaxation techniques, spending time in nature, or pursuing creative outlets, can help individuals manage stress and maintain emotional well-being.

Building resilience: Resilience refers to the ability to bounce back from setbacks and adversity. Developing resilience involves cultivating a positive outlook, maintaining social connections, seeking support when needed, and viewing challenges as opportunities for growth.

Meaningful relationships: Building and nurturing positive relationships with friends, family, and community members is essential for emotional well-being. Healthy relationships provide support, connection, and a sense of belonging.

Setting boundaries: Establishing clear boundaries in relationships and commitments is crucial for maintaining emotional well-being. Setting limits on time, energy, and emotional resources helps prevent burnout and fosters self-care.

Practicing gratitude: Cultivating an attitude of gratitude involves acknowledging and appreciating the positive aspects of life, even during difficult times. Regularly practicing gratitude has been linked to improved emotional well-being and overall happiness.

Seeking help when needed: It's important to recognize when additional support is necessary and to seek help from mental health professionals, such as therapists, counselors, or support groups when experiencing persistent or severe emotional difficulties.

Engaging in self-care: Prioritizing self-care activities that promote physical, mental, and emotional well-being is essential for overall health. This includes getting enough sleep, eating nutritious foods, engaging in enjoyable activities, and managing stress effectively.

Cultivating mindfulness: Mindfulness involves being fully present and engaged in the present moment without judgment. Mindfulness practices, such as meditation, yoga, or tai chi, can help individuals reduce stress, enhance self-awareness, and improve emotional regulation.

By prioritizing self-awareness, healthy coping mechanisms, supportive relationships, and self-care practices, individuals can cultivate greater emotional well-being and resilience to navigate life's challenges more effectively.

Box 2.4. Developing Empathy

Developing empathy towards others is a valuable skill that involves understanding and sharing the feelings, thoughts, and perspectives of others. It allows individuals to connect with and support others more effectively, fostering stronger relationships and promoting compassion and understanding. Here are some strategies for developing empathy towards others:

Active listening: Practice active listening by giving your full attention to the person speaking without interrupting or judging. Focus on understanding their perspective and emotions, and reflect on what they are saying to demonstrate understanding.

Put yourself in their shoes: Try to imagine yourself in the other person's situation, considering their experiences, background, and emotions. This can help you better understand their perspective and empathize with their feelings.

Ask open-ended questions: Encourage others to share their thoughts and feelings by asking open-ended questions that invite deeper conversation and reflection. Avoid jumping to conclusions or making assumptions about their experiences.

Validate their feelings: Acknowledge and validate the other person's feelings, even if you don't necessarily agree with them. Show empathy by expressing understanding and empathy for their emotional experience.

Practice perspective-taking: Actively practice putting yourself in the shoes of others to understand their thoughts, feelings, and motivations. This can help broaden your perspective and enhance your empathy towards others.

Cultivate curiosity: Approach interactions with genuine curiosity and interest in understanding the other person's perspective. Ask questions and seek to learn more about their experiences and emotions.

Be nonjudgmental: Suspend judgment and avoid criticizing or blaming others for their feelings or experiences. Instead, focus on understanding and supporting them without imposing your values or beliefs.

Show empathic concern: Demonstrate empathy by showing concern for the other person's well-being and offering support and assistance when needed. Let them know that you are there for them and willing to help in any way you can.

Practice self-reflection: Take time to reflect on your thoughts, feelings, and biases that may impact your ability to empathize with others. Cultivating self-awareness can help you become more empathetic and understanding towards others.

Practice empathy daily: Make a conscious effort to practice empathy in your daily interactions with others, whether it's with family, friends, coworkers, or strangers. The more you practice empathy, the more natural it will become over time.

By actively practicing these strategies, you can develop greater empathy toward others, fostering deeper connections, understanding, and compassion in your relationships and interactions.

The Ripple of Empathy

At Wallingford College, Riya was known for her academic brilliance. She aced every exam, submitted projects on time, and was always prepared for class. However, as focused as she was on her studies, she often found herself disconnected from the people around her. She rarely interacted with classmates beyond group projects and kept to herself most of the time.

One day, a new student named Sam joined the class. Sam struggled from the start—missing deadlines, failing quizzes, and having trouble fitting in. He often sat alone in the cafeteria and avoided eye contact in class. Most students, including Riya, barely noticed him.

One afternoon, their professor announced a group assignment. Sam was placed in Riya's group. She wasn't happy about it, thinking his lack of focus would drag their project down. But as they started working together, she noticed something—Sam wasn't lazy or uninterested. He was just overwhelmed. Riya overheard him talking quietly to a classmate about how he was juggling his studies with a part-time job and taking care of his younger siblings at home.

For the first time, Riya saw Sam not as a slacker, but as a person carrying more weight than most students. She realized she had been too quick to judge him based on his grades and participation, without considering the challenges he faced outside the classroom.

After class one day, Riya approached Sam and offered to help with the project, explaining the parts he found difficult. They started meeting regularly and, slowly, Sam opened up more. He wasn't just struggling with time management; he felt out of place in college, unsure if he belonged. Riya didn't have all the answers, but she listened. She shared some of her struggles, and for the first time, Sam felt like someone genuinely understood him.

Over the next few weeks, something surprising happened. Not only did Sam improve in their project, but he started participating more in class. Other students began noticing his efforts, and slowly, he found his place among them.

Through her interaction with Sam, Riya learned a valuable lesson: empathy could bridge gaps where academic success and logic couldn't. By putting herself in someone else's shoes, she was able to connect in a way that made both of them better students and people. Sam, too, found confidence and motivation through that simple act of kindness.

After that moment, Riya made a conscious effort to be more mindful of others, not just focusing on grades or performance. She realized that every person had a story, a struggle, or a challenge, and a little empathy could make a world of difference. In a way, that simple shift in perspective made her college experience richer and more meaningful than any exam or grade ever could.

Her empathy started a ripple effect. Other students began helping and supporting each other, and soon, the campus felt more like a community—a place where everyone was valued, regardless of where they came from or what they were going through.

Learning: Riya learned that empathy is a powerful force that can quietly change everything.

Conflict Resolution

Conflict resolution is the process of addressing and resolving disagreements or disputes in a constructive and mutually satisfactory manner. Effective conflict resolution skills are essential for maintaining healthy relationships, whether in personal, professional, or social contexts. By following the steps given below and practicing effective communication and conflict-resolution skills, you can navigate conflicts more successfully and strengthen your relationships with others. Here are some steps and strategies for resolving conflicts:

Stay calm: Maintain your composure and avoid reacting impulsively or emotionally. Take a few deep breaths to calm yourself down if necessary. Remaining calm can help you think more clearly and rationally, which is essential for resolving conflicts effectively.

Active listening: Practice active listening by giving the other person your full attention and focusing on understanding their perspective. Avoid interrupting or formulating your response while they're speaking. Show empathy and validation by acknowledging their feelings and concerns.

Clarify the issues: Make sure you understand the root cause of the conflict by asking clarifying questions and paraphrasing what the other person has said. Encourage open and honest communication by creating a safe and nonjudgmental environment for discussion.

Express your perspective: Share your thoughts, feelings, and needs respectfully and assertively. Use "I" statements to express how the conflict is impacting you personally without blaming or accusing the other person. Be honest and transparent about your concerns and desires.

Seek level playing ground: Look for areas of agreement or shared interests that can serve as a basis for finding a resolution. Focus on finding win-win solutions that address the needs and concerns of all parties involved. Collaborate with the other person to brainstorm possible solutions together.

Explore alternative solutions: Be open to considering alternative solutions or compromises that may satisfy both parties' interests. Brainstorm creative solutions and be willing to think outside the box. Evaluate the pros and cons of each option and choose the solution that best meets everyone's needs.

Negotiate and compromise: Negotiate in good faith and be willing to make concessions if necessary to reach a mutually acceptable agreement. Be flexible and open-minded during the negotiation process, and be prepared to give and take to find a middle ground.

Focus on the future: Once a resolution has been reached, focus on moving forward and rebuilding the relationship. Let go of any lingering resentment or grudges and commit to learning from the conflict to prevent similar issues from arising in the future.

Follow-up: Check in with the other person periodically to ensure that the resolution is working for both parties and to address any new issues that may arise. Keep the lines of communication open and be willing to revisit the resolution if necessary.

Bridging the Divide: A Lesson in Conflict Resolution

Once upon a time in a peaceful village, there were two neighboring families: the Kumars and the Patels. They had lived side by side for many years, and their friendship was the cornerstone of the community. They shared meals, helped each other during hard times, and celebrated festivals together. However, one day, a simple misunderstanding turned their bond into a bitter conflict.

The conflict started when **Mr. Kumar** decided to build a new fence along the boundary between their properties. He wanted to extend his garden and thought a fence would create a clear division. However, he accidentally placed the fence a few feet into the Patel family's land. **Mr. Patel**, seeing the fence encroaching on his property, felt disrespected and angry.

Mr. Patel removed the fence overnight and put up his markers, claiming what he believed was rightfully his, without discussing it with Mr. Kumar. When **Mr. Kumar** woke up the next day and saw the fence gone, he felt offended. He thought, "How dare he touch my fence without asking!" Tempers flared, and soon the two families were no longer speaking to each other.

The small issue escalated into a major feud, causing both families to stop attending village gatherings. Their children, who were once best friends, were no longer allowed to play together. The once united village now felt divided as neighbors took sides. It was clear to everyone that the situation was getting out of hand, but neither family was willing to back down.

One day, the village elder **Ammaji**, who was respected for her wisdom, decided to intervene. She called both families to her house for a discussion. At first, neither **Mr. Kumar** nor **Mr. Patel** wanted to attend, but their wives convinced them that it was better to at least hear what Ammaji had to say.

When they arrived, **Ammaji** welcomed them with a calm and warm smile. She sat them down together and said, "I've seen you two live in harmony for years. But now, because of this small issue, your friendship and the peace of our village are in danger. Before we solve this problem, I want each of you to tell me what happened, one at a time."

Mr. Kumar spoke first, explaining how he felt hurt that **Mr. Patel** had removed his fence without discussing it with him. "I was trying to improve my garden, but now I feel like he doesn't respect my efforts," he said.

Then, **Mr. Patel** shared his side. "When I saw the fence on my land, I felt like you were trying to take what belongs to me without even asking. That's why I acted so quickly to remove it."

Ammaji listened carefully, nodding as each man spoke. After they finished, she asked them a simple question: "Why didn't you talk to each other first?"

Both men were silent, realizing for the first time that their anger had come from assumptions, not facts. Neither had taken the time to understand the other's perspective.

Ammaji then shared a story with them: "When I was younger, my sister and I had a similar argument over a piece of land our father left us. We fought for months, each believing the other was wrong. But then one day, we realized that by fighting, we were destroying the very thing our father had given us to cherish together. We made peace, and in the end, we shared the land, each planting different crops but helping each other's harvests."

The story deeply affected **Mr. Kumar** and **Mr. Patel**. They had let a minor problem escalate into something much larger than it should have been. They came to understand that their friendship and the welfare of their families were more significant than a boundary fence.

Ammaji then suggested a solution: "Why don't you both work together to rebuild the fence, but this time, make sure it's on the correct boundary? That way, you both have a say in how the land is divided."

At first, there was hesitation, but both men agreed it was fair. They decided to spend the next day re-measuring the land and working together on the fence. Their children, who had missed playing together, helped with the task, turning it into a bonding moment rather than a fight.

As they worked side by side, **Mr. Kumar** and **Mr. Patel** began to talk again. They apologized for their actions, admitting that their pride had gotten in the way of resolving the issue peacefully. By the time the fence was rebuilt, their old friendship had returned. The conflict that had once seemed so big now felt trivial.

As the sun dipped below the horizon, casting a warm orange glow over the village, both families came together to share a hearty meal. Laughter and chatter filled the air as they sat around the table, the lingering tension from their past feud dissipating into the night. Once fractured by conflict, the village felt united and whole, with lightened hearts and the bonds of friendship and kinship stronger than ever before.

Learning: Conflicts often arise from misunderstandings and assumptions. The best way to resolve them is through open communication, empathy, and cooperation. When we listen to each other and work together, even the most difficult problems can be solved.

Mental Health

Mental health encompasses being functional at the physical, emotional, and psychological levels and a connection beyond, touching the spiritual aspect of well-being. Staying connected with oneself is crucial for maintaining overall balance. Mental health is not the responsibility of one individual it is a collective effort. It requires commitment from all of us from family, educational institutions, employers, and society to create environments where people can thrive. When focusing on mental health, we can contribute to healthier families, stronger communities, and an improved quality of life.

Mental health refers to a person's emotional, psychological, and social well-being. It affects how people think, feel, and act, influencing how they handle stress, relate to others, and make decisions. Mental health is important at every stage of life, from childhood and adolescence through adulthood. Good mental health helps individuals manage daily life challenges, maintain relationships, and achieve a balanced, productive life. Common mental health challenges include:

1. **Anxiety disorders**: Persistent feelings of worry or fear that interfere with daily activities.
2. **Depression**: A mood disorder causing persistent sadness, loss of interest, and a lack of motivation.
3. **Bipolar disorder**: A mental health condition causing extreme mood swings, including emotional highs (mania) and lows (depression).
4. **Schizophrenia**: A severe mental health disorder characterized by distorted thinking, perceptions, emotions, and behavior.
5. **Post-traumatic stress disorder (PTSD)**: A disorder triggered by experiencing or witnessing a traumatic event, leading to flashbacks, nightmares, and severe anxiety.

Importance of Mental Health

Mental health plays a vital role in shaping the well-being and academic success of students and staff in educational institutions. In a competitive academic environment, individuals often face pressures from coursework, exams, and social dynamics, which can lead to stress, anxiety, and burnout. Addressing mental health in schools, colleges, and universities is essential to creating a supportive atmosphere where students can thrive emotionally, socially, and academically.

Prioritizing mental health helps improve focus, resilience, and overall productivity. When students are mentally well, they are better equipped to handle academic challenges, develop positive relationships, and make sound decisions. Similarly, teachers and staff who receive mental health support are more engaged, motivated, and capable of fostering a nurturing learning environment.

Educational institutions can play a key role by providing mental health services, offering peer support programs, promoting work-life balance, and raising awareness about mental well-being. Ensuring that mental health resources are accessible and stigma-free creates a culture of openness, where seeking help is normalized and students feel empowered to address their challenges. Ultimately, promoting mental health in educational institutions contributes to a well-rounded educational experience, leading to better outcomes for both individuals and the broader academic community.

Strategies to Cope with Mental Health at Educational Institutions

Coping with mental health challenges at educational institutions is crucial for both students and staff, as academic pressure, social dynamics, and other factors can significantly impact mental well-being. Here are some effective strategies for managing and supporting mental health in educational settings:

1. Establish Mental Health Programs and Services

- **Counseling and Therapy Services**: Offer on-campus mental health counseling for students and staff, providing access to professional therapists.

- **Mental Health Hotlines**: Set up hotlines or virtual chat services that provide confidential support and crisis intervention.
- **Workshops and Awareness Campaigns**: Organize regular workshops and awareness campaigns to educate the community about mental health, stress management, and wellness.

2. Promote Peer Support Networks

- **Peer Counseling Programs**: Train students to provide emotional support to their peers through structured peer-counseling initiatives.
- **Support Groups**: Establish peer-led support groups where students can openly share experiences and challenges related to stress, anxiety, or other issues.
- **Mentorship Programs**: Pair students with mentors (older students or faculty) who can provide guidance, advice, and emotional support.

3. Create a Healthy Learning Environment

- **Flexible Academic Policies**: Allow flexibility in deadlines, exam retakes, or project extensions for students facing significant mental health challenges.
- **Reduce Stigma**: Foster a culture of openness where mental health is discussed without stigma. Encourage students to seek help without fear of judgment.
- **Mindfulness and Stress-Reduction Programs**: Introduce mindfulness practices, yoga, or meditation sessions to help students manage stress.

4. Train Faculty and Staff

- **Mental Health Training**: Provide mental health awareness and sensitivity training for teachers and administrative staff to recognize signs of distress and offer appropriate support.

- **Early Intervention**: Train educators to identify early warning signs of mental health issues, such as a decline in academic performance or social withdrawal, and take preventive action.
- **Staff Wellness Programs**: Offer wellness initiatives for teachers and staff, helping them cope with their mental health challenges.

5. Encourage Work-Life Balance

- **Promote Breaks and Downtime**: Ensure students have adequate breaks between classes and encourage participation in extracurricular activities for relaxation.
- **Time Management Workshops**: Offer training on time management, helping students manage their academic workload without feeling overwhelmed.
- **Physical Activity**: Encourage regular exercise through sports clubs, fitness programs, or access to gym facilities, as physical health is closely linked to mental well-being.

6. Focus on Inclusive and Supportive Policies

- **Non-discriminatory Policies**: Implement policies that address the needs of students with mental health conditions, ensuring they receive reasonable accommodations.
- **Support for Marginalized Groups**: Recognize that minority groups may face additional pressures and provide tailored support to ensure inclusivity and belonging.
- **Accessible Resources**: Ensure that mental health resources are accessible, including for those with disabilities or limited access to technology.

7. Encourage Open Communication

- **Regular Check-ins**: Teachers and counselors should regularly check in with students, especially those struggling academically or socially, to provide emotional support.

- **Anonymous Feedback Systems**: Create platforms where students can anonymously share their concerns about mental health and well-being without fear of repercussions.
- **Parental Involvement**: In some cases, involve parents or guardians in mental health discussions to provide a support system at home.

8. Utilize Technology for Support

- **Mental Health Apps**: Promote the use of mental health apps that provide tools for relaxation, stress reduction, and mental health tracking.
- **Online Counseling**: Provide access to teletherapy or virtual mental health support for students who may not feel comfortable with in-person sessions.

9. Build a Supportive Physical Environment

- **Create Safe Spaces**: Designate quiet, stress-free zones on campus where students can relax, meditate, or unwind.
- **Green Spaces**: Incorporate nature into the campus environment, as access to green spaces has been shown to reduce stress and anxiety.

Maintaining mental health involves practices like seeking therapy or counseling and staying physically active, Practicing mindfulness and relaxation techniques, Building and maintaining supportive relationships, and prioritizing sleep and nutrition. Addressing mental health issues often requires professional help, such as therapy or medication, and societal support to reduce stigma around mental health. By implementing appropriate strategies, educational institutions can create a supportive atmosphere that promotes the mental well-being of both students and staff, fostering a healthier, more resilient academic community.

Mindfulness and Wellness

Mindfulness is a mental state of focusing on the present moment without judgment, and it can help with wellness. Mindfulness and wellness together create a holistic approach to maintaining and enhancing overall well-being. While mindfulness focuses on being present and aware at the moment, wellness encompasses the broader concept of maintaining a healthy balance in the physical, mental, emotional, and spiritual dimensions of life.

Yoga and meditation are two powerful practices that work hand-in-hand to promote mindfulness and overall wellness. Together, they help cultivate a deeper connection between the mind, body, and spirit, fostering a balanced and healthy life. By combining yoga and meditation, you can cultivate mindfulness in both movement and stillness, promoting physical, mental, and emotional wellness. This holistic approach leads to reduced stress, better emotional balance, improved physical health, and a deeper sense of inner peace and fulfillment.

Key Takeaways

- Emotion is the feelings we experience in response to different situations. Understanding emotions can help us navigate life with greater ease and stability.

- Paul Ekman is a renowned psychologist known for his groundbreaking work on emotions and facial expressions. He proposed six basic emotions: happiness, sadness, fear, anger, surprise, and disgust.

- The concept of the three minds, associated with Dialectical Behavior Therapy (DBT), developed by Marsha M. Linehan is to help individuals develop and strengthen their wise minds by integrating emotional and rational aspects of thinking, to achieve greater balance, resilience, and well-being in their lives.

- Emotional Intelligence (EI), measured by Emotional Quotient (EQ), refers to the ability to recognize, understand, and manage one's own emotions, as well as to recognize, understand, and influence the emotions of others.

- EI is a key determinant of success and fulfillment in both personal and professional life. By cultivating self-awareness, self-regulation, self-motivation, empathy, and social skills.

- Daniel Goleman played a pivotal role in bringing the concept of emotional intelligence to a broader audience. Goleman published his groundbreaking book (1995), ***"Emotional Intelligence: Why it can matter more than IQ,"*** which catapulted him to international acclaim.

- IQ (Intelligence Quotient) and EQ (Emotional Quotient) are two different measures that assess different aspects of human abilities, capabilities, and characteristics. Research has shown that IQ is just like the tip of the iceberg, whereas EQ is bigger and hidden inside the base.

- The Emotional competence framework comprises personal competence and social competence. The personal competencies are self-awareness, self-regulation, and self-motivation. The social competencies are: empathy and social skills

- Stress management refers to a variety of techniques and strategies aimed at reducing, coping with, or preventing the negative effects of stress on mental, emotional, and physical well-being.

- Emotional well-being refers to the state of being in good mental and emotional health, characterized by a positive sense of self, the ability to cope with life's challenges, resilience in the face of adversity, and the capacity to form and maintain healthy relationships.

- Conflict resolution is the process of addressing and resolving disagreements or disputes in a constructive and mutually satisfactory manner which is essential for maintaining healthy relationships, whether in personal, professional, or social contexts.

- Mental health refers to a person's emotional, psychological, and social well-being. Mental health plays a vital role in shaping the well-being and academic success of students and staff in educational institutions

- Coping with mental health challenges at educational institutions is crucial for both students and staff, as academic pressure, social dynamics, and other factors can significantly impact mental well-being

Key Terms

Emotions, Three Minds (DBT), Emotional Intelligence (EI), IQ vs. EQ, Mental Health, Personal Competence, Social Competence, Stress Management, Emotional Well-being, Conflict Resolution, Self-awareness, Self-regulation, Empathy, Social Skills, Resilience, Mindfulness.

Quiz – Multiple Choice Questions

1. Which of the following is a positive emotion?

    a. Fear
    b. Sadness
    c. Happiness
    d. Anger

2. Which emotion is typically associated with a response to perceived danger or threat?

    a. Joy
    b. Fear
    c. Love
    d. Surprise

3. The wise mind is a balance between which two aspects?

    a. Conscious mind and unconscious mind
    b. Emotional mind and rational mind
    c. Reflexive mind and reactive mind
    d. Logical mind and creative mind

4 . What does Emotional Intelligence (EI) primarily focus on?

    a. Cognitive abilities
    b. Social skills
    c. Emotional awareness
    d. Physical fitness

5. Which of the following is NOT a component of Emotional Intelligence according to Daniel Goleman?

    a. Self-awareness
    b. Self-regulation
    c. Social awareness
    d. Self-care

6. Which of the following is an example of intrapersonal EI?

a. Empathy
b. Self-motivation
c. Conflict resolution
d. Team collaboration

7. How does emotional intelligence differ from IQ?

a. Emotional intelligence is fixed, whereas IQ can be developed
b. Emotional intelligence is solely based on academic performance
c. Emotional intelligence focuses on understanding and managing emotions, whereas IQ measures cognitive abilities
d. Emotional intelligence is irrelevant in personal and professional settings

8. Which of the following is a key aspect of social awareness?

a. Self-control
b. Empathy
c. Self-motivation
d. Decision making

9. What does self-regulation in Emotional Intelligence refer to?

a. Ability to understand others' emotions
b. Ability to control one's impulses and emotions
c. Ability to motivate oneself
d. Ability to work effectively with others

10. Which of the following statements best describes empathy?

a. Understanding and sharing the feelings of others
b. Controlling one's own emotions effectively
c. Ability to motivate oneself towards achieving goals
d. Ability to work well with diverse teams

11. What is the significance of Emotional Intelligence in leadership?

    a. It helps leaders manipulate others' emotions

    b. It improves communication and relationship building

    c. It reduces the need for decision-making skills

    d. It has no impact on leadership effectiveness

12. Which of the following is an example of emotional intelligence in the workplace?

    a. Avoiding emotional conversations

    b. Reacting impulsively to criticism

    c. Offering constructive feedback

    d. Micromanaging employees

13. How does Emotional Intelligence contribute to personal well-being?

    a. By suppressing emotions

    b. By increasing self-awareness and self-regulation

    c. By avoiding social interactions

    d. By ignoring others' emotions

14. Which of the following is a common symptom of depression?

    a. Increased energy and excitement

    b. Persistent sadness and loss of interest

    c. Excessive fear of social situations

    d. Obsession with cleanliness and order

15. What is the primary goal of cognitive-behavioral therapy (CBT) in treating mental health disorders?

    a. Altering brain chemistry through medication

    b. Helping individuals change negative thought patterns and behaviors

    c. Encouraging clients to avoid stressful situations

    d. Using hypnosis to uncover unconscious memories

Answers:

1. c
2. b
3. b
4. c
5. d
6. b
7. c
8. b
9. b
10. a
11. b
12. c
13. b
14. b
15. b

Exercise 2.1

<u>Assess Your Emotional Intelligence</u>

This self-assessment questionnaire is designed to get you thinking about the various competencies of emotional intelligence as they apply to you. Effectiv leaders are always distinguished by a high degree of emotional intelligence (Daniel Goleman "Emotional Intelligence, 1995), which includes:

Self-awareness: The ability to recognize what you are feeling, to understand your habitual emotional responses to events, and to recognize how your emotions affect your behavior and performance. When you are self-aware, you see yourself as others see you, and have a good sense of your abilities and current limitations.

Managing emotion: The ability to stay focused and think even when experiencing powerful emotions. Being able to manage your emotional state is essential for taking responsibility for your actions, and can save you from hasty decisions that you later regret.

Self-motivation: The ability to use your deepest emotions to move and guide you towards your goals. This ability enables you to take the initiative and persevere despite obstacles and setbacks.

Empathy: The ability to sense, understand, and respond to what other people are feeling. Self-awareness is essential to having empathy with others. If you are not aware of your own emotions, you will not be able to read the emotions of others.

Social Skills: The ability to manage, influence, and inspire emotions in others. Being able to handle emotions in relationships and being able to influence and inspire others are essential foundation skills for successful teamwork and leadership.

Methodology

1. Assess and score each of the questionnaire's statements. Score your assessment, using the scale below:

1 indicates that the statement does NOT apply at all

3 indicates that the statement applies about half the time

5 indicates that the statement ALWAYS applies to you

2. Total and interpret your results

Transfer your scores to the calculation table and total your results. Remember, this tool is not a validated psychometric test - the answers you give are likely to vary depending on your mood when you take it.

3. Consider your results

Identify one or two actions you can take immediately to strengthen your emotional intelligence. Put your actions into your plan.

Assess and score how much each statement applies to you

#	How much does each statement apply to you	Mark your score				
Read each statement and decide how strongly the statement applies to you. Score yourself 1-5 based on 1= Does not apply 3= Applies half of the time 5= Always applies						
1	I realize immediately when I lose my temper	1	2	3	4	5
2	I can 'reframe' bad situations quickly	1	2	3	4	5
3	I can always motivate myself to do difficult tasks	1	2	3	4	5
4	I am always able to see things from the other person's viewpoint	1	2	3	4	5
5	I am an excellent listener	1	2	3	4	5
6	I know when I am happy	1	2	3	4	5
7	I do not wear my 'heart on my sleeve'	1	2	3	4	5
8	I am usually able to prioritise important activities at work and get on with them	1	2	3	4	5

		1	2	3	4	5
9	I am excellent at empathising with someone else's problem	1	2	3	4	5
10	I never interrupt other people's conversations	1	2	3	4	5
11	I usually recognise when I am stressed	1	2	3	4	5
12	Others can rarely tell what kind of mood I am in	1	2	3	4	5
13	I always meet deadlines	1	2	3	4	5
14	I can tell if someone is not happy with me	1	2	3	4	5
15	I am good at adapting and mixing with a variety of people	1	2	3	4	5
16	When I am being 'emotional' I am aware of this	1	2	3	4	5
17	I rarely 'fly off the handle' at other people	1	2	3	4	5
18	I never waste time	1	2	3	4	5
19	I can tell if a team of people are not getting along with each other	1	2	3	4	5
20	People are the most interesting thing in life for me	1	2	3	4	5
21	When I feel anxious, I usually can account for the reason(s)	1	2	3	4	5
22	Difficult people do not annoy me	1	2	3	4	5
23	I do not fabricate	1	2	3	4	5
24	I can usually understand why people are being difficult towards me	1	2	3	4	5
25	I love to meet new people and get to know what makes them 'tick'	1	2	3	4	5
26	I always know when I'm being unreasonable	1	2	3	4	5
27	I can consciously alter my frame of mind or mood	1	2	3	4	5
28	I believe you should do the difficult things first	1	2	3	4	5
29	Other individuals are not 'difficult' just 'different'	1	2	3	4	5
30	I need a variety of work colleagues to make my job interesting	1	2	3	4	5
31	Awareness of my own emotions is very important to me at all times	1	2	3	4	5
32	I do not let stressful situations or people affect me once I have left work	1	2	3	4	5
33	Delayed gratification is a virtue that I hold to	1	2	3	4	5
34	I can understand if I am being unreasonable	1	2	3	4	5

35	I like to ask questions to find out what it is important to people	1	2	3	4	5
36	I can tell if someone has upset or annoyed me	1	2	3	4	5
37	I rarely worry about work or life in general	1	2	3	4	5
38	I believe in 'Action this Day'	1	2	3	4	5
39	I can understand why my actions sometimes offend others	1	2	3	4	5
40	I see working with difficult people as simply a challenge to win them over	1	2	3	4	5
41	I can let anger 'go' quickly so that it no longer affects me	1	2	3	4	5
42	I can suppress my emotions when I need to	1	2	3	4	5
43	I can always motivate myself even when I feel low	1	2	3	4	5
44	I can sometimes see things from others' point of view	1	2	3	4	5
45	I am good at reconciling differences with other people	1	2	3	4	5
46	I know what makes me happy	1	2	3	4	5
47	Others often do not know how I am feeling about things	1	2	3	4	5
48	Motivations has been the key to my success	1	2	3	4	5
49	Reasons for disagreements are always clear to me	1	2	3	4	5
50	I generally build solid relationships with those I work with	1	2	3	4	5

Total and interpret your results

1. ***Record*** your 1, 2, 3, 4, and 5 scores for the questionnaire statement in the grid below. The grid organizes the statements into emotional competency lists.

SA		ME		MO		E		SS	
1		2		3		4		5	
6		7		8		9		10	
11		12		13		14		15	
16		17		18		19		20	
21		22		23		24		25	

26		27		28		29		30	
31		32		33		34		35	
36		37		38		39		40	
41		42		43		44		45	
46		47		48		49		50	

2. ***Calculate*** a total for each of the 5 emotional competencies.

Total = (SA)		Total = (ME)		Total = (MO)		Total = (E)		Total = (SS)	

3. ***Interpret*** your totals for each area of competency using the following guide.

35-50	This area is a ***strength*** for you.
18-34	***Giving attention*** to where you feel you are weakest will pay dividends.
10-17	Make this area a ***development priority***.

4. ***Record*** your result for each of the emotional competencies: strength, needs attention or development

	Strength	Needs attention	Development priority
Self-awareness			
Managing emotions			
Self-Motivation			
Empathy			
Social Skill			

5. ***Consider*** your results and identify one or two actions you can take immediately to strengthen ***emotional intelligence***. Put them into your action plan.

Activity 2.1

<u>Group Discussion: The Role of Empathy in Emotional Intelligence (EI)</u>

Objective: The objective of this group discussion is to explore and deepen our understanding of the role of empathy in Emotional Intelligence (EI) and its significance in personal and professional contexts.

Introduction: The Facilitator welcomes everyone to the group discussion on the role of empathy in Emotional Intelligence (EI). Let's start by briefly defining empathy and Emotional Intelligence. Empathy is the ability to understand and share the feelings of another person, putting oneself in their shoes and experiencing their emotions. Emotional Intelligence (EI) refers to the ability to recognize, understand, and manage our own emotions, as well as understand and influence the emotions of others. Empathy is a component of EI.

Guided Discussion Questions:

1. What is your understanding of empathy, and how do you think it contributes to Emotional Intelligence?
2. How does empathy differ from sympathy, and why is empathy considered a crucial component of EI?
3. Can you share examples of how empathy has positively impacted your personal or professional relationships?
4. In what ways can empathy enhance communication skills and conflict resolution abilities?
5. How do you think developing empathy can benefit individuals in leadership roles or positions of influence?
6. What challenges or barriers might individuals face in practicing empathy, and how can they overcome these obstacles?
7. How can we cultivate empathy in ourselves and encourage it in others, both within and outside of formal education settings?

8. Can you think of any real-life examples of individuals or organizations demonstrating high levels of empathy as part of their Emotional Intelligence?

Open Discussion and Reflection: Now, let's open up the floor for any additional thoughts, questions, or reflections on the role of empathy in Emotional Intelligence. Feel free to share your personal experiences, insights, or examples related to empathy and EI.

Conclusion: Thank you all for your valuable contributions to our discussion today. We've explored the multifaceted role of empathy in Emotional Intelligence and its importance in fostering understanding, connection, and effective communication. Let's continue to cultivate empathy in ourselves and others as we strive to develop our Emotional Intelligence and create positive impacts in our lives and communities.

Situation 2.1

Bharati's Dilemma is IQ better than EQ?

Bharati, a successful manager in a multinational company, finds herself in a challenging situation. She's facing a dilemma with her intellectual quotient (IQ) against her emotional quotient (EQ).

On one hand, Bharati's high IQ has always been her greatest asset. It has enabled her to analyze complex problems, analyse data, and excel in her career. However, in this particular situation, relying solely on her IQ might not be sufficient. The issue she's dealing with involves interpersonal dynamics, team morale, and sensitive emotions.

Bharati knows that addressing these aspects effectively requires a high level of emotional intelligence (EQ). She needs to navigate through conflicting perspectives, manage egos, and foster a positive work environment. While she's confident in her analytical skills, she's less certain about her ability to connect with others on an emotional level.

Her dilemma lies in finding the right balance between IQ and EQ. Should she approach the situation purely from a logical standpoint, focusing on data and rational arguments? Or should she tap into her emotional intelligence, demonstrating empathy, understanding, and effective communication?

What is your suggestion to Bharati?

Learning: Bharati should understand that successful leadership often demands a synthesis of both intellect and empathy. While her IQ might help her devise strategic plans, it's her EQ that will enable her to implement those plans successfully by garnering support, inspiring trust, and fostering collaboration among her team members.

Bharati should decide to leverage both her IQ and EQ. She should approach the situation with a logical analysis of the problem, but she should also take the time to listen to her team members' perspectives, validate their feelings, and communicate her decisions with empathy and clarity. By integrating her intellectual and emotional capacities, Bharati has to find a resolution that not only addresses the immediate challenge but also strengthens the bonds within her team.

Situation 2.2

<u>**Empathy in Action**</u>

Scenario: Comforting a Friend

Situation: Your friends have recently experienced a personal setback, such as failing an important exam or facing a breakup. They are feeling upset and discouraged, and they confide in you for support and comfort. This scenario provides an opportunity for individuals to reflect on their ability to demonstrate empathy, provide emotional support, and communicate effectively in a comforting role.

Questions for Analysis

Self-awareness:

1. How do you recognize and understand your own emotions when your friend confides in you about their setback?

2. Are you aware of any personal biases or assumptions that might influence your response to your friend's situation?

Empathy:

1. How do you demonstrate empathy towards your friend's feelings of upset and discouragement?
2. Can you identify and understand the emotions your friend is experiencing, such as sadness, frustration, or disappointment?

Social Skills:

1. How do you effectively communicate your support and comfort to your friend?
2. What actions or words do you use to show that you are there for them and that you care about their well-being?

Reflection:

1. After comforting your friend, how do you evaluate your response and effectiveness in providing support?
2. What were the key strengths and areas for improvement in your approach to comforting your friend?

Simulation Game 2.1

Mindful Journey: Exploring Meditation Techniques

Overview: Mindful Journey is a simulation game designed to introduce participants to various meditation techniques and guide them through the practice of mindfulness. Through immersive gameplay and interactive exercises, participants learn how to cultivate inner peace, reduce stress, and enhance their overall well-being through regular meditation practice.

Introduction to Meditation: Participants are introduced to the concept of meditation through virtual or physical guides who explain its benefits and importance. They learn about different meditation techniques, including mindfulness meditation, loving-kindness meditation, body scan meditation, and focused breathing exercises.

Guided Meditation Sessions: Mindful Journey offers a variety of guided meditation sessions tailored to different themes and purposes. Players can choose from sessions focused on stress reduction, relaxation, self-compassion, concentration, and emotional balance. Each session is led by a virtual or physical meditation instructor who provides gentle guidance and encouragement.

Real-Life Application: This game encourages participants to apply the meditation techniques they learn to their real lives. Through regular practice and integration into daily routines, participants can experience the benefits of meditation firsthand, improving their focus, resilience, and overall well-being.

By providing a safe and immersive environment for participants to explore meditation techniques and cultivate mindfulness, mindful Journey empowers them to embark on a journey of self-discovery and inner transformation. Through guided meditation sessions, interactive exercises, and reflection activities, participants develop the skills and resilience needed to navigate life's challenges with calmness, clarity, and compassion.

Note: Watch YouTube You will be OK! (10 Minute Guided Meditation), https://www.youtube.com/watch?v=0xD57-A3cx4

Role Play 2.1

Navigating Internship Opportunities (Guiding with Empathy)

Objective: Internships play an important role in initiating students into the professional world. With the National Education Policy (NEP) 2020, internships have become increasingly important in education and upskilling. The NEP 2020 mandates the integration of internships into undergraduate curricula to bolster academic learning with skill-based learning.

Characters:

1. **Veena:** An empathetic coordinator for career guidance.
2. **Chetan:** A proactive and ambitious student with a keen interest in internships.
3. **Deepak:** A strategic and analytical thinker, focused on maximizing internship opportunities.
4. **Arjun:** A thoughtful and observant student, contemplating the best-fit internship for students' goals.
5. **Rohini:** A confident and well-networked student, eager to share internship insights.

Setting: A placement cell of the college campus, where Ms. Veena, Chetan, Deepak, Arjun, and Rohini are gathered to discuss internship prospects. A Conflict Resolution session among College Students, who are looking for internship opportunities and seeking guidance from Ms Veena, coordinator for career guidance as part of the placement cell.

Veena: [Starting the conversation with enthusiasm] Hey, everyone! With summer approaching, I thought it'd be great to discuss about internship opportunities. If there are any issues, I want to resolve. How does everyone feel about their search?

Chetan: [Excitedly] I've been researching like crazy! There are so many interesting internships out there, but I'm struggling to narrow down my options.

Deepak: [Nodding in agreement] I hear you, Chetan. It's important to find an internship that aligns with one's interests and career goals.

Arjun: [Thoughtfully] I'm still unsure about what I want to pursue after graduation, so I'm finding it challenging to pick the right internship.

Rohini: [Offering support] Don't worry, Arjun. Exploring different fields through internships can help you figure out your interests and strengths.

Veena: [Encouraging] Exactly! Internships are a great way to gain real-world experience and test the waters in different industries. Have any of you reached out to your network for opportunities?

Chetan: [Eagerly] Yes, I've been leveraging LinkedIn and reaching out to alumni for advice and potential referrals.

Deepak: [Adding] Networking is key. It's not just about what you know, but who you know. Building relationships can open doors to exciting opportunities.

Arjun: [Reflecting] I haven't tapped into my network much yet. Maybe I should start reaching out to mentors and peers for guidance.

Rohini: [Sharing her experience] Networking has been invaluable for me. I've landed some great internships through connections and informational interviews.

Veena: It sounds like we're all on the right track. Let's keep exploring, networking, and applying to internships that excite us. And remember, it's okay to seek guidance from career services or mentors along the way.

Chetan: [Feeling motivated] Thanks, Veena! I'm feeling more confident about my internship search now.

Deepak: [Optimistically] Absolutely. Let's keep pushing forward and seizing those opportunities. Our internships could be the first step toward our dream careers.

Arjun: [Feeling encouraged] I'm excited to see where this journey takes us. Thanks for the support, Ms. Veena.

Rohini: [With a smile] Cheers to new experiences and growth! We've got this.

Veena: Anyway, to sum up, our discussion, I will give you how you can begin: Decide your field of interest, personalize your resume, and add a cover letter to your resume stating your interest and passion for the role. Next look for vacancies on job search portals like LinkedIn and Internshala to research the company and industry. Apply to multiple companies with a recommendation letter from your mentors, which can improve your chances of getting an internship. Then follow up periodically, and in the meantime build core skills and technical skills indicating your career readiness. Best of luck! We will review it next week.

Project 2.1

Emotional Intelligence Empowerment Program for College Students

Project Overview: The "Emotional Intelligence Empowerment Program" aims to equip college students with essential emotional intelligence (EI) skills to navigate academic, personal, and professional challenges effectively. Through a series of workshops, activities, and reflections, students will develop self-awareness, self-regulation, empathy, social skills, and motivation, fostering a positive and supportive campus culture. By implementing the "Emotional Intelligence Empowerment Program," college students can develop essential life skills that will not only enhance their academic performance but also contribute to their overall well-being and success in future endeavors.

Objectives:

1. Enhance students' understanding of emotional intelligence and its importance in personal and academic success.
2. Cultivate self-awareness to recognize and understand one's emotions, strengths, and areas for growth.
3. Develop self-regulation techniques to manage stress, anxiety, and other negative emotions effectively.
4. Foster empathy and understanding of others' perspectives to build strong interpersonal relationships.
5. Improve social skills, including communication, teamwork, and conflict resolution, essential for collaboration and leadership.
6. Motivate students to set and pursue meaningful goals aligned with their values and aspirations.

Project Components

Workshop Series:

a. Introduction to Emotional Intelligence: Exploring the five components of EI and their significance.

b. Self-Awareness and Self-Reflection: Activities and exercises to help students identify their emotions, triggers, and values.

c. Self-Regulation Techniques: Mindfulness practices, stress management strategies, and relaxation techniques.

d. Empathy and Understanding Others: Role-playing, perspective-taking exercises, and active listening activities.

e. Social Skills Development: Communication workshops, team-building exercises, and conflict resolution simulations.

f. Goal Setting and Motivation: Guided goal-setting sessions, vision board creation, and motivational talks.

Peer Support Groups:

a. Formation of small peer support groups for ongoing discussions, reflections, and accountability.

b. Facilitated by trained peer mentors or counselors to provide guidance and encouragement.

Guest Speaker Sessions:

a. Inviting experts in emotional intelligence, psychology, leadership, and personal development to share insights and experiences.

b. Q&A sessions and networking opportunities for students to interact with professionals in related fields.

Service-Learning Projects:

a. Collaborative projects that allow students to apply their EI skills in real-world contexts, such as community service initiatives, mentoring programs, or campus wellness campaigns.

Reflection and Feedback:

a. Regular reflection activities to encourage students to assess their progress, challenges, and growth throughout the program.

b. Feedback mechanisms to gather input from participants for program improvement and refinement.

Culminating Event:

a. Showcase event to celebrate students' achievements, share success stories, and inspire ongoing commitment to emotional intelligence development.

b. Recognition of outstanding contributions and participation.

Outcome Evaluation:

1. Pre- and post-program assessments to measure changes in participants' self-awareness, self-regulation, empathy, social skills, and motivation.

2. Surveys and focus groups to gather qualitative feedback on the program's impact, relevance, and effectiveness.

3. Long-term follow-up to track participants' continued application of EI skills and their academic and personal growth.

Quick Case 2.1

Building Bridges: Resolving Interdepartmental Conflict with Emotional Intelligence

Abstract: This case study examines how a large retail company addressed longstanding interdepartmental conflicts using Emotional Intelligence (EI) principles. By fostering self-awareness, empathy, and effective communication, the company successfully transformed the contentious relationship between the Sales and Operations departments, resulting in improved collaboration and organizational harmony.

Introduction: Conflict between departments is a common challenge faced by many organizations, often stemming from differences in goals, priorities, and communication styles. Addressing such conflicts requires a strategic approach that acknowledges the emotional dynamics at play. This case study illustrates how a retail company leveraged EI principles to mitigate interdepartmental tensions and foster a culture of collaboration.

Case Background: The retail company, Orion Retailers, has been grappling with friction between its Sales and Operations departments for several years. Sales employees often complained about Operations' perceived inefficiency and lack of responsiveness, while Operations staff felt undervalued and overwhelmed by the demands placed upon them. The resulting animosity hindered workflow, strained interdepartmental communication, and jeopardized customer satisfaction.

Recognizing the detrimental impact of these conflicts on organizational performance, the company's leadership sought to intervene proactively. They appointed a cross-functional team led by HR manager Meena to facilitate conflict resolution using an EI-based approach.

Application of EI Principles: Meena began by conducting emotional intelligence workshops for members of both departments, aimed at enhancing self-awareness and empathy. Through exercises and discussions, employees learned to recognize and manage their emotions, as well as understand the perspectives and experiences of their colleagues in the other department.

Meena organized joint meetings and team-building activities to promote cross-departmental collaboration and foster a sense of unity. These activities provided opportunities for Sales and Operations employees to interact in a neutral and non-threatening environment, breaking down barriers and building mutual respect.

Meena also facilitated open dialogues between department heads, encouraging them to communicate openly and empathetically. By fostering a culture of transparent communication and active listening, she created a platform for resolving grievances and finding common ground.

Outcome and Impact: Over time, the concerted efforts to apply EI principles yielded positive results. Sales and Operations employees began to view each other more positively, recognizing the value of each department's contributions to the company's success. Interactions became more collaborative and constructive, with employees proactively seeking solutions to shared challenges.

The transformation in interdepartmental dynamics translated into tangible benefits for the organization. Workflow efficiency improved as Sales and Operations teams worked together more seamlessly, resulting in faster order processing and enhanced customer satisfaction. Moreover, employee morale and engagement increased as individuals felt valued and supported within a more cohesive work environment.

Conclusion: This case study highlights the transformative potential of Emotional Intelligence in resolving interdepartmental conflicts and fostering collaboration within organizations. By cultivating self-awareness, empathy, and effective communication skills, companies can bridge divides between departments, unlock synergies, and drive sustainable growth. The success of Orion Retailers in transforming the relationship between its Sales and Operations departments serves as a testament to the power of EI in building bridges and fostering organizational harmony.

Case Questions

1. What were the main sources of conflict between the Sales and Operations departments at Orion Retailers?
2. How did the leadership of Orion Retailers recognize the need to address the interdepartmental conflicts, and why did they choose to apply Emotional Intelligence principles in resolving them?
3. What specific EI principles and techniques were utilized to address the conflicts between the Sales and Operations departments?
4. What were the measurable outcomes and impacts of implementing Emotional Intelligence strategies in resolving interdepartmental conflicts at Orion Retailers?

Discussion Questions

1. What is Emotional Intelligence (EI), and how does it differ from traditional intelligence measures like IQ?

2. How can developing Emotional Intelligence positively impact personal relationships, both in professional and personal settings?

3. What role does self-awareness play in Emotional Intelligence, and how can individuals enhance their self-awareness?

4. Discuss the importance of empathy in EI and its implications for effective communication and collaboration in teams.

5. How does Emotional Intelligence contribute to effective leadership and team building, and what specific EI competencies are crucial for leaders?

6. Can Emotional Intelligence be learned and improved over time? What are some strategies or practices that can help individuals enhance their EI?

7. Explore the connection between Emotional Intelligence and mental health. How does EI influence resilience and coping mechanisms during times of stress or adversity?

8. How can emotional intelligence help entrepreneurs succeed in their businesses?

9. How do cultural differences influence the perception and expression of Emotional Intelligence? Are there universal EI principles, or does EI vary across cultures?

10. Discuss the potential drawbacks or limitations of focusing too much on Emotional Intelligence in personal and professional development.

11. In what ways can organizations incorporate Emotional Intelligence assessments and training into their talent development programs to foster a more emotionally intelligent workforce?

References

1. Bar-On, R., & Parker, J. D. A. (Eds.). (2000). The handbook of emotional intelligence: Theory, development, assessment, and application at home, school, and in the workplace. Jossey-Bass.

2. Biswas-Diener, R., & Dean, B. (2007). Positive psychology coaching: Putting the science of happiness to work for your clients. John Wiley & Sons.

3. Bradberry, T., & Greaves, J. (2009). Emotional intelligence 2.0. Talent Smart.

4. Brackett, M. A., & Katulak, N. A. (2006). Emotional intelligence in the classroom: Skill-based training for teachers and students. In J. Ciarrochi, J. P. Forgas, & J. D. Mayer (Eds.), Emotional intelligence in everyday life: A scientific inquiry (pp. 255-273). Psychology Press.

5. Brackett, M. A., & Rivers, S. E. (Eds.). (2014). Emotional intelligence in education: Integrating research with practice. Springer.

6. Clark, J., & Ives, B. (2001). Neuro-Linguistic Programming and Emotional Intelligence: Harnessing the Power of the Mind to Enhance Emotional Awareness and Communication Skills. New York, NY: HarperCollins.

7. Ekman, P. (1999). Basic emotions. In T. Dalgleish & M. J. Power (Eds.), Handbook of cognition and emotion (pp. 45-60). John Wiley & Sons.

8. Goleman, D. (1995). Emotional intelligence: Why it can matter more than IQ. Bantam Books.

9. Goleman, D. (2013). Emotional Intelligence and Working with Emotional Intelligence, Two International Bestsellers in One Volume, Bloomsbury.

10. Mayer, J. D., Roberts, R. D., & Barsade, S. G. (2008). Human abilities: Emotional intelligence. Annual Review of Psychology, 59, 507-536.

11. Petrides, K. V., & Furnham, A. (2001). Trait emotional intelligence: Psychometric investigation concerning established trait taxonomies. European Journal of Personality, 15(6), 425-448.

12. Salovey, P., & Grewal, D. (2005). The science of emotional intelligence. *Current Directions in Psychological Science, 14*(6), 281-285.

13. Salovey, P., & Mayer, J. D. (1990). Emotional intelligence. *Imagination, Cognition and Personality, 9*(3), 185-211.

WORKSHEETS

Chapter 3

Creativity

Creative Sparks: Turning Darkness into Light

During exam week at Northside University, a sudden power outage plunged the campus into darkness, leaving students unable to study for their finals. Panic spread as students were left without lights, and with no power expected until morning, they feared losing crucial study time.

Maya, a quick-thinking physics student, remembered a stash of unused glowsticks from a campus event. She and her friends quickly distributed them across the library and dorms, lighting up study spaces with neon colors. What began as a simple solution soon turned into a campus-wide "Glowstick Rally"—students shared glowsticks, posted fun photos online, and turned the crisis into a moment of community bonding. Maya became a campus hero, not only for her glowstick idea but for inspiring other students to think creatively in the face of unexpected challenges.

While the glowsticks provided enough light for basic tasks, Maya knew they weren't a long-term solution. So she thought of another idea: What if they could generate power using bicycles? The university had a set of stationary bikes in the gym, and Maya realized they could be rigged to create a temporary power source.

But Maya didn't stop there. Maya and her team approached the engineering students, who eagerly jumped on board. Using basic electrical engineering concepts, they worked through the night to hook up the stationary bikes to small generators. By morning, they had created a makeshift system that allowed students to charge their phones and laptops. They called it the **"Pedal for Power"** project, and students volunteered to take turns riding the bikes to keep the power flowing.

The university was so impressed by the innovative idea of **Pedal for Power** that they decided to make it a permanent feature. Additionally, the Glowstick Rally became an annual tradition, serving as a powerful symbol of student resilience and teamwork in the face of unexpected challenges. This tradition stands as a reminder that during times of crisis, the combination of creativity and collaboration has the potential to transform the most difficult situations into opportunities for growth and connection.

Learning Objectives

1. Explain Key Concepts and Analyze the Components of the Process of Creativity.
2. Recognize Different Types of Creative Thinking Techniques.
3. Apply Creative Problem-Solving Tools to Generate Novel Ideas
4. Generate Original Solutions to Complex Problems.
5. Develop Opportunity from Idea

"Creativity is Thinking Outside the Box, then Realizing there is no Box."

Introduction

Creativity is a fundamental human trait that can be cultivated and harnessed to solve complex problems, drive innovation, and enhance personal growth. This chapter aims to explore the nature of creativity, understand its cognitive and psychological underpinnings, and develop practical strategies to foster creative thinking in various contexts. Through a blend of theoretical knowledge, interactive exercises, and real-world applications, students will embark on a transformative journey to unlock their creative potential.

Creativity is the spark that ignites new ideas and possibilities, while innovation is the process of harnessing and transforming those ideas into meaningful outcomes. Both are essential drivers of progress and growth in every aspect of human endeavor, felling advancements, solving complex problems, and enriching lives. Cultivating a culture that values and nurtures creativity and innovation is critical for fostering sustainable success and adaptability in an ever-changing world.

Creative Mind

A creative mind can generate original ideas, solutions, or expressions. It involves thinking outside the box, making unconventional connections, and exploring novel perspectives. Creative minds often exhibit curiosity, openness to new experiences, imagination, flexibility, and persistence in facing challenges. They thrive on exploring possibilities, experimenting with different approaches, and embracing ambiguity. Creative individuals may express their creativity in various fields such as art, science, technology, literature, or business, bringing fresh insights and innovations to the world around them.

Cultivating a creative mindset involves nurturing certain habits, practices, and attitudes that foster creativity and innovation. Here are some strategies to help you develop creative thinking:

- **Embrace Curiosity:** Stay curious and ask questions. Curiosity fuels creativity by encouraging you to explore new ideas, learn new things, and seek out different perspectives.

- **Open-mindedness:** Be open to new experiences, ideas, and ways of thinking. Avoid being overly critical or judgmental, as this can limit your creative potential.

- **Embrace Constraints:** Sometimes, limitations can fuel creativity by forcing you to think more creatively within the boundaries. Embracing constraints can lead to innovative solutions and approaches.

- **Change Your Environment:** Changing your environment can stimulate creativity by exposing you to new stimuli and breaking up routine patterns of thinking. Try working in a different location or taking a walk outdoors to refresh your mind.

- **Embrace Failure:** See failure as a learning opportunity rather than a setback. Embrace challenges and view them as chances to grow and improve.

- **Practice Mindfulness:** Mindfulness can help you become more aware of your thoughts, feelings, and surroundings, allowing you to tap into your creative potential more effectively.

- **Foster a Growth Mindset**: Adopt a growth mindset, believing that your abilities and intelligence can be developed through dedication and hard work. This mindset encourages resilience and a willingness to take on challenges.

- **Engage in Diverse Activities:** Explore a variety of activities, hobbies, and interests to stimulate your mind and expose yourself to different experiences that can inspire creativity.

- **Collaborate with Others**: Collaborating with others can provide new perspectives, insights, and ideas that can spark creativity. Surround yourself with people who challenge and inspire you.

- **Set Aside Time for Creativity:** Dedicate regular time for creative activities, whether it's writing, drawing, brainstorming, or experimenting with new ideas. Consistency is key to developing and maintaining a creative mindset.

- **Keep an Idea Journal**: Keep a journal or notebook to jot down ideas, observations, and inspirations. This can help you capture and develop ideas over time.

- **Challenge Assumptions**: Question your assumptions and beliefs to challenge conventional thinking and explore alternative viewpoints.

The Doodler's Revolution

In a lively community college located in a bustling city, Leela, a graphic designer, was renowned for her whimsical doodles that spilled out of her sketchbook. Her illustrations, brimming with intricate patterns and fantastical characters, captivated the imagination of those around her. While her classmates concentrated on traditional art forms, Leela's creativity was truly unique.

As the semester drew to a close, anticipation and enthusiasm mounted for the highly anticipated annual college art exhibition. However, the entire college community was caught off guard when the administration revealed unforeseen budget cuts, casting a shadow of uncertainty over the event. The unexpected news reverberated through the student body, leaving many budding artists in a state of concern, as the exhibition served as a vital platform for them to present and celebrate their dedication and creativity.

Leela was determined to ensure that the exhibition would not fade into obscurity. She rallied her classmates and put forward an ingenious idea: creating a "**Doodle Wall.**" Rather than showcasing individual pieces of art in frames, they envisioned covering an entire wall with a collaborative mural, inviting every student to contribute their doodles and illustrations. What began as a simple concept soon blossomed as students from diverse fields of study came together, infusing the mural not just with visual art but also with elements of poetry and music, resulting in a harmonious and multifaceted creative expression.

Leela took the initiative to plan and facilitate brainstorming sessions, encouraging everyone to contribute their ideas. As the Doodle Wall concept started to come to life, they reached out to local businesses to secure sponsorships to finance the project. Despite facing constraints in terms of resources, they effectively marketed the event using visually appealing materials adorned with Leela's unique doodles. This approach proved successful in capturing the attention and support of art supply stores, which provided supplies in exchange for promotional exposure.

On the day of the exhibition, the campus was filled with excitement and anticipation. The Doodle Wall stood as a vibrant tapestry of colors and creativity, welcoming students, faculty, and members of the local community. The event featured live music, food stalls, and interactive stations where attendees could add their doodles, further enriching the mural.

The exhibition was a resounding success, drawing large crowds and receiving enthusiastic praise. The Doodle Wall became a powerful symbol of resilience and community spirit, showcasing the collaborative efforts of the students and their diverse talents.

Inspired by the success, the college decided to incorporate collaborative art projects into future exhibitions, fostering creativity and teamwork among students. The Doodle Wall remained a permanent feature on campus, a lasting testament to the power of imagination and collaboration.

Leela's creative and imaginative approach transformed what could have been a crisis into a remarkable and memorable celebration of artistic expression. Her initiative inspired others to not only embrace their creativity but also to come together and collaborate amid adversity. The Doodler's Revolution was far more than just an art exhibition; it served as a powerful reminder of the extraordinary outcomes that can emerge when a community fosters and supports creativity.

Doodler's Revolution not only saved the art exhibition but also enriched the college experience, instilling a spirit of collaboration and creativity that would resonate for years to come.

Divergent and Convergent Thinking

Divergent thinking and convergent thinking are two distinct cognitive processes involved in creative problem-solving and idea generation. **Figure 3.1** provides the patterns of Divergent thinking and Convergent thinking.

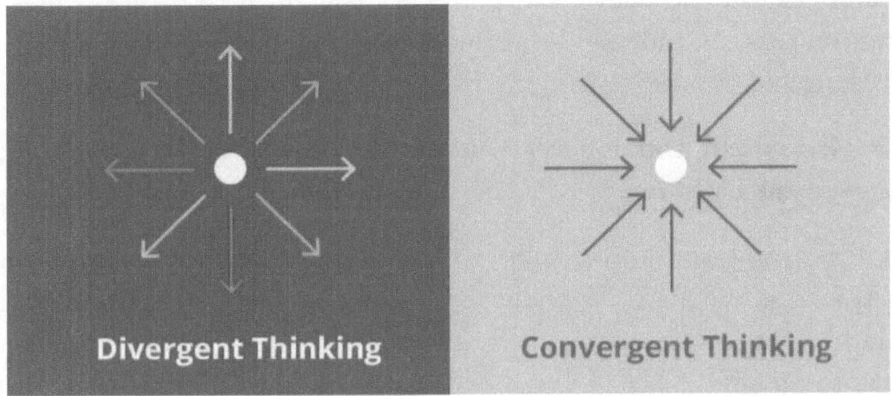

Figure 3.1. Divergent Thinking and Convergent Thinking

Divergent Thinking: Refers to the ability to generate a wide variety of ideas or solutions to a problem. It involves exploring multiple perspectives, thinking outside the box, and producing creative and original ideas. Divergent thinking focuses on quantity over quality of ideas.

Example: A group brainstorming session where participants are encouraged to share as many ideas as possible for a new product. Creative writing and ideation workshops often utilize divergent thinking to explore numerous possibilities and generate innovative solutions.

Convergent Thinking: It is the process of narrowing down multiple ideas or options to find the best solution to a problem. It focuses on evaluating and selecting the most appropriate and effective solution based on criteria and constraints. Decision-making processes, problem-solving tasks, and critical thinking exercises often require convergent thinking to analyze information, assess alternatives, and make informed choices.

Convergent thinking emphasizes accuracy and efficiency, the use of established methods, and criteria for evaluation. It is applied commonly in problem-solving scenarios that require a clear, definitive answer.

Example: Solving a mathematical equation or answering multiple-choice questions on a test.

Both divergent and convergent thinking are essential components of the creative process, and they often work together to facilitate innovative thinking and problem-solving.

The Greenfield Community Garden: A Journey of Divergent and Convergent Thinking

In the quaint and picturesque town of Greenfield, a passionate and dedicated group of college students belonging to the **Environmental Club** became acutely aware of a significant and urgent problem plaguing their community. They observed that numerous families in the town were grappling with the harsh reality of food insecurity. Fueled by a deep sense of empathy and a resolute determination to bring about positive change, these students embarked on a noble mission. Their vision was to establish a flourishing community garden, not only to address the pressing issue of food insecurity but also to cultivate a communal spirit of unity and support.

Divergent Thinking: Brainstorming Solutions

To launch their green project initiative, the students gathered in the bustling college cafeteria for an invigorating brainstorming session. With an atmosphere filled with excitement and anticipation, they urged everyone to unleash their creativity without any limitations. The room reverberated with energy as a myriad of ideas began to cascade forth:

- **Types of Crops**: Suggestions ranged from common vegetables like tomatoes and carrots to more exotic options like kale and specialty herbs.
- **Garden Layout**: Some students proposed a simple row garden, while others envisioned a circular garden with pathways and benches for relaxation.
- **Community Involvement**: Ideas included involving local schools, hosting workshops, and even starting a "Sponsor a Plot" program for families in need.

- **Events and Activities**: The group thought of organizing seasonal festivals, cooking classes, and a "Harvest Day" to celebrate the community's efforts.

This brainstorming session exemplified **divergent thinking**, as the students generated a wealth of ideas, embracing possibilities without judgment.

Convergent Thinking: Focusing on a Plan

After the brainstorming session, the group encountered the challenge of refining their ideas to develop a workable plan. They gathered again to assess each idea, discussing its feasibility and potential impact. Using sticky notes, they organized their suggestions and voted on the best options:

1. **Crop Selection**: They chose to grow a mix of tomatoes, peppers, and zucchini, which were popular and easy to maintain.
2. **Garden Design**: The group settled on a rectangular layout that included designated areas for each type of crop, as well as a small communal seating area for gatherings.
3. **Community Engagement**: They decided to partner with local schools and the food bank to maximize participation and outreach, focusing on families most in need.
4. **Workshops and Events**: They planned to host a kickoff planting day and a seasonal harvest festival, ensuring a fun and educational experience for all participants.

This phase showcased **convergent thinking**, where the students critically analyzed their options, made decisions, and developed a clear, cohesive plan to move forward.

Execution and Impact

The students had a solid plan in place and rallied the community for support. They secured a plot of land from the town council and organized volunteers for the planting. Over several weekends, they built raised beds, planted seeds, and painted signs to mark their progress.

As the garden flourished, community involvement. also grewLocal families came together to tend to the crops, sharing gardening tips and stories. The students organized educational workshops on sustainable gardening practices and healthy cooking, drawing even more residents into the fold.

The inaugural **Harvest Festival** was a resounding success, attracting families from all over Greenfield. The event featured fresh produce from the garden, cooking demonstrations, and activities for children, transforming the garden into a vibrant community hub.

The **Greenfield Community Garden** became a shining example of how **divergent and convergent thinking** can drive positive change. By first generating a multitude of creative ideas and then focusing on the most feasible solutions, the students turned their vision into reality. The project not only alleviated food insecurity but also fostered a sense of community and collaboration, leaving a lasting legacy of teamwork and sustainability in Greenfield.

The Creative Process

The creative process is a journey of transforming ideas into reality, encompassing various stages that individuals typically go through when generating and developing new ideas, solutions, or artworks. The creative process is not always linear; it can be iterative, with stages overlapping and revisiting previous steps as needed. Everyone's creative journey is unique, so find what works best for you and embrace the process with curiosity, passion, and perseverance. Ideas usually evolve through a creative process.

Throughout the creative process, it's important to maintain an open mind, embrace ambiguity and uncertainty, and be willing to experiment and take risks. Creativity often involves trial and error, persistence, and resilience in the face of challenges. While the creative process can vary from person to person and across different fields, it often involves several key stages. In his book, "Creativity," Mihaly Csikszentmihalyi says that an effective creative process usually consists of five steps. These are:

1. **Preparation (Finding Problems)**: This is the initial stage where you gather information, explore different sources, and seek out new experiences. Finding problems and issues that are interesting and that arouse curiosity. This stage is also termed the seeding process. The exact manner in which an idea is germinated is a mystery. However, most creative ideas can be traced to an individual's interest in or curiosity about a specific problem or study.

2. **Incubation:** After gathering initial ideas, the incubation stage involves letting these ideas simmer in your mind. It's a period of subconscious processing where your brain continues to work on the problem or idea in the background, even when you're not actively thinking about it.

3. **Ideation:** In this stage, you actively brainstorm and generate a variety of ideas without filtering or judging them. The focus is on quantity rather than quality, encouraging free thinking and exploring different possibilities. In this stage, the idea resurfaces as a realistic creation.

4. **Evaluation:** After generating a range of ideas, the evaluation stage involves assessing and refining them. You consider the feasibility, relevance, and potential of each idea, narrowing down the options to those that are most promising.

5. **Implementation:** Once you've selected the most promising ideas, the implementation stage involves turning them into action. This may involve planning, experimenting, prototyping, and refining your ideas to bring them to life. After implementing your ideas, it's essential to reflect on the process and outcomes. Reflecting allows you to learn from your experiences, identify what worked well, and areas for improvement. It can also provide insights for future creative endeavors.

Box 3.1. Creative Storytelling

Creative storytelling involves weaving together narrative elements compellingly and imaginatively to captivate the audience's attention and evoke emotions. Pitching a story effectively requires a combination of planning, preparation, clarity, and effective communication. Pitching is not just about selling your story; it's about building relationships and fostering collaboration. Approach each pitch with professionalism, confidence, and enthusiasm, and you'll increase your chances of success. Here's a step-by-step guide to help you pitch your story:

Know Your Audience: Find out to whom you are pitching. Whether it's an employee, a mentor, an editor, a producer, or an investor, tailor your pitch to their interests, preferences, and expectations. Infuse your story with emotion to create a powerful connection with your audience.

Research: Every story begins with a strong concept or an idea. Gather information about the outlet, audience, and publication, you're pitching to. Familiarize yourself with their previous work, target audience, and editorial guidelines. This will help you tailor your pitch to fit their style and preferences.

Building an Engaging Plot: Craft a plot that is full of twists, turns, and surprises to keep the audience hooked. Start your pitch with a strong hook that grabs the attention of your audience. This could be a surprising fact, a figure, a compelling question, or a thought-provoking statement related to your story.

Outline the Story: Clearly outline the main points of your story. Highlight the key elements such as the plot, memorable characters, setting, and themes. Keep it concise but informative, providing enough detail to give the listener a clear understanding of what the story is about.

Highlight the Unique Angle: Emphasize what makes your story novel, unique or different from others. Whether it's a fresh perspective, exclusive access, or timely relevance, make sure to highlight the distinctive elements that set your story apart.

Provide Supporting Evidence: Back up your pitch with concepts, and relevant evidence, such as research findings, statistics, expert quotes, or anecdotes. This helps to build credibility and demonstrates that your story is well-researched and backed by reliable sources.

Showcase Your Expertise: If you have relevant experience or expertise related to the story, mention it briefly to establish your credibility as a storyteller. This could include previous publications, prizes, awards, or specialized knowledge in the subject matter.

Address Potential Concerns: Anticipate any potential objections or concerns your audience may have and address them proactively in your pitch. This shows that you've thought critically about your story and are prepared to overcome any challenges.

Be Flexible: Be open to feedback and willing to adapt your pitch based on the preferences of your audience. Listen attentively to any comments, suggestions, or requests for changes, and be prepared to revise your pitch accordingly.

Edit and Revise: Finally, don't underestimate the importance of editing and revising your story. After delivering your pitch, follow up with a thank-you email and any additional information requested. Maintain open communication and be prepared to answer any further questions or provide clarification as needed. Take the time to polish your writing, tighten the plot, and refine the language to ensure that every word serves a purpose and contributes to the overall impact of your storytelling.

Importance of Creativity

Creativity is a fundamental human trait that drives progress, enriches our lives, and shapes our future. It empowers individuals to explore their potential, make meaningful contributions to society, and lead fulfilling lives. Embracing and nurturing creativity is essential for personal growth, societal advancement, and the well-being of our global community. Creativity plays a crucial role in various aspects of our lives, society, and economy. Here are some key reasons highlighting the importance of creativity:

- **Problem-solving:** Creativity enables individuals to think outside the box and come up with innovative solutions to complex problems. It encourages flexible thinking, adaptability, and the ability to approach challenges from different perspectives.

- **Innovation:** Creativity is the driving force behind innovation, leading to the development of new products, services, technologies, and processes that improve our lives, drive economic growth, and address societal challenges.

- **Personal Growth and Self-Expression:** Engaging in creative activities fosters personal growth, self-expression, and self-discovery. It allows individuals to explore their interests, passions, and emotions, leading to greater self-awareness and fulfillment.

- **Economic Growth:** Creativity fuels economic growth by stimulating entrepreneurship, job creation, and the development of new industries and markets. It drives competitiveness and enables businesses to differentiate themselves in the marketplace.

- **Social and Cultural Impact:** Creativity contributes to the richness and diversity of cultures, promoting understanding, empathy, and appreciation of different perspectives. It plays a vital role in shaping cultural identity, fostering social cohesion, and promoting positive social change.

- **Learning and Education:** Creativity enhances learning by encouraging curiosity, critical thinking, and problem-solving skills. It fosters a love for learning and empowers individuals to explore, experiment, and discover new ideas and knowledge.

- **Adaptability and Resilience:** In an ever-changing world, creativity equips individuals with the skills and mindset needed to adapt to new situations, embrace uncertainty, and overcome challenges. It fosters resilience and the ability to thrive in dynamic environments.

- **Health and Well-being:** Engaging in creative activities has been shown to have numerous health benefits, including reducing stress, improving mental health, enhancing cognitive function, and boosting overall well-being. Creativity can serve as a therapeutic outlet and a source of joy and fulfillment.

Creative Problem-Solving Tool Kit

In business, creativity is used to solve problems. Therefore, the greater the amount of creativity that can be unleashed, the better the solution is likely to be. Several tools have been developed to enhance and extract the creative talents among individuals and groups. The effectiveness of these tools is a function of the people, the environment, the process needs and the problem being addressed. These tools help in developing creative focus, setting direction, exercising the mind, shattering paradigms, and gaining new insights. These tools assist in creating a framework that over time has consistently yielded better results. Creative problem-solving automatically involves value because a creative solution that fails to bring about improvement is not a solution. The following considerations need to be kept in mind while using the term "creative problem solving":

- The element of value is not forgotten when the word creativity is used.
- Improvement is kept in mind as an essential part of creative problem-solving.
- The word problem is used in its broader meaning as an improvable situation.

1. **The Six Thinking Hats**

The Six Thinking Hats method is a creativity technique to solve problems and arrive at decisions. Dr Edward de Bono invented this method in the early 1980s. The method is a framework for thinking and can incorporate lateral thinking. Judgmental thinking has its place in the system. However, it is not allowed to dominate as in normal thinking.

Organizations such as Prudential Insurance, IBM, Federal Express, British Airways, Polaroid, PepsiCo, DuPont, and Nippon Telephone, and Telegraph, possibly the world's largest companies, use this methodology to creatively solve problems.

The six hats represent six modes of thinking and are directions to think rather than labels. The method promotes fuller input from more people. According to de Bono, "it separates ego from performance." Everyone can contribute to the exploration without denting egos as they are just using one of the coloured hats from among the six mentioned hats.

People can contribute irrespective of a hat even though they may initially support the opposite view. Where six coloured, metaphorical hats represent the styles of thinking, the thinker can put on or take off one of these hats to indicate the type of thinking being used. This putting on and taking off of hats is essential. The hats must never be used to categorize individuals, even though their behaviour may seem to invite this. When done in a group, everybody wears the same hat at the same time. The six hats are briefly explained below:

    i. **White Hat (Facts and Information):** The white thinking hat represents data, information, and facts and identifies the gaps and information needs. This is used to analyze past trends and to extrapolate from historical data.

   ii. **Red Hat (Emotions and Intuition):** The red thinking hat represents intuition, feelings, and emotions brought on by the current discussions. Feelings need not be justified, allowing for valuable input. This input is valuable only when grounded in logic.

  iii. **Black Hat (Critical Thinking):** The black hat indicates looking at things pessimistically, cautiously, and defensively. One must try to see why ideas and approaches might not work. This is important because it highlights the weak points in a plan or course of action. It allows you to eliminate them, alter your approach, or prepare contingency plans to counter problems that arise.

iv. **Yellow Hat (Positive Thinking):** The yellow hat stands for sunshine thinking and helps to think positively. It is the optimistic viewpoint that helps to see all the benefits of the decision, the value in it, and spot the opportunities that arise from it. Yellow hat thinking helps everyone to keep going when things look gloomy and difficult.

v. **Green Hat (Creativity and Innovation):** The green hat represents creativity. This is where creative solutions to a problem can be developed. There is little criticism of ideas.

vi. **Blue Hat (Control):** The blue hat stands for process control. This is the hat worn by people chairing meetings. Blue hat thinking is utilized when an overview and process control are needed. This thinking is not focused on the subject but rather on the thinking about the subject. Blue hat thinking identifies "other hat thinking" needed to facilitate and make progress.

Suggested sequence: The following hat sequence is advised:

1. **White hat:** Presents information and data
2. **Green hat:** Provides creative thinking
3. **Yellow hat:** Gives rationale for why it may work
4. **Red hat:** Feedback feelings and intuition
5. **Black hat:** Gives rationale for why it may not work
6. **Blue hat:** Guide the direction taken by the thinking process

The Six Thinking Hats method is a good technique for looking at the effects of a decision from different points of view. It allows necessary emotion and skepticism to be brought into what would otherwise be purely rational decisions. It opens up the opportunity for creativity within decision-making. It also helps, for example, persistently pessimistic people to be positive and creative.

Plans developed using the "Six Thinking Hats" method are considered to be sounder and more resilient. This technique helps to avoid public relations mistakes and also enables you to spot good reasons not to follow a course of action before you have committed to it. The key theoretical reasons to use the Six Thinking Hats are to:

- Encourage parallel thinking
- Encourage full-spectrum thinking
- Separate ego from performance

Example: Six Thinking Hats Approach

Problem: Selecting a location for an industrial visit for students.

White Hat (Facts): Gather information about potential industrial visit locations: Manufacturing Plant, Technology Park, and Research Laboratory. Consider factors such as distance, accessibility, safety regulations, and educational value.

Red Hat (Feelings): Students express their initial feelings about each location. Some might feel excited about seeing how products are made at a Manufacturing Plant, while others might be interested in the cutting-edge technology at a Technology Park or the innovative research at a Research Laboratory.

Black Hat (Critique): Identify potential drawbacks of each location. The Manufacturing Plant might have safety concerns or limited accessibility to certain areas. The Technology Park might be too technical or complex for some students to understand. The Research Laboratory might have restricted access to certain areas due to confidentiality.

Yellow Hat (Positives): Highlight the positives of each location. The Manufacturing Plant offers insight into real-world production processes and job opportunities in the manufacturing industry. The Technology Park showcases the latest advancements in technology and innovation, inspiring students to pursue careers in STEM fields. The Research Laboratory provides a glimpse into groundbreaking research and potential future career paths in scientific research.

Green Hat (Creativity): Brainstorm ways to enhance the experience at each location. For the Manufacturing Plant, organize guided tours of the production line and hands-on activities demonstrating manufacturing processes. For the Technology Park, arrange interactive demonstrations of emerging technologies and opportunities for students to engage with industry professionals. For the Research Laboratory, coordinate discussions with researchers and hands-on experiments related to ongoing projects.

Blue Hat (Control): Facilitate the discussion, ensuring all perspectives are considered, and guide the group towards making a decision based on the gathered information and insights.

Decision: After considering all perspectives, the group decides to visit the **Technology Park** for the industrial visit. It offers a balance of educational value, innovative technology demonstrations, and opportunities for students to engage with industry professionals, making it an enriching experience for all participants.

2. Brainstorming: Brainstorming is a method for developing creative solutions to problems. It works by focusing on a problem, and then deliberately coming up with as many unusual solutions as possible by pushing the ideas as far as possible. Brainstorming is a group technique for generating creative ideas spontaneously and quickly. Participants freely share thoughts without criticism, encouraging a diverse range of ideas. Ideas are then evaluated and refined for further development.

According to Alex F. Osborne, brainstorming is a tool for maximizing a group's creativity in problem-solving. It is a conference technique by which a group attempts to find a solution for a specific problem by amassing all the ideas spontaneously by its members Most problems are not solved automatically by the first idea that comes to mind. It is important to consider many possible solutions to get to the best solution. One of the best ways to do this is called brainstorming. Brainstorming is the act of defining a problem or idea and coming up with anything related to the topic—no matter how remote the suggestion may sound. All these ideas are recorded and evaluated only after the brainstorming session is completed.

Brainstorming combines a relaxed, informal approach to problem-solving with lateral thinking. It encourages people to come up with thoughts and ideas that can, at first, seem a bit crazy. Some of these ideas can be crafted into original, creative solutions to a problem, while others can spark even more ideas. This helps to get people unstuck by "jolting" them out of their normal ways of thinking. The following rules are important to brainstorm successfully:

a. Make sure everyone understands and is satisfied with the central questions before you open up for ideas.

b. You may want to give everyone a few seconds to jot down a few ideas before getting started.

c. Begin by going around the table or room, giving everyone a chance to voice their ideas or pass.

d. Open the floor after a few rounds.

e. More ideas are better. Encourage radical ideas and piggybacking.

f. Suspend judgement of all ideas.

g. Record exactly what is said. Clarify only after everyone is out of ideas.

h. Don't stop until ideas become sparse. Allow for ideas that come late.

i. Eliminate duplicates and ideas that are irrelevant to the topic.

Step-by-step Guide to Brainstorming

i. Define your problem. Write out your problem concisely and make sure that everyone understands the problem and is in agreement with the way it is worded. There is no need to put a lot of restrictions on your problem at this time.

ii. Give yourselves a time limit. Larger groups may need more time to get everyone's ideas out.

iii. Everyone must shout out solutions to the problem while one person records them. Ideas must not be criticized. If participants begin to fear criticism of their ideas, they will stop generating ideas. Ideas that may seem silly initially may prove to be very good or may lead to very good ideas.

iv. Select the five ideas that you like best once the time is up. Make sure everyone involved in the brainstorming session is in agreement.

v. Write down five criteria for deciding on the ideas that best solve your problem. Each criterion should start with the word "should." For example, "it should be cost-effective," "it should be legal," etc.

vi. Give each idea a score between 0 and 5 points depending on how well it meets each criterion. Add up the scores once all the ideas have been scored for each criterion.

vii. The idea with the highest score will best solve the problem. However, a record must be maintained of all the five ideas in case the idea selected does not turn out to be workable.

When managed well, brainstorming can help you generate radical solutions to problems. It can also, encourage people to commit to solutions because they have provided input and played a role in developing them

Example:

Scenario: This example illustrates how a simple brainstorming session can generate ideas and facilitate decision-making in a fun and collaborative way. A group of friends is brainstorming ideas for a weekend trip destination.

Generate Ideas: Beach, camping in the mountains, exploring a nearby village, visiting a national park, trekking in the Forest

Build Upon Ideas:

- **Beach:** Rent a beach house, plan a bonfire, and go swimming.
- **Camping in the mountains:** Bring along telescopes for stargazing, and plan a hike to a waterfall.
- **Exploring a nearby village:** Research farms, canteens, and landmarks to visit.
- **Visiting a national park:** Plan a picnic, go birdwatching, and rent bicycles to explore the trails.

- **Trekking in the forest:** Identify nearby forests, carry water and eatables, and safety precautions

Defer Judgment: All ideas are welcomed without criticism or evaluation during the brainstorming session.

Encourage Wild Ideas: Participants are encouraged to think creatively and suggest any destination or activity that comes to mind.

Record Ideas: Ideas are written down on a whiteboard or notepad for everyone to see and reference.

Evaluate and Select Ideas: After generating a list of ideas, the group discusses the pros and cons of each option and decides on the best destination based on preferences, budget, and logistics.

Follow-Up: The group plans the details of their chosen trip, including transportation, accommodations, and activities, and sets a date for their adventure.

3. Mind Mapping: A visual tool where ideas are organized around a central concept, allowing for the exploration of relationships and connections between different elements. The technique is used to develop new ideas or to break down and better understand existing information. Here's how to create a mind map in five simple steps:

i. Choose the topic of the mind map and place it in the middle of the drawing
ii. Come up with three to five main ideas, then evenly space them in a circular formation around the mind map topic
iii. Draw a line from the mind map topic to each main idea
iv. Brainstorm supporting details such as ideas, tasks, and questions for each main idea
v. Draw lines connecting each main idea to its supporting details

Example: A mind map for creating a better earth is given in **Figure 3.2**

Figure 3.2. Creating a Better Earth

4. SCAMPER: An acronym for Substitute, Combine, Adapt, Modify, Put to Another Use, Eliminate, and Reverse, which prompts individuals to explore different ways to modify and improve existing ideas or products.

Substitute: What can I Substitute?

Combine: How can I Combine?

Adapt: What can I Adopt from someone else?

Modify: What can I Modify for other uses?

Put to Another Use: How can I Put to other uses?

Eliminate: What can I Eliminate or simplify?

Reverse: How can I change reorder or reverse?

Example

The SCAMPER technique can be used to generate creative ideas for bringing innovative improvements to a backpack tailored to the needs and preferences of college students, enhancing both functionality and convenience for their everyday use.

Substitute: Substitute traditional backpack straps with adjustable ergonomic straps that provide better support and comfort for students carrying heavy loads of books and laptops.

Substitute the standard backpack material with a waterproof and durable fabric to protect books and electronic devices from rain or spills.

Combine: Combine the backpack with a portable charging station integrated into a side pocket, allowing students to charge their devices on the go.

Combine the backpack with a built-in laptop sleeve that includes RFID-blocking technology to protect against electronic theft.

Adapt: Adapt the backpack to include a dedicated compartment for a refillable water bottle, promoting hydration throughout the day.

Adapt the design to include a removable organizer pouch for pens, pencils, and other small items, making it easy to switch between backpacks or carry essentials separately.

Modify: Modify the backpack's interior layout to include padded compartments specifically designed to protect laptops, tablets, and other electronic devices from damage.

Modify the backpack's closure system to include a combination lock or biometric scanner for added security, particularly for valuable items stored inside.

Put to Another Use: Repurpose the backpack's outer pocket as a detachable mini cooler for storing snacks or lunches, especially useful for long days on campus.

Use the backpack's side pockets to hold reusable containers or utensils, encouraging sustainable eating habits and reducing single-use plastic waste.

Eliminate: Eliminate excess exterior pockets and zippers to streamline the backpack's design and reduce bulkiness while maintaining functionality.

Eliminate the need for a separate laptop sleeve by integrating padded laptop storage directly into the main compartment, maximizing space efficiency.

Reverse/Rearrange: Reverse the backpack's design to have a clamshell opening for easier access to contents, allowing students to see and retrieve items without rummaging. Rearrange the layout of the backpack's compartments to prioritize organization, with designated sections for textbooks, notebooks, electronics, and personal items.

Box. 3.2. Idea Lab

Creating an Idea Lab within a Higher Education Institution is a fantastic idea! It can serve as a hub for innovation, entrepreneurship, and interdisciplinary collaboration among students, faculty, and the community. Here's a step-by-step guide to help you establish an Idea Lab:

1. Define Objectives and Scope

- **Objectives:** Clearly define the goals of the Idea Lab. Is it to foster innovation, support entrepreneurial ventures, promote interdisciplinary collaboration, or something else?
- **Scope:** Determine the scope of the Idea Lab, including the disciplines it will cover, the types of projects it will support, and the resources it will provide.

2. Secure Institutional Support

- **Stakeholder Engagement:** Engage key stakeholders, such as university administrators, faculty members, and students, to gain their support and input.
- **Funding:** Secure initial funding either from the institution, grants, or partnerships with industry sponsors.

3. Develop a Business Plan

- **Mission and Vision:** Clearly articulate the mission, vision, and values of the Idea Lab.

- **Services and Offerings:** Define the services, resources, and support the Idea Lab will provide to students, faculty, and staff.
- **Budget:** Develop a detailed budget outlining the initial and ongoing costs of operating the Idea Lab.

4. Design the Physical Space

- **Location:** Choose a suitable location that is accessible to students and faculty.
- **Layout and Amenities:** Design the space to facilitate collaboration, creativity, and innovation. Consider including areas for brainstorming, prototyping, meetings, and presentations.

5. Hire Staff

- **Team:** Recruit a diverse team of skilled professionals, including a director, program coordinators, mentors, and technical experts.
- **Training:** Provide training and professional development opportunities to equip the staff with the necessary skills and knowledge.

6. Develop Programs and Services

- **Workshops and Training:** Organize workshops, training sessions, and seminars on topics such as design thinking, entrepreneurship, and innovation.
- **Mentorship:** Establish a mentorship program connecting students with industry professionals, alumni, and faculty members.
- **Funding and Resources:** Provide access to funding opportunities, resources, and tools necessary for developing and scaling innovative projects.

7. Promote and Market the Idea Lab

- **Awareness Campaigns:** Launch marketing campaigns to raise awareness about the Idea Lab among the university community and beyond.
- **Partnerships:** Collaborate with other departments, organizations, and industry partners to expand the reach and impact of the Idea Lab.

8. Evaluate and Iterate

- **Metrics and KPIs:** Establish key performance indicators (KPIs) to measure the success and impact of the Idea Lab.
- **Feedback:** Collect feedback from users and stakeholders regularly to identify areas for improvement and make necessary adjustments.

9. Scale and Expand

- **Growth:** Monitor the success of the Idea Lab and explore opportunities for scaling and expanding its programs, services, and impact.
- **Community Engagement:** Foster a vibrant community of innovators, entrepreneurs, and collaborators within the Idea Lab and the broader university ecosystem.

By following these steps, you can create a thriving Idea Lab that serves as a hub for innovation and creativity within your higher education institution.

5 Storyboarding: A visual technique commonly used in design and filmmaking, where ideas are presented sequentially through a series of sketches or images. Storyboarding helps creators visualize and plan their ideas, identify potential issues or gaps in the story, and communicate their vision to others involved in the project. It serves as a blueprint for the final product, whether it's a film, animation, advertisement, or digital experience. It involves creating a series of sketches or illustrations arranged in a sequence to represent scenes or key moments in the story.

Example: Title: "A Day on the Campus: College Edition"

This storyboard offers a glimpse into a typical day in the life of a college student, capturing the various activities and experiences they encounter throughout the day. It provides a visual outline for a potential short film or animation project depicting college life.

The storyboard follows a college student named Sunaina as she navigates through a typical day on campus, from waking up in the morning to attending classes, studying in the library, socializing with friends, and finally returning to her dormitory in the evening.

Scene 1: Morning Routine
Sketch: Sunaina's alarm clock rings, Sunaina groggily wakes up in her dormitory room.
Caption: "Sunaina's morning routine begins."

Scene 2: Breakfast
Sketch: Sunaina having breakfast in the college cafeteria with a friend.
Caption: "Sunaina grabs breakfast with her friend before class."

Scene 3: Class Time
Sketch: Sunaina sitting in a lecture hall, listening attentively to the professor.
Caption: "Sunaina attends her morning classes."

Scene 4: Study Session
Sketch: Sunaina studying alone in the library, surrounded by books and notes.
Caption: "Sunaina hits the books in the library."

Scene 5: Lunch Break
Sketch: Sunaina chatting with friends over lunch at an outdoor garden table.
Caption: "Sunaina takes a break to eat lunch with friends."

Scene 6: Afternoon Classes
Sketch: Sunaina participated in a group discussion in a seminar room.
Caption: "Sunaina engages in afternoon classes and discussions."

Scene 7: Extracurricular Activity
Sketch: Sunaina attending a club meeting or sports practice on campus.
Caption: "Sunaina participates in her favorite extracurricular activity."

Scene 8: Evening Unwind
Sketch: Sunaina relaxing in her dormitory room, maybe watching TV or reading a book.
Caption: "Sunaina unwinds in her dormitory after a long day."

6. Role-playing: Role-playing is a creative activity where participants assume the roles of characters and act out scenarios either predetermined or improvised. It's a fun way to explore different situations, characters, and narratives, often used in storytelling, gaming, therapeutic settings, and more. Participants assume different roles or perspectives related to the problem at hand, allowing them to explore solutions from diverse viewpoints. When engaging in role-playing, it's essential to establish clear guidelines and boundaries to ensure that all participants feel comfortable and respected. It's also crucial to maintain open communication and be mindful of the feelings and reactions of others involved. It's a versatile activity that can be used for various purposes, such as:

- **Creative Expression**: Role-playing allows participants to explore and express themselves creatively by stepping into different roles and experiencing situations from various perspectives.
- **Skill Development**: It can be used as a tool for learning and development, helping participants improve communication, problem-solving, empathy, and social skills.
- **Entertainment**: Role-playing can be a fun and engaging form of entertainment, whether it's through tabletop role-playing games, improvisational theater, or online role-playing games.

- **Therapeutic Applications:** Some therapists use role-playing as a therapeutic technique to help clients explore and address emotional and interpersonal issues in a safe and controlled environment.
- **Educational Purposes**: Role-playing can be incorporated into educational settings to make learning more interactive and engaging. It can help students better understand historical events, literary works, or scientific concepts by immersing them in relevant scenarios.

Example

Scenario: Conflict Resolution in a Group Project

Characters:

Amit: A proactive and organized student who takes leadership roles in group projects.

James: A laid-back student who tends to procrastinate and relies on others to take the lead.

Chandana: A studious and detail-oriented student who prefers to work independently.

Setting: Classroom or any suitable meeting space.

Objective: The role play aims to simulate a scenario where students must resolve a conflict within their group project team.

Script: Amit, James, and Chandana are gathered to discuss their group project progress.

Amit: Okay, team, let's start our meeting. How's everyone doing with their assigned tasks?

James: Well, I haven't started yet. I was busy with other classes.

Chandana: I've made some progress on my part, but I'm still working out some details.

Amit: James, we need everyone to contribute to the project. Can you commit to completing your tasks by the deadline?

James: Sure. I'll try to catch up this weekend.

Chandana: I think we should divide the remaining tasks more evenly. Amit, can you delegate some of James's tasks to me?

Amit: That's a good idea, Chandana. James, would you be okay with that?

James: Yeah, I guess so.

Amit: Great. Let's also set up regular check-ins to make sure we're all on track. How about we meet again on Wednesday to review our progress?

James: Sounds good to me.

Chandana: OK

Amit: Perfect. Let's aim to have everything finalized by the end of the week. Thanks, everyone!

Conclusion: In this role-play scenario, the three students addressed the conflict of unequal contribution by openly discussing their concerns and finding a solution together. They agreed on a plan of action and established clear expectations moving forward, demonstrating effective communication and teamwork skills.

7. Prototyping: Prototyping is the process of creating a preliminary version or model of a product, system, or project to test its functionality, design, and usability before proceeding with full-scale development. Prototypes can range from simple sketches or wireframes to more complex interactive models, depending on the needs of the project. Rough models of potential solutions may be created to test their feasibility and gather feedback for further refinement. Prototyping allows quick testing and refinement of ideas before full development.

Example

Project: "Task Tracker" Mobile App

Objective: Create a basic prototype to demonstrate key features of the Task Tracker app.

Steps:

    i.   **Sketching:** Draw rough sketches of app screens on paper.
    ii.   **Wireframing:** Create digital wireframes using tools like Balsamiq.
    iii.   **Designing:** Add basic visual elements like colors and fonts.
    iv.   **Linking:** Use a prototyping tool to link screens for interaction.
    v.   **Testing:** Gather feedback from users on usability.
    vi.   **Iterating:** Make revisions based on feedback.

Example Prototype Screens:

    a.   **Home Screen:** Displays task list.
    b.   **Task Detail Screen:** Shows details of a selected task.
    c.   **Add Task Screen:** Allows users to add new tasks.
    d.   **Settings Screen:** Provides options for customization.

8. Reverse Thinking: Reverse thinking can be a valuable problem-solving tool in situations where traditional methods have been unsuccessful or when faced with complex or ambiguous problems. It encourages creative thinking and can lead to innovative solutions by challenging individuals to consider problems from a different perspective. Rather than starting with the problem and trying to find a solution, reverse thinking starts with the desired outcome and works backward to identify the actions or conditions necessary to achieve that outcome.

Example

Problem: Choosing a career path.

By using reverse thinking, the student starts with their desired career outcome and works backward to identify the necessary steps to achieve it.

This approach can help students set clearer goals and take more intentional actions toward their future careers.

Traditional Approach:

  i.   Explore different career options.
  ii. Consider personal interests, skills, and values.
  iii. Research job prospects and educational requirements.
  iv. Make a decision based on the gathered information.

Reverse Thinking Approach:

Define the Desired Outcome: Start by imagining yourself in the future with a fulfilling career.

Work Backward: Think about what steps you would need to take to reach that desired career.

Identify Preconditions: Consider what qualifications, skills, and experiences you would need to have to excel in that career.

Implement the Steps: Begin taking actions that align with your desired career path, such as gaining relevant education, skills, and experiences.

Evaluate Progress: Continuously assess your progress towards your desired career and make adjustments as necessary.

Box. 3.3. How to be a Creative Problem Solver?

Navigating through challenges and finding creative solutions is a valuable skill in today's dynamic and complex world. Being a creative problem solver involves adopting a mindset that fosters curiosity, critical thinking, collaboration, and adaptability. Whether you're facing personal dilemmas, professional obstacles, or societal issues, these tips aim to empower you with strategies to approach problems creatively, explore diverse perspectives, and devise effective solutions. Let's delve into these actionable insights to enhance your problem-solving capabilities and unlock your creative potential.

- **Develop a Growth Mindset:** Embrace challenges, learn from failures, and seek feedback.
- **Cultivate Curiosity:** Ask questions, explore new ideas, and stay informed about diverse topics.
- **Practice Divergent Thinking:** Generate multiple solutions and think outside the box.
- **Enhance Critical Thinking Skills:** Analyze problems, evaluate information, and make informed decisions.
- **Collaborate and Communicate:** Work with others, share ideas, and value teamwork.
- **Embrace Adaptability:** Adapt to change, remain resilient, and persevere through challenges.
- **Engage in Creative Activities:** Explore artistic pursuits and stimulate imagination.
- **Seek Continuous Learning:** Pursue learning opportunities and develop new skills.
- **Practice Problem-Solving:** Identify problems, analyze challenges, and implement creative solutions.
- **Reflect and Evaluate:** Assess outcomes, learn from experiences, and refine your approach.

9. Design thinking: It is a process of creative problem solving that starts with people and their needs. It is a human-centered approach to problem-solving that emphasizes empathy, defining, ideating, prototyping, and testing. Design thinking is characterized by its iterative nature, with the stages often overlapping and informing each other. The process is flexible and can be adapted to suit the specific needs and constraints of different projects. By focusing on understanding user needs, fostering creativity, and embracing experimentation, design thinking enables teams to develop innovative solutions that truly resonate with users. Moving through the phases of design thinking can take you from a blank slate to a new, innovative solution.

The core stages of Design Thinking were originally proposed by the Hasso-Plattner Institute of Design at Stanford. David Kelley the founder of IDEO, played a significant role in popularizing design thinking in the 1990s through practical applications in product design and innovation. IDEO is often credited with inventing the term "design thinking" and its practice. IDEO is a design and consulting firm that uses design thinking to help clients create products, services, and experiences. Design Thinking is a human-centered design process consisting of five core stages Empathize, Define, Ideate, Prototype, and Test. The five core stages of design thinking are given in **Figure 3.3** and comprise of:

i. Empathize (learn about the audience for whom you are designing)
ii. Define (construct a point of view that is based on user needs and insights)
iii. Ideate (brainstorm and come up with creative solutions)
iv. Prototype (build a representation of one or more of your ideas to show to others),
v. Test (return to your original user group and test your ideas for feedback)

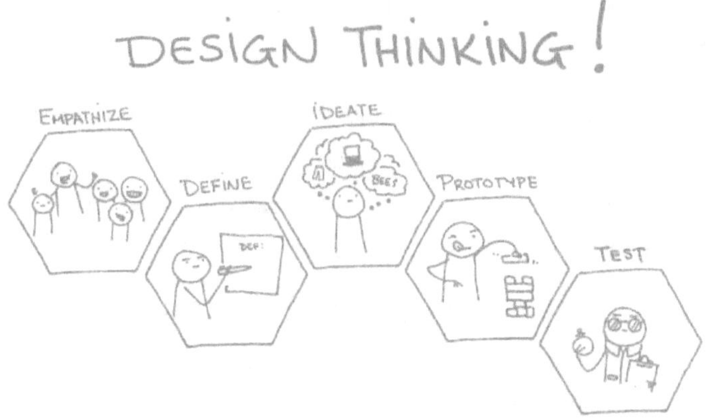

Figure 3.3. Design Thinking Model

Example

Problem: Designing a better college cafeteria experience.

Design Thinking Approach

Empathize: Start by understanding the needs and preferences of students using the cafeteria. This could involve conducting surveys, interviews, or observations to gather insights into their experiences and pain points.

Define: Based on the research, define the specific problem or opportunity to address. For example, after gathering insights, you might identify that students feel rushed during lunchtime and lack healthy food options.

Ideate: Brainstorm potential solutions to improve the cafeteria experience. Encourage creativity and open-mindedness in generating ideas. Ideas could include extending lunch hours, offering more diverse menu options, or redesigning the cafeteria layout to encourage social interaction.

Prototype: Select one or more promising ideas and create simple prototypes or mock-ups to visualize how they might work in practice. For example, you could create a prototype of a new cafeteria layout using cardboard cutouts or design a sample menu with healthier food choices.

Test: Gather feedback from students and other stakeholders by testing the prototypes. Observe how they interact with the prototypes and gather their thoughts and opinions. This feedback will help refine and improve the ideas further.

Implement: Based on the feedback received during testing, refine the prototypes and develop an implementation plan. This might involve working with school administrators, cafeteria staff, and other stakeholders to implement the changes in the cafeteria.

Conclusion: By applying the principles of design thinking, students can approach the problem and encourage creativity, collaboration, and empathy, ultimately leading to innovative solutions that better meet the needs of students.

10. TRIZ (Theory of Inventive Problem Solving): TRIZ is the Russian acronym for the "Theory of Inventive Problem Solving,". According to TRIZ, universal principles of creativity form the basis of innovation. TRIZ identifies and codifies these principles, using them to make the creative process more predictable. TRIZ is a systematic method for analyzing and solving technical problems by identifying patterns of invention across different domains. Using TRIZ consists of learning these repeating patterns of problem and solution, understanding the contradictions present in a situation, and developing new methods of using scientific effects.

Key Principles of TRIZ

a. **Contradiction Resolution**: TRIZ identifies contradictions as the root cause of problems. These contradictions can be physical (e.g., a system requires both flexibility and rigidity) or technical (e.g., increasing strength increases weight). TRIZ offers principles to resolve these contradictions.

b. **40 Inventive Principles:** These are a set of guidelines developed by Genrich Altshuller, a soviet engineer and inventor that provide solutions to overcome technical contradictions. For example, one principle is "segmentation," where a complex object is broken down into simpler components. The 40 inventive principles are given in **Table 3.1.**

c. **Separation Principles:** In cases of physical contradictions, TRIZ suggests four types of separation: in time, in space, between the parts and the whole, or through changing conditions.

d. **Ideality:** TRIZ encourages designers to work toward "ideality," the concept of a perfect system that delivers all benefits without any drawbacks. This pushes for solutions that are minimal, resource-efficient, and highly effective.

e. **Patterns of Evolution:** TRIZ posits that technology evolves following certain patterns. By recognizing where a technology is in its evolutionary path, future developments can be anticipated and guided.

    f. **Knowledge Database:** TRIZ is supported by a vast database of problem-solving patterns derived from analyzing patents and innovations. By tapping into this knowledge, innovators can leverage tried-and-tested solutions.

TRIZ is a system of creative problem-solving, commonly used in engineering and process management. The central concepts behind TRIZ: generalizing problems and solutions, and eliminating contradictions. TRIZ recognizes two categories of contradictions: Technical contradictions and Physical contradictions. The key technical contradictions are summarized in the TRIZ Contradiction Matrix. You can solve physical contradictions with the TRIZ Separation Principles according to space, time, and scale. **Figure 3.4** provides the process of TRIZ. It follows four basic steps:

    i.   Define your specific problem.

    ii.   Find the TRIZ generalized problem that matches it.

    iii.   Find the generalized solution that solves the generalized problem.

    iv.   Adapt the generalized solution to solve your specific problem

Table 3.1. Forty Inventive Principles

#	Principle	#	Principle
1	Segmentation	21	Skipping
2	Taking Out	22	Blessing in Disguise
3	Local Quality	23	Feedback
4	Asymmetry	24	Intermediary
5	Merging	25	Self-Service
6	Universality	26	Copying
7	Nesting	27	Cheap Short-Lived Objects
8	Counterbalance	28	Mechanics Substitution
9	Prior Counteraction	29	Pneumatics and Hydraulics
10	Preliminary Anti-Action	30	Flexible Shells and Thin Films
11	Beforehand Compensation	31	Porous Materials
12	Equipotentiality	32	Color Change
13	The Other Way Around	33	Homogeneity

#	Principle	#	Principle
14	Spheroidality	34	Discarding and Recovering
15	Dynamics	35	Parameter Changes
16	Partial or Excessive Action	36	Phase Transitions
17	Another Dimension	37	Thermal Expansion
18	Mechanical Vibration	38	Enriched Atmosphere
19	Periodic Action	39	Inert Atmosphere
20	Continuity of Useful Action	40	Composite Materials

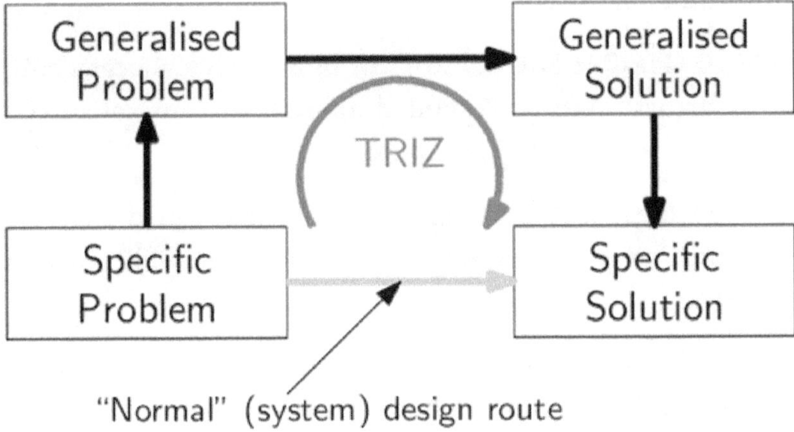

Figure 3.4. The Process of TRIZ

Source: https://help4study.online/homework/triz-theory-of-inventive-problem-solving

Application of TRIZ

- **Engineering:** TRIZ is often used in mechanical, electrical, and software engineering to develop innovative products.
- **Business and Management:** It is also applied in business contexts to optimize processes, solve organizational problems, and foster innovation.
- **Creative Industries:** TRIZ can enhance problem-solving in creative domains like design, marketing, and even entertainment.

Example: Creative Industry: Packaging Design (Consumer Goods)

Problem: A food company wants to develop eco-friendly packaging that is both strong enough to protect the product during transport but can also decompose easily in an environmentally friendly way.

TRIZ Approach:

Technical Contradiction: Strong packaging typically doesn't decompose easily.

Inventive Principles Used:

Principle 30 (Flexible Shells and Thin Films): Use biodegradable films that offer strength and protection during transit but can decompose naturally once exposed to the environment.

Principle 23 (Feedback): Design packaging that can change form or structure based on environmental triggers, such as humidity, to speed up decomposition.

Solution: The company introduces a biodegradable packaging material that remains durable during shipping but begins to decompose when exposed to moisture in landfills, achieving both protection and eco-friendliness.

11. 5W2H Technique

The 5W and 2H framework is a critical thinking framework. It helps in systematically analyzing and understanding a situation or problem by asking seven fundamental questions. Each question guides the thinker to gather essential details, enabling a comprehensive view and promoting deeper insights. The 5W and 2H a questioning and problem-solving methods that aim to view ideas and issues from different perspectives. It helps you to understand a problem better and find the root cause of it. 5W is an acronym for What, Where, When, Why, and Who, while the letter 2H stands for How and How much/How many.

This structured approach ensures that all critical aspects of the product development process are carefully considered and planned for. While product managers can use the 5Ws and 2H framework at any stage of the development process, it can be most beneficial during product definition. During this stage, the team is trying to figure out what they are building, who they're making it for, when it should be released, where it will be used, and why they're building it. Does that sound familiar?

By asking the **5 W** questions during the product definition stage, the team can understand what they're setting out to achieve. They will be able to identify key factors, align with the product vision, and stay focused on the matter at hand. Once they've figured out the W's, they can work on **How and How much** to create the product. An example of 5W and 2H for New Product/Service Development is given in **Table 3.2.**

Table 3.2. 5W and 2H for New Product/Service Development

a.	**WHO**	Identifies the People Involved or Responsible.	Who is the target user(s)?
b	**WHAT**	Defines what needs to be done or what the issue is.	What problem will your product solve for the user?
c	**WHEN**	Determines the timing or deadlines or sequence of the events.	When will users be using your product? (ex. before going to restaurants, before their commute …)
d	**WHERE**	Specifies the location or context involved.	Where will users be using your product? (ex. in the car, on a desktop, on a mobile device, at the bar…)
e	**WHY**	Explain the reasons, causes, or purposes.	Why should users use your product? (ex. because it will save them time/money because the current solutions aren't effective enough)
f	**HOW**	Describes the process, techniques, or manner in which something is to be done.	How will users access your product? (ex. from an existing social network, from their company, by downloading the app to their phone)

g	**HOW MUCH?/ HOW MANY**	Considers the cost, number of resources, or amount needed.	How much is the resource allocation (Budget and Pricing)

12. Lateral Thinking

Lateral thinking is a creative problem-solving approach that encourages creativity and innovative thinking by moving away from traditional, linear reasoning. The term was coined by Edward de Bono in the 1960s. Lateral thinking is often contrasted with vertical thinking, which is a more linear and logical approach to problem-solving. Lateral thinking is about fostering creativity and innovation by breaking away from conventional thought processes, making it a valuable tool for problem-solving in dynamic and complex environments.

Lateral thinking involves looking at problems from different angles and making unexpected connections. It's a way to think outside the box and come up with unique and practical solutions. Lateral thinking (horizontal thinking) is a form of ideation where designers approach problems by using reasoning that is disruptive or not immediately obvious. Lateral thinking can be applied in various fields, including business, education, design, and everyday problem-solving. It helps teams and individuals think outside the box to develop innovative products, strategies, and solutions. Key features of lateral thinking are:

- **Non-linear approach**: Lateral thinking emphasizes looking at problems from different angles rather than following a direct path to a solution. It encourages exploring unexpected and unconventional routes.
- **Creative Problem Solving:** This mode of thinking aims to generate unique ideas and solutions. It often involves brainstorming, idea generation, and the use of analogies to break free from established thought patterns.
- **Challenging Assumptions**: Lateral thinking encourages questioning assumptions and norms that may limit creativity.

This includes re-evaluating how problems are framed and seeking alternative perspectives.

- **Techniques and Tools:**

  a. **Random Entry:** Introducing random stimuli to spark new ideas.

  b. **Provocation:** Making provocative statements to stimulate new thinking (e.g., "What if we did the opposite?")

  c. **Challenge:** Questioning existing norms or practices to find new solutions.

Example: An example of lateral thinking could be finding a way to reduce traffic congestion in a city. Instead of simply adding more roads or increasing public transport, a lateral thinking approach might involve encouraging remote work, implementing flexible hours, or creating incentives for carpooling.

Common Obstacles to Creative Thinking

Creative thinking can be hindered by various obstacles. Some of the common obstacles include:

Fear of failure: The fear of making mistakes or failing can prevent people from taking risks and exploring new ideas.

Lack of confidence: Doubting one's abilities and ideas can stifle creativity and prevent individuals from expressing their thoughts openly.

Fixed mindset: Believing that abilities and intelligence are fixed traits can limit the willingness to learn and adapt, hindering creative thinking.

Overthinking: Overanalyzing situations and focusing too much on details can impede the flow of creative ideas.

Perfectionism: Striving for perfection can be paralyzing, making it difficult to complete projects or share ideas that may be seen as imperfect.

Lack of motivation or interest: Without a genuine interest or passion for a subject, it can be challenging to engage in creative thinking.

External pressures: Pressure from peers, supervisors, or societal expectations can influence individuals to conform to established norms rather than explore new and innovative ideas.

Narrow-mindedness: Being closed off to different perspectives and ideas can limit creativity and prevent collaboration.

Lack of time or resources: Constraints in time, budget, or resources can restrict the ability to experiment and innovate.

Negative environment: A negative or unsupportive work or social environment can suppress creativity and discourage individuals from sharing and exploring new ideas.

Overcoming these obstacles requires self-awareness, resilience, openness to new experiences, and a willingness to challenge conventional thinking. Developing a growth mindset, embracing failure as a learning opportunity, seeking feedback, collaborating with others, and creating a supportive environment can help foster creative thinking and innovation.

<u>Box 3.4. Ideathon</u>

Organizing an Ideathon can be an exciting way to encourage creativity, innovation, and problem-solving among participants. Ideations can inspire creativity, collaboration, and innovation by engaging participants in problem-solving and entrepreneurial activities. Here's a guide to help you plan and execute a successful Ideathon:

- **Define Objective & Theme:** Set clear goals and choose a relevant theme for the Ideathon.
- **Identify Participants:** Target specific audiences and promote the event for registrations.

- **Organize Logistics:** Choose a suitable venue with the necessary amenities and provide the required tools and technologies.
- **Develop Agenda:** Create a structured schedule with activities, workshops, and presentations.
- **Engage Mentors:** Invite experts to guide participants and conduct skill-building sessions.
- **Promote Collaboration:** Facilitate team formation and encourage networking among participants.
- **Provide Resources:** Offer access to research materials, data sets, and support throughout the event.
- **Evaluate Ideas:** Establish judging criteria and offer prizes for innovative solutions.
- **Capture Insights:** Document the event and share success stories to inspire future participation.
- **Collect Feedback:** Gather feedback to evaluate the event's success and identify areas for improvement.

Improve Your Creativity

1. **Walk outside**: Breaking free of your work, moving around, and observing your surroundings can give you mental clarity and boost creativity.
2. **Write a list of things that annoy you**: You can identify new patterns by identifying these things. This exercise can lead to new ideas previously unseen.
3. **Play with the lyrics to your favorite song**: Playing with the lyrics of your favorite song opens your mind to new possibilities and breaks you out of your comfort zone.
4. **Create a video montage of your day**: This can be a fun way to document your life and see how your creativity manifests itself. Trying different techniques and making edits will improve your creativity skills.

5. **Write about what scares you and why it scares you:** Some creatives sharpen creativity muscles by writing about what scares them and why (or writing about what doesn't scare them). Exploring scary things can open new avenues that would otherwise be closed.

6. **Play games that require creativity:** Many creatives play games such as chess or scrabble. These games sharpen the mind and improve problem-solving.

7. **Do something that makes you laugh:** If you are struggling with a creativity block, you can watch funny videos or do other things that release endorphins.

8. **Draw something you see every day but don't pay attention:** When we see the same things repeatedly, they become mundane. If we examined the objects and scenes that make up our everyday lives, we'd be surprised at how much creativity hides in plain sight.

9. **Exercise your brain with a puzzle:** Puzzles exercise the creative side of your brain by forcing you to come up with new ideas and solutions. Doing this can help you break out of a rut.

10. **Make crafts out of old things lying around the house:** Crafts help you tap into your creativity and improve your ideation.

Converting Idea to Opportunity

An idea is a creative thought or a concept, whereas an opportunity is a chance to bring that idea to life and make it a reality. Generating business ideas is one of the most important steps for any entrepreneur. If you don't have any good ideas, it's going to be tough to get your business off the ground.

Business Idea

A million-dollar idea is one with an unquestionable utility and one that increases effectiveness in a manner unprecedented. An idea is a thought, an impression, or a notion. A business idea is a concept that can be tested for commercial purposes. All ideas may not become an opportunity.

How to Identify Business Ideas?

Generating business ideas is one of the most important steps for any entrepreneur. If you don't have any good ideas, it's going to be tough to get your business off the ground. Business ideas can be generated by environmental analysis, industry analysis, and SWOT analysis.

1. **Ask family and friends**: The first place any entrepreneur should look when coming up with new business ideas is their network of family and friends. After all, these are the people who know you best and will be most likely to support your new venture.

2. **Consider problems in your everyday life - then solve them**: The best business ideas come from solving problems that you or others face every day. If there's something in your life that frustrates you, chances are there are plenty of other people who feel the same way.

3. **Build on your hobbies**: It is important to look at your hobbies and interests when trying to come up with a business idea. It's much easier (and more enjoyable) to build a business around something you're passionate about.

4. **Consider if there are tasks you could make easier**: A great way to come up with new business ideas is to think about ways you could make existing tasks easier or more efficient.

5. **Identify changes in the business environment**: Changes in the environment such as climate change, competition, technological changes, disruption, regulatory and political change, social and demographic change, and economic changes will lead to new business ideas.

6. **Build on existing products or services:** A great way to do this is by looking at the current services or products you're already using and asking yourself the "What if?" questions. What if this service was available in my city? What if this product was cheaper/better quality/easier to use?

Opportunity

An opportunity has the potential to generate income and create value for customers. Turning an idea into an opportunity involves a mix of creativity, analysis, planning, and execution. The difference between Idea and Opportunity is furnished in **Table 3.3.**

Table 3.3. Idea Vs Opportunity

Aspect	Idea	Opportunity
Definition	A concept or thought that may or may not be feasible.	A favorable situation that allows for the realization of an idea.
Nature	Abstract and often untested.	Concrete and actionable, with potential for implementation.
Focus	Creativity and innovation.	Market demand and practicality.
Development Stage	Early stage of the creative process.	Advanced stage, often validated by research or market analysis.
Risk	Typically high, as it is untested.	Generally lower, as it is based on existing market needs.
Implementation	May require significant resources and time to develop.	More likely to have clear pathways for execution.
Value	Can be subjective and may not translate to economic value.	Has potential economic value and can lead to profit.
Assessment	Evaluated based on creativity, originality, and feasibility.	Evaluated based on market viability, potential return on investment, and competitive advantage.
Example	A new app concept for social networking.	A growing demand for mental health apps in the current market.

RedBus, founded in 2006 by Phanindra Sama, Sudhakar Pasupunuri, and Charan Padmaraju, revolutionized bus ticketing in India by providing an online platform for booking bus tickets. The idea stemmed from Phanindra Sama's frustration with the unorganized and unreliable offline bus ticketing system when he missed a bus home for Diwali. Recognizing the need for a more accessible and systematic approach, the founders developed RedBus to connect travelers with a vast network of bus operators, making the booking process seamless and efficient. In 2013, RedBus reached a significant milestone when it was acquired by the Ibibo Group.

Ola, founded by Bhavish Aggarwal and Ankit Bhati in December 2010, emerged as one of India's largest ride-hailing companies. The idea originated when Aggarwal experienced issues with traditional taxi services during a road trip, highlighting the need for a reliable cab service. Starting as an online cab aggregator in Mumbai, Ola aimed to provide a customer-friendly alternative to conventional taxis, revolutionizing urban transportation in India.

Practo, co-founded by Shashank ND and Abhinav Lal in 2008, began as a platform for booking doctor appointments. The inspiration came from Shashank ND's struggle to find the right doctor for his father's treatment, revealing a gap in accessible healthcare information. Initially a doctor search engine and appointment booking service, Practo has since expanded to offer a variety of healthcare services, aiming to simplify and enhance the healthcare experience.

Characteristics of a Good Opportunity

An opportunity arises when there's a demand in the market for your idea. It's the chance to introduce your product or service to consumers who are willing to pay for it. Identifying and seizing opportunities is crucial for turning ideas into successful ventures. The five basic elements of the recipe to turn ideas into tangible opportunities that further allow you to make strategic plans:

1. **Market Demand**: The business idea needs to have market attractiveness. There's a significant need or desire for your offering.
2. **Competitive Advantage**: Your idea has a unique value proposition that sets it apart from competitors.
3. **Feasibility and Profitability**: Can be implemented with available resources and technology. The opportunity has the potential to generate revenue and profits.

4. **Timeliness:** The business idea should be implemented within the time frame to get market acceptance. Timeliness is essential to gain a first-mover advantage.

5. **Scalability and Sustainability:** The market conditions are favorable to scale for long-term success.

Connecting Idea to Opportunity

You can turn a business idea into a business opportunity by conducting market research and a feasibility study on your idea, writing a business plan, and assembling a business team that will work with you on your idea. Only then will such an idea become an opportunity that will attract investors and probably get the needed financing.

1. **Proof of Concept (POC):** Before pursuing an opportunity, validate your idea to ensure there's a genuine demand for it. Conduct market research, surveys, and feasibility studies to assess its viability. Proof of concept refers to a demonstration or experiment that shows the feasibility or potential of a particular idea, design, theory, or project. It's often used in business, technology, and scientific contexts to validate whether a concept can be implemented effectively before committing resources to full-scale development

2. **Gap Analysis:** Identify gaps in the market that your idea can fill. Look for underserved customer needs, inefficient processes, or emerging trends that present opportunities.

3. **Prototype:** Prototypes are early-stage models of a product used to test design, functionality, and user experience. They can vary from basic sketches to interactive mockups. Developed in the early stages, prototypes help refine ideas and gather feedback before significant investment. Feedback from prototypes informs design improvements and can influence subsequent Most Viable Product (MVP) development.

4. **Building MVP:** MVPs follow prototyping and are the first version of a product released to real users for testing and feedback. They're

the simplest version that still delivers value, allowing teams to gather early feedback, validate assumptions, and iterate quickly. This lean approach ensures efficient resource use and real-world user input for product evolution.

5. **Lean Business Model Canvas**: Create a business model that outlines how you plan to monetize your idea. Consider factors like pricing, distribution channels, and revenue streams.

6. **Building a Team and Execution**: Once you've validated your idea and identified a promising opportunity, focus on execution. Build a strong team, secure funding, and launch your product or service in the market.

7. **Iterate and Adapt**: Continuously monitor market dynamics, customer preferences, and competition. Adapt your idea and business strategy as needed to seize new opportunities and stay ahead of the curve.

Million Dollar Business Ideas

A million-dollar business idea refers to a concept that has the potential to generate substantial revenue, often surpassing the million-dollar mark, by addressing real-world problems, leveraging emerging trends, or exploiting market gaps. These ideas are typically innovative, profitable, scalable, and sustainable, making them highly attractive to investors and entrepreneurs alike. Some of the million-dollar business ideas are:

1. **E-commerce platform:** Build an online marketplace that connects customers with various sellers.

2. **Subscription-based service:** Offer a service that customers can subscribe to on a monthly or annual basis. This can be anything from a meal delivery service to a virtual event platform.

3. **Health and wellness:** Develop a health and wellness product or service, such as a fitness app, healthy meal delivery service, or a line of supplements.

4. **Clean energy solutions:** Invest in renewable energy and offer green energy solutions to individuals and businesses.

5. **Edtech:** Develop an educational technology platform that helps students learn more effectively.

6. **Remote work tools**: Create tools and platforms that make remote work easier and more efficient.

7. **Digital marketing agency**: Offer digital marketing services to businesses looking to reach more customers online.

8. **E-learning platform:** Create an online platform where people can learn new skills and gain knowledge.

9. **Personal finance**: Develop a financial management tool that helps people manage their money and reach their financial goals.

10. **Agriculture technology:** Invest in agricultural technology that can help farmers improve crop yields and reduce waste.

Key Takeaways

- Creativity is a fundamental human trait that can be cultivated and harnessed to solve complex problems, drive innovation, and enhance personal growth.
- Creativity is the spark that ignites new ideas and possibilities, while innovation is the process of harnessing and transforming those ideas into meaningful outcomes.
- A creative mind can generate original ideas, solutions, or expressions. It involves thinking outside the box, making unconventional connections, and exploring novel perspectives.
- The creative process is a journey of transforming ideas into reality, encompassing various stages that individuals typically go through when generating and developing new ideas, solutions, or artworks.
- The creative process is not always linear; it can be iterative, with stages overlapping and revisiting previous steps as needed.
- Divergent thinking and convergent thinking are two distinct cognitive processes involved in creative problem-solving and idea generation.
- Both divergent and convergent thinking are essential components of the creative process, and they often work together to facilitate innovative thinking and problem-solving.
- The creative process often involves several stages: Inspiration, Germination, Incubation, Ideation, Evaluation, Implementation, and Reflection.
- Creative problem-solving is essential for overcoming challenges and generating innovative solutions.
- The generally used creative problem-solving tools are: The six thinking hats, Brainstorming, Mind mapping, SCAMPER, Role-play Storyboarding, Prototyping, Reverse thinking, Design thinking, TRIZ, and 5W2H, Lateral thinking method.
- Fear of failure, self-doubt, routine, negative self-talk, fear of judgment, perfectionism, limited perspective, external pressures,

lack of time, and uninspiring environments can all act as roadblocks to creativity.

- Overcoming roadblocks to creativity requires self-awareness, resilience, and a willingness to embrace change and uncertainty.

- By cultivating a growth mindset, fostering a supportive environment, and practicing creative techniques, individuals can unlock their creative potential and overcome barriers.

- A business idea is a concept that can be tested for commercial purposes. All ideas may not become an opportunity.

- An opportunity has the potential to generate income and create value for customers. Turning an idea into an opportunity involves a mix of creativity, analysis, planning, and execution.

- A million-dollar ideas are typically innovative, profitable, scalable, and sustainable, making them highly attractive to investors and entrepreneurs.

Key Terms

Business Idea, Brainstorming, Creativity, Creative Mind, Creative Process, Creative Problem-Solving Tools, Convergent Thinking, Design Thinking, Divergent Thinking, Evaluation, Inspiration, Germination, Incubation, Ideation, Implementation, Business Opportunity, Reflection, The Six Thinking Hats, Mind Mapping, Minimum Viable Product (MVP), Proof of Concept (POC), Prototyping, Reverse Thinking, SCAMPER, Storyboarding, TRIZ, 5W2H, Opportunity.

Quiz – Multiple Choice Questions

1. What is considered the first step in the creative process?

- a.   Evaluation
- b.   Ideation
- c.   Implementation
- d.   Preparation

2. Which of the following best describes divergent thinking?

a. A process that focuses on finding a single, correct solution to a problem
b. A method that encourages generating multiple ideas and solutions
c. A systematic approach to logical reasoning
d. A technique used primarily in mathematical problem-solving

3. In which scenario would convergent thinking be most appropriate?

a. Brainstorming ideas for a new marketing campaign
b. Developing a detailed plan for a project with a specific goal
c. Exploring different perspectives on a social issue
d. Generating a list of potential products for a startup

4. What is the primary goal of the "Empathize" stage in the Design Thinking process?

a. To generate as many ideas as possible
b. To define the problem statement
c. To understand the needs and experiences of users
d. To create prototypes for testing

5. Which tool is commonly used to generate a large number of ideas quickly?

a. Mind mapping
b. Brainstorming
c. SWOT analysis
d. Six thinking hats

6. What does the acronym SCAMPER stand for in creative problem-solving?

a. Systematic creative method of problem exploration and resolution
b. Substitution, Combination, Adaptation, Modification, Purpose, Evaluation, Redesign

   c. Sequential creative approach to meaningful problem exploration and resolution

   d. Systematic combination of adaptive methods for problem exploration and resolution

7. Which stage of the creative process involves testing and refining ideas?

   a. Ideation

   b. Implementation

   c. Inspiration

   d. Evaluation

8. Which tool encourages looking at problems from different perspectives?

   a. Mind mapping

   b. SWOT analysis

   c. Six thinking hats

   d. SCAMPER

9. What is a common obstacle to creativity?

   a. Routine

   b. Collaboration

   c. Experimentation

   d. Flexibility

10. Who developed the "six thinking hats" method?

   a. Edward de Bono

   b. Roger von Oech

   c. Tom Kelley

   d. Alex Osborn

11. Which stage of the creative process involves coming up with new ideas?

   a. Evaluation

   b. Ideation

  c. Implementation

  d. Inspiration

12. What is the primary purpose of using mind mapping in creativity?

  a. Evaluation

  b. Organization of ideas

  c. Implementation

  d. Inspiration

13. What does TRIZ stand for?

  a. Theory of Real Innovative Zones

  b. Technical Resolution for Innovative Zones

  c. Theory of Inventive Problem Solving

  d. Technical Resolution for Inventive Zones

14. Which of the following best defines a business opportunity?

  a. a business challenge to overcome

  b. a favorable set of circumstances for starting or expanding a business

  c. a financial risk associated with a business venture

  d. a legal requirement for business operations

15. Which of the following is a key step in transforming an idea into a business opportunity?

  a. Ignoring market research

  b. Avoiding feedback from potential customers

  c. Developing a prototype

  d. Skipping the business planning phase

Answers:

  1. d

  2. b

  3. b

  4. c

  5. b

6. b
7. d
8. c
9. a
10. a
11. b
12. b
13. c
14. b
15. c

Exercise 3.1

<u>How Creative You Are?</u>

Instructions: For each statement given below, tick in the column that best describes you. Please answer questions as you are (rather than how you think you should be), and don't worry if some questions seem to score in the 'wrong direction.' When you are finished, please calculate the total at the end of the test.

1= Not at all   2= Rarely   3= Sometimes
4= Often   5=Very often

Sl. No.	Statements	1	2	3	4	5
1	Creative people should specialize in coming up with lots of ideas. Other people should then implement these.					
2	If I have a problem, I allow myself to back off active problem-solving, and I create some mental distance between myself and the issue.					
3	When I'm coming up with ideas, I find myself using phrases like "we can't" or "we don't."					
4	I'm busy. As soon as I have a good idea, I move forward with implementation.					
5	I gather information from a wide variety of sources to stay current with what's happening in my field of work.					
6	I see problems, complaints, and bottlenecks as opportunities rather than as issues.					
7	When solving a problem, I try to rethink my current understanding of an issue to develop a deeper insight into it.					
8	I often ignore good ideas because I don't have the resources to implement them.					
9	I find problems and issues distracting. They cause me to lose focus on my real work.					

10	I'm confident that I can develop creative ideas to solve problems, and I'm motivated to implement solutions.						
11	I take time to investigate how things are working, even when there are no current problems.						
12	I always look for the causes of problems, so that I can understand what's really going on.						
13	I look for things in my environment to inspire me to find new interpretations of problems.						
14	I focus on issues that are important right now, preferring to worry about future problems as they arise.						
15	When gathering information about an issue, I explore solutions that have worked elsewhere in the past.						
16	When I generate ideas, I evaluate them and I quickly discard ideas that I don't like.						

Calculate a total for each of the 5 creative competencies.

Competency	Preparation	Incubation	Ideation	Evaluation	Implementation
Add Scroes of Questions	6+9+11+14+15	2+5	3+7+12	4+13+16	1+8+10
Total					

Results: Consider your results and identify one or two actions you can take immediately to strengthen your creativity. Put them into your action plan. Find out your strong areas and weaker areas and try to fill the gap.

Activity 3.1

Connect the Dots

Thinking outside the box is one of the biggest creativity cliches. The basic idea is that to be creative you need to challenge your assumptions and look at things from a fresh angle. You need to break out of conventional thinking and take off the blinkers formed by experience. Look at the picture below with the nine dots. Can you connect the nine dots using four straight lines without lifting your pencil from the paper and without retracing any lines?

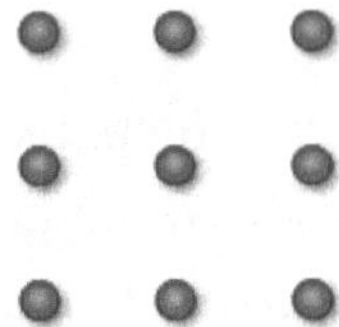

Situation 3.1

Brainstorming Session: Addressing the Water Crisis for Sky Scrapers Housing Association

Objective: To generate creative ideas by brainstorming with members of the housing association to mitigate the water crisis faced by the Sky Scrapers Housing Association in Bangalore City.

Materials:

- Whiteboard or flip chart
- Markers
- Sticky notes
- Timer
- Projector (optional for displaying data or visuals)

Venue: Clubhouse of the Sky Scrapers Housing Association

Participants: One facilitator and nine members of the housing association

Agenda: Facilitator prepares agenda for brainstorming session

1. Introduction :

- A facilitator briefly explains the purpose of the brainstorming session and the importance of addressing the water crisis.

- Provide relevant background information, such as current water consumption, challenges faced, and any existing solutions or initiatives.

2. Empathize :

- The facilitator facilitates so that each member participates and discusses the impact of the water crisis on residents' daily lives.
- Each member shares personal experiences and stories related to water scarcity.
- Facilitate to Identify key stakeholders and their perspectives (e.g., residents, maintenance staff, local authorities).

3. Define :

- Facilitator narrowed down the focus to specific challenges or problems related to the water crisis.
- Formulate clear problem statements that capture the essence of the issues identified (e.g., "How might we reduce water consumption by 50% without compromising residents' needs?").

4. Ideate :

- The facilitator encourages participants to brainstorm as many solutions as possible.
- Use sticky notes to capture individual ideas and place them on the whiteboard or flip chart.
- Foster an open and collaborative environment, emphasizing quantity over quality at this stage.

5. Prioritize :

- Review and group similar ideas together.
- Allow participants to vote on the most promising or feasible solutions using dot stickers or markers.

6. Develop :

- Select 3-5 top ideas based on the prioritization.

- Discuss potential implementation strategies, required resources, and potential challenges for each selected solution.

7. Wrap-up and Next Steps:

- Summarize the brainstorming session and the key ideas generated.
- Discuss the next steps, including assigning responsibilities, setting timelines, and planning follow-up meetings or actions.

Guidelines for Participants:

- Encourage everyone to participate actively and contribute ideas without judgment.
- Emphasize the importance of building upon each other's ideas and collaborating as a team.
- Remind participants to stay focused on solutions and avoid getting sidetracked by challenges or limitations during the ideation phase.

Benefits:

- Encourages collaborative problem-solving and creativity.
- Promotes empathy by considering the needs and perspectives of all stakeholders.
- Generates actionable solutions to address the water crisis effectively.

Note: After the brainstorming session, it's essential to document the ideas generated and share them with the housing association members who couldn't attend. Consider creating a report or presentation summarizing the brainstorming outcomes and proposed solutions to ensure transparency and collective decision-making moving forward.

Situation 3.2

Decline in Sales at Energy Drinks

Scenario: A company called Energy Drinks facing a decline in sales. Use the 5W2H technique to analyze the problem. Using the 5W2H technique for problem-solving can help you systematically analyze and address issues by asking key questions.

By using the 5W1H technique for problem-solving, you can gain a comprehensive understanding of the issue, identify root causes, and develop effective solutions to address the decline in sales.

Situation 3.3

Is this a Potential Business Idea?

Shilpa completed her Bachelor's Degree in Dietician from a prestigious medical college based in Bangalore. She was very interested in starting her own business. She discussed her idea with her parents, teachers, and mentors. She wants to know whether her Business Idea will become a Business Opportunity.

Shilpa has developed a subscription-based, healthy meal delivery service. The service could cater to busy individuals and families who want to eat healthy but don't have the time to plan and prepare meals. The company could partner with local farms to source fresh, seasonal ingredients and offer a variety of meal plans to meet different dietary requirements. Customers would receive weekly deliveries of pre-portioned, ready-to-eat meals that are healthy, delicious, and convenient.

Learning: This business idea takes advantage of the growing demand for healthy and convenient food options, as well as the increasing number of people who are looking to improve their health and wellness through better eating habits. This a potential business idea, which can be turned into a business opportunity. Shilpa should build a team and brainstorm to turn the idea into a business opportunity.

Simulation Game 3.1

Mind Mapping Madness

Introduction: Mind Mapping Madness involves teams creating visual diagrams to explore connections between different ideas and concepts.

Objective: This game aims to visually organize thoughts and stimulate innovative solutions by encouraging participants to think spatially and make connections between seemingly unrelated concepts.

Benefits: Mind Mapping Madness enhances visual thinking and the ability to identify new opportunities by recognizing relationships between ideas.

How to Play:

1. Provide participants with a central topic, issue, or challenge.
2. Encourage them to create a mind map, starting with the central theme and branching out with related ideas, keywords, and concepts.
3. Teams can use various tools, from whiteboards to digital mind-mapping software.

4. Facilitate a discussion where teams present their mind maps and discuss the insights they gained.

Implementation Tips: Ensure that teams have access to suitable mind-mapping tools or materials. Emphasize the importance of non-linear thinking and encourage participants to explore unexpected connections between concepts.

Role Play 3.1

The Six Thinking Hats to Generate Creative Solutions for Traffic Congestion and Pollution

Scenario: A city is facing increasing traffic congestion, leading to longer commute times and air pollution. Use the technique of the Six Thinking hats to analyze the problem. This role-play demonstrates how The Six Thinking Hats method can help identify the root causes of a problem, explore various perspectives, and generate creative solutions to address complex challenges like traffic congestion and pollution in a city.

Instructions:

1. **White Hat (Facts and Information):** Focus on data, facts, and information available. What do we know? What do we need to know?

2. **Red Hat (Feelings and Emotions):** Consider intuition, gut reactions, and emotional responses to the situation. How do we feel about this?

3. **Black Hat (Critical Judgment):** Look at the negative aspects, risks, and potential problems. What could go wrong? What are the downsides?

4. **Yellow Hat (Optimism):** Focus on positive aspects, benefits, and opportunities. What are the benefits? What can go right?

5. **Green Hat (Creativity):** Generate new ideas, alternatives, and possibilities. What are some creative solutions? How can we innovate?

6. **Blue Hat (Process Control):** Manage the thinking process, set agendas, and guide the discussion. What is our goal? What steps should we take?

Participants:

- **Anita** (wearing the White Hat)
- **Bhavani** (wearing the Red Hat)
- **Catherine** (wearing the Black Hat)
- **Dravid** (wearing the Yellow Hat)
- **Eve** (wearing the Green Hat)
- **Frank** (wearing the Blue Hat)

Anita (White Hat): Let's start by examining the traffic data and air quality reports. The data shows a significant increase in vehicles on the road and a decline in air quality.

Bhavani (Red Hat): I'm frustrated with the daily traffic jams. It's stressful and time-consuming for everyone.

Catherine (Black Hat): The increasing traffic congestion poses risks such as accidents, increased fuel consumption, and environmental damage due to pollution.

Dravid (Yellow Hat): There's an opportunity to improve public transportation, promote carpooling, and invest in green initiatives like electric buses and bike lanes to reduce traffic and pollution.

Eve (Green Hat): What if we implement congestion pricing for driving in high-traffic areas during peak hours? We could also improve public transportation by adding more routes and increasing frequency. Additionally, launching a public awareness campaign on the benefits of carpooling and using alternative modes of transportation could encourage behavioral change.

Frank (Blue Hat): Excellent insights, team! Let's prioritize our ideas and develop an action plan. Our goal is to reduce traffic congestion, improve air quality, and enhance the overall commuting experience for residents. We'll start by exploring Eve's suggestion of implementing congestion pricing and investing in public transportation improvements.

Project 3.1

Redesigning College Canteen by Design Thinking

Introduction: Design thinking is a creative problem-solving approach that focuses on empathy, ideation, and experimentation. Redesigning a college canteen is a relevant and engaging design-thinking activity. Here's a detailed activity plan for college students to redesign their college canteen experience a design thinking activity tailored for college students.

Objective: To enhance the college canteen experience by focusing on the needs and preferences of the students.

Materials:

- Sticky notes
- Markers

- Whiteboards or large sheets of paper
- User personas (profiles of different students)
- Timer

Steps:

1. Empathize :

- Divide students into small groups.
- Assign each group a user persona (e.g., vegetarian student, vegan student, athlete, international student).
- Discuss and list the needs, pain points, and desires of that persona regarding the canteen experience.

2. Define: Based on the discussions, each group defines a specific problem statement related to the canteen experience for their chosen persona. For example: "How might we offer more diverse and healthy food options for vegetarian students?"

3. Ideate :

- Encourage each group to brainstorm solutions to their defined problem.
- Use sticky notes to jot down ideas and place them on the whiteboard or large paper.

4. Prototype:

- Each group selects one idea from their brainstorming session.
- Create a simple prototype using drawings, sketches, or any available materials to visualize the solution.

5. Test:

- Groups present their prototypes to the class.
- Collect feedback and discuss potential improvements.

6. Reflect:

- Conclude the activity by reflecting on the design thinking process.

- Discuss the insights gained, the challenges faced, and the importance of catering to diverse needs and preferences.

Discussion Questions:

1. How did considering the user's perspective influence your design?
2. What innovative ideas emerged during the ideation phase?
3. How might you overcome potential implementation challenges?

Benefits:

- Enhances critical thinking and problem-solving skills.
- Promotes empathy and user-centered design.
- Encourages creativity and innovation in addressing real-world challenges.
- Provides practical experience in the design thinking process.

Optional Extension: After the activity, students can be encouraged to gather feedback from their peers about the redesigned canteen concepts. This can be done through surveys or informal discussions to gain further insights and refine the proposed solutions.

The goal of this activity is not just to come up with creative ideas but also to understand the importance of empathy, user-centered design, and iterative feedback in creating meaningful solutions.

Quick Case 3.1

Converting a Business Idea into a Business Opportunity -Airbnb

In 2007, Brian Chesky and Joe Gebbia, two young entrepreneurs living in San Francisco, were struggling to pay their rent. With a design conference coming to town and hotels booked to capacity, they saw an opportunity. They decided to turn their loft into a makeshift bed-and-breakfast, offering guests a unique and affordable place to stay. This idea evolved into what is now known as Airbnb, a global online marketplace for lodging and tourism experiences.

Identifying the Idea: Brian and Joe recognized a problem: the high cost and limited availability of accommodations during peak travel times. They identified an opportunity to leverage underutilized space in people's homes as an alternative lodging option.

Validating the Concept: To validate their idea, Brian and Joe created a simple website advertising their air mattresses for rent. They received three bookings for the design conference, confirming that there was demand for their concept.

Developing the Opportunity: Encouraged by their initial success, Brian and Joe launched Airbnb in 2008, allowing individuals to list their properties for short-term rentals. They focused on creating a user-friendly platform and building trust through user reviews and verification processes.

Overcoming Challenges: Airbnb faced numerous challenges, including regulatory hurdles, safety concerns, and scaling issues. However, the founders persevered, adapting their business model and collaborating with regulators to address concerns and expand their market reach.

Achieving Success: Today, Airbnb is a global leader in the sharing economy, with millions of listings in over 220 countries and regions. It has transformed the way people travel and has become a household name synonymous with peer-to-peer lodging.

Highlights

- Identifying a problem and offering a unique solution can lead to a successful business opportunity.
- Validating the concept through a minimum viable product can provide valuable insights into market demand.
- Overcoming challenges requires resilience, adaptability, and collaboration with stakeholders.
- Success is achieved through continuous innovation, customer-centricity, and a commitment to delivering value.

Brian Chesky and Joe Gebbia's journey from renting air mattresses to founding Airbnb exemplifies how a simple idea can be transformed into a thriving business opportunity through innovation, perseverance, and a deep understanding of customer needs.

Case Questions

1. How did Airbnb identified and validated the market opportunity for its peer-to-peer lodging platform?
2. What insights did the founders gain from their initial test with air mattresses in their loft?
3. How did Airbnb differentiate itself from traditional lodging options, and what strategies did it employ to build trust among hosts and guests?

Discussion Questions

1. What does creativity mean to you personally, and why do you think it's important?
2. Can creativity be taught, or is it an innate ability that some people are born with?
3. What are the phases in the creative process, and how can we embrace it as a learning opportunity?
4. How do collaborative environments and teamwork impact creativity compared to individual efforts?
5. How do different disciplines, such as science, art, and business, approach creativity differently?
6. How does a growth mindset contribute to fostering creativity, and how can we cultivate it in ourselves and others?
7. Discuss some common creative problem-solving tools and techniques.
8. How do brainstorming sessions contribute to generating creative solutions, and what are some best practices to ensure effective brainstorming?
9. How do creative problem-solving tools, such as the Six Thinking Hats and SCAMPER, facilitate the creative process?

10. How can prototyping and storyboarding help visualize and refine creative concepts?

11. What is design thinking, and how can it be applied to solve complex problems and innovate?

12. How does the TRIZ methodology contribute to systematic problem-solving and creative innovation?

13. Discuss the importance of divergent thinking and convergent thinking in the creative problem-solving process. How do they complement each other?

14. What role do prototyping and experimentation play in testing and refining creative solutions to complex problems?

15. How do storytelling and narrative techniques aid in communicating solutions effectively and gaining stakeholder buy-in?

16. What are the roadblocks to creativity and how to overcome?

17. How can asking the 5W2H questions (Who, What, When, Where, Why, How, How much) help clarify and structure creative projects?

18. How does an initial idea evolve into a viable business opportunity? What steps or factors play a crucial role in this transformation process?

References

1. Adams, F. (2020). Storyboarding for Success: Visualizing Creative Concepts. Visionary Books.

2. Amabile, T. M. (1996). Creativity in context: Update to the social psychology of creativity. Westview Press.

3. Brown, T. (2019). Design Thinking: A Guide to Creative Problem-Solving. Creative Solutions Publishing.

4. Csikszentmihalyi, M. (1996). Creativity: Flow and the psychology of discovery and invention. HarperCollins Publishers.

5. De Bono, E. (1985). Six thinking hats. Little, Brown and Company.

6. De Bono, E. (1992). Serious creativity: Using the power of lateral thinking to create new ideas. HarperCollins Publishers.

7. Dweck, C. S. (2006). Mindset: The new psychology of success. Random House.

8. Foster, G. (2021). Asking the 5W1H Questions: A Structured Approach to Creative Projects. Thoughtful Publications.

9. Green, T. (2021). Brainstorming and Mind Mapping: Tools for Creative Thinking. Thoughtful Publications.

10. Johnson, L. & Clark, M. (2019). Divergent Thinking in the Modern World. Insightful Publications.

11. Kaufman, J. C., & Sternberg, R. J. (Eds.). (2006). The international handbook of creativity. Cambridge University Press.

12. Lewis, M. (2021). The TRIZ Methodology: Systematic Problem-Solving for Innovation. Insightful Publications.

13. Mitchell, P. (2019). SCAMPER: Creative Techniques for Idea Generation and Innovation. Innovative Books.

14. Pink, D. H. (2005). A whole new mind: Why right-brainers will rule the future. Riverhead Books.

15. Roberts, L. (2018). Reverse Thinking: Flipping the Script on Creative Problem-Solving. Breakthrough Books.

16. Robinson, K., & Aronica, L. (2009). The element: How finding your passion changes everything. Penguin Books.

17. Sawyer, R. K. (2012). Explaining creativity: The science of human innovation (2nd ed.). Oxford University Press.

18. Smith, J. A. (2020). The Creative Mind: Exploring the Power of Imagination. Creative Press.

19. Sternberg, R. J. (Ed.). (1999). Handbook of creativity. Cambridge University Press.

20. Tharp, T. (2003). The creative habit: Learn it and use it for life. Simon & Schuster.

21. Turner, A. (2019). Overcoming Creative Blocks: Strategies for Unleashing Your Creativity. Breakthrough Books.

22. Williams, S. (2021). Inspiration and Innovation: Unlocking Creativity in the Workplace. Innovative Books.

WORKSHEETS

Chapter 4

Innovation

3M: A Legacy of Inventive and Innovation Spirit

3M's innovation journey is a testament to its enduring commitment to creativity, collaboration, and customer-centricity, driving continuous improvement, and fostering a culture of innovation that empowers individuals to make a meaningful difference. As 3M continues to innovate and adapt to evolving global challenges and opportunities, its legacy of innovation and commitment to excellence will undoubtedly inspire future generations of innovators, entrepreneurs, and change-makers to embrace the power of innovation to shape a better future for humanity.

Let's explore the innovation journey of 3M, a multinational conglomerate known for its innovative culture and diverse range of products across various industries, and highlight some of its notable innovators who have contributed to its legacy of innovation.

3M, originally known as the Minnesota Mining and Manufacturing Company, was founded in 1902 in Two Harbors, Minnesota, with a vision to mine corundum for grinding wheels and eventually diversify into other industries. Over the years, 3M has evolved into a global powerhouse in innovation, offering various products, including adhesives, abrasives, films, and healthcare solutions, catering to various industries and consumer needs.

3M's culture of innovation is rooted in its commitment to fostering creativity, encouraging experimentation, and embracing failure as a learning opportunity, empowering employees to pursue new ideas and solutions. 3M's core values, including integrity, collaboration, and innovation, serve as guiding principles that inspire its workforce to push the boundaries of what's possible, driving continuous improvement and sustainable growth. 3M's Notable Innovators and Their Contributions:

Richard Drew (Scotch Tape): Invented the world's first masking tape in 1925, which later evolved into Scotch Tape, revolutionizing the adhesive tape industry and introducing a versatile solution for various applications.

Spencer Silver (Post-it Notes): Accidentally discovered a low-tack adhesive in 1968, which led to the development of Post-it Notes, a ubiquitous office, and household product that has become synonymous with innovation and creativity.

Art Fry (Post-it Notes): Collaborated with Spencer Silver to develop and commercialize Post-it Notes in the late 1970s, leveraging the unique properties of the low-tack adhesive to create a simple yet transformative product for everyday use.

Dr. Jayshree Seth (Sustainability and Innovation): As a Corporate Scientist and Chief Science Advocate at 3M, Dr. Jayshree Seth has been a champion for sustainability and innovation, driving initiatives to address global challenges through science and technology.

Source: https://www.3m.com/3M/en_US/company-us/about-3m/history

Learning Objectives

1. Define the Concept of Innovation and its Significance
2. Differentiate between types of Innovation
3. Apply the Innovation Tool Kit and Innovation Frameworks
4. Select Intellectual Property Rights (IPR)
5. Choose Innovation Metrics

"Innovation is the Key Differentiator to Compete"

Introduction

Innovation is the key differentiator that will demarcate the winners giving exponential value proposition. Innovation is going to be critical not only for growth and competitive advantage but also to ensure that future development is sustainable and inclusive. There are 17 Sustainable Development Goals (SDGs) set by the United Nations in total, covering a wide range of interconnected issues such as poverty, inequality, climate change, environmental degradation, peace, and justice to be accomplished by 2030 to save the planet. To meet our unique needs, we require a growth mindset to develop a new model of innovation that focuses on affordability and inclusive growth and lifts people at the bottom of the pyramid.

Creativity Vs Innovation

Creativity involves generating original and unique ideas, while innovation is about implementing those ideas to create value. Understanding these distinctions is essential for organizations and individuals looking to remain competitive in their respective fields. Creativity is the process of generating original and novel ideas, emphasizing imagination and ideation. On the other hand, innovation focuses on applying these creative ideas to develop new or improved products, services, or processes, highlighting the importance of practical implementation and value creation. Innovation can occur in various fields, such as technology, business, healthcare, and education. Key aspects of innovation include:

- **Creativity:** Generating new ideas and thinking outside the box to address challenges and opportunities. Creativity involves generating original and unique ideas, while innovation is about implementing those ideas to create value.
- **Research and Development (R&D):** Investing time and resources in research to explore new possibilities and develop innovative solutions.
- **Collaboration:** Working together with others to share knowledge, skills, and insights that can lead to breakthrough innovations.
- **Adaptability:** Being open to change and adapting to new technologies, trends, and market demands to stay ahead of the competition.
- **Implementation:** Turning innovative ideas into reality through effective planning, execution, and commercialization.

Table 4.1. summarises the key differences and relationships between creativity and innovation.

Table 4.1. Creativity Vs Innovation

Aspect	Creativity	Innovation
Definition	Generating new, original, and valuable ideas	Implementing creative ideas to provide tangible benefits
Focus	Imagination, ideation, thinking outside the box	Practical application, value creation
Process	Divergent thinking, exploring multiple possibilities	Convergent thinking, developing, testing, and launching ideas
Examples	Writing a novel, composing music, brainstorming	Developing new technology, launching a business model, improving processes
Nature	Idea generation	Idea implementation
Outcome	Ideas or concepts	Products, services, processes, or business models
Scope	Individual or collective activity, not necessarily tied to implementation	Requires collaboration and resources for execution

Aspect	Creativity	Innovation
Measurement	Subjective, qualitative	Objective, quantitative (market impact, financial performance)
Interdependence	Serves as the foundation for innovation	Channels creativity into practical solutions
Cycle	Inspires further creativity	Encourages continuous cycle of creativity and innovation

Source: Compiled from various sources

Turning Ideas into Action: A Campus Tale of Creativity and Innovation

At Great Mountain University, two close friends, Priya and Amar, were renowned for their exceptional problem-solving abilities. Priya, a passionate design student, was always overflowing with creative and imaginative ideas. On the other hand, Amar, an accomplished engineering student, possessed a remarkable talent for bringing those ideas to life through practical and effective solutions. Their collaborative efforts consistently produced groundbreaking innovations that left a lasting impact on the university community.

While studying in the campus café, Priya observed the overcrowding during lunchtime and the consequent time wasted in waiting for orders. She proposed the concept of a café with a floating table system, enabling students to sit while food is delivered through tubes directly to their tables, thus offering a futuristic and efficient dining experience.

Amar couldn't help but chuckle at the imaginative idea that Priya had just shared. "That sounds amazing, Priya," he said, "but building a floating table system with tubes might be quite complicated and expensive. However, what if we brainstormed an app that allows students to conveniently order food from anywhere on campus, pay in advance, and simply pick it up when it's ready? This way, there's no need to endure long lines for food."

Priya expressed enthusiasm, stating, "That's practical! Perhaps we could implement a color-coded system within the app to indicate the café's level of busyness at any given time, allowing patrons to plan their visits accordingly."

Priya's original floating table idea represented creativity—an imaginative concept without constraints. Amar's suggestion of a food-ordering app was innovation—applying a creative idea in a practical, feasible way to solve a real problem.

Together, they presented the concept to their university's business incubator, and within a short period, their food-delivery application proved to be highly successful within the campus community. This demonstrates how addressing common challenges within an academic environment can stimulate innovative problem-solving, leading to tangible advancements.

This story highlights the difference between creativity and innovation. Creativity is about thinking in unconventional ways and coming up with original ideas, while innovation is about taking those ideas and finding practical ways to turn them into reality.

Significance of Innovation

Innovation plays a crucial role in driving progress, fostering growth, and shaping the future across various sectors and industries. The significance of innovation lies in its transformative power to drive progress, unlock potential, and create positive impact across individuals, organizations, industries, and societies, inspiring creativity, fostering collaboration, and shaping a brighter, more resilient, and sustainable future for humanity. Here are some key significances of innovation:

Driving Economic Growth: Innovation stimulates economic growth by creating new industries, jobs, and opportunities, fueling productivity, competitiveness, and prosperity.

Fostering Competitive Advantage: Innovation enables organizations to differentiate themselves, gain a competitive edge, and adapt to changing market dynamics, consumer preferences, and technological advancements.

Solving Complex Challenges: Innovation addresses societal, environmental, and global challenges by developing novel solutions, technologies, and approaches that improve quality of life, sustainability, and well-being.

Enhancing Productivity and Efficiency: Innovation optimizes processes, enhances efficiency, and streamlines operations by introducing new methods, tools, and technologies that drive productivity and performance improvements.

Creating Value and Impact: Innovation generates value by delivering innovative products, services, and experiences that meet evolving customer needs, exceed expectations, and create meaningful impact for individuals, communities, and society at large.

Fostering Continuous Improvement: Innovation promotes a culture of continuous improvement, learning, and adaptation by encouraging experimentation, embracing failure as a learning opportunity, and fostering a growth mindset within organizations.

Catalyzing Collaboration and Partnerships: Innovation fosters collaboration, partnerships, and knowledge sharing among stakeholders, including employees, customers, suppliers, and communities, driving collective efforts to co-create and implement innovative solutions.

Empowering Individuals and Teams: Innovation empowers individuals and teams to unleash their creativity, explore new ideas, and take calculated risks to challenge the status quo, disrupt conventional thinking, and unlock new potentials for growth and success.

Adapting to Change and Uncertainty: Innovation enables organizations to adapt to change, navigate uncertainty, and seize new opportunities by fostering agility, resilience, and the ability to anticipate, respond, and capitalize on emerging trends, disruptions, and market shifts.

Shaping the Future: Innovation shapes the future by envisioning possibilities, driving transformational changes, and influencing the direction of industries, economies, and societies, laying the foundation for a more sustainable, inclusive, and prosperous future for all.

Invention and Innovation

Invention and innovation are closely related concepts but have distinct meanings and roles in the development and advancement of technology, products, and ideas.

Invention refers to the creation of a new product, system, process, or method that did not previously exist. It involves coming up with a novel idea or solution to a particular problem. Inventions are typically the result of research, experimentation, and creativity. An invention can be tangible, like a new gadget or device, or intangible, like a new method or algorithm.

Innovation, on the other hand, refers to the process of improving, adapting, or applying an existing invention or idea to create value. It involves transforming an idea into a marketable product or service or improving upon an existing product, process, or service to make it more efficient, effective, or user-friendly. Innovation often involves combining existing technologies or ideas in new ways to address current challenges or meet new demands.

Invention and innovation are interconnected and often build upon each other. While invention lays the foundation by creating something new, innovation takes it a step further by bringing that invention to market, refining it, and adapting it to meet changing needs and preferences.

For example, the invention of the personal computer laid the groundwork for innovation in computing technology. Over time, innovators have improved and adapted the initial invention, leading to the development of laptops, tablets, and smartphones, among other advancements.

Invention lays the groundwork by creating something new, while innovation takes that invention to the next level by making it marketable, scalable, and impactful. Both are essential for progress and play a crucial role in driving economic growth, improving quality of life, and addressing global challenges. **Table 4.2** furnishes the difference between Invention and Innovation

Table 4.2. Invention vs Innovation

Basis for Comparison	Invention	Innovation
Meaning	The idea for a product or process that has never been made before	Implementation of a new idea for a product/process/business model
What is it?	Creation of a new product	Adding value to something already existing
Concept	An original knowledge and idea	Practical implementation of a new idea
Skills Required	Scientific skills	Set of marketing, technical, and strategic skills
Occurs when	A new idea strikes a scientist	Improvement in existing product
Concerned with	Single product or process	Combination of various products or process
Activities	Limited to R&D department	Spread across organisation

Invention and Innovation: A Campus Story of Creating and Improving

At Riverside University, two engineering students, Riya and Kiran, worked on their final-year projects. Both had a passion for technology, but their approaches to problem-solving were quite different.

Riya had been working on something entirely new: a solar-powered backpack that could charge electronic devices on the go. After months of research and prototyping, she created a working model. Her backpack had small solar panels embedded into it, converting sunlight into power that could charge laptops and phones. It was something no one had seen before—an invention that pushed the boundaries of what was possible.

Kiran, who had always been fascinated by transportation issues on campus, was thinking of ways to improve the existing bike-sharing system. The bikes were popular but often unavailable when students needed them the most.

Instead of inventing something entirely new, Kiran focused on innovating the system by creating an app. This app would allow students to reserve bikes in advance, track bike availability in real-time, and even pay for their rides through their smartphones.

When it was time to present their projects, Riya's solar-powered backpack caught everyone's eye due to its novelty - it was an original invention that had never been created before. However, it was still in the early stages and would need further development before it could be mass-produced.

Kiran's app was quickly adopted by the university's transportation department. His innovation didn't introduce a new product, but it improved an existing service by making it more efficient, accessible, and user-friendly. Within weeks, students started using his app, and it revolutionized the campus bike-sharing system.

Riya's solar-powered backpack represented an invention, introducing a completely novel concept. In contrast, Kiran's app exemplified innovation by enhancing an existing system, the bike-sharing service, to deliver increased value and utility to the student community.

Both Riya and Kiran have made notable contributions. While invention pertains to the creation of something entirely original, innovation involves the application of new ideas to enhance or advance existing solutions.

This story clearly shows the distinction: invention is the creation of something new, while innovation is the practical application or improvement of something that already exists.

Box 4.1. Groundbreaking Inventions and Innovations

Groundbreaking inventions and innovations that have had a significant impact on society and technology:

1. **Personal Computer (1970s-1980s):** The development of personal computers by companies like Apple and Microsoft

revolutionized computing, making it accessible and affordable for individuals and businesses, leading to the digital revolution.

2. **Internet (1960s-1990s):** The creation and expansion of the Internet transformed communication, information sharing, and global connectivity, paving the way for the digital age and the emergence of the information society.

3. **Mobile Phones (1980s-2000s):** The invention and evolution of mobile phones enabled wireless communication on the go, connecting people worldwide and laying the foundation for the mobile revolution and the smartphone era.

4. **World Wide Web (1990):** Developed by Sir Tim Berners-Lee, the World Wide Web revolutionized information access and sharing, creating a global platform for communication, collaboration, and commerce.

5. **Digital Cameras (1980s-2000s):** The invention of digital cameras replaced film-based photography, making it easier, faster, and more convenient to capture, store, and share images digitally.

6. **GPS Technology (1970s-1990s):** The development and commercialization of GPS technology enabled accurate location tracking and navigation, transforming transportation, logistics, and outdoor recreation.

7. **3D Printing (1980s-2000s):** The advent of 3D printing technology allowed for rapid prototyping and customized manufacturing, revolutionizing design, production, and distribution processes across various industries.

8. **CRISPR-Cas9 Gene Editing (2010s):** CRISPR-Cas9 gene editing technology revolutionized genetic engineering and biomedical research, offering unprecedented precision, efficiency, and potential for treating genetic diseases and advancing personalized medicine.

9. **Electric Vehicles (2000s-2010s):** The development and adoption of electric vehicles (EVs) by companies like Tesla and

Nissan have transformed the automotive industry, promoting sustainability and reducing dependence on fossil fuels.

10. **Artificial Intelligence (AI) and Machine Learning (2010s):** The advancements in AI and machine learning technologies have led to breakthroughs in automation, data analysis, natural language processing, and robotics, driving innovation across sectors and shaping the future of work, healthcare, transportation, and more.

Four Basic Types of Innovation

The four basic types of innovation are Incremental, Architectural, Radical, and Disruptive Innovation. These are the various ways the companies can innovate as shown in Figure 4.1. These types of innovation are dependent on two factors:

1. **Market** – does the innovation create a new market, or address the existing market?

2. **Technology** – does the innovation use a new technology or an existing technology?

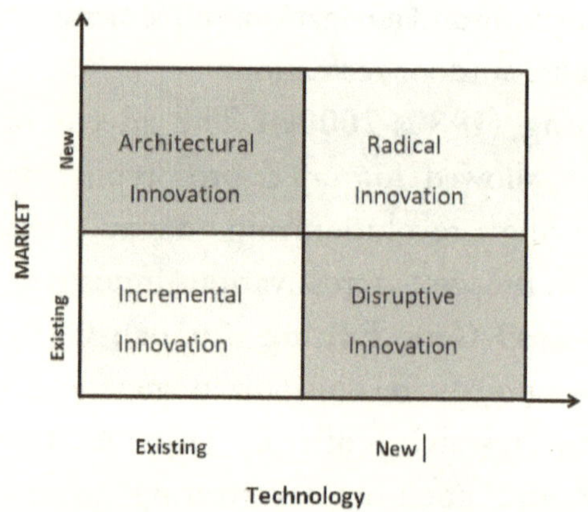

Figure 4.1. Types of Innovation

Incremental innovation refers to the process of making small improvements. These may be enhancements to existing products, services, or processes in the existing market. It enables organizations to continuously evolve and adapt to changing market needs while maximizing the value of their existing assets and capabilities. One of the most famous examples of incremental innovation is the Apple iPhone. Every year, Apple makes small but significant changes to the iPhone to improve it. When Gillette went from a single razor blade to a double blade, to now up to six blades, no new markets were created, as the same consumers are buying the blades. There was no new technology involved,

Architectural innovation occurs when new products or services use existing technology to create new markets and/or new consumers who have not purchased that item before. For example, the smartwatch used existing cell phone technology and was repackaged into a watch. Copiers used to be large and expensive machines purchased only for large offices. Canon and others reconfigured copiers to be small, portable, and usable on desktops, creating a whole new market of people buying personal copiers/printers.

Radical innovation refers to the development and implementation of entirely new products, services, or processes that introduce revolutionary changes to an industry or market. Radical innovation is an invention that destroys or supplants an existing business model. Netflix remains an excellent example of radical innovation. Apple's Airpods can be considered a radical innovation. Apple developed an earpiece that could use wireless technology to receive Bluetooth signals. We see people wearing Airpods now, while previously they rarely used wired earphones.

Disruptive Innovation occurs when firms introduce offerings that are so unique and superior that they threaten to replace traditional approaches. Existing markets are disrupted by new technology. In this process, new products, services, or technologies emerge to fundamentally disrupt and reshape existing markets, industries, or business models. Coined by Clayton Christensen, disruptive innovation typically starts by targeting overlooked or underserved customer segments with simpler, more affordable, or more convenient alternatives. Digital cameras disrupted the photography industry by offering instant gratification and eliminating the cost of getting film developed. Tablet computers disrupted laptop sales due to their versatility and portability. Reading books can be awkward on traditional computers, but user-friendly devices such as iPad, Nook, and Kindle are popular platforms for aggressive textbook publishers.

Box 4.2. Common Types of Innovation

Innovation can take various forms, each serving a different purpose and driving progress in different ways. Here are some common types of innovation:

Product Innovation

1. **Definition:** Product innovation involves the development and introduction of new or improved products or services to meet customer needs or create new market opportunities.

Examples: Introduction of a new smartphone model with enhanced features, development of a new medicine to treat a specific disease, or creation of a novel software application.

2. **Process Innovation**

Definition: Process innovation focuses on improving or reengineering existing processes, methods, or systems to increase efficiency, reduce costs, or improve quality.

Examples: Implementation of automated manufacturing processes, adoption of lean manufacturing principles, or optimization of supply chain logistics.

3. **Business Model Innovation**

Definition: Business model innovation involves creating new ways to deliver value to customers, generate revenue, or capture market share by rethinking and redesigning business models.

Examples: Transitioning from a traditional retail model to an e-commerce platform, introducing subscription-based services, or implementing a freemium pricing strategy.

4. Service Innovation

Definition: Service innovation focuses on developing new or improved services, processes, or methods to enhance customer experience, satisfaction, and loyalty.

Examples: Introduction of online banking services, implementation of telehealth solutions, or development of personalized customer support experiences.

5. Technological Innovation

Definition: Technological innovation involves the invention or adoption of new technologies, tools, or systems to create novel solutions, improve performance, or enable new capabilities.

Examples: Development of renewable energy technologies, advancement of artificial intelligence and machine learning algorithms, or creation of new materials with unique properties.

6. Social Innovation

Definition: Social innovation focuses on addressing social, environmental, or community challenges by developing innovative solutions, programs, or initiatives that deliver positive societal impact.

Examples: Implementation of sustainable development projects, creation of community-based programs to address poverty or inequality, or development of innovative healthcare solutions for underserved populations.

Innovation Tool Kit

1. Juggad

'**jugaad**' is a mindset to do more about creative improvisation. Amid rising global competition and swelling Research and Development budgets, Jugaad Innovation presents ways to innovate, be flexible, and do more with fewer resources (less). Jugaad is a word often heard in general conversation in India. Whether to find ingenious solutions to problems or turn adversity into opportunity. Jugaad innovation involves finding quick, low-cost solutions using whatever materials or resources are readily available.

jugaad innovation has been used in India to address various challenges, from healthcare and agriculture to transportation and energy. Jugaad solutions often leverage local resources and ingenuity to create practical, affordable, and sustainable solutions to everyday problems. While jugaad innovation can be effective in certain contexts, it's important to note that it's not always suitable for complex or high-stakes situations. Jugaad represents a bottom-up innovation model that India excels. Key characteristics of jugaad innovation include:

- **Unconventional:** Jugaad involves seeking opportunity in adversity making the most of limited resources to give more value and finding unconventional solutions to problems.
- **Flexibility and Adaptability:** Jugaad innovators are adaptable and act flexibly and open to improvisation, often combining existing technologies or repurposing materials in new ways.
- **Simplicity:** Creative simplicity is key to Jugaad solutions. Jugaad innovations tend to be simple and easy to implement, focusing on addressing the immediate need rather than striving for perfection.
- **Ingenuity:** Jugaad innovation often involves thinking outside the box by creative problem-solving and finding innovative ways to overcome constraints. Jugaad innovators don't just think outside the box, with nonlinear thinking creating whole new boxes.

- **Frugality**: Jugaad solutions are typically low-cost or even cost-neutral, making them accessible to people with limited financial resources and pulling them into the mainstream.

Examples: Here are some examples of jugaad innovation from India:

1. **The MittiCool Refrigerator**: Invented by Mansukhbhai Prajapati, the MittiCool refrigerator is made entirely from clay and doesn't require electricity to operate. It works on the principle of evaporative cooling, keeping food items fresh without the need for a refrigerator.

2. **NirNal Water Filter**: In many places in India or across the world, safe or pure drinking water is a big concern for most of us. The company always wanted to revolutionize the idea of a cost-effective filter for those living in rural areas and envisioned this social problem as an opportunity. Thus, for the above problem, the founder Niranjan Karagi came up with a solution - the NirNal Water Filter - a reusable water bottle with an integrated disposal filter.

3. **Modified Scooter Ambulance**: In rural areas where access to medical facilities is limited, locals have repurposed old scooters into makeshift ambulances. These modified vehicles are equipped with a stretcher and basic medical supplies, allowing them to transport patients to nearby clinics or hospitals quickly and efficiently.

4. **Bamboo Drip Irrigation**: In regions with erratic rainfall patterns, farmers have developed bamboo drip irrigation systems to efficiently water their crops. By perforating bamboo poles and connecting them with hoses, farmers can deliver water directly to the roots of plants, minimizing wastage and maximizing crop yield.

5. **Jugaad Vehicles:** In many parts of India, people have ingeniously modified vehicles to serve multiple purposes called **Chakada.** For example, trucks may be converted into mobile cinemas, equipped with screens and speakers to entertain villagers in remote areas. Similarly, autorickshaws are often repurposed as mobile shops,

selling everything from groceries, and books to clothing. The **Chukudu** is a two-wheeled handmade vehicle used in the east of the Democratic Republic of Congo. It is made of wood and is used for transporting cargo.

6. **Solar-powered ATMs**: To address the issue of power outages in rural areas, some Indian banks have installed solar-powered ATMs. These ATMs are equipped with solar panels that generate electricity to operate the machines, ensuring that customers have access to banking services even when the grid is down.

7. **The Jaipur Foot:** Developed by the Bhagwan Mahaveer Viklang Sahayata Samiti (BMVSS), the Jaipur Foot is a low-cost prosthetic limb designed for amputees in India. Made from locally available materials such as rubber, wood, and aluminum, the Jaipur Foot is not only affordable but also durable and comfortable to wear.

8. **Embrace:** It is a portable and reusable baby incubator that doesn't require electricity to function. It uses a phase-change material to maintain a constant temperature for up to six hours, providing a stable and safe environment for newborns. This innovation has been particularly beneficial in regions with unreliable power sources or limited access to healthcare facilities. The Embrace Warmer aligns with several SDGs, including Goal 3 (Good Health and Well-being), Goal 9 (Industry, Innovation, and Infrastructure), and Goal 17 (Partnerships for the Goals), as it addresses a critical healthcare need through innovative technology and collaborative efforts.

2. Frugal Innovation

It is also known as frugal engineering is an approach to product development and problem-solving. Frugal innovation emphasizes simplicity, affordability, and resourcefulness. It originated in emerging economies like India but has gained attention worldwide as a means to address global challenges and reach underserved markets. Here are some key characteristics of frugal innovation:

- **Simplicity:** Frugal innovations are often simpler in design and functionality compared to traditional products. They focus on essential features that address the core needs of users.
- **Affordability:** Frugal innovations are designed to be affordable, especially for consumers in low-income or resource-constrained regions. This often involves minimizing costs in materials, manufacturing, and distribution.
- **Resourcefulness:** Frugal innovators leverage available resources creatively. Whether it's repurposing materials, using existing technologies in new ways, or adopting unconventional approaches to problem-solving.
- **Scalability:** Frugal innovations are often scalable, allowing for widespread adoption and impact across different markets and contexts.
- **Sustainability:** Frugal innovations are sometimes more environmentally sustainable than traditional solutions, as they may use fewer resources, generate less waste, and have lower carbon footprints.

Examples: The following examples demonstrate how frugal innovation can address complex challenges and improve the lives of people. Especially those in resource-constrained environments. By prioritizing simplicity, affordability, and resourcefulness, frugal innovators can create solutions that are not only effective but also sustainable and inclusive.

1. **Tata Nano:** Marketed as the world's cheapest car, the Tata Nano was designed to provide affordable transportation to millions of people in India and other emerging markets. By simplifying the design and manufacturing process, Tata Motors was able to offer the Nano at a significantly lower price point than other cars.
2. **Mobile Money:** Services like M-Pesa in Kenya have revolutionized banking for millions of people in underserved communities. By using basic mobile phones and existing telecommunication infrastructure, M-Pesa allows users to transfer money, make payments, and access other financial services without needing a traditional bank account.

3. **Solar Lanterns:** Solar lanterns are a popular frugal innovation that provides affordable and clean lighting to off-grid communities. By harnessing available solar energy, these lanterns eliminate the need for expensive and polluting kerosene lamps, improving indoor air quality and reducing household expenses.

4. **IKEA's Better Shelter:** IKEA's Better Shelter is a flat-pack refugee shelter designed to provide safe and dignified housing for displaced populations. Made from lightweight and durable materials, the Better Shelter is easy to transport, assemble, and maintain, offering an innovative solution to the global refugee crisis.

5. **Aravind Eye Care System:** The Aravind Eye Care System founded in India, provides high-quality, low-cost eye care to millions of people, including those in rural and underserved areas. By streamlining processes, leveraging economies of scale, and cross-subsidizing services, Aravind has been able to make eye care accessible and affordable to all.

Jugaad and Frugal Innovation share common principles of simplicity, affordability, and resourcefulness. They differ in their origins, approaches, scope, and formality. Jugaad tends to be more ad-hoc and localized, while Frugal Innovation is often more systematic, scalable, and aimed at addressing broader societal challenges.

3. Agile Innovation

Agile innovation refers to an approach to innovation that emphasizes flexibility, adaptability, and responsiveness to changes. It draws heavily from the principles of agile software development, which prioritize collaboration, customer feedback, and iterative development to deliver value quickly and efficiently. Agile innovation is based on the active fusion of innovation and agility.

Innovation + Agility = Agile Innovation

Agile innovation results from applying the "Lean" principles to accelerate the innovation process and all the related ones. Agility is introducing the concept of value and flow in all processes, freeing resources and integrating them, especially into the innovation process. Agile innovation offers a dynamic and responsive approach to driving innovation, enabling organizations to quickly adapt to changing market conditions and customer needs. By embracing agility, businesses can increase their chances of success in an increasingly competitive and VUCA environment.

In the context of innovation, agile methodologies can be applied to various stages of the innovation process, including idea generation, product development, and market launch. Some key characteristics of agile innovation include:

Iterative Development: Agile innovation involves breaking down the innovation process into small, manageable increments called iterations. Each iteration typically involves planning, execution, evaluation, and feedback allowing for continuous improvement.

Customer-Centricity: Agile innovation is a customer-centric approach that places a strong emphasis on understanding and meeting the needs of customers. This often involves gathering feedback early and frequently, then incorporating it into subsequent iterations of the innovation process.

Cross-Functional Collaboration: Agile teams are typically interdisciplinary, bringing together individuals with diverse backgrounds, skills, and perspectives. Collaboration between team members is essential for generating new ideas, solving problems, and delivering innovative solutions.

Adaptive Planning: Agile innovation recognizes that requirements and priorities may change over time. Rather than following a rigid plan, agile teams prioritize flexibility and adaptability, adjusting their approach as needed based on new information or changing situations.

Rapid Prototyping: Agile innovation promotes the rapid development of prototypes or Minimum Viable Products (MVPs) to test ideas, and samples and then gather feedback from stakeholders. This allows teams to validate assumptions and make informed decisions about the direction of the innovation effort.

Continuous Learning: Agile innovation fosters a culture of continuous learning and improvement. Teams reflect on their experiences, identify potential areas for growth, and implement suitable changes to enhance their effectiveness and efficiency.

Examples: India has seen numerous examples of agile innovation across various industries. These examples demonstrate how agile innovation is driving transformative changes across various sectors in India, enabling companies to stay competitive, meet customer needs, and capitalize on emerging opportunities. Here are a few notable examples:

Digital Payments Revolution: India has witnessed a rapid transformation in the way people make payments, largely due to agile innovation in the fintech sector. Services such as Phone Pay and Google Pay have revolutionized digital payments by offering convenient, secure, and user-friendly mobile payment solutions. These platforms continuously iterate based on user feedback and technological advancements, driving widespread adoption across the country.

Jio's Disruption in Telecom: Reliance Jio, a telecommunications company in India, disrupted the market with its agile approach to innovation. Jio introduced affordable data plans, high-speed internet, and innovative digital services, significantly altering the competitive landscape of the telecom industry. By leveraging agile methodologies, Jio rapidly expanded its network infrastructure and introduced new features and services to meet evolving customer demands.

Ola and Uber: The city ride in India, dominated by Ola and Uber, exemplifies agile innovation in the transportation sector. These companies revolutionized urban mobility by providing on-demand transportation services through mobile apps. Agile approach enable them to continuously enhance their platforms, introduce new features, and optimize operations to deliver seamless experiences for both riders and drivers.

E-commerce Disruption: Companies like Flipkart and Amazon India have transformed the retail sector landscape in India through agile innovation in e-commerce. They continuously iterate on their platforms, optimize logistics and supply chain processes, and introduce innovative features to enhance the shopping experience for customers. Their ability to quickly adapt to changing market needs and consumer preferences has enabled them to maintain a competitive edge in the rapidly evolving e-commerce market.

Healthcare Innovations: Startups in India are leveraging agile methodologies to drive innovation in healthcare delivery, diagnostics, and telemedicine. Companies like Practo, Portea Medical, LiveHealth, MUrgency, and 1mg are using technology to improve access to healthcare services, streamline appointment booking, provide remote consultations, and deliver personalized healthcare solutions. Their agile approach allows them to iterate on their solutions based on user feedback and emerging healthcare trends.

4. Systematic Innovation

Systematic innovation refers to an organized and structured approach to generating new ideas, solving problems, and creating innovative solutions. Unlike ad-hoc or random methods, systematic innovation follows a disciplined process aimed at consistently producing valuable and novel outcomes.

By following systematic processes and leveraging diverse inputs and tools, organizations can increase their capacity for innovation and drive sustained growth and competitiveness. Several methodologies and frameworks have been developed to facilitate systematic innovation. Each methodologies have its own set of principles and techniques. Here are some key aspects of systematic innovation:

Structured Process: Systematic innovation involves following a structured process or framework that guides individuals or teams through the innovation process. This process typically includes stages such as problem identification, idea generation, evaluation, prototyping, testing, and implementation.

Problem-Centric Approach: Instead of focusing solely on ideas or solutions, systematic innovation emphasizes understanding and defining the problem or challenge. By clearly articulating the problem, innovators can generate more targeted and effective solutions.

Diverse Inputs: Systematic innovation encourages gathering inputs from diverse sources, including customers, stakeholders, experts from different fields, and interdisciplinary teams. This diversity of perspectives helps in generating a wide range of ideas and identifying innovative solutions to situations.

Use of Tools and Techniques: Various tools and techniques are employed in systematic innovation to stimulate creativity, analyze problems, generate ideas, and evaluate solutions. There are various tools such as brainstorming, mind mapping, TRIZ (Theory of Inventive Problem Solving), design thinking, etc.

Iterative Approach: Systematic innovation often involves iterative cycles of ideation, prototyping, testing, and refinement. This iterative approach allows innovators to learn from their failures, make incremental changes and improvements, and converge toward optimal solutions in their journey.

Metrics and Evaluation: Systematic innovation emphasizes the use of metrics and evaluation criteria to assess the effectiveness and viability of potential solutions. By systematically measuring and evaluating ideas against predefined criteria, innovators can make informed decisions and prioritize resources effectively.

Culture and Environment: Creating a mindset, conducive culture in the ecosystem is crucial for fostering systematic innovation within organizations. This includes promoting openness to new ideas, encouraging risk-taking and experimentation, providing resources and support for innovation initiatives, and recognizing and rewarding innovative efforts.

Examples

Cognizant, started the Manage Innovation program. They realized that they had many ideas and plenty of talent floating around, but they needed to direct those to customer solutions. IT service is driven largely by customer requirements. Cognizant re-defined innovation as using skills to create additional value for the customer. They have an elaborate program to measure innovation right from individual to team to manager to corporate level. They give rewards to employees at different levels for innovations they create. Cognizant has, 'one idea, per person, per year'. They are tracking a lot of ideas to build innovative capabilities systematically.

Titan Industries, India's largest jewelry and watch manufacturer, is an innovation in branding, marketing, advertising, product design, and manufacturing. They have done this by encouraging everyone to be a part of innovation and democratizing the whole process. The philosophy is very simple: Everyone has the potential to be creative and innovative and it is up to the organization to harness that. Titan runs a lot of training programs on creative problem-solving, where the employees develop systematic creative problem-solving skills. This is right from the shop floor to the managerial level.

The skills are practiced and improved when working on projects. Almost 10% of work time is allotted to the trainees to work on these challenges. So, it is partly an issue of training, believing in people's innovation, and setting the right kind of challenges. It is running these innovation campaigns year after year, on different themes, that drives systematic innovation at Titan.

Box 4.3. Global Innovation Index (GII)

The Global Innovation Index (GII) uses various metrics to show the overall innovation of a nation. This metric uses various factors to calculate the GII, including multiple subcategories of innovation input and output. The Global Innovation Index (GII), of 132 economies is published annually by INSEAD, the World Intellectual Property Organization (WIPO), and Cornell University. Switzerland has often been ranked as the most innovative country in the world. The GII considers a range of factors, including institutions, human capital and research, infrastructure, market sophistication, business sophistication, knowledge and technology outputs, and creative outputs.

The GII ranking reflects the ability of a country to make innovations and how well the people in that nation follow through with creation. High GII values show countries that have systems in place to encourage the creation of novel ideas, methods, or products. Countries that lack internal structures or innovation output have lower GII scores. While these countries may have some innovators within them, they do not meet the innovation performance of countries with higher GII values. The GII ranking guides policymakers and business leaders in stimulating human ingenuity.

The countries that topped the GII ranking for the year 2023 are Switzerland, United States of America, Sweden, United Kingdom, Netherlands, South Korea, Singapore, Germany, Finland, and Denmark. India retained its 40th position on the annual Global Innovation Index (GII) 2023 due to its vibrant start-up ecosystem, knowledge capital, and the work done by public and private research organizations.

These GII rankings of 132 economies are based on a combination of 80 quantitative and qualitative indicators, providing a comprehensive assessment of a country's innovation ecosystem. It's important to note that innovation is a complex and multifaceted phenomenon influenced by various factors, including government policies, education systems, business environment, and cultural attitudes towards risk-taking and entrepreneurship. While these rankings offer valuable insights into the global landscape of innovation, they should be interpreted with caution, recognizing that innovation is not confined to specific geographic locations and can emerge from anywhere with the right mix of talent, resources, and a conducive environment.

India has been on a rising trajectory over the past several years, from a rank of 81 in 2015 to 40 in 2023, as all government departments have played a pivotal role in enriching the national innovation ecosystem. Most importantly, the Atal Innovation Mission has played a major role in expanding the innovation ecosystem. NITI Aayog has been working tirelessly to ensure the optimization of national efforts for bringing policy-led innovation in different areas such as electric vehicles, biotechnology, nanotechnology, space, and alternative energy sources. The world's five biggest science and technology clusters are all located in East Asia, including the Bengaluru, Delhi, Chennai, and Mumbai clusters.

Innovation Frameworks

Innovation frameworks are structured methodologies, models, or approaches that guide organizations through the process of generating, developing, and implementing innovative ideas, products, services, or solutions. These frameworks provide a systematic and disciplined approach to managing innovation, helping organizations foster creativity, drive collaboration, and optimize resources to achieve desired outcomes and competitive advantage. Here are some commonly used innovation frameworks: Assured Framework, Innovation S Curve, Innovation Funnel, and Ten Faces of Innovation.

1. Assured Framework

We live in a VUCA world, that is Volatile, Uncertain, Complex, and Ambiguous. Some innovations have firmly withstood the winds of time. In his seminal work *'Leapfrogging to Pole-vaulting: Creating the Magic of Radical yet Sustainable Transformation'*, Dr. R A Mashelkar, a global thought leader presented a framework for innovation and termed as **ASSURED** Total Innovation.

ASSURED Framework is an assured success in Innovation. It is a transformation innovation concept that has seven important attributes namely: **A**ffordable, **S**calable, **S**ustainable, **U**niversal, **R**apid, **E**xcellent, and

Distinctive. It is commendable to note that the framework has its roots deeply planted in empathy. This is how empathy drives innovation.

The "ASSURED Total Innovation" model has been successfully implemented by various government agencies and private entities in India. Central Government's Department of Drinking Water and Sanitation adopted it for evaluation of innovations in the drinking water sector.

Examples

Two illustrative contemporary Indian examples, the first is a growing startup, and the second is a startup turned into a successful company, that became successful rapidly and massively by implementing ASSURED.

Dozee By Shell Technologies: A Growing Startup

It is estimated that India has only 2 million hospital beds and 0.12 million ICU beds (2023). What's worse, most of the ICU beds are concentrated in the private sector, with substantial variation in available resources across states. While this presented a healthcare problem even before the COVID-19 pandemic, it has become even more critical in during COVID.

The lack of ICU beds was a major concern even before the pandemic. Anjani Mashelkar Inclusive Innovation Award (AMIIA) winner for 2020 has the potential to partly address this bleak situation. Dozee is a continuous, contact-free vitals monitor with remote monitoring capabilities and an alert system that converts any bed into a step-down ICU in less than 2 minutes. In COVID times, 5000 beds were enabled with health monitoring, helping patients across India in 220 hospitals so far.

Let's view it in the ASSURED framework.

A: It is Priced at 2 USD per day, which is about 1/10th of the cost of conventional alternatives.

S: 75000 patients have been monitored so far

S: Aim to install 50,000 ICU beds across India in the next 6 months and reach one million in the next 3 years. Currently, 1400 out of 5000 beds have been supported by CSR funds so far. The demand in public hospitals is large but the slow purchase procedures there are slowing down the scale up.

U: The user has to put the device under the mattress. Vital parameters are collected automatically. Setting up Dozee requires minimal technical expertise and it can be used in home settings.

R: Can convert any bed into a step-down ICU in just 2 minutes

E: Uses sophisticated Ballistocardiograph technology. Medical-grade accuracy of 98.4%contact-free vitals monitors with remote monitoring capabilities. The device also lets clinicians set thresholds to trigger alerts for body vitals. Incorporated AI technology brings in predictive capability.

D: Contact-free vitals monitor with remote monitoring capabilities. Dozee monitors critical parameters so reliably that one nurse can handle 100 patients, tenfold more than normal.

Jio: A Successful Enterprise

Jio was launched in 2016 and it has become the world's second-largest mobile data carrier in less than five years. In 2020 about 450 million Indians enjoyed the benefits of free voice calling and extremely affordable high-speed 4G internet. The Jio platform raised $ 15 Billion in 2019-2020 from leading global investors for the business in just two months, while in 2019 the entire Indian startup ecosystem raised $12.7 Billion.

Let us view Jio in the ASSURED framework

A: Jio offers free voice calling for life. Jio also did away with national 'roaming charges', marking the first time in India's history that the length and breadth of the nation are truly connected.

S: World's largest all-IP network. Acquired 100 million subscribers in just 170 days. Currently about 450 million subscribers (2023)

S: Jio's network is uniquely positioned to quickly and seamlessly upgrade from 4G to 5G. The entire 5G Standalone Network has been installed in Jio data centers across the nation and trial sites in Navi Mumbai. To develop the end-to-end 5G ecosystem, Jio has worked with leading global partners to develop a full range of 5G-capable devices. The Jio 5G technology has created compelling applications for consumers and enterprises spanning Healthcare, Education, Entertainment, Retail, and other key verticals of the economy

U: Simple, customer-friendly plans – pay for one service. 'Ecosystem of entertainment, payment, and other services

R: Jio became the number one player in India in less than 5 years deployed through technological, product, and business model innovations.

E: One of the most important innovations at Jio was its configuration- Jio's greenfield LTE network is the first countrywide deployment of VoLTE or voice-over LTE in India. It provides 15-20 MBPS speed that enables high-definition voice calls. Jio deployed microcell technology to enhance connectivity

D: Fast-tracked Aadhaar-based e-KYC (Know Your Customer) which allowed SIM activation in 5 minutes instead of a few days.

2. Innovation S Curve

The Innovation S-curve is a conceptual framework used to illustrate the life cycle of innovation and technology adoption over time. It describes the trajectory of innovation from its initial development and introduction to market adoption and eventual maturity. The curve is shaped like an "S," representing the slow initial growth phase, followed by a rapid growth phase, and ending with a saturation phase as the innovation reaches its limits. Figure 4.2 furnishes Innovation S Curve.

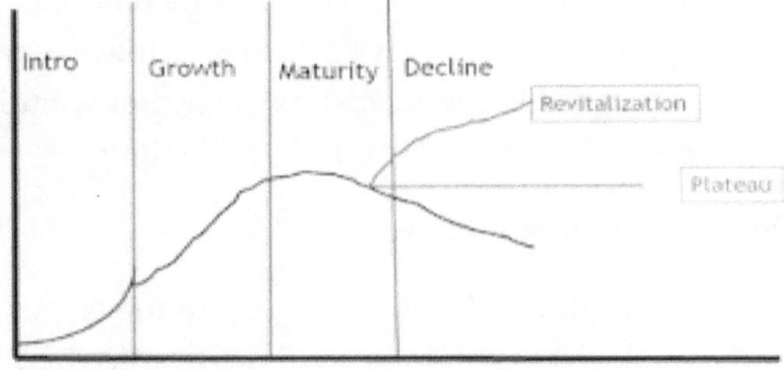

Figure 4.2. Innovation S Curve

Source: https://www.consumerpsychologist.com/cb_Diffusion_of_Innovation.html

Here's a breakdown of the key phases of the Innovation S-curve:

1. **Introduction Phase (Slow Growth):**

   - **Description:** In this phase, an innovation is introduced to the market, but initial growth is slow due to limited awareness, high costs, or technological limitations.
   - **Characteristics:** Early adopters and innovators are the primary users, and there may be skepticism or resistance from mainstream consumers or businesses.

2. **Growth Phase (Rapid Growth):**

   - **Description:** As the innovation gains traction, awareness spreads, costs decrease, and improvements are made, leading to accelerated adoption and market growth.
   - **Characteristics:** More consumers or businesses begin to adopt the innovation, leading to increasing sales, market share, and profitability. Competition may intensify as more players enter the market.

3. **Maturity Phase (Saturation):**

   - **Description:** Eventually, the innovation reaches a point where market saturation occurs, growth slows down, and the market becomes saturated with similar offerings.

- **Characteristics:** The market becomes more competitive, and differentiation becomes challenging. Innovation focuses on incremental improvements, cost reductions, or diversification to maintain market share and profitability.

4. **Decline or Renewal Phase:**

- **Description:** Over time, innovations or disruptive technologies may emerge, leading to the decline of the existing innovation or the need for renewal through reinvention or adaptation.
- **Characteristics:** The innovation may become obsolete, replaced by newer technologies or solutions. Organizations may need to pivot, innovate, or transition to new opportunities to stay relevant and competitive.

The Innovation S-curve is not only applicable to products but can also be used to understand the life cycle of technologies, industries, business models, and even individual careers. It highlights the importance of continuous innovation, adaptation, and strategic planning to navigate through different phases and sustain growth over the long term.

Organizations can use the Innovation S-curve as a strategic tool to identify opportunities, allocate resources, manage risks, and plan for future growth by understanding where they are on the curve and what actions are needed to drive innovation, competitiveness, and sustainability.

3. Innovation Funnel

The innovation funnel, also known as the idea-to-launch process or innovation pipeline, is a systematic approach used by organizations to manage and nurture ideas from conception to market implementation. It serves as a structured framework for guiding innovation initiatives through various stages of development, evaluation, and refinement to bring new products, services, or solutions to market successfully. The innovation funnel and its key components are furnished in **Figure 4.3.** Here's an overview of the innovation funnel and its key components:

Stage 1: Ideation. The Birthplace of Ideas

Every innovative concept starts with an idea. The ideation phase, often supported by design thinking sessions or open innovation platforms, is where numerous new concepts emerge. Here, teams don't just have a lot of ideas; they generate a constant stream of them.

Stage 2: Evaluation. Sifting Through the Potential

With the influx of so many ideas, it's important to assess them critically. The evaluation stage is where any available data comes into play. Alongside specific set criteria, each idea's potential impact and feasibility are assessed. It's not always about the best ideas or great ideas, but the most actionable ones.

You will need to set the evaluation criteria for your business, in line with your mission, vision, and goals, because each company is different. Decide how you will measure the success of your innovations, then work back from there to structure your evaluation framework.

Stage 3: Prototyping. Bringing Thoughts to Life

It's one thing to have a brilliant idea and another to see it in action. This is where the prototyping stage of the innovation funnel comes in. Ideas that have been deemed promising are molded into tangible prototypes or trial service propositions. The prototype might represent a new service or product with the potential to transform an entire industry.

Stage 4: Testing. The Crucible

The only way to know if an idea is truly viable is to test it. Before going all in, these ideas are subject to rigorous testing. Feedback mechanisms, like focus groups and early-stage initiatives, become invaluable. They refine the concept, making it ready for a full-scale launch.

Stage 5: Implementation. The Final Frontier

With the prototype tested and refined, the idea finally sees the light of day. It moves from being just another proposal in the innovation portfolio to a fully-fledged product or service offering.

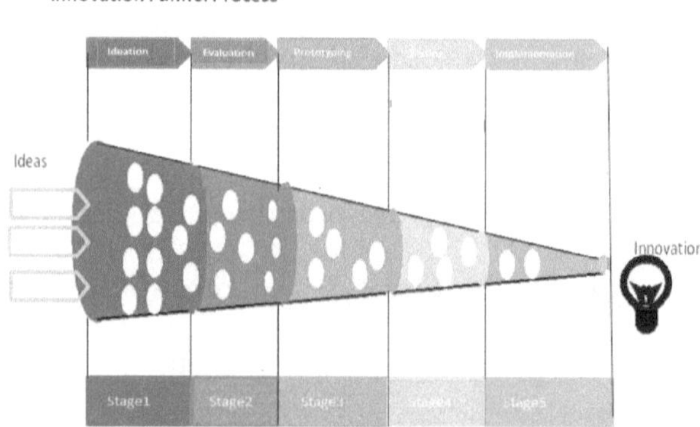

Figure 4.3. Innovation Funnel

4. Ten Faces of Innovation

Ten Faces of Innovation offers a framework for individuals and organizations to cultivate a culture of innovation, embracing diversity, collaboration, experimentation, and empathy. By adopting these roles, teams can approach challenges with a fresh perspective, generate new ideas, and drive meaningful change.

"The Ten Faces of Innovation" is a book by Tom Kelley, the general manager of IDEO, a renowned design and innovation consulting firm. In this book, Kelley discusses ten personas or roles that people can adopt to foster innovation within organizations. These personas help individuals and teams to approach challenges creatively and drive innovation forward. Here are the ten personas described in the book:

i. **The Anthropologist:** This persona involves observing human behavior, immersing oneself in unfamiliar environments, and gaining insights into how people interact with products, services, and experiences.

ii. **The Experimenter:** Experimenters take risks and prototype new ideas quickly. They learn by doing and are not afraid to fail, seeing failures as opportunities to learn and iterate.

iii. **The Cross-Pollinator:** Cross-Pollinators draw connections between seemingly unrelated fields or ideas. They bring insights from one area to another, sparking fresh perspectives and innovative solutions.

iv. **The Hurdler**: Hurdles are problem-solvers who overcome obstacles and challenges with determination. They find creative ways to navigate constraints and make things happen despite limited resources.

v. **The Collaborator**: Collaborators thrive on teamwork and building connections with others. They value diverse perspectives and work well in interdisciplinary teams, fostering a collaborative environment.

vi. **The Director**: Directors provide vision and leadership. They inspire and motivate teams, setting clear goals and guiding the innovation process from conception to implementation.

vii. **The Experience Architect**: Experience Architects design compelling experiences that engage users emotionally and intellectually. They focus on creating memorable interactions that resonate with people on a deeper level.

viii. **The Set Designer**: Set Designers create physical and virtual spaces that foster creativity and collaboration. They understand the importance of the environment in shaping behavior and promoting innovation.

ix. **The Caregiver**: Caregivers empathize with users' needs and concerns. They prioritize user-centric design, ensuring that products and services address real-world problems and improve people's lives.

x. **The Storyteller**: Storytellers communicate ideas and concepts effectively through compelling narratives. They use storytelling to inspire, persuade, and create a shared vision around innovation.

Box 4.4. Institution's Innovation Council (IIC)

Ministry of Education, Govt. of India has established an 'Innovation cell' to systematically foster the culture of Innovation in all Higher Education Institutions (HEIs) across the country. Ministry of

Education's Innovation Cell (MIC) will focus on creating a complete ecosystem that will foster a culture of Innovation across all educational institutions from ideas generation to pre-incubation, incubation, and graduating from the incubator as a successful start-up. MIC also has designed a ranking system to identify institutions at the forefront of innovation.

The Ministry of Education has established 'MoE's Innovation Cell'(MIC) with the mandate to work closely with our Higher Education Institutions (HEIs) to encourage the creative energy of our student population to work on new ideas and innovation and promote them to create start-ups and entrepreneurial ventures.

In the year 2018, the Ministry of Education (MoE) through MoE's Innovation Cell (MIC) launched the Institution's Innovation Council (IIC) program in collaboration with AICTE for Higher Educational Institutions (HEIs) to systematically foster the culture of innovation and start-up ecosystem in education institutions. Primarily, IIC's role is to engage a large number of faculty, students, and staff in various innovation and entrepreneurship-related activities such as ideation, Problem-solving, Proof of Concept development, Design Thinking, IPR, project handling and management at Pre-incubation/Incubation stage, etc., so that innovation and entrepreneurship ecosystem gets established and stabilized in HEIs. The IIC is led by 10-12 faculty members also working as IIC council members.

Major Focus of IIC

- To create a vibrant local innovation ecosystem
- Start-up/ entrepreneurship supporting mechanism in HEIs
- Establish a function ecosystem for scouting ideas and pre-incubation of ideas
- Develop better cognitive ability among technology students

Functions of IIC

- Promote innovation in the institution through multitudinous modes leading to an innovation promotion eco-system in the campus
- To conduct various innovation and entrepreneurship-related activities prescribed by central MIC in time-bound fashion.
- Identify and reward innovations and share success stories.
- Organize periodic workshops/ seminars/ interactions with entrepreneurs, investors, and professionals and create a mentor pool for student innovators.
- Network with peers and national entrepreneurship development organizations.
- Create an Institution's Innovation portal to highlight innovative projects carried out by the institution's faculty and students.
- Organize hackathons, idea competitions, mini-challenges, etc., with the involvement of industries.

Intellectual Property Rights (IPR)

IPR refers to the legal rights granted to creators and owners of creative works, inventions, and other intangible assets to control the use and distribution of their creations. IPR is important for protecting the interests of creators, owners, and investors in creative works, inventions, and other intangible assets. It incentivizes innovation, creativity, and investment by ensuring that the fruits of these efforts can be protected and commercially exploited.

Intellectual Property Rights play a crucial role in fostering innovation, creativity, and economic growth by providing incentives for individuals and institutions to invest in research, development, and creative endeavors. Proper protection and enforcement of IPR help ensure that creators and inventors are rewarded for their efforts and contributions to society. The types of IPR include:

a. **Copyright** - Protects original works of authorship, such as literature, music, and software.

b. **Trademark** - Protects brands, logos, and other identifying marks associated with goods or services.

c. **Patent** - Protects new and useful inventions, such as products, processes, or technologies.

d. **Trade Secret** - Protects confidential business information, such as recipes, formulas, or manufacturing processes.

e. **Industrial Design** - Protects the appearance of a product, such as its shape, ornamentation, or configuration.

f. **Geographical Indications (GI)**: Provide a level of legal protection to products that are associated with a specific geographical location, ensuring that their unique characteristics and reputation are not misused or imitated by other products. This helps to promote and preserve the cultural heritage and traditional skills associated with these products. Examples of Geographical Indications from India include:

   ✓ **Darjeeling Tea** - Tea grown in the Darjeeling district of West Bengal, India, is protected under GI and is known for its unique flavor and aroma.

   ✓ **Basmati Rice** - Rice grown in the Punjab, Haryana, and Himachal Pradesh regions of India is protected under GI and is known for its long grain, fragrance, and taste.

   ✓ **Alphonso Mango** - Mangoes are grown in the Ratnagiri and Devgad districts of Maharashtra, India, are protected under GI, and are known for their juicy, sweet, and aromatic flavor.

   ✓ **Kancheepuram Silk Sarees** - Silk saris woven in the Kancheepuram district of Tamil Nadu, India, are protected under GI and are known for their intricate designs and fine quality.

- ✓ **Chanderi Fabric** - Fabrics woven in the Chanderi town of Madhya Pradesh, India, are protected under GI and are known for their delicate designs and lightweight.
- ✓ **Channapattana Toys:** Channapatna toys are a particular form of wooden toys and dolls that are manufactured in the town of Channapatna in the Ramanagara district of Karnataka state, India.

The following acts deal with the protection of intellectual property in India

1. Trade Marks Act, 1999
2. The Patents Act, 1970 (as amended in 2005)
3. The Copyright Act, 1957
4. The Designs Act, 2000
5. The Geographical Indications of Goods (Registration and Protection) Act, 1999
6. The Semiconductor Integrated Circuits Layout Design Act, 2000
7. The Protection of Plant Varieties and Farmers' Rights Act, 2001
8. The Information Technology Act, 2000

Innovation Metrics

Innovation metrics are used to measure and evaluate the success, effectiveness, and impact of innovation efforts within an organization. These metrics help businesses understand how well their innovation initiatives are performing and identify areas for improvement. These metrics help organizations assess their innovation performance, make data-driven decisions, allocate resources effectively, and foster a culture of continuous improvement and innovation. Common innovation metrics include:

1. **Return on Investment (ROI):** Measures the financial return generated from an innovation project compared to the investment made.
2. **Number of Patents Filed:** Counts the number of patents filed or granted, indicating the organization's commitment to protecting its intellectual property.

3. **Time to Market**: Evaluate the speed at which a new product or service is developed and launched, indicating efficiency in innovation processes.

4. **Revenue from New Products**: Tracks the revenue generated from new products or services launched, indicating market acceptance and success.

5. **Customer Adoption Rate**: Measures the rate at which customers adopt and use a new product or service, indicating its market relevance and appeal.

6. **Innovation Pipeline:** Assesses the number and quality of ideas or projects in the innovation pipeline, indicating the organization's innovation capacity and future potential.

7. **Employee Engagement in Innovation:** Measures the level of employee involvement and contribution to innovation initiatives, indicating organizational culture and commitment to innovation.

8. **Cost Savings from Innovation**: Calculates the cost savings achieved through innovative processes, technologies, or ideas implemented within the organization.

9. **Partnerships and Collaborations**: Tracks the number and quality of partnerships or collaborations established for innovation, indicating the organization's networking and external engagement capabilities.

10. **Customer Satisfaction and Feedback**: Gauges customer satisfaction and collects feedback on new products or services, providing insights into customer preferences, needs, and areas for improvement.

Key Takeaways

- Innovation is the development of new ideas or methods that bring about positive change and improvement.
- Innovation involves creativity, problem-solving, and the implementation of novel solutions to address challenges or seize opportunities.
- The significance of innovation lies in its ability to drive progress, competitiveness, and growth across various sectors and industries.
- Invention is the creation of a new product or process, while innovation is the improvement or application of an existing invention to create value.
- The four basic types of innovation are Incremental, Architectural, Radical, and Disruptive Innovation.
- The common types of innovation are: Product Innovation, Process Innovation, Business Model Innovation, Service Innovation, Technological Innovation, Social Innovation
- Juggad Innovation, Frugal Innovation, Agile Innovation, and Systematic Innovation are the various innovation tools used depending on the situation
- ASSURED Framework, Innovation S Curve, Innovation Funnel, and Ten Faces of Innovation are different types of Innovation Framework
- Intellectual Property Rights (IPR) are legal protections for creations of the mind, granting creators exclusive rights to their intellectual property, such as inventions, artistic works, and trademarks, enabling them to control and profit from their creations.
- Patents, trademarks, copyrights, trade secrets, industrial designs, and geographic indications are the main types of Intellectual Property Rights (IPR) protecting various forms of intellectual creations.
- Innovation Metrics measure the success and impact of innovation efforts of an organization using indicators such as ROI, patents filed, time to market, and customer adoption rates.

Key Terms

Invention, Innovation, Incremental Innovation, Architectural innovation, Radical Innovation, Disruptive Innovation, Product Innovation, Process Innovation, Business Model Innovation, Service Innovation, Technological Innovation, Social Innovation, Juggad Innovation, Frugal Innovation, Agile Innovation, Systematic Innovation, ASSURED Framework, Innovation S Curve, Innovation Funnel, Ten Faces of Innovation, Intellectual Property Rights (IPR), Patents, Trademarks, Copyrights, Trade secrets, Industrial Designs, Geographic Indications, Innovation Metrics.

Quiz – Multiple Choice Questions

1. What is innovation?

    a. Replicating existing ideas
    b. Implementing new ideas or methods
    c. Stagnation
    d. Reducing costs

2. What does invention refer to?

    a. Replicating existing products
    b. Improving existing technologies
    c. Creating or discovering a new product, process, or idea
    d. Marketing existing products

3. What is Jugaad Innovation?

    a. Following established rules and procedures
    b. Finding quick and inexpensive solutions using limited resources
    c. Implementing complex and elaborate processes
    d. Relying heavily on external funding

4. Frugal innovation refers to:

    a. Creating solutions that are overly complex and expensive
    b. Developing products or services that are affordable and accessible
    c. Exclusively targeting high-income markets

d.   Ignoring cost considerations during the innovation process

5. Which of the following best describes Agile Innovation?

a.   A structured and linear approach to innovation
b.   A flexible and iterative approach to adapting to changes quickly
c.   A method that focuses solely on cost reduction
d.   A strategy that prioritizes long-term planning over short-term results

6. What is a key feature of Systematic Innovation?

a.   Random and unplanned approach to problem-solving
b.   Ignoring customer feedback and preferences
c.   A structured and methodical approach to generating new ideas
d.   Focusing solely on incremental improvements

7. What does the ASSURED Framework primarily focus on?

a.   Identifying customer needs
b.   Evaluating market opportunities
c.   Assessing the feasibility of innovation projects
d.   Ensuring the sustainability and scalability of innovations

8. What does the Innovation S Curve depict?

a.   The relationship between cost and quality of innovation
b.   The life cycle of an innovation from introduction to decline
c.   The speed of technological advancement over time
d.   The stages of innovation from ideation to implementation

9. What is the primary purpose of the Innovation Funnel?

a.   Filtering out unfeasible ideas
b.   Generating new ideas through brainstorming sessions
c.   Evaluating the market potential of innovations
d.   Assessing the technical feasibility of projects

10. Which of the following is NOT one of the Ten Faces of Innovation?

    a. The Hurdler

    b. The Anthropologist

    c. The Storyteller

    d. The Explorer

11. Which type of Intellectual Property Rights protects the visual design of objects?

    a. Patents

    b. Trademarks

    c. Copyrights

    d. Industrial Designs

12. What does Return on Investment (ROI) measure in the context of innovation?

    a. Speed of product development

    b. Market share of new products

    c. Financial return generated from an innovation project

    d. Number of patents filed

13. Which type of Intellectual Property Rights protects new inventions and discoveries?

    a. Patents

    b. Trademarks

    c. Copyrights

    d. Trade Secrets

14. Which type of Intellectual Property Rights protects symbols, names, and slogans used to identify goods or services?

    a. Patents

    b. Trademarks

    c. Copyrights

    d. Trade Secrets

15. Which type of Intellectual Property Rights protects original literary, artistic, and musical works?

    a. Patents

    b. Trademarks

    c. Copyrights

    d. Trade Secrets

16. Which type of Intellectual Property Rights protects confidential information, such as formulas and processes?

    a. Patents

    b. Trademarks

    c. Copyrights

    d. Trade Secrets

17. What does GI stand for in the context of Intellectual Property Rights?

    a. General Infringement

    b. Geographic Indicator

    c. Genuine Innovation

    d. Global Investment

18. What type of innovation focuses on finding inventive and cost-effective solutions with limited resources?

    a. Product innovation

    b. Process innovation

    c. Business model innovation

    d. Jugaad innovation

19. Which type of innovation focuses on developing new technologies or improving existing ones?

    a. Social innovation

    b. Service innovation

   c. Technological innovation

   d. Product innovation

20. What type of innovation addresses social needs and challenges, aiming to improve the well-being of individuals and communities?

   a. Product innovation

   b. Process innovation

   c. Business model innovation

   d. Social innovation

<u>ANSWERS</u>

1. b.
2. c
3. b
4. b
5. b
6. c
7. d
8. b
9. a
10. d
11. d
12. c
13. a
14. b
15. c
16. d
17. b
18. d
19. c
20. d

Exercise 4.1

How Innovative You Are?

Instructions: Read each statement and select the option that best describes you. Be honest with your answers.

1. How do you approach problems?

A. Stick to conventional solutions.
B. Experiment with different approaches.
C. Create new solutions that challenge the norm.

2. How often do you seek out new challenges or experiences?

A. Rarely
B. Occasionally
C. Frequently

3. How do you handle unexpected changes?

A. Prefer stability and routine.
B. Adapt and find new ways to manage.
C. Thrive on change and see it as an opportunity.

4. How do you react to feedback or criticism?

A. Avoid feedback to prevent criticism.
B. Consider feedback and look for ways to improve.
C. Actively seek feedback to innovate and refine.

5. How do you approach learning?

A. Focus on mastering existing knowledge.
B. Explore new ideas outside my comfort zone.
C. Continuously seek opportunities to learn and grow.

6. How do you feel about taking risks?

A. Avoid risks whenever possible.
B. Take calculated risks when necessary.
C. Embrace risks as a chance to innovate and grow.

7. How do you stay updated with industry trends?

A. Rely on established practices and ignore new trends.
B. Keep an eye on emerging trends but prefer proven methods.
C. Actively seek out new trends and incorporate them into my work.

8. How do you foster creativity?

A. Stick to structured routines and processes.
B. Engage in brainstorming and explore diverse ideas.
C. Encourage experimentation and out-of-the-box thinking.

9. How do you handle failure?

A. Give up easily after facing failure.
B. Learn from mistakes and try again.
C. View failure as a learning opportunity and pivot accordingly.

10. How do you collaborate with others?

A. Prefer working alone and avoid collaboration.
B. Collaborate occasionally but value independent work.
C. Thrive on collaboration and value diverse perspectives.

Scoring:

For each question:
A = 1 point
B = 2 points
C = 3 points

Interpretation:

10-20 points: You have a more traditional approach and may benefit from exploring new ideas and methods to foster innovativeness.
21-30 points: You demonstrate a balanced approach to innovation, combining traditional methods with a willingness to explore new ideas.

31-30 points: You exhibit strong innovativeness, actively seeking opportunities to innovate and embracing change and challenges.

This quiz offers a quick assessment of innovativeness, but remember, it's a simplified tool and should be used as a starting point rather than a definitive measure.

Activity 4.1

Identify Innovations

Instructions: Examples of different types of innovation are given below. Identify the type of innovation.

Number	Example
1	Introduction of the iPhone by Apple
2	Development of automated customer service chatbots
3	Development of online education platforms (e.g., Coursera, Udemy)
4	Implementation of the freemium model by apps such as LinkedIn
5	Adoption of remote work policies and flexible work arrangements
6	Creation of microfinance initiatives to support entrepreneurs in underserved communities
7	Introduction of blockchain technology in finance and other industries
8	Development of Artificial Intelligence (AI) and Machine Learning (ML) technologies
9	Introduction of online streaming services
10	Development of electric vehicles

Answers

1. Product Innovation
2. Process Innovation
3. Service Innovation
4. Business Model Innovation
5. Organisational Innovation
6. Social Innovation

7. Technological Innovation
8. Technological Innovation
9. Service Innovation
10. Product Innovation

Situation 4.1

Strategic Innovation Decision

Mind Tech Corp, a leading technology company, has been facing increasing competition in its core market of smartphone manufacturing. Sales have plateaued, and customer feedback indicates a desire for more advanced features, improved user experience, and longer battery life.

The company has the opportunity to invest in innovations to regain market share and satisfy customer demands. However, the leadership team is divided on which type of innovation to pursue: Incremental Innovation, Architectural Innovation, or Radical Innovation.

Situation Analysis: Divide the class into three groups. The first group to analyse Incremental Innovation and second on Architectural Innovation and the third on Radical Innovation. And each group present their ideas in the class. The following instructions provide a discussion for analysis.

Instructions:

Incremental Innovation: This approach focuses on making small improvements to existing products or processes. For Mind Tech Corp, this could mean upgrading current smartphone models with better cameras, faster processors, or longer battery life.

Architectural Innovation: This involves reconfiguring existing technologies or processes in a novel way. Mind Tech Corp could explore new designs that integrate hardware and software more seamlessly, leading to a more intuitive user experience.

Radical Innovation: This type of innovation involves developing entirely new technologies or business models. Mind Tech Corp could invest in developing a revolutionary new smartphone design or explore alternative energy sources for longer battery life.

Situation 4.2

Protect Your IPR

Tejas Inc., a LLP firm has developed a new and innovative technology for water filtration. To protect its rights over the technology, Tejas Inc. has filed for a patent in India. Soon after, a local company, Ashwin Ltd., starts selling a similar water filtration system in the Indian market. Upon investigation, Tejas Inc. finds out that Ashwin Ltd. has been using its patented technology without permission. The company decides to take legal action to protect its intellectual property rights.

Tejas Inc. files a lawsuit against Ashwin Ltd. for patent infringement under the Patents Act, of 1970. The court examines the evidence presented by both parties and determines that Aswin Ltd. has indeed infringed upon Tejas Inc.'s patent rights.

The court orders Ashwin Ltd. to stop selling the infringing product and pay damages to Tejas Inc. for the unauthorized use of its technology. In addition, the court imposes an injunction on Ashwin Ltd. to prevent it from using the technology in the future.

Learning: In this situation, Tejas Inc. was able to successfully enforce its intellectual property rights in India and protect its innovative technology from infringement. This demonstrates the importance of obtaining proper IPR protection in India and taking legal action to enforce it when necessary. This situation highlights the crucial role of IPR in promoting innovation and protecting the rights of creators and owners of original works in India. Companies operating in the country should be aware of the laws and regulations governing IPR and take appropriate measures to protect their rights.

Simulation Game 4.1

<u>**Innovation Odyssey**</u>

Objective: Navigate the innovation landscape to revitalize Mind Tech Corp's market position by making strategic decisions on Incremental, Architectural, and Radical Innovations.

Materials Needed

- Game board depicting the innovation landscape
- Innovation cards (Incremental, Architectural, Radical)
- Market demand cards
- Resource cards (time, money, talent)
- Competition cards
- Customer feedback cards

Setup

- Place the game board in the center, representing the innovation landscape with three paths: Incremental, Architectural, and Radical.
- Shuffle the Innovation cards and place them face-down.
- Shuffle the Market demand cards and place them face-down.
- Shuffle the Resource cards and place them face-down.
- Shuffle the Competition cards and place them face-down.
- Shuffle the Customer feedback cards and place them face-down.

Gameplay

Turn Sequence: Players take turns drawing cards and making decisions based on the information provided.

Draw Cards

- **Innovation Cards:** Determine the type of innovation available (Incremental, Architectural, Radical).

- **Market Demand Cards:** Provide insights into customer preferences and market trends.
- **Resource Cards:** Allocate resources (time, money, talent) to pursue innovations.
- **Competition Cards:** Present challenges and opportunities based on competitors' actions.
- **Customer Feedback Cards:** Offer feedback on current products and potential innovations.

Decision Making

- Choose which innovation path to pursue based on the drawn Innovation cards.
- Allocate resources wisely to develop and implement innovations.
- Consider market demand, competition, and customer feedback when making decisions.

Implementation

- Advance along the chosen innovation path by investing resources.
- Face challenges and opportunities presented by market demand and Competition cards.
- Adjust strategies based on customer feedback and resource availability.

Evaluation:

- After a set number of turns or when all Innovation cards are drawn, evaluate the outcomes.
- Measure success based on market share, customer satisfaction, and innovation impact.

Winning the Game: Achieve the highest market share and customer satisfaction by strategically navigating the innovation landscape, making informed decisions, and effectively implementing innovations.

Debrief: Discuss the decisions made during the game, lessons learned, and insights gained about the importance of choosing the right innovation path for business success.

Learning Outcomes:

- Understand the different types of innovation (Incremental, Architectural, Radical) and their impact on business strategy.
- Develop strategic thinking and decision-making skills.
- Learn to balance resource allocation, market demand, competition, and customer feedback when pursuing innovation.
- This simulation game provides an interactive and engaging way to explore the complexities of innovation strategy, helping participants grasp the challenges and opportunities involved in choosing the right path for business growth and success.

Role Play 4.1

The Ten Faces of Innovation in Action

Objective: Explore the ten personas of innovation from Tom Kelley's "The Ten Faces of Innovation" and understand their roles in fostering creativity and driving innovation within Mind Tech Corp. By engaging in this role play, participants will gain a deeper understanding of the Ten Faces of Innovation and learn how to apply these personas to real-world challenges, fostering a culture of creativity and innovation within Mind Tech Corp.

Mind Tech Corp is facing stiff competition and needs to innovate to stay ahead in the market. The company is struggling with product development, customer engagement, and employee morale.

Participants:

- Innovator (Lead role)
- Observer
- Team members (Roles based on the Ten Faces of Innovation)
- Facilitator

Materials Needed:

- Character cards representing the ten personas of innovation
- Scenario cards depicting various challenges and opportunities within XYZ Tech Corp
- Innovation toolkit (props to represent different innovative tools and techniques)

Setup:

1. Distribute character cards to the team members, assigning each one a persona from the Ten Faces of Innovation.
2. Review the roles and responsibilities of each persona to ensure understanding.
3. Prepare scenario cards that describe specific situations within Mind Tech Corp where innovation is needed.

Roles and Responsibilities:

1. **Innovator (Lead role):** Drive the innovation process, inspire the team, and ensure collaboration among the personas.
2. **Observer:** Monitor the interactions, identify strengths and weaknesses in the innovation process, and provide feedback.
3. **The Anthropologist:** Study the company culture, customer behaviors, and market trends to gain insights.
4. **The Experimenter:** Test new ideas, prototype solutions, and iterate based on feedback.
5. **The Cross-Pollinator:** Bring external perspectives and ideas from different industries to spark innovation.
6. **The Hurdler:** Overcome obstacles, navigate challenges, and find creative solutions to problems.
7. **The Collaborator:** Foster teamwork, encourage collaboration, and build relationships across departments.
8. **The Director:** Provide vision, set goals, and guide the team towards achieving innovation objectives.

9. **The Experience Architect:** Design user experiences, improve customer engagement, and enhance product usability.
10. **The Set Designer:** Create inspiring workspaces, foster creativity, and promote a culture of innovation.

Gameplay:

1. **Introduction:** The Innovator sets the stage, explains the scenario, and outlines the objectives.
2. **Role Play:** Team members assume their roles and interact based on the scenario, applying the principles of their personas to address the challenges and opportunities presented.
3. **Innovation Toolkit:** Utilize props and tools to facilitate discussions, brainstorming sessions, and idea generation.
4. **Reflection:** After the role-play, the Observer provides feedback on the team's performance, highlighting strengths and areas for improvement.
5. **Debrief:** Discuss the experience, share insights, and identify lessons learned about the role of each persona in driving innovation.

Learning Outcomes:

- Understand the importance of diverse personas in fostering a culture of innovation.
- Explore the different roles and responsibilities involved in the innovation process.
- Gain insights into how to effectively collaborate, overcome challenges, and drive creativity within a team.

Project 4.1

National Institutional Ranking Framework (NIRF)-Innovation

Introduction: Atal Ranking of Institutions on Innovation Achievements (ARIIA) is an initiative of the Ministry of Education (MoE), Govt. of India to systematically rank all major higher educational institutions and universities in India on indicators related to "Innovation and

Entrepreneurship Development" amongst students and faculties. The first edition was launched in 2019.

Objective: ARIIA ranking will certainly inspire Indian institutions to reorient their mindset and build ecosystems to encourage high-quality research, innovation, and entrepreneurship. More than quantity, ARIIA will focus on the quality of innovations and will try to measure the real impact created by these innovations nationally and internationally. Moreover, ARIIA will set the tone and direction for institutions for future development making them globally competitive and at the forefront of innovation.

All recognized Higher Educational Institutions of India are eligible to participate in the ARIIA ranking. The 4th edition of ARIIA is renamed as the 'NIRF-Innovation' ranking and it has adopted the framework, parameters, and Key Performance Indicators (KPIs) of ARIIA. This 4th edition has received participation from 1417 HEIs with very good representation from 6 different types of institutions. The NIRF-Innovation Ranking Framework captures data by using 22 Key Performance Indicators under seven broad parameters. Assessment of innovation and startup ecosystem in HEIs will be based on Seven parameters with certain weights allocated as below.

No.	KPI	Weightage %
1	Policy and Institutionalization of I&E Activities in HEIs	10
2	Teaching and Learning Courses on Innovation and Entrepreneurship	10
3	Pre-Incubation and Incubation Infrastructure & Facilities are Currently in Operation to Promote I&E Agenda	10
4	Generation and Support of Ideas/Prototypes / Innovations at HEI and Recognition received	20

5	Start-ups/Ventures Established and Supported at HEI and & Recognitions Received	20
6	Collaboration with other Incubation Units, HEIs, and Industry Associations to Strengthen Services and Support Innovation & Start-ups at HEI	05
7	Intellectual Property (IP), Generation and Commercialization	25
	TOTAL	100

Visit the website https://www.ariia.gov.in/ to identify the gaps and present them in the class to develop awareness of NIRF-Innovation among stakeholders.

Quick Case 4.1

Flipkart's Disruptive Innovation in e-commerce

Introduction: Flipkart's commitment to disruptive innovation, customer-centricity, and continuous improvement has enabled the company to navigate challenges, capitalize on opportunities, and establish itself as a leader in the competitive Indian e-commerce market. By embracing change, leveraging technology, and fostering partnerships. Flipkart has redefined the shopping experience and set new benchmarks for success in the digital era.

Background: Flipkart, founded in 2007 by Sachin Bansal and Binny Bansal, started as an online bookstore and quickly expanded into a comprehensive e-commerce platform, revolutionizing the Indian retail landscape. Facing intense competition and evolving customer expectations, Flipkart needed to innovate continuously to maintain its market leadership.

The Challenges Faced by Flipkart:

- Intense competition from global and local e-commerce players
- Rapidly changing consumer preferences and expectations
- Infrastructure and logistics challenges in India's diverse market

Disruptive Innovation: Flipkart adopted a disruptive innovation strategy, introducing new business models, technologies, and services to redefine the e-commerce experience in India.

Implementation:

1. Customer-Centric Approach:

- Flipkart focused on understanding and anticipating customer needs, offering a wide range of products, competitive pricing, and personalized shopping experiences.
- The company introduced features like easy returns, cash on delivery, and robust customer support to enhance user satisfaction.

2. Innovative Business Models:

- Flipkart launched initiatives such as 'Flipkart Plus loyalty program, 'Flipkart Wholesale for B2B customers, and 'Flipkart Video' for original content, diversifying its offerings and attracting a broader audience.
- The company invested in technology and AI-driven solutions to optimize operations, improve recommendations, and personalize the shopping experience.

3. Logistics and Infrastructure Development:

- Flipkart invested heavily in building a robust logistics network, warehousing facilities, and last-mile delivery solutions to ensure timely and efficient order fulfillment across India.
- The company collaborated with local partners and leveraged technology to overcome infrastructure challenges and enhance supply chain efficiency.

4. Marketplace Expansion and Partnerships:

- Flipkart expanded its marketplace model, allowing third-party sellers to list products, increasing product assortment, and driving growth.

- The company formed strategic partnerships with brands, retailers, and local artisans to offer exclusive products, expand reach, and foster innovation.

Results

- Established as a market leader in the Indian e-commerce industry
- Expanded customer base and increased market share
- Enhanced brand reputation for innovation, reliability, and customer satisfaction
- Attracted significant investments and achieved unicorn status

Case Questions

1. How did Flipkart's customer-centric approach contribute to its success and differentiation in the competitive e-commerce market in India?
2. In what ways did Flipkart leverage innovative business models and technology to drive growth, diversify offerings, and enhance the shopping experience for customers?
3. How did Flipkart overcome logistics and infrastructure challenges to build a robust supply chain network, ensuring efficient order fulfillment and customer satisfaction?
4. What role did marketplace expansion, strategic partnerships, and collaborations play in Flipkart's strategy to expand reach, drive innovation, and maintain market leadership in the Indian e-commerce industry?

Discussion Questions

1. What distinguishes invention from innovation, and why is understanding this distinction crucial for businesses?
2. How do Incremental, Architectural, Radical, and Disruptive Innovations differ from each other, and when should each be pursued?

3. What are the key differences between Product and Process Innovations, and how do they contribute to organizational growth?

4. How can Business Model Innovation transform industries and create new opportunities for growth and sustainability?

5. How do Service Innovation and Technological Innovation complement each other in delivering value to customers?

6. What role do Social Innovation and Jugaad Innovation play in addressing societal challenges and fostering inclusive growth?

7. How do Frugal Innovation and Agile Innovation enable organizations to do more with less and respond quickly to market changes?

8. What are the key principles of Systematic Innovation, and how can organizations implement systematic approaches to foster creativity and problem-solving?

9. How does the ASSURED Framework help organizations ensure the successful adoption and implementation of innovations?

10. How does the Innovation S Curve illustrate the evolution of technologies and the lifecycle of innovation within industries?

11. What role does the Innovation Funnel play in the innovation process, and how can organizations effectively manage and prioritize ideas?

12. How can understanding the Ten Faces of Innovation help organizations cultivate a culture of creativity, collaboration, and continuous improvement?

13. What are Intellectual Property Rights, and why are they essential for protecting innovations and fostering innovation ecosystems?

14. How do patents, trademarks, copyrights, trade secrets, and industrial designs differ in their protection of intellectual property, and when should each be used?

15. What are Geographic Indications, and how do they contribute to preserving cultural heritage, promoting local products, and fostering innovation?

16. How can organizations measure the impact and success of their innovation efforts using relevant metrics, and why is it essential to track innovation performance systematically?

References

1. Christensen, C. M. (1997). *The innovator's dilemma: When new technologies cause great firms to fail.* Harvard Business School Press.

2. Dyer, J. H., Gregersen, H. B., & Christensen, C. M. (2011). *The innovator's DNA: Mastering the five skills of disruptive innovators.* Harvard Business Press.

3. Tidd, J., & Bessant, J. (2018). *Managing innovation: Integrating technological, market and organizational change.* John Wiley & Sons.

4. Chesbrough, H. (2010). *Business model innovation: Opportunities and barriers.* Long Range Planning, 43(2-3), 354-363.

5. Edvardsson, B., & Olsson, J. (1996). *Key concepts for new service development.* Service Industries Journal, 16(2), 140-164.

6. Mair, J., & Marti, I. (2006). *Social entrepreneurship research: A source of explanation, prediction, and delight.* Journal of World Business, 41(1), 36-44.

7. Bhatti, Y., & Ventresca, M. (2015). *The socio-emotional dynamics of juggad: A study of entrepreneurs in Pakistan.* Journal of Business Ethics, 127(1), 177-190.

8. Chesbrough, H., & Appleyard, M. M. (2007). *Open innovation and strategy.* California Management Review, 50(1), 57-76.

9. Plattner, H., Meinel, C., & Leifer, L. (Eds.). (2012). *Design thinking: Understand – improve – apply.* Springer Science & Business Media.

10. Brem, A., & Wolfram, P. (2014). *Research and development from the bottom up—Introduction of terminologies for new product development in emerging markets.* R&D Management, 44(3), 250-262.

11. Khanna, T., & Palepu, K. (2010). *Winning in emerging markets: A roadmap for strategy and execution.* Harvard Business Press.

12. Kelley, T., & Littman, J. (2005). *The ten faces of innovation: IDEO's strategies for beating the devil's advocate and driving creativity throughout your organization.* Currency.

13. Landes, D. S. (2003). *The wealth and poverty of nations: Why some are so rich and some so poor.* WW Norton & Company.

14. Rigby, D. K., Sutherland, J., & Takeuchi, H. (2016). *Embracing agile.* Harvard Business Review, 94(5), 40-50.

15. Miller, G. J. (2012). *The development of indicators for the measurement of innovation.* Science and Public Policy, 39(6), 765-779.

WORKSHEETS

Business Plan

EcoTech Solutions Pvt. Ltd.

EcoTech Solutions Pvt. Ltd. is a forward-thinking Indian company committed to revolutionizing urban sustainability through advanced technology. Founded in 2024, the primary focus is to address pressing environmental challenges in India's rapidly growing cities. The core product offering includes a range of innovative, eco-friendly solutions designed to enhance urban infrastructure while minimizing ecological impact.

The flagship product, the Smart Waste Management System (SWMS), leverages the power of IoT (Internet of Things) and AI (Artificial Intelligence) to optimize waste collection and recycling processes. The SWMS uses real-time data to monitor waste levels, optimize collection routes, and reduce carbon emissions from waste vehicles. By integrating predictive analytics, the company ensures efficient resource management and fosters a circular economy.

In addition to waste management, Eco Tech Solutions offers solar-powered street lighting that utilizes renewable energy to reduce electricity consumption and lower municipal costs. The solar lights are equipped with motion sensors and intelligent controls to adapt to varying traffic conditions, further enhancing energy efficiency.

EcoTech Solution's Intelligent Water Management System employs advanced sensors and data analytics to monitor and control water distribution, detect leaks, and optimize usage. This system helps municipalities conserve water resources, prevent wastage, and ensure reliable access to clean water.

EcoTech Solutions is dedicated to fostering collaborations with municipal authorities, real estate developers, and private enterprises to implement technologies on a large scale. The goal is to contribute to sustainable urban development, improve quality of life, and support India's vision for a greener future. Through continuous innovation and a commitment to excellence, the company aim to be a leader in creating smart, sustainable cities across India.

Source: https://ecotechsolutions.net

Learning Objectives

1. Explain the Significance of a Business Plan
2. Identify different types of Business Plan
3. Explain the Contents of a Business Plan
4. Distinguish the Significance of an Executive Summary in a Business Plan
5. Develop and Present a Business Plan

"A solid business plan is crucial for turning your goals into actionable steps and achieving your objectives."

Introduction

A business plan is a road map and blueprint of the project. It is a comprehensive document that outlines a company's goals, strategies, and the steps necessary to achieve them. It serves as a roadmap for the business and is essential for both starting a new venture and guiding an existing one. A well-crafted business plan not only helps in securing funding but also serves as a blueprint for managing and growing the business.

Purpose of a Business Plan

A business plan is a vital document that supports strategic planning, financial management, and operational efficiency, contributing to the overall success and growth of the business. A business plan serves several key purposes:

1. **Direction**: It provides a clear roadmap for the business, outlining goals, strategies, and the steps needed to achieve them. This helps in staying focused and organized as the business grows.

2. **Attracting Investors:** A well-prepared business plan is essential for securing funding from investors or lenders. It demonstrates that the business idea is viable and that the entrepreneur has a solid strategy for success.

3. **Benchmark for Success:** It establishes benchmarks and milestones to measure progress. By comparing actual performance to the projections outlined in the plan, the business can assess its performance and make necessary adjustments.

4. **Operational Planning:** It helps in detailing the operational aspects of the business, including organizational structure, processes, and resource allocation. This ensures that all operational aspects are well thought out and managed efficiently.

5. **Strategic Planning**: It helps in identifying potential challenges and opportunities in the market, allowing the business to develop strategies to address them. This proactive approach can lead to better decision-making and risk management.

6. **Communication Tool:** It serves as a communication tool to share the business vision, strategy, and goals with stakeholders, including partners, employees, and advisors. This helps in aligning everyone with the business objectives.

7. **Understanding the Market:** It provides an in-depth analysis of the market, including target customers, competition, and industry trends. This understanding is crucial for developing effective marketing and sales strategies.

8. **Resource Allocation**: It helps in planning and allocating resources efficiently, including financial, human, and material resources. This ensures that resources are used effectively to support business goals.

Types of Business Plans

Business plans come in various types, each serving different purposes and audiences. Each type of business plan serves a specific purpose and can be tailored to meet the needs of the business and its stakeholders. Here are the main types:

1. **Traditional Business Plan**

   - **Detailed and Comprehensive:** Includes all sections like executive summary, market research, marketing strategy, operations, and financial projections.
   - **Purpose:** Used for seeking investment or loans, guiding long-term strategy, and managing complex businesses.

2. **Lean Business Plan**

   - **Concise and Focused:** Covers key components such as value proposition, customer segments, channels, revenue streams, and key metrics.
   - Purpose: Ideal for startups or businesses in the early stages looking for a streamlined approach to plan and pivot quickly.

3. **Startup Business Plan**

   - **Detailed Overview:** Focuses on the initial setup, including market analysis, business model, and financial projections.

- o **Purpose:** Used for launching new businesses and attracting initial funding.

4. **Internal Business Plan**

   - o **Operational Focused:** Targets internal stakeholders, detailing day-to-day operations, goals, and procedures.
   - o **Purpose:** Helps manage and guide internal processes and track performance.

5. **Strategic Business Plan**

   - o **Long-Term Focus:** Concentrates on the overall strategy, including vision, mission, and long-term goals.
   - o **Purpose:** Used for guiding long-term growth and aligning organizational objectives with strategic goals.

6. **Growth Business Plan**

   - o **Expansion Focused:** Details plans for business expansion, including new markets, products, or services.
   - o **Purpose:** Aim to secure funding for growth and manage the scaling process.

7. **Feasibility Business Plan**

   - o **Assessing Viability:** Evaluates the feasibility of a business idea or project, including market demand and financial viability.
   - o **Purpose:** Used to determine whether a business idea is worth pursuing before investing significant resources.

8. **One-Page Business Plan**

   - o **Brief Overview:** Summarizes key aspects of the business, such as goals, strategies, and key metrics, on a single page.
   - o **Purpose:** Useful for quick reference and as a pitch tool for investors or partners.

Box 5.1 One-Page Business Plan Template

Section	Details
Business Name	(Your Business Name Here)
Mission Statement	(A clear statement of your business's purpose and the value you offer)
Problem	(What is the main problem your business is solving?)
Solution	(What product or service are you offering to solve this problem?)
Target Market	(Who are your ideal customers? Describe your target market)
Competitive Advantage	(What makes your business unique? Why will customers choose you over competitors?)
Objectives	1. (Specific, measurable, and time-bound short-term goal) 2. (Medium-term) 3. (Long-term)
Revenue Model	Primary revenue streams: (e.g., product sales, subscriptions, services) Pricing strategy: (How will you price your products or services?)
Marketing Strategy	Channels: (e.g., social media, online ads, email campaigns, partnerships) Key marketing activities: (How will you promote your business?)
Operations Plan	**Key Activities:** (Daily tasks to run the business) **Key Resources:** (People, technology, or tools you need) **Suppliers/Partners:** (Important partners)
Financial Plan	Startup costs: (How much capital do you need to launch?) Revenue projections: (Expected income in year one) Break-even point: (When will you be profitable?)
Team	(Key members and their roles)
Milestones	1. (First key milestone in the next 6–12 months) 2. (Second key milestone) 3. (Third key milestone)
SWOT Analysis	

Contents of a Business Plan

A business plan is a comprehensive document that outlines a company's goals and the strategies to be achieved. It serves as a roadmap for the business and is often used to secure funding from investors or lenders. Business plans follow a broadly similar structure. Different business plans may have additional content based on their goals and the needs of their audience. The key sections in a business plan along with the average number of pages to be included in each section are furnished in **Table 5.1.**

Table 5.1. Contents of a Business Plan

Sl. No.	Contents	No. of Pages
1	Cover Page and Table of Contents	2
2	Executive Summary	1-2
3	Business Description	2-3
4	Organization and Management	2
5	Industry and Market Analysis	2-3
6	Product/Services	2
7	Marketing Plan	2-3
8	Operational Plan	2-3
9	Financial Plan	2-3
10	Appendices	4-3

Each section of the business plan should be tailored to fit the specific needs and circumstances of the business. The plan should be clear, concise, and well-organized to effectively communicate the business's vision and strategy to stakeholders. Here are the typical sections of a business plan:

1. Cover Page and Table of Contents

Every business plan should have a cover page. The cover page presents the first impression of your business plan to readers. The cover page should have a professional appearance. The table of contents is a roadmap to help the recipient peruse the list and easily find each section. The cover page should include the following:

- Company name
- Logo
- Contact person
- Website address, email, fax, and phone number
- Date and state of incorporation (if you have not formed yet, list where you will form)
- Confidentiality and nondisclosure statement

2. Executive Summary

The executive summary is a standalone document of two pages and is probably the most important section of the business plan. It is designed to be a complete yet concise business plan by itself. It is a snapshot of the entire business plan and is usually written last. The purpose of the executive summary is to give the reader a quick understanding of the business proposal and provide the whole picture. Bankers, and venture capitalists, competition readers, go through the executive summary. A full business plan is required to be submitted only by the shortlisted finalists. The executive summary is a formal document and should include the following information:

- **Overview**: Summary of the business, its mission, and vision.
- **Business Name and Location**: Basic details about the business.
- **Products or Services**: A concise description of what the business offers.
- **Market Opportunity**: Brief overview of the market and target customers.
- **Business Strategy**: Strategic Goals
- **Financial Highlights**: Summary of financial projections and funding requirements.
- **Management Team**: Key team members and their roles.

3. Business Description

Provide details on the history of the company, including how the company was formed and its locations of operation. If you have many locations, list your headquarters and states. If the company still needs to be formed, briefly explain how you got the idea for the business and where you will operate. This section should include the following information:

- **Company Overview**: Detailed information about the company, its history, and structure.
- **Mission and Vision**: The core purpose and long-term aspirations of the business.
- **Business Strategy**: Stakeholder analysis, SWOT analysis to achieve sustainable competitive advantage
- **Business Model**: Explanation of how the business makes money.
- **Business Objectives**: Short-term, medium-term and long-term goals.

4. Organization and Management

The management team is very important in any business. The success of the business mainly depends on the quality of the management team. This section should include the following information:

- **Business Structure**: The legal structure of the business (e.g., sole proprietorship, partnership, corporation).
- **Ownership**: Information about the business owners.
- **Management Team**: Detailed profiles of the management team and their expertise.
- **Advisors**: Information on any advisory board members or consultants.

5. Industry and Market Analysis

The Industry and Market Analysis section of a business plan is crucial as it provides a comprehensive overview of the environment in which your business will operate. This section demonstrates your understanding of the market, helps to identify opportunities and threats, and supports the feasibility of your business idea. Here's a detailed breakdown of what this section should include:

- **Industry Overview**: Insights into the industry, trends, and growth projections.
- **Target Market**: Detailed analysis of the target customer segments.
- **Market Needs**: Problems or needs that the business aims to address.
- **Competitive Analysis**: Identification and analysis of competitors, their strengths, and weaknesses.
- **Key Success Factors:** Identify critical factors for success within the industry, such as cost control, innovation, or customer service.
- **Regulations and Compliance**: Outline any regulations, standards, or compliance requirements that impact your industry and how your business will adhere to them.
- **Licensing and Permits**: Detail any necessary licenses or permits required to operate in your industry and the steps you have taken to secure them.
- **Market Size and Growth Potential**: Data and analysis on the size and growth potential of the target market.

6. Products or Services

A business plan's Products and Services section provides detailed information about what your business offers. This section should clearly explain your products or services, their unique features, and the benefits they provide to customers. Here's a detailed breakdown of what to include:

- **Product/Service Description**: Detailed information about the products or services offered.
- **Unique Selling Proposition (USP)**: What sets the product or service apart from competitors?
- **Lifecycle**: The stage of development or life cycle of the product or service.
- **Research and Development (R&D)**: Plans for future products or services and ongoing R&D.

- **IPR:** List any patents, trademarks, or other intellectual property protections related to your products or services. Explain your strategy for protecting and leveraging intellectual property.

7. Marketing Plan

The Marketing Plan should provide a clear roadmap for your marketing efforts, helping you to effectively reach and engage your target audience, drive sales, and achieve your business objectives. The Marketing Plan section of a business plan outlines how you intend to attract and retain customers, as well as how you will communicate your brand and product offerings to the market. It includes strategies for reaching your target audience, the tactics you'll use to implement these strategies, and the metrics you'll track to measure success. Here's a detailed breakdown of what to include:

- **Marketing Strategy:** Strategies for reaching the target market, including pricing, promotion, advertising, and distribution.
- **Sales Strategy:** The sales process, sales channels, and sales tactics.
- **Customer Acquisition and Retention:** Strategies for acquiring and retaining customers.
- **Branding:** The business's brand strategy and positioning.
- **Marketing Budget:** Provide a detailed breakdown of your marketing budget, specifying the amount allocated to each marketing tactic. Include projections for marketing spend versus expected returns, such as increased sales or market share.
- **Future Plan:** Introducing additional sizes and capabilities to cater to different industry needs. Exploring opportunities in international markets.

8. Operational Plan

The Operational Plan section of a business plan details how your business will function daily to achieve its goals. This includes the processes, resources, and logistics necessary to run the business efficiently. The Operational Plan should provide a clear blueprint for how your business will operate on a day-to-day basis, ensuring efficiency, quality, and compliance with all relevant regulations. Here's a comprehensive guide on what to include:

- **Operational Process**: How the business operates on a day-to-day basis.
- **Location**: The business's physical location(s) and facilities.
- **Technology**: Key technology and tools used in the business.
- **Suppliers and Vendors**: Key suppliers and vendors, and their relationships with the business.
- **Quality Assurance**: Measures in place to ensure product or service quality.

9. Financial Plan

The Financial Plan section of a business plan outlines the financial goals, projections, and strategies of your business. It provides a detailed analysis of the financial feasibility and sustainability of your business idea. This section is crucial for attracting investors and securing financing. The Financial Plan should provide a clear picture of your business's financial health, funding needs, and profitability potential. It will help you to manage your finances effectively and demonstrate the viability of your business to potential investors and lenders. Here's a comprehensive guide on what to include:

- **Revenue Model**: How the business generates revenue.
- **Financial Projections**: Detailed financial forecasts, including income statements, balance sheets, and cash flow statements.
- **Funding Requirements**: Amount of funding needed, how it will be used, and potential sources.
- **Break-even Analysis**: When the business expects to break even.
- **Exit Strategy**: Plan for investors to exit their investment.

10. Appendices

The Appendices section of a business plan contains supplementary materials that provide additional details and support the main content of the plan.

This section helps to keep the core sections of the business plan concise while allowing interested readers to delve deeper into specific areas if they wish. Appendices will provide comprehensive support and validation for the claims and projections made in your business plan, giving potential investors and stakeholders confidence in your business's potential. Here's what you might include in the Appendices:

- **Supporting Documents**: Additional documents such as resumes of the management team, organization chart, legal agreements, product photos, technical specifications, etc.
- **Legal Documents:** Copies of relevant business licenses and permits, Information on any IPR, copies of key contracts, agreements, or letters of intent with suppliers, customers, or partners.
- **Market Research Data**: Detailed data supporting market analysis, customer testimonials, and case studies.
- **Detailed Financial Projections**: Extended financial data and assumptions.
- **Press Coverage**: A feature article in industry weekly, interview with the CEO on local news channel.

Sample Business Plan

This business plan outlines the strategic approach Eco Tech Solutions Pvt. Ltd. will take to become the leading provider of sustainable urban solutions in India. With a focus on innovation, environmental responsibility, and customer satisfaction, Eco Tech Solutions is poised to make a significant impact on urban sustainability in India. This business plan provides a comprehensive overview of EcoTech Solutions, outlining its vision, market potential, products, marketing strategies, operational plans, and financial projections. It serves as a roadmap for the company's growth and a persuasive document for potential investors and stakeholders.

<u>Eco Tech Solutions Pvt. Ltd. Business Plan</u>

1. Cover Page and Table of Contents

Title: Eco Tech Solutions Pvt. Ltd.

Business Plan

Date: [Insert Date]

Prepared by: [Your Name]

Contact Information: [Your Contact Information]

Table of Contents

1. Executive Summary
2. Business Description
3. Organization and Management
4. Industry and Market Analysis
5. Products/Services
6. Marketing Plan
7. Operational Plan
8. Financial Plan
9. Appendices

2. Executive Summary

Company Overview

Eco Tech Solutions Pvt. Ltd. was founded in 2024 with a mission to drive sustainable technological advancements that benefit both businesses and the environment. It is a forward-thinking company committed to innovation in the eco-tech industry, providing solutions that address environmental challenges while promoting economic growth. It is a forward-thinking Indian company dedicated to revolutionizing urban sustainability through advanced technology. The mission is to address pressing environmental challenges in India's rapidly growing cities by providing innovative, eco-friendly solutions that enhance urban infrastructure while minimizing ecological impact. The core product offerings include smart waste management systems, green building technologies, and renewable energy solutions. The company aim to become the leading provider of sustainable urban solutions in India within the next five years. Founded by four members with a passion for bringing socio-economic and environmental transformation.

Vision and Mission

Vision: To be a global leader in sustainable technology solutions, creating a healthier planet for future generations.

Mission: To deliver cutting-edge, eco-friendly technologies that reduce carbon footprints, enhance energy efficiency, and promote sustainable practices across various industries.

Core Values

- **Sustainability:** Prioritizing environmental health in all our business practices.
- **Innovation:** Continuously developing advanced technologies to meet the needs of a changing world.
- **Integrity:** Maintaining transparency, honesty, and ethical practices in all operations.
- **Collaboration:** Building strong partnerships with stakeholders to drive collective progress.
- **Customer Focus:** Ensuring customer satisfaction through tailored solutions and exceptional service.

Team

Eco Tech Solutions was founded by a team of five members passionate about socio-economic and environmental transformation. The team combines expertise in technology, environmental science, finance, and market and business management, ensuring a well-rounded approach to addressing urban sustainability challenges.

Products and Services

Eco Tech Solutions offers a diverse range of products and services aimed at promoting sustainability:

- **Renewable Energy Systems:** Solar panels, wind turbines, and bioenergy solutions for residential, commercial, and industrial use.
- **Energy Efficiency Solutions:** Smart grids, energy management systems, and energy-efficient appliances.
- **Waste Management Technologies:** Advanced recycling systems, waste-to-energy solutions, and sustainable waste disposal methods.
- **Water Conservation Technologies:** Innovative irrigation systems, water purification, and rainwater harvesting solutions.
- **Sustainable Construction Materials:** Eco-friendly building materials and sustainable architecture consulting.

Market Analysis

Eco Tech Solutions targets urban municipalities, real estate developers, and businesses committed to sustainability. The market for green technologies in India is projected to grow at a CAGR of 15% over the next decade, driven by government initiatives and increasing consumer demand for eco-friendly solutions. The comprehensive market research indicates strong demand for products, particularly in metropolitan areas facing acute environmental challenges.

The global market for eco-friendly technologies is rapidly expanding, driven by increased environmental awareness, regulatory support, and technological advancements. Eco Tech Solutions is well-positioned to capitalize on this growth, with a focus on key markets including:

a. **North America:** High demand for renewable energy and sustainable construction materials.
b. **Europe:** Strong regulatory framework supporting eco-friendly technologies.
c. **Asia-Pacific:** Rapid urbanization and industrialization creating opportunities for waste management and water conservation solutions.

Competitive Advantage

Eco Tech Solutions differentiates itself through innovation, quality, and a deep understanding of the Indian market. The products are designed to meet local needs and regulatory requirements, offering superior performance and cost-effectiveness compared to international competitors. The company leverage strategic partnerships with local governments and businesses to ensure the successful implementation and adoption of our solutions. Eco Tech Solutions stands out in the market due to its:

- **Innovative R&D:** Commitment to research and development ensures cutting-edge solutions.
- **Strategic Partnerships**: Collaborations with leading tech firms, research institutions, and government bodies.
- **Experienced Team**: A skilled workforce with expertise in sustainability, engineering, and technology.
- **Customer-Centric Approach**: Tailored solutions to meet the specific needs of diverse clients.
- **Business Strategy**: SWOT analysis, Stakeholder analysis

Financial Projections

The financial model forecasts rapid revenue growth over the next five years, with profitability achieved by year three. Initial funding will be used to scale operations, invest in R&D, and expand the marketing efforts. We projected annual revenues of ₹100 crore by year five, driven by strong sales of waste management systems and renewable energy solutions. Eco Tech Solutions aims for steady growth with a focus on profitability and sustainability. Key financial projections for the next five years include:

Year 1: Establishing market presence and achieving breakeven.

Year 2-3: Expansion of product lines and market reach, targeting a 20% annual growth in revenue.

Year 4-5: Consolidation of market leadership with an expected 30% increase in net profit.

Strategic Goals

- **Innovation:** Launch new products and services that address emerging environmental challenges.
- **Market Expansion:** Enter new geographical markets and increase market share in existing ones.
- **Sustainability Leadership:** Set industry standards for sustainable practices and corporate social responsibility.
- **Customer Engagement:** Enhance customer satisfaction and loyalty through continuous improvement and feedback.

Conclusion: Eco Tech Solutions Pvt. Ltd. is dedicated to making a significant impact on the environment and the economy through innovative eco-tech solutions. With a clear vision, strong values, and strategic goals, the company is poised to lead the way in sustainability and technological advancement.

3. Business Description

Company Name: Eco Tech Solutions Pvt. Ltd.

Location: [Insert Location]

Business Structure: Private Limited Company

Vision: To lead the transformation of urban environments into sustainable, eco-friendly spaces.

Mission: To deliver cutting-edge, environmentally sustainable technologies that address urban challenges and promote green living.

Objectives:

- Achieve a 20% market share in India's urban sustainability sector within three years.
- Develop partnerships with at least ten major Indian cities for implementing our solutions.
- Reduce urban carbon footprint by 10% in partner cities within five years.

4. Organization and Management

CEO: Dr. Brijesh Patel

COO: Mr. Anil Goel

CTO: Dr. Rohini Gogte

CMO: Mr. Rajendra Singh

CFO: Mr. James Robert (CA)

Management Team: Comprises professionals with expertise in environmental science, urban planning, engineering, and business development.

Organisation Structure is given in Figure 5.1

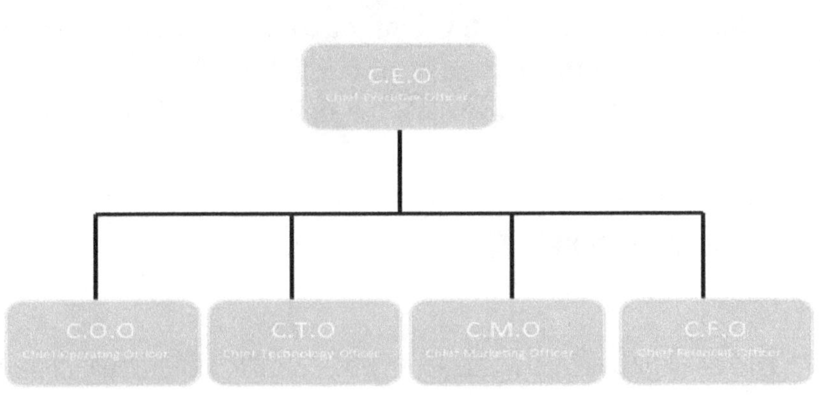

Figure 5.1. Organisation Structure

5. Industry and Market Analysis

Industry Overview: The urban sustainability sector in India is rapidly growing, driven by increasing urbanization and the need for sustainable development solutions.

Market Trends:

- Rising awareness and demand for eco-friendly urban solutions.
- Government initiatives promoting sustainable cities.

- Technological advancements in renewable energy and smart city infrastructure.

Target Market: Municipal governments, real estate developers, and urban planners in major Indian cities.

Stakeholder analysis of Eco Tech Solutions Pvt. Ltd

Stakeholder analysis for Eco Tech Solutions Pvt. Ltd. can help identify and understand the interests, influences, and potential impact of various stakeholders on the company's mission to drive sustainable technological advancements. Here's a detailed stakeholder analysis:

Key Stakeholders

1. Founders and Management Team

- **Interests:** Success and growth of the company, innovation in eco-tech, achieving the mission of sustainability.
- **Influence:** High – responsible for strategic decision-making and direction.
- **Impact:** Direct impact on the company's vision, operations, and market positioning.

2. Employees

- **Interests:** Job security, career growth, contribution to sustainability goals, fair compensation.
- **Influence:** Moderate to High – their performance and innovation drive the company's success.
- **Impact:** Essential in executing the company's projects and initiatives effectively.

3. Investors and Shareholders

- **Interests:** Return on investment, company growth, sustainability impact.
- **Influence:** High – provide necessary capital and influence major financial decisions.

- **Impact:** Financial stability and capability to scale operations and innovate.

4. Customers

- **Interests:** Reliable and innovative eco-friendly solutions, cost-effectiveness, and support for their own sustainability goals.
- **Influence:** High – customer satisfaction and adoption drive the company's revenue and market position.
- **Impact:** Directly impact the company's market reputation and sales.

5. Government and Regulatory Bodies

- **Interests:** Compliance with environmental regulations, promotion of sustainable practices, and economic development.
- **Influence:** High – can affect the company through policies, subsidies, and regulations.
- **Impact:** The regulatory environment can create opportunities or barriers for company operations.

6. Local Communities

- **Interests:** Environmental benefits, job creation, improved urban infrastructure, and reduced pollution.
- **Influence:** Moderate – support from the community can enhance the company's social license to operate.
- **Impact:** Positive community relations can lead to smoother project implementations and better public perception.

7. Environmental NGOs and Advocacy Groups

- **Interests:** Environmental protection, promotion of sustainable technologies and practices.
- **Influence:** Moderate – can influence public opinion and government policy.
- **Impact:** Partnerships can enhance the credibility and reach of sustainability initiatives.

8. Suppliers and Partners

- **Interests:** Long-term business relationships, fair trading terms, collaboration on sustainability.
- **Influence:** Moderate – reliability and quality of supply affect the company's operations.
- **Impact:** Strong partnerships can lead to better product offerings and operational efficiency.

Stakeholders Matrix is given in Table 5.2.

Table 5.2. Stakeholders Matrix

Stakeholders	Interest Level	Influence Level	Impact on Company
Founders and Management Team	High	High	Direct
Employees	High	Moderate to High	Essential
Investors and Shareholders	High	High	Financial Stability
Customers	High	High	Market Position
Government and Regulatory Bodies	High	High	Regulatory Environment
Local Communities	High	Moderate	Public Perception
Environmental NGOs and Advocacy Groups	High	Moderate	Credibility and Reach
Suppliers and Partners	Moderate	Moderate	Operational Efficiency

a. **High Influence/High Interest (Manage closely):** Founders, Leadership Team, Customers, Investors, and Government Bodies. These stakeholders are critical to the company's strategic direction and operational success.

b. **High Influence/Moderate Interest (Keep satisfied):** Media and PR can significantly impact public perception but may not be as interested in the company's specific operational details.

c. **Moderate Influence/High Interest (Keep Informed)**: Employees, as they are crucial for day-to-day operations and innovation, and local communities, whose support and advocacy can impact the company's operations.

d. **Moderate Influence/Moderate Interest (Monitor)**: Suppliers and Partners, whose collaboration is essential for operational success.

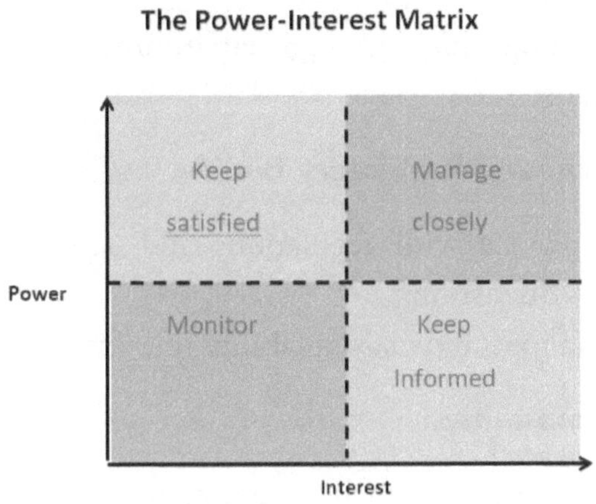

The Power-Interest Matrix

Figure 5.2. The Power-Interest Matrix

Strategies for Engagement

Eco Tech Solutions Pvt. Ltd. should engage with these stakeholders through targeted communication, collaboration, and transparent reporting to align interests and ensure mutual benefits.

1. **Founders and Management Team:**

   - Regular strategic meetings and clear communication of vision and goals.
   - Incentives tied to sustainability performance and innovation.

2. **Employees:**

   - Training and development programs focused on sustainability.
   - Open communication channels and recognition programs.

3. **Investors and Shareholders:**

   - Transparent reporting on financial performance and sustainability impact.
   - Engagement in strategic decisions and growth plans.

4. **Customers:**

   - Customer feedback mechanisms and continuous improvement of products.
   - Marketing highlighting environmental and economic benefits.

5. **Government and Regulatory Bodies:**

   - Compliance with regulations and active participation in policy discussions.
   - Collaboration on sustainability initiatives and projects.

6. **Local Communities:**

   - Community outreach programs and involvement in local sustainability projects.
   - Clear communication of benefits and contributions to the local environment.

7. **Environmental NGOs and Advocacy Groups:**

   - Partnerships on sustainability projects and campaigns.
   - Regular dialogue and collaboration on common goals.

8. **Suppliers and Partners:**

   - Long-term contracts and fair-trade practices.
   - Joint development of sustainable supply chains and technologies.

SWOT Analysis of Eco Tech Solutions Pvt. Ltd.

Strength	Opportunities
1. Innovative Product 2. Clear Mission and Vision 3. Founding Team 4. First Mover Advantage	1. Growing Urbanisation 2. Government Policies 3. Partnerships and Collaborations 4. Education and Awareness
Weakness	Threats
1. New Market 2. Resource Constraint 3. Scalability Issues 4. Branding	1. Competitive Market 2. Regulatory Changes 3. Economic Uncertainty 4. Technological Advancement

Strengths

1. **Innovative Product Offerings**: Strong focus on smart waste management systems, green building technologies, and renewable energy solutions, addressing critical urban sustainability issues.

2. **Clear Mission and Vision**: Dedicated to socio-economic and environmental transformation, which resonates well with current global and local sustainability trends.

3. **Founding Team**: Established by five passionate members, likely providing a strong foundation of commitment and diverse expertise.

4. **First Mover Advantage**: Being an early player in India's eco-tech sector could allow for establishing a strong market presence and brand recognition.

Weaknesses

1. **New Market Entrant**: As a company founded in 2024, it may face challenges related to brand recognition and trust compared to established competitors.

2. **Resource Constraints**: Potential limitations in funding, human resources, and technology infrastructure as a new startup.

3. **Scalability Issues**: Rapid growth ambitions might face operational and logistical challenges.

Opportunities

1. **Growing Urbanization**: Increasing urban populations in India drive demand for innovative and sustainable urban infrastructure solutions.
2. **Government Policies and Incentives**: Favorable government policies and subsidies for green technologies and sustainable practices can be leveraged.
3. **Partnerships and Collaborations**: Opportunities to partner with government bodies, NGOs, and other tech companies to expand reach and impact.
4. **Awareness and Education**: Increasing awareness and education on sustainability issues among businesses and consumers can drive demand for eco-friendly solutions.

Threats

1. **Competitive Market**: High competition from both local and international players in the eco-tech and sustainability sectors.
2. **Regulatory Changes**: Potential changes in government policies and regulations that could impact operations and growth.
3. **Economic Uncertainty**: Economic fluctuations and uncertainties can affect investment, consumer spending, and business operations.
4. **Technological Advancements**: Rapid technological changes may require continuous innovation and adaptation, posing a challenge for resource management.

By focusing on leveraging strengths and opportunities while addressing weaknesses and threats, Eco Tech Solutions Pvt. Ltd. can strategically position itself for growth and leadership in the sustainable urban solutions market in India.

Competitive Analysis: Key competitors include local sustainability consultancies and multinational firms. Eco Tech Solutions differentiates itself through its focus on cutting-edge technology and customized solutions for the Indian market.

5. Products/Services

i. **Smart Waste Management Systems**: Automated waste collection, sorting, and recycling technologies.

ii. **Green Building Technologies**: Energy-efficient building materials, water conservation systems, and sustainable construction practices.

iii. **Renewable Energy Solutions**: Solar, wind, and bioenergy systems tailored for urban environments.

iv. **Future Offerings**: Smart grid technologies, urban green spaces, and pollution control systems.

6. Marketing Plan

Target Audience: Municipal governments, real estate developers, and urban planners.

Value Proposition: Innovative, eco-friendly solutions that enhance urban infrastructure and sustainability, leading to cost savings and environmental benefits.

Marketing Channels:

- **Digital Marketing**: SEO, social media, email campaigns focused on sustainability.
- **Networking**: Participation in industry conferences, trade shows, and environmental forums.
- **Partnerships**: Collaborations with government agencies, NGOs, and industry leaders.

Sales Strategy:

- Demonstration projects to showcase the effectiveness of our solutions.
- Customized proposals based on the specific needs of each client.

- Long-term maintenance and support contracts to ensure ongoing success.

Operational Plan

- **Location**: Headquarters in [City, State].
- **Facilities**: Eco-friendly office space equipped with the latest technology.
- **Technology**: Use of state-of-the-art engineering tools and sustainability software.

Processes:

- **Project initiation:** Client consultation, needs assessment, proposal, and agreement.
- **Project execution:** Design, development, testing, and implementation.
- **Support and maintenance:** Regular system checks, updates, and customer support.

Staffing: Recruitment of skilled professionals in environmental science, engineering, and sales.

9. Financial Plan

Startup Costs: [Detailed list of startup expenses]

Revenue Projections:

- Year 1: ₹X
- Year 2: ₹Y
- Year 3: ₹Z

Expense Projections:

- Salaries
- Office rent
- Marketing
- Equipment and technology

Break-Even Analysis: Expected to break even within [X] months.

Funding Requirements: Seeking ₹X to cover initial startup costs and working capital.

10. Appendices

1. Resumes of Key Management
2. Detailed Financial Statements
3. Market Research Data
4. Legal Documents
5. Service Brochures and Marketing Materials

Box 5.2. Importance of Executive Summary in a Business Plan

a. The executive summary is a standalone document of one or two pages and is probably the most important and undeniably the most critical section of the business plan.

b. An executive summary is essentially an outline of your business plan. If your full business plan is a roadmap, your executive summary is your roadmap's roadmap

c. It provides a concise overview, including key elements such as the business concept, mission, vision, market opportunities, offered products and services, financial projections, and noteworthy achievements or milestones.

d. The executive summary is the first section to be read and must engage readers and excite them about the potential business idea. It should be the most carefully written of all the sections.

e. An executive summary is a written version of what is sometimes referred to as an elevator pitch. It should be able to explain the key ideas and features of business concepts in two or three minutes.

f. Keep the Executive Summary concise, one page.

g. It should capture the essence of your business plan, providing an overview without too many details.

h.   Tailor the Executive Summary to the audience, especially if pitching to investors or partners.

i.   The executive summary needs to demonstrate why this investment would be a smart financial decision.

j.   It is designed to be a complete yet concise business plan by itself. It is a snapshot of the entire business plan and is usually written last.

k.   The primary goals of the executive summary are to provide a condensed version of the main document, and to grab the attention of the reader(s).

l.   The purpose of the executive summary is to give the reader a quick understanding of the business proposal and provide the whole picture.

m.   Investors will read the executive summary to decide if they will even bother reading the rest of the business plan.

Box 5.3. Executive Summary Template

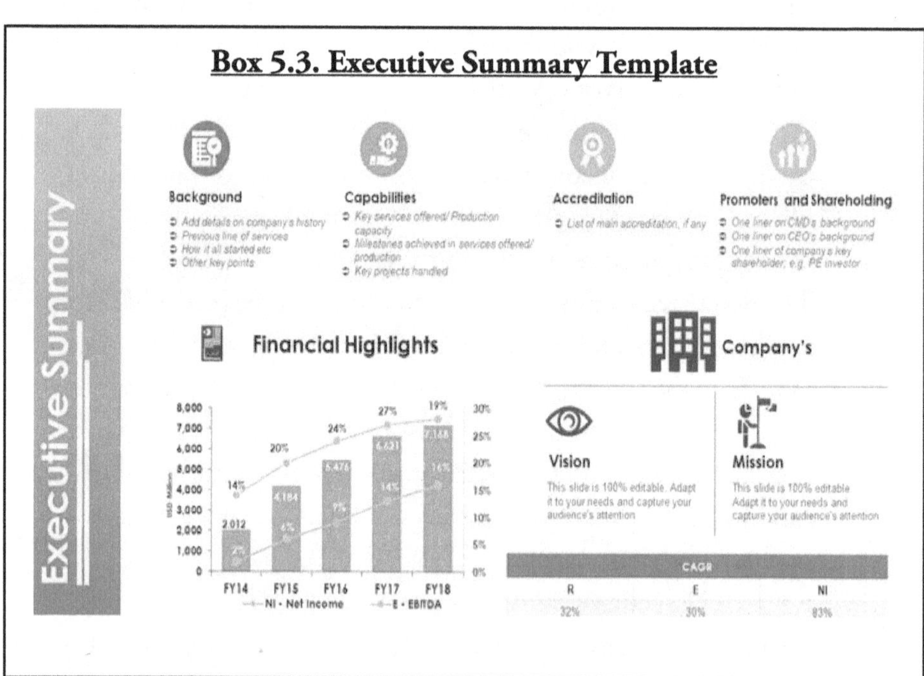

Presenting a Business Plan: Elevator Pitch

An elevator pitch is a brief, persuasive speech that succinctly describes an idea, product, or business in a short amount of time, typically 1 to 3 minutes—the approximate duration of an elevator ride. The goal of an elevator pitch is to capture the listener's interest and prompt further conversation or action. An elevator pitch is a succinct summary of a business proposal. An elevator pitch should be clear, compelling, and tailored to the audience you are addressing. Key elements of an effective elevator pitch include:

1. **Introduction**: Quickly introduce yourself and your company.
2. **Value Proposition**: Explain what your business does and the unique value it offers.
3. **Problem and Solution**: Identify the problem your target market faces and how your product or service solves it.
4. **Team**: The expertise, skills, and passion of the team members
5. **Call to Action**: Market you are going to serve, Funding required. End with a clear call to action, such as a request for a meeting, investment, or partnership.

Pitching your proposal effectively involves clear communication, engaging storytelling, and addressing the needs and interests of your audience. Here are steps to help you craft and deliver a compelling pitch:

1. Preparation

Know Your Audience: Understand who you are pitching to—investors, potential clients, partners, or stakeholders—and tailor your pitch accordingly.

Research: Gather relevant data, market research, and insights to support your proposal. Be ready to answer potential questions.

2. Structure Your Pitch

Start with a Hook: Capture attention immediately with a compelling story, interesting fact, or bold statement.

Problem Statement: Clearly articulate the problem or need that your proposal addresses. Make it relatable and urgent.

Solution: Present your solution, highlighting what makes it unique and effective. Explain how it solves the problem better than existing alternatives.

Value Proposition: Emphasize the benefits and value your proposal brings. Explain how it will improve the current situation.

Market Opportunity: Provide insights into the market size, target audience, and growth potential. Show that there is a demand for your solution.

Business Model: Explain how you plan to make money. Outline your revenue streams and pricing strategy.

Traction: If applicable, showcase any early success, such as user numbers, sales, partnerships, or testimonials. This demonstrates proof of concept.

Team: Introduce your team and their qualifications. Highlight relevant experience and why they are capable of executing the proposal.

Financial Projections: Provide a high-level overview of your financial projections, including revenue, expenses, and profitability.

Call to Action: End with a clear call to action. Specify what you are asking for, whether it's funding, a partnership, or another form of support.

3. Delivery

Be Clear and Concise: Keep your pitch focused and to the point. Avoid jargon and complex language.

Engage Your Audience: Make eye contact, use positive body language, and be enthusiastic about your proposal.

Use Visuals: If possible, incorporate visual aids like slides or prototypes to make your points more vivid and understandable.

Practice: Rehearse your pitch multiple times to build confidence and ensure smooth delivery. Time yourself to make sure you stay within the allotted time.

4. Follow-Up

Q&A Session: Be prepared to answer questions. Listen carefully and respond thoughtfully.

Provide Materials: Offer to send additional information, such as a detailed business plan, executive summary, or product demo.

Follow-Up: Send a thank-you email and any promised materials after the pitch. Keep the lines of communication open for further discussions.

Example of a Pitch Structure for Eco Tech Solutions Pvt. Ltd. Follow the steps given below

1. **Hook**: "Imagine a city where waste management is automated, buildings are energy-efficient, and renewable energy powers homes and businesses."

2. **Problem Statement**: "India's urban areas are growing rapidly, but this growth comes with significant environmental challenges, including waste management issues, inefficient buildings, and reliance on non-renewable energy sources."

3. **Solution**: "Eco Tech Solutions offers smart waste management systems, green building technologies, and renewable energy solutions that enhance urban infrastructure while minimizing ecological impact."

4. **Value Proposition**: "Our innovative solutions not only improve environmental sustainability but also reduce costs and improve quality of life for city residents."

5. **Market Opportunity**: "With India's urban population expected to reach 600 million by 2030, the demand for sustainable urban solutions is immense."

6. **Business Model**: "We generate revenue through the sale and maintenance of our technology solutions, as well as consulting services."

7. **Traction**: "We have successfully implemented our solutions in two major Indian cities, reducing their carbon footprint by 15%."

8. **Team**: "Our team consists of experts in environmental science, engineering, and urban planning, with a proven track record in sustainability projects."

9. **Financial Projections**: "We project revenues of ₹50 million in the first year, growing to ₹200 million by year three."

10. **Call to Action**: "We are seeking ₹100 million in funding to scale our operations and bring sustainable solutions to more cities across India. Join us in transforming urban living for a better future."

Box 5.4. Tips for Elevator Pitch

The most important things to be considered, while you are pitching your business proposal are:

1. Introduce yourself and find out to whom you are pitching.
2. Pitch with passion. The first impression is the best.
3. Demonstrate that you understand customer needs. Show how their needs are unmet by your competitors.
4. Explain the concept and the salient features of your business plan.
5. Customize the pitch based on whom you are pitching.
6. Summarize your business plan in a few sentences.
7. Explain, how you are going to raise finance for your venture.
8. Be clear about, what you want to get out of the pitch.
9. Explain why a potential investor should invest in your business proposal.
10. Develop a script for your pitch, to describe the problem and how you can solve it and market it.
11. Rehearse your elevator pitch and make it interesting.
12. Keep refining your pitch based on the feedback you receive and the results you achieve.
13. Remember you are not giving your whole pitch in the elevator; you are just trying to make them listen.
14. It is just like a trailer or teaser and the movie comes later.
15. At the end make an appointment for a detailed discussion.

16. Offer your business card at the end and also do not forget to collect a business card of the person to whom you have pitched.
17. The best place to pitch a business plan is at business conferences, business plan competitions, professional forums, meetings, and in front of investors and stakeholders.

Why Do Some Business Plans Fail?

Successful business planning requires thorough research, realistic financial projections, a clear value proposition, effective execution, and adaptability. Addressing these common pitfalls can help increase the likelihood of business plan success and overall sustainability. Business plans can fail for a variety of reasons, often related to shortcomings in planning, execution, or external factors. Here are some common reasons why business plans fail:

1. Lack of Market Research

Insufficient Understanding: Failing to thoroughly research and understand the target market can lead to misaligned products or services and poor customer acquisition strategies.

Overestimating Demand: Incorrectly estimating market demand can result in underperformance and financial losses.

2. Unclear Value Proposition

Lack of Differentiation: If the business doesn't clearly articulate what makes it unique or how it addresses customer pain points, it may struggle to attract and retain customers.

Poor Communication: Failing to effectively communicate the value of the product or service can lead to a lack of interest from potential customers.

3. Inadequate Financial Planning

Underestimating Costs: Misjudging initial costs, operational expenses, and cash flow requirements can lead to financial difficulties and insufficient funding.

Overly Optimistic Projections: Unrealistic revenue projections and timelines can result in poor financial management and unexpected shortfalls.

4. Weak Business Model

Unclear Revenue Streams: Failing to define how the business will generate revenue and sustain profitability can result in financial instability.

Ineffective Pricing Strategy: Incorrect pricing models can either deter potential customers or erode profit margins.

5. Poor Execution

Inadequate Management: Weak leadership and management can lead to poor decision-making, inefficiencies, and operational challenges.

Execution Gaps: Problems in implementing the business plan, such as delays in product development or operational inefficiencies, can hinder progress and success.

6. Lack of Adaptability

Failure to Pivot: Inability to adapt to changing market conditions, customer feedback, or unexpected challenges can prevent a business from staying relevant and competitive.

Rigid Strategies: Sticking too rigidly to the original plan without considering new information or changing circumstances can lead to missed opportunities.

7. Poor Marketing and Sales

Ineffective Marketing: Failing to effectively reach and engage the target audience can result in low brand awareness and poor customer acquisition.

Weak Sales Strategy: An ineffective sales approach or lack of a clear sales process can result in low conversion rates and revenue.

8. Inadequate Risk Management

Ignoring Risks: Not identifying or mitigating potential risks, such as market fluctuations, competitive threats, or regulatory changes, can jeopardize the business.

Lack of Contingency Plans: Failing to prepare for unexpected challenges or setbacks can lead to crises that are difficult to manage.

9. Unrealistic Goals and Timelines

Overambitious Objectives: Setting overly ambitious goals without a realistic plan for achieving them can lead to failure.

Unachievable Milestones: Setting unrealistic timelines and milestones can result in frustration and failure to meet objectives.

10. Poor Customer Focus

Neglecting Customer Needs: Failing to prioritize and address customer needs and feedback can lead to dissatisfaction and loss of business.

Inadequate Customer Support: Poor customer service and support can damage the company's reputation and customer loyalty.

Business Plan Softwares

Writing a business plan not only helps you stay on track as you start a new business but it can also help you secure funding. You can create one from scratch with a simple template, but business plan software often has features to make it easier, more nuanced, and overall better. Several business plan software options can help streamline the process of creating and managing a business plan. These tools can help with structuring, writing, and formatting business plans, making it easier to present a professional and comprehensive document. Some popular ones include:

a. **LivePlan:** Offers customizable templates, financial forecasting tools, and collaboration features.

b. **Bizplan:** Provides a visual builder, guided templates, and progress tracking.

c. **Enloop:** Features automated business plan writing, financial forecasting, and performance scoring.

d. **PlanGuru:** Focuses on budgeting, forecasting, and financial planning.

e. **Cuttles**: Offers step-by-step guidance and templates for creating business plans and financial models.

f. **Wrike:** It is a project management app that doubles as a collaborative work management tool and works well for businesses of all sizes.

g. **Smartsheet:** Powerful project management software

Procedure for Setting Up an Enterprise

Setting up an enterprise involves careful planning, legal and financial setup, operational arrangements, and effective marketing. By following these steps and staying adaptable, you can build a strong foundation for your business and work towards long-term success. **Figure 5.3** provides a Procedure and Formalities for Setting up a Business Enterprise. The steps involved in setting up an enterprise are given below

1. Selection of a Project: product or service selection, location selection, project feasibility study, business plan preparation, prepare project profile
2. Decide on the constitution
3. Obtain online registration to get an eight-digit DIN unique number
4. Obtain clearances from departments as applicable
5. Infrastructure - Land & Building, Water and Power Supply
6. Sourcing Process, Raw Materials, Machineries and Equipment
7. Prepare project report
8. Apply and obtain funding
9. Comply with legal aspects
10. Implement and obtain final clearances

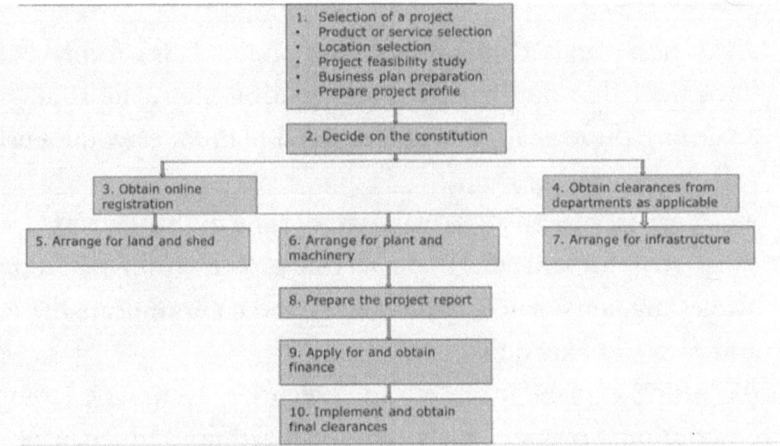

Figure 5.3. Procedure for Setting up an Enterprise

Key Takeaways

- A business plan is a blueprint of your project. It is a formal written document that outlines the goals of a business, the strategy for achieving those goals, and the detailed plan for how the business will operate and grow.

- The purpose of a business plan is to outline the business's goals and the strategy for achieving them, serve as a roadmap for management, attract investors or secure financing, and communicate the vision and plan to stakeholders.

- A business plan includes an executive summary, company description, market analysis, organization and management details, description of products or services, marketing and sales strategy, funding request, financial projections, and appendices with additional documents.

- The executive summary is a standalone document one or two pages, crucial in a business plan as it provides a concise overview of the key points, capturing the essence of the plan.

- The executive summary highlights the business's mission, objectives, products or services, market potential, financial projections, and funding needs, aiming to engage and inform investors and stakeholders quickly.

- An elevator pitch is a brief, compelling summary of a business or idea, delivered in 2 to 3 minutes, aimed at capturing interest and conveying key points quickly.

- Business plans come in several types: Traditional (detailed and comprehensive), Lean (concise and focused), Startup (for new ventures), Strategic (long-term goals), Internal (guiding operations), Feasibility (assessing viability), one-page (concise in a single page)

- A one-page business plan condenses the business concept, target market, value proposition, revenue model, strategy, and key financials into a single, concise page.

- Business plans fail due to unrealistic assumptions, inadequate market research, poor planning, insufficient financial forecasting, lack of adaptability, and weak execution.
- Business plan software, such as LivePlan, Bizplan, Enloop, PlanGuru, Wrike, Smartsheet, and Cuttles, helps streamline the creation, formatting, and management of business plans with various features like templates, financial forecasting, and progress tracking.
- The procedure for setting up a business enterprise involves the identification of business opportunities, researching and planning, forming a team, registering the business, obtaining necessary licenses and permits, securing funding, setting up operations, and launching the business.

Key Terms

Executive Summary, Organisation Structure, Stakeholder Analysis, Market Analysis, Marketing Plan, Business Description, Business Plan, Business Model, Target Market, Competitive Analysis, SWOT Analysis, Industry Analysis, Forecasting, Marketing Strategy, Sales Strategy, Financial Projections, Revenue Streams, Revenue Model, Financial Projections, Market Research, Stakeholder Matrix, Operational Plan, Product Development, Management Team, Financial Plan, Funding Requirements, Business Objectives, Risk Management, Customer Segmentation, Value Proposition, Vision, Mission, Values, Strategic Goals, Objectives, Lean Business Plan, Startup Business Plan, Internal Business Plan, Traditional Business Plan, Strategic Business Plan, Growth Business Plan, Feasibility Business Plan, Contents of a Business Plan, Customer Acquisition, Customer Retention, Branding, Marketing Budget, Quality Assurance, Business Strategy, Business Plan Software, Break Even Analysis, Elevator Pitch, One Page Business Plan, Pricing Strategy, Market Trends, Strategic Partnerships, Key Performance Indicators (KPIs), Legal Structure, Exit Strategy.

Quiz – Multiple Choice Questions

1. What is the primary purpose of a business plan?

    a.   To impress potential customers
    b.   To serve as a blueprint for the business
    c.   To comply with government regulations
    d.   To outline marketing strategies

2. Which section of a business plan outlines the company's long-term goals?

    a.   Executive Summary
    b.   Marketing Plan
    c.   Financial Plan
    d.   Vision Statement

3. A business plan is typically used by:

    a.   Potential investors
    b.   Company management
    c.   Bank loan officers
    d.   All of the above

4. What should be included in the executive summary of a business plan?

    a.   Detailed financial statements
    b.   A brief overview of the business
    c.   A list of employees
    d.   Technical specifications

5. Which part of the business plan details the products or services offered?

    a.   Marketing Plan
    b.   Operations Plan

   c. Product/Service Line

   d. Executive Summary

6. The section that explains the company's organizational structure is:

   a. Executive Summary

   b. Management Team

   c. Marketing Plan

   d. Financial Plan

7. In a business plan, what is a SWOT analysis used for?

   a. Assessing financial performance

   b. Identifying strengths, weaknesses, opportunities, and threats

   c. Evaluating marketing strategies

   d. Outlining operational procedures

8. What is the main focus of the marketing plan section?

   a. Hiring employees

   b. Managing daily operations

   c. Promoting and selling products or services

   d. Financial forecasting

9. How often should a business plan be updated?

   a. Every month

   b. Only when seeking investors

   c. Annually or as needed

   d. Never, it's a one-time document

10. Which section of the business plan projects future revenue and expenses?

   a. Marketing Plan

   b. Financial Plan

   c. Managesent Team

   d. Executive Summary

11. A business plan should include which of the following to attract investors?

    a. Prsonal history of the owner

    b. Market analysis and growth potential

    c. Detailed product descriptions

    d. Customer testimonials

12. The operational plan section of a business plan focuses on:

    a. Day-to-day business activities

    b. Financial projections

    c. Marketing strategies

    d. Long-term goals

13. What is a key characteristic of a well-written business plan?

    a. Lengthy and detailed

    b. Clear, concise, and realistic

    c. Vague and general

    d. Full of technical jargon

14. Which section would detail the company's legal structure?

    a. Executive Summary

    b. Financial Plan

    c. Company Description

    d. Marketing Plan

15. The purpose of the financial projections in a business plan is to:

    a. Predict future profitability

    b. Determine employee salaries

    c. Identify market trends

    d. Plan for daily operations

16. In a business plan, what is a break-even analysis?

    a. The point where total revenue equals total expenses

    b. An evaluation of product features

   c. A strategy for entering a new market

   d. A method of setting product prices

17. Which section would discuss the business's competitive advantage?

   a. Executive Summary

   b. Market Analysis

   c. Product/Service Line

   d. Financial Plan

18. What role do appendices play in a business plan?

   a. Summarize the business objectives

   b. Provide additional detailed information

   c. Outline the marketing strategy

   d. Describe the management team

19. The section that outlines the target market and customer demographics is:

   a. Executive Summary

   b. Market Analysis

   c. Financial Plan

   d. Operations Plan

20. What is the significance of a business plan for a startup?

   a. It's a formality with no real use

   b. It's a tool to guide the startup's growth and secure funding

   c. It's only needed for legal reasons

   d. It's optional and often skipped

ANSWERS:

   1. b) To serve as a blueprint for the business

   2. d) Vision Statement

   3. d) All of the above

   4. b) A brief overview of the business

   5. c) Product/Service Line

6. b) Management Team
7. b) Identifying strengths, weaknesses, opportunities, and threats
8. c) Promoting and selling products or services
9. c) Annually or as needed
10. b) Financial Plan
11. b) Market analysis and growth potential
12. a) Day-to-day business activities
13. b) Clear, concise, and realistic
14. c) Company Description
15. a) Predict future profitability
16. a) The point where total revenue equals total expenses
17. b) Market Analysis
18. b) Provide additional detailed information
19. b) Market Analysis
20. b) It's a tool to guide the startup's growth and secure funding

Exercise 5.1

Create a Business Plan

Objective: To create a comprehensive business plan for a new business venture, covering all essential components. This exercise will help participants understand the structure and importance of each section of a business plan.

Instructions:

1. **Form Groups**: Divide participants into small groups of 3-5 members.
2. **Choose a Business Idea**: Each group should brainstorm and select a unique business idea.
3. **Develop a Business Plan**: Using the guidelines below, each group will create a detailed business plan for their chosen business idea.

Business Plan Components:

1. **1. Executive Summary**

   - Briefly describe the business idea.
   - State the mission and vision of the business.
   - Highlight the unique value proposition.

2. **Company Description**

   - Provide an overview of the business.
   - Outline the business model and legal structure.
   - Explain the industry and market needs the business will address.

3. **Market Analysis**

   - Identify the target market and customer demographics.
   - Conduct a SWOT analysis (Strengths, Weaknesses, Opportunities, Threats).
   - Analyze competitors and market trends.

4. **Organization and Management**

   o   Describe the organizational structure.

   o   Detail the management team and their roles.

   o   Include brief profiles highlighting relevant experience.

5. **Products or Services**

   o   Describe the products or services offered.

   o   Explain the benefits and features.

   o   Discuss the product lifecycle and any plans for future products/services.

6. **Marketing and Sales Strategy**

   o   Develop a marketing strategy to reach the target audience.

   o   Outline sales tactics and channels.

   o   Explain the pricing strategy and promotional activities.

7. **Operations Plan**

   o   Detail the day-to-day operations of the business.

   o   Discuss the location, facilities, and technology needed.

   o   Include supply chain and logistics plans.

8. **Financial Plan**

   o   Provide financial projections including income statements, cash flow statements, and balance sheets for the next 3-5 years.

   o   Outline the funding requirements and potential sources of funding.

   o   Conduct a break-even analysis.

9. **Appendices**

   o   Include any additional documents such as resumes, legal agreements, product photos, or other relevant information.

Presentation:

Each group will present their business plan to the class, simulating a pitch to potential investors. Presentations should be 10-15 minutes long, followed by a Q&A session.

Evaluation Criteria:

- **Clarity and Completeness**: Is the business plan well-organized and comprehensive?
- **Creativity and Innovation**: How unique and innovative is the business idea?
- **Market Understanding**: Does the group demonstrate a thorough understanding of their target market and competitive landscape?
- **Feasibility**: Is the business plan realistic and achievable?
- **Presentation Skills**: How effectively does the group communicate their business plan?

Submission:

Each group should submit a written business plan document, including all the components listed above, by the end of the exercise period.

Reflection:

After the presentations, each group should reflect on the process, discussing what they learned and how they can apply these lessons to real-world business planning.

Activity 5.1

Develop and Deliver an Elevator Pitch

Objective: To develop and deliver a concise and compelling elevator pitch for a business idea, focusing on key elements of the business plan.

Instructions:

1. **Form Groups**: Divide participants into small groups of 3-5 members.

2. **Choose a Business Idea**: Each group should brainstorm and select a unique business idea.

3. **Develop an Elevator Pitch**: Each group will create a 3 minutes elevator pitch for their business idea, incorporating the essential elements listed below.

Key Elements of the Elevator Pitch:

1. **Introduction**

   - Introduce the name of the business.
   - State the mission of the business concisely.

2. **Problem Statement**

   - Identify the problem or need in the market that the business aims to address.
   - Explain why this problem is significant.

3. **Solution**

   - Describe the product or service offered by the business.
   - Highlight how it solves the problem or meets the need identified.

4. **Unique Value Proposition**

   - Explain what makes the business unique.
   - Emphasize the key benefits and advantages over competitors.

5. **Market Opportunity**

   - Briefly outline the target market.
   - Mention the market size and growth potential.

6. **Business Model**

   - Summarize how the business will make money.
   - Highlight the key revenue streams.

7. **Call to Action**

   o End with a clear call to action, such as inviting potential investors to a meeting or requesting contact information.

Activity Steps:

1. **Brainstorming and Development (20 minutes)**

   o Each group brainstorms their business idea and drafts their elevator pitch.

   o Ensure the pitch is clear, concise, and compelling, staying within the 3 minutes limit.

2. **Practice and Refinement (10 minutes)**

   o Groups practice their pitch internally, refining it based on feedback from group members.

   o Focus on clarity, delivery, and staying within the time limit.

3. **Pitch Presentation (30 minutes)**

   o Each group presents their elevator pitch to the class.

   o Timekeepers ensure each pitch does not exceed 3 minutes.

4. **Feedback and Discussion (20 minutes)**

   o After each pitch, the audience (other participants and facilitator) provides constructive feedback.

   o Discuss strengths, areas for improvement and overall effectiveness of the pitch.

Evaluation Criteria:

- **Clarity**: Is the pitch easy to understand?
- **Conciseness**: Does the pitch stay within the three-minute limit?
- **Engagement**: Is the pitch engaging and compelling?
- **Problem-Solution Fit**: Does the pitch identify a problem and present an effective solution?

- **Unique Value Proposition**: Is the unique value of the business communicated?
- **Delivery**: Is the pitch delivered confidently and professionally?

Reflection:

After all pitches are presented and feedback is given, each group should reflect on the following:

- What went well in their pitch?
- What could be improved?
- How can they apply the feedback to improve their business plan and future pitches?

Submission:

Each group should submit a written version of their elevator pitch, including the key elements outlined above, by the end of the activity period.

Situation Analysis 5.1

Business Plan for a Sustainable Packaging Company

Objective: To conduct a situational analysis for a new sustainable packaging company, identifying internal and external factors that can impact the business.

Instructions:

1. **Form Groups**: Divide participants into small groups of 3-5 members.
2. **Assign Roles**: Assign specific roles within each group (e.g., Market Researcher, SWOT Analyst, Competitor Analyst, Environmental Analyst, etc.).
3. **Develop Situational Analysis**: Each group will conduct a comprehensive situational analysis based on the components listed below.

Components of the Situational Analysis:

1. **Company Overview**

   - Briefly describe the business idea.
   - State the mission and vision of the company.
   - Define the core products and services.

2. **Market Analysis**

   - **Market Size and Growth**: Assess the size and growth potential of the sustainable packaging market.
   - **Target Market**: Identify and describe the target market segments.
   - **Customer Needs and Preferences**: Analyze customer needs and preferences regarding sustainable packaging solutions.

3. **Competitive Analysis**

   - **Key Competitors**: Identify and profile key competitors in the market.
   - **Competitive Advantage**: Evaluate the strengths and weaknesses of competitors.
   - **Market Position**: Determine the market position of the new company relative to competitors.

4. **SWOT Analysis**

   - **Strengths**: Internal capabilities that provide an advantage (e.g., innovative technology, strong management team).
   - **Weaknesses**: Internal limitations that could hinder progress (e.g., limited funding, lack of market presence).
   - **Opportunities**: External factors that the company can capitalize on (e.g., growing demand for eco-friendly products, regulatory support).
   - **Threats**: External factors that could pose challenges (e.g., economic downturn, intense competition).

5. **PESTLE Analysis**

   o **Political**: Government policies, regulations, and political stability affecting the business.

   o **Economic**: Economic factors such as market trends, inflation rates, and economic growth impact the industry.

   o **Social**: Societal trends and cultural factors influencing customer behavior and market demand.

   o **Technological**: Technological advancements and innovations relevant to sustainable packaging.

   o **Legal**: Legal requirements and regulations specific to the industry.

   o **Environmental**: Environmental considerations and sustainability practices.

6. **Internal Analysis**

   o **Resources and Capabilities**: Assess the company's resources and capabilities (e.g., financial resources, human capital, technology).

   o **Operational Efficiency**: Evaluate the efficiency of current operations and processes.

   o **Organizational Structure**: Describe the organizational structure and management team.

Activity Steps:

1. **Research and Data Collection (30 minutes)**

   o Each group researches their assigned areas using available resources (internet, market reports, etc.).

   o Gather relevant data and information for each component of the situational analysis.

2. **Analysis and Discussion (30 minutes)**

   o Groups analyze the collected data, discussing their findings and implications for the business.

- Complete each component of the situational analysis based on the research.

3. **Presentation and Feedback (30 minutes)**

    - Each group presents their situational analysis to the class.
    - Presentations should be 5-10 minutes long, followed by a Q&A session.
    - The audience (other participants and facilitator) provides constructive feedback.

Evaluation Criteria:

- **Thoroughness**: Is the analysis comprehensive and well-researched?
- **Relevance**: Are the findings relevant to the sustainable packaging industry and the new business?
- **Insightfulness**: Does the analysis provide valuable insights and strategic implications?
- **Presentation**: Is the information presented clearly and professionally?

Reflection:

After all presentations, each group should reflect on the following:

- What were the key insights from their situational analysis?
- How can these insights inform the development of their business plan?
- What areas of the analysis were most challenging, and how can they improve their research and analytical skills?

Submission:

Each group should submit a written report of their situational analysis, including all components listed above, by the end of the activity period.

Simulation Game 5.1

<u>Launch Your Startup</u>

Objective: To simulate the experience of launching a startup, allowing students to apply their knowledge of business plans in a dynamic and interactive environment.

Instructions:

4. **Form Teams**: Divide participants into small teams of 4-6 members.
5. **Select a Business Idea**: Each team will brainstorm and choose a business idea for their startup.
6. **Develop Business Plan Components**: Teams will develop key components of their business plan through various stages of the simulation.

Game Structure:

The simulation will be divided into four main stages, with specific tasks and challenges in each stage. Teams will earn points based on their performance in each stage.

Stage 1: Business Concept and Planning (30 minutes)

Tasks:

1. **Brainstorming Session**: Teams brainstorm and select a unique business idea.
2. **Mission and Vision**: Define the mission and vision statements for the business.
3. **SWOT Analysis**: Conduct a SWOT analysis to identify strengths, weaknesses, opportunities, and threats.

Deliverables:

- Business idea description
- Mission and vision statements
- SWOT analysis report

Scoring Criteria:

- Creativity and originality of the business idea (10 points)
- Clarity and relevance of mission and vision statements (10 points)
- Depth and insightfulness of SWOT analysis (10 points)

Stage 2: Market Research and Analysis (30 minutes)

Tasks:

1. **Market Analysis**: Research the market size, growth potential, and target market segments.
2. **Competitive Analysis**: Identify key competitors and evaluate their strengths and weaknesses.
3. **Customer Survey**: Design a short survey to understand customer needs and preferences.

Deliverables:

- Market analysis report
- Competitor analysis report
- Summary of customer survey findings

Scoring Criteria:

- Thoroughness of market research (10 points)
- Insightfulness of competitor analysis (10 points)
- Relevance and clarity of customer survey findings (10 points)

Stage 3: Product Development and Marketing Strategy (30 minutes)

Tasks:

1. **Product/Service Description**: Define the core product or service and its unique value proposition.
2. **Marketing Strategy**: Develop a marketing strategy, including pricing, promotion, and distribution plans.
3. **Sales Forecast**: Create a sales forecast for the first year of operation.

Deliverables:

- Detailed product/service description
- Marketing strategy plan
- Sales forecast report

Scoring Criteria:

- Clarity and differentiation of the product/service (10 points)
- Feasibility and creativity of the marketing strategy (10 points)
- Accuracy and realism of the sales forecast (10 points)

Stage 4: Financial Planning and Pitch (30 minutes)

Tasks:

1. **Financial Projections**: Develop financial projections, including income statements, cash flow statements, and balance sheets for the first year.
2. **Funding Plan**: Outline the funding requirements and potential sources of funding.
3. **Elevator Pitch**: Prepare a 3 minutes elevator pitch to present to potential investors.

Deliverables:

- Financial projections report
- Funding plan
- Elevator pitch presentation

Scoring Criteria:

- Accuracy and completeness of financial projections (10 points)
- Viability of the funding plan (10 points)
- Persuasiveness and clarity of the elevator pitch (10 points)

Game Flow:

1. **Introduction (10 minutes)**: Explain the rules and objectives of the simulation game.

2. **Stage 1 (30 minutes)**: Teams work on the business concept and planning tasks.
3. **Stage 2 (30 minutes)**: Teams conduct market research and analysis.
4. **Stage 3 (30 minutes)**: Teams develop their product and marketing strategy.
5. **Stage 4 (30 minutes)**: Teams work on financial planning and prepare their elevator pitch.
6. **Presentations and Scoring (30 minutes)**: Each team presents an elevator pitch, and judges score their performance based on the criteria.

Final Evaluation:

At the end of the simulation, the scores for each stage are tallied. The team with the highest total score wins the game. Provide constructive feedback to all teams, highlighting strengths and areas for improvement.

Reflection:

After the simulation, hold a reflection session where teams discuss:

- What they learned about developing a business plan
- Challenges they faced during the simulation
- How they can apply these lessons to real-world business planning

Submission:

Each team should submit a complete business plan document, including all components developed during the simulation, by the end of the activity period.

Role Play 5.1

Founders' Meeting to Develop a Business Plan

Objective: To engage students in a role, play that simulates the process of developing a business plan by five founders of a new venture. Each founder will take on a specific role with distinct responsibilities, fostering collaboration and strategic thinking.

Roles and Responsibilities:

1. **CEO (Chief Executive Officer):**

   o Lead the discussion and ensure all aspects of the business plan are covered.

   o Focus on the overall vision, mission, and strategic direction of the company.

   o Make final decisions and ensure team alignment.

2. **CFO (Chief Financial Officer):**

   o Handle financial projections, funding requirements, and financial strategy.

   o Develop income statements, cash flow statements, and balance sheets.

   o Identify potential investors and funding sources.

3. **CMO (Chief Marketing Officer):**

   o Conduct market research and develop marketing strategies.

   o Define the target market, customer needs, and competitive analysis.

   o Create marketing and sales plans, including pricing and promotion.

4. **COO (Chief Operating Officer):**

   o Oversee operational planning and logistics.

   o Detail the day-to-day operations, supply chain, and production processes.

   o Ensure operational efficiency and resource allocation.

5. **CTO (Chief Technology Officer):**

   o Focus on product development and technological innovation.

- Outline the product/service features, development roadmap, and technical requirements.
- Ensure the technology aligns with the company's vision and market needs.

Scenario:

The founders of "EcoSmart Packaging," a sustainable packaging company, are meeting to develop a comprehensive business plan. They need to address all critical components to attract investors and guide their startup to success.

Role Play Instructions:

1. **Introduction (10 minutes):**

   - Explain the objectives and rules of the role play.
   - Assign roles to participants and provide role-specific guidelines.

2. **Preparation (20 minutes):**

   - Founders individually prepare their points and gather necessary information based on their roles.
   - They can use provided templates and research materials.

3. **Role Play (40 minutes):**

   - Founders convene for the meeting, led by the CEO.
   - Each founder presents their findings and proposals in their area of responsibility.
   - Collaborative discussion to integrate each section into a cohesive business plan.

4. **Presentation and Feedback (30 minutes):**

   - Founders present their final business plan to a panel of judges or the class.

- ○ Judges provide constructive feedback on the business plan's feasibility, comprehensiveness, and strategic alignment.

Meeting Agenda:

1. **Opening Remarks by CEO (5 minutes):**

   - ○ Introduce the company's mission, vision, and overall business idea.
   - ○ Outline the meeting agenda and objectives.

2. **Market Analysis by CMO (10 minutes):**

   - ○ Present market research findings.
   - ○ Define target market segments, customer needs, and competitive landscape.

3. **Product Development by CTO (10 minutes):**

   - ○ Describe the product/service features and development roadmap.
   - ○ Discuss technological innovations and requirements.

4. **Operational Plan by COO (10 minutes):**

   - ○ Detail the day-to-day operations, supply chain, and logistics.
   - ○ Discuss operational efficiency and resource allocation.

5. **Financial Plan by CFO (10 minutes):**

   - ○ Present financial projections, including income statements, cash flow statements, and balance sheets.
   - ○ Outline funding requirements and potential sources.

6. **Discussion and Integration (20 minutes):**

   - ○ Open floor for collaborative discussion to integrate each section.
   - ○ Address any gaps, or overlaps, and ensure alignment with the overall strategy.

7. **Closing Remarks by CEO (5 minutes)**:

   o   Summarize key points and next steps.

   o   Assign any follow-up tasks and set deadlines.

Evaluation Criteria:

- **Comprehensive Coverage**: Does the business plan cover all essential components?
- **Strategic Alignment**: Are all sections aligned with the company's mission and vision?
- **Feasibility**: Is the plan realistic and achievable?
- **Collaboration**: How well did the founders work together to develop the plan?
- **Presentation**: Is the business plan presented clearly and professionally?

Reflection:

After the role-play, hold a reflection session where participants discuss:

- What they learned about developing a business plan.
- The challenges they faced in their roles.
- How collaboration and role-specific responsibilities contribute to a successful business plan.

Submission:

Each team should submit a final written business plan, incorporating feedback received during the presentation, by the end of the activity period.

Project 5.1

Market Research for Your Business Plan

Objective: Designing a market research project for students developing a business plan involves several key steps. This project will help them gather essential information to understand the market, identify target customers, and evaluate the competitive landscape. Here's a structured approach for them:

Market Research Project Outline

1. Define Research Objectives

Purpose: Understand the market to develop a viable business plan.

Objectives:

- Identify target market demographics.
- Assess market size and growth potential.
- Analyze competitors.
- Understand customer needs and preferences.
- Evaluate potential market entry barriers.

2. Research Design

Types of Research:

a. Primary Research: Surveys, interviews, focus groups.
b. Secondary Research: Industry reports, market analysis, academic journals, and government publications.

3. Develop Research Questions

- What are the key demographics of the target market?
- What is the current market size and projected growth?
- Who are the main competitors and what are their strengths/ weaknesses?
- What are the customer pain points and needs?
- What trends are influencing the market?

4. Data Collection Methods

a. Primary Research:

- **Surveys:** Online or paper questionnaires to gather quantitative data.

- **Interviews**: One-on-one conversations with industry experts, potential customers, and stakeholders.
- **Focus Groups**: Small group discussions to gain qualitative insights.

b. Secondary Research:

Literature Review: Analyze existing studies and reports.

Competitive Analysis: Review competitor websites, marketing materials, and financial reports.

5. Sampling Plan

Target Population: Define who will be included in the research (e.g., age, gender, location, income level).

Sample Size: Determine the number of participants needed for reliable data.

Sampling Method: Decide on random sampling, stratified sampling, or convenience sampling.

6. Data Analysis

a. **Quantitative Analysis**: Use statistical tools to analyze survey data (e.g., SPSS, Excel).
b. **Qualitative Analysis:** Identify themes and patterns from interviews and focus groups.
c. **SWOT Analysis:** Assess strengths, weaknesses, opportunities, and threats.

7. Interpretation and Reporting

Findings: Summarize key insights from the data analysis.

Recommendations: Provide actionable recommendations based on the research findings.

Business Plan Integration: Incorporate research insights into the business plan sections (market analysis, marketing strategy, etc.).

8. Timeline and Budget

Timeline: Create a detailed timeline with milestones for each stage of the research project.

Budget: Estimate costs for surveys, incentives for participants, software tools, and other expenses.

9. Presentation

Report: Prepare a comprehensive report detailing the research process, findings, and recommendations.

Presentation: Develop a PowerPoint presentation to share key insights with stakeholders and potential investors.

Example Activities for Students

Week 1-2: Planning

- Define research objectives and questions.
- Develop a research plan and timeline.

Week 3-4: Data Collection

- Conduct primary research (surveys, interviews).
- Gather secondary data from reliable sources.

Week 5-6: Data Analysis

- Analyze quantitative and qualitative data.
- Perform SWOT analysis.

Week 7: Reporting

- Summarize findings and develop recommendations.
- Integrate insights into the business plan.

Week 8: Presentation

- Prepare the final report and presentation.
- Present findings to peers and advisors for feedback.

- This structured approach will guide students through the market research process, ensuring they gather relevant data to create a solid business plan.

Quick Case 5.1

<u>Executive Summary of a Business Plan of HealthTech Innovations Pvt. Ltd.</u>

Company Overview

HealthTech Innovations Pvt. Ltd., founded in 2024, is a pioneering healthcare technology company based in Mumbai, India. The company is dedicated to transforming healthcare delivery through innovative technology solutions, improving patient outcomes, and enhancing operational efficiency for healthcare providers.

Mission Statement

Our mission is to revolutionize healthcare in India by developing cutting-edge technology solutions that improve patient care, streamline healthcare operations, and reduce costs. We aim to be the leading provider of healthcare technology solutions in India within the next five years.

Products and Services

HealthTech Innovations offers a diverse range of products and services designed to address critical aspects of healthcare delivery:

a. **Telemedicine Platform:** A comprehensive telemedicine solution enabling remote consultations, diagnostics, and monitoring, improving access to healthcare services.

b. **Electronic Health Records (EHR) System:** An integrated EHR system that enhances patient data management, streamlines workflows, and ensures secure data sharing among healthcare providers.

c. **AI-Powered Diagnostics:** Advanced AI algorithms for early disease detection and diagnosis, helping doctors make informed decisions and improving patient outcomes.

Market Analysis

The Indian healthcare market is rapidly growing, driven by increasing demand for quality healthcare services, government initiatives, and advancements in technology. The Indian health-tech market is projected to reach $25 billion by 2025, representing a doubling in size on account of factors such as rising internet penetration, the demand for enhanced accessibility, and the increasing prevalence of chronic diseases in the country. In addition to the growth drivers, the Indian government is actively working towards establishing the country as a global hub for healthcare services. Our target market includes hospitals, clinics, diagnostic centers, and healthcare professionals seeking innovative solutions to improve patient care and operational efficiency.

Competitive Advantage

HealthTech Innovations distinguishes itself through:

- Cutting-edge technology and continuous innovation.
- Strong partnerships with leading healthcare institutions and technology providers.
- A multidisciplinary team with expertise in healthcare, technology, and business management.
- A holistic approach to healthcare solutions, addressing various aspects of healthcare delivery.

Financial Projections

We project significant revenue growth over the next five years, with an anticipated annual growth rate of 30%. Initial funding of Rs 50 Lakhs will be allocated to research and development, market expansion, and scaling operational capabilities.

Management Team

The company was founded by a team of four experienced professionals with backgrounds in healthcare, technology, finance, and business management. Their collective experience and passion for improving healthcare drive the company's strategic vision.

Goals and Objectives

i. Achieve market leadership in healthcare technology solutions in India within five years.
ii. Expand product offerings to include more advanced and integrated healthcare technologies.
iii. Foster a culture of innovation and excellence.
iv. Develop strategic partnerships to strengthen market presence and capabilities.

Case Questions

1. What are the key challenges HealthTech Innovations might face in achieving market leadership in healthcare technology solutions?
2. How does HealthTech Innovations plan to differentiate itself in the competitive healthcare technology market?
3. What are the major milestones and timelines for achieving the company's financial projections?
4. What strategies will be implemented to ensure customer adoption and satisfaction of HealthTech Innovations' products and services?

Discussion Questions

1. What are the key components of a successful business plan? What is the common software available to develop a business plan and which one do you recommend and why?
2. How does a business plan help in securing funding from investors? How to pitch a business plan to investors?
3. What role does market analysis play in the development of a business plan?

4. How should a company define its mission and vision in a business plan?

5. What are the common pitfalls to avoid when creating financial projections in a business plan?

6. How important is the management team's experience and background in a business plan?

7. What strategies can a company use to differentiate itself from competitors in its business plan?

8. How can a business plan address potential risks and challenges?

9. What are the benefits of including a detailed marketing strategy in a business plan?

10. How does a business plan evolve from the startup phase to an established business?

11. What are the essential elements of a market analysis section in a business plan?

12. How should a business plan outline the company's operational strategy?

13. What is the significance of a SWOT analysis in a business plan?

14. How can a business plan be used as a roadmap for business growth?

15. What metrics should be used to measure the success of a business plan?

16. How can a business plan address regulatory and compliance issues?

17. What role does customer feedback play in shaping a business plan?

18. How can a business plan incorporate technological advancements and innovation?

19. What are the key financial documents to include in a business plan?

20. How often should a business plan be reviewed and updated?

References

1. Abrams, R. (2014). The successful business plan: Secrets & strategies. The Planning Shop.

2. Barringer, B. R., & Ireland, R. D. (2012). Entrepreneurship: Successfully launching new ventures (4th ed.). Pearson Education.

3. Blank, S., & Dorf, B. (2012). The startup owner's manual: The step-by-step guide for building a great company. K&S Ranch.

4. Burns, P. (2016). Entrepreneurship and small business: Start-up, growth, and maturity (4th ed.). Palgrave Macmillan.

5. Charantimath, P. M. (2019). Entrepreneurship development and small business enterprises (3rd ed.). Pearson Education India.

6. Hatten, T. S. (2015). Small business management: Entrepreneurship and beyond (6th ed.). Cengage Learning.

7. Hisrich, R. D., Peters, M. P., & Shepherd, D. A. (2016). Entrepreneurship (10th ed.). McGraw-Hill Education.

8. Hormozi, A. M., Sutton, G. S., McMinn, R. D., & Lucio, W. (2002). Business plans for new or small businesses: Paving the path to success. Management Decision, 40(8), 755-763. doi:10.1108/00251740210437752

9. Kuratko, D. F. (2016). Entrepreneurship: Theory, process, and practice (10th ed.). Cengage Learning.

10. Mullins, J. (2017). The new business road test: What entrepreneurs and executives should do before launching a lean start-up (5th ed.). FT Press.

11. Osterwalder, A., & Pigneur, Y. (2010). Business model generation: A handbook for visionaries, game changers, and challengers. John Wiley & Sons.

12. Pinson, L. (2008). Anatomy of a business plan: The step-by-step guide to building a business and securing your company's future (7th ed.). Out of Your Mind and Into the Marketplace.

13. Scarborough, N. M., & Cornwall, J. R. (2018). Essentials of entrepreneurship and small business management (9th ed.). Pearson Education.

14. Sahlman, W. A. (1997). How to write a great business plan. Harvard Business Review, 75(4), 98-108.

15. Timmons, J. A., & Spinelli, S. (2009). New venture creation: Entrepreneurship for the 21st century (8th ed.). McGraw-Hill/Irwin.

16. Wickham, P. A. (2006). Strategic entrepreneurship (4th ed.). Pearson Education.

WORKSHEETS

Chapter 6

Building and Growing a Start-Up

Building and Growing a Start-up: The Story of RedBus

In the early 2000s, India was facing a burgeoning problem: a lack of organized transportation, particularly in the intercity bus sector. Passengers often faced challenges in booking tickets, finding reliable bus operators, and ensuring a smooth travel experience. Amidst this chaos, three young entrepreneurs, Phanindra Sama, Charan Padmaraju, and B. V. Naidu, identified an opportunity that would change the way people traveled by bus in India—thus, RedBus was born.

The idea for RedBus emerged when Phanindra Sama experienced the hassles of booking bus tickets while traveling home for a festival. He realized that there was no centralized platform for bus ticket booking, unlike the air and train travel sectors, which were already more organized. Recognizing the immense potential, he teamed up with Charan Padmaraju and B. V. Naidu to create a solution. With limited funding, the founders manually gathered data from bus operators in Bangalore, launching the platform in 2006. The initial response was slow, but they persisted.

RedBus focused on forging relationships with bus operators and providing excellent customer service, which helped build trust and a loyal user base. As demand grew, RedBus developed an app and improved its platform with features like real-time tracking, enhancing the overall user experience.

The company diversified its offerings to include hotel bookings and travel packages, creating a comprehensive travel ecosystem. In 2013, RedBus was acquired by Naspers, which provided resources for further growth and expansion. RedBus revolutionized bus travel in India and inspired a wave of tech-driven innovations, becoming a prominent case study in entrepreneurship.

The RedBus story highlights how identifying a problem and leveraging technology can lead to significant impact and success in the start-up landscape.

Learning Objectives

1. Identify Steps in Building a Start-up
2. Conduct Feasibility Analysis and Build a Lean Business Model Canvas
3. Identify Your Market
4. Arrange and Assess Finance for Your Startup
5. Building a Team and Constitution of the Unit
6. Formulate a Growth Strategy for your Business by Applying AI Tools

"If you want to walk fast, walk alone. But if you want to walk far, walk together."

Introduction

Starting with a generated business idea to a business opportunity, the journey to creating a Minimum Viable Product (MVP) involves several key stages. Firstly, opportunity assessment entails evaluating market potential and target audience while identifying the problem the product will solve. Then, through Proof of Concept (POC), feasibility is validated, often with small-scale user experiments. Following this, Prototyping visualizes the product's features and user experience, ranging from low-fidelity sketches to high-fidelity simulations.

Changes based on prototype feedback can influence the development of subsequent MVPs. Finally, the MVP is developed, focusing on core features to address the target market's needs while minimizing resource investment. Throughout this iterative process, feedback guides refinement, ensuring the MVP effectively solves the identified problem while remaining adaptable to market dynamics.

Steps in Building a Startup

Startup means an entity, incorporated or registered in India not before five years, with annual turnover not exceeding ₹25 crore in any preceding financial year, working towards innovation, development, deployment, or commercialization of new products, processes, or services driven by technology or intellectual property (Startup India, 2016).

By following these steps and leveraging the lean business model canvas framework, you can systematically build and scale your startup while maximizing efficiency and minimizing risk. Remember to remain agile and adaptable, as the startup journey is often filled with unexpected twists and turns. To build a startup the following steps are usually involved.

1. **Feasibility Analysis: Idea Generation to business opportunity and Validation**

   - Identify a problem or opportunity in the market.
   - Conduct market research to validate the demand for your solution.

- Gather feedback from potential customers to refine your idea.
- Move from business idea to business opportunity to Proof of Concept (POC) to Prototyping to a Most Viable Product (MVP).

2. **Create a Lean Business Model Canvas**

- Define your value proposition: What problem are you solving, and how are you solving it better than existing solutions?
- Identify your customer segments: Who are your target customers, and what are their needs and preferences?
- Determine your distribution channels: How will you reach and acquire customers?
- Outline your revenue streams: How will you generate revenue from your product or service?
- Define the key resources, activities, and partnerships needed to deliver your value proposition.
- Determine your cost structure: What are your primary costs and expenses?

3. **Go-to-Market Strategy**

- Develop a marketing plan to raise awareness and generate interest in your product or service.
- Identify your initial target market and tailor you're messaging and positioning accordingly.
- Determine your pricing strategy based on market research and competitive analysis.
- Launch a Minimum Viable Product (MVP) to gather feedback and iterate based on user response.
- Implement customer acquisition strategies, such as digital marketing, partnerships, or direct sales efforts.

4. **Financing the Venture**

- Bootstrap: Use personal savings or funds from friends and family to get started.

- Seek angel investors: Pitch your idea to high-net-worth individuals willing to invest in early-stage startups.
- Explore venture capital: Approach venture capital firms specializing in your industry or sector for larger funding rounds.
- Consider crowdfunding: Launch a crowdfunding campaign on platforms like Kickstarter or Indiegogo to raise funds from a large number of backers.

5. **Building a Core Team**

- Identify the key roles and expertise needed to support your startup's growth.
- Recruit talented individuals passionate about your mission and bring complementary skills to the team.
- Prioritize diversity and inclusion to foster a culture of innovation and creativity.
- Establish clear roles, responsibilities, and communication channels within the management team.
- Continuously evaluate and evolve your team as the startup grows and new challenges arise.

Feasibility Analysis

Feasibility analysis examines the viability or sustainability of an idea, project, or business. The study examines whether there are enough resources to implement it and whether the concept has the potential to generate reasonable profits. In addition, it will demonstrate the benefits received in return for taking the risk of investing in the idea.

Feasibility Study analyses whether the proposed business ideas will succeed or fail. It determines the practicality by assessing the opportunities and threats of the proposed plan.

There are different types of studies to check feasibility, such as technical feasibility, market feasibility, organizational feasibility, and financial feasibility, that help to build a lean canvas business model.

1. **Technical Feasibility:** Technical feasibility study checks for accessibility of technical resources in the organization. Many factors need to be taken into consideration here, like staffing requirements, software, hardware, transportation, and technological competency.

2. **Market Feasibility:** It assesses the industry type, the existing marketing characteristics and improvements to make it better, the growth evident and needed, potential market, market share, and competitive environment of the company's products and services.

3. **Organizational Feasibility:** It focuses on the organization's structure, including the legal system, management team's competency, etc. It checks whether the existing conditions will suffice to implement the business idea.

4. **Financial Feasibility:** It allows an organization to determine risk, return, and cost-benefit analysis. It gives details about the investment that has to go in to get the desired level of profit.

Why is a feasibility study important?

It is crucial to check whether the proposed business plan is within the achievable limits of the company. The companies can do studies regarding resources, return on investment, technical capabilities, organizational competencies, whether they can complete the plan within a proposed time frame, etc.

What are the Benefits of a Feasibility Study?

1. Point out the valid reason to go ahead with the idea
2. Saves time money and resources
3. Enhances the team's focus
4. Helps in the identification of new opportunities
5. Helps to make an informed decision
6. Narrow down the business alternatives
7. Enhances the probability of success in a short period

Lean Business Model Canvas

As an entrepreneur, one of the most important tasks you can perform is getting your idea(s) into a tangible format so that you can communicate that with others. In the past, this usually meant a well-researched business plan, that would usually take weeks (more like months) to create. Lean Business Model Canvas was created by Ash Maurya for start-ups. The canvas focuses on problems, solutions, key metrics, and competitive advantages.

Business plans take too long to write, are seldom updated, and are rarely read by others. When you're going fast and under conditions of extreme uncertainty, you need dynamic models, not static plans. The Lean Canvas replaces long and boring business plans with a 1-page business model that takes less time to create and gets read.

Lean Canvas is a visual guide to help me quickly formulate possible business models, product launches, campaigns, and variations, and communicate this with stakeholders. The key fundamental to Lean methodology is the elimination of waste — this includes time, processes, inventory, and more. So as a lean startup, you need a quicker way to get ideas out of your head, you need to stay lean & avoid waste — so, it's time to create Lean Canvas.

The Lean Business Model Canvas is a versatile tool that encourages iterative refinement and adaptation as entrepreneurs gather feedback and test their business hypotheses in the real world. It's often used in conjunction with lean startup methodologies to foster rapid experimentation and learning.

The Lean Business Model Canvas is a streamlined version of the traditional business plan, designed to help entrepreneurs quickly and effectively validate their business ideas. It consists of nine key building blocks as shown in **Figure 6.1.**

1. **Problem**: The problem that the product or service solves for the customer.
2. **Customer Segments**: The specific group of people who have the problem that the product or service solves.
3. **Unique Value Proposition:** The unique value the product or service provides the customer.
4. **Solutions:** The product or service that solves the customer's problem.
5. **Channels:** The path through which a product or service is delivered to the customer.
6. **Revenue Streams:** The sources of revenue for the business.
7. **Cost Structure:** The cost of delivering the product or service and operating the business.
8. **Key Metrics:** The key performance indicators that measure the business's success.
9. **Unfair Advantage:** The factors that give the business a competitive advantage in the market.

PROBLEM	SOLUTION	UNIQUE VALUE PROPOSITION	UNFAIR ADVANTAGE	CUSTOMER SEGMENTS
	KEY METRICS		CHANNELS	
COST STRUCTURE		REVENUE STREAMS		

Figure 6.1. Lean Business Model Canvas

Types of Business Models

There are various types of business models, each designed to suit different industries, markets, and strategies. Many businesses may combine elements of multiple models or innovate with entirely new approaches to meet evolving market demands. Some common types include:

1. **E-commerce**: Businesses sell products or services online, often without physical storefronts. Example: **Amazon.com** - A massive online marketplace that sells a wide range of products to customers worldwide.

2. **Subscription-based**: Customers pay a recurring fee for access to a product or service over time. Example: **Netflix** - Offers streaming services for movies and TV shows on a monthly subscription basis.

3. **Freemium**: Offers basic services for free, while charging for premium features or upgrades. Example: **Dropbox** - Provides cloud storage services for free with limited storage space, while offering premium plans with additional features for a fee.

4. **Marketplace**: Facilitates transactions between buyers and sellers, taking a commission or fee for each transaction. Example: **Etsy** - A platform where artisans and craftsmen can sell handmade or vintage goods directly to customers.

5. **Franchise**: Allows individuals to operate under an established brand and business model in exchange for fees and royalties. Example: **McDonald's** - Operates on a franchise model, allowing individuals to own and operate McDonald's restaurants under the company's brand and business model.

6. **Platform**: Connects multiple parties, such as users and service providers, and facilitates transactions or interactions. Example: **Airbnb** - Connects travellers with hosts who rent out their homes or properties for short-term stays.

7. **On-demand**: Provides immediate access to goods or services, often through digital platforms, in response to customer demand. Example: **Uber** - Offers on-demand transportation services

through a mobile app, connecting passengers with drivers for rides.

8. **Brick-and-Mortar**: Traditional businesses with physical locations, selling products or services directly to customers. Example: **Walmart** - A retail giant with physical stores across the globe, selling a wide range of products to customers in-store.

9. **Razor and Blade**: Offers a product at a low initial cost (the "razor") and generates recurring revenue from complementary products or services (the "blades"). Example: **Gillette** - Sells razors at a low cost but generates recurring revenue from the sale of replacement blades.

10. **Asset-light**: Focuses on leveraging existing resources or infrastructure rather than heavy investments in physical assets. Example: **Airbnb** - Utilizes existing residential properties as accommodations, without needing to own or invest heavily in physical properties.

Box 6.1. Role of Entrepreneurship Development (ED) Cell in HEIs

The Entrepreneurship Development (ED) Cell plays a pivotal role in Higher Education Institutions (HEIs) by fostering an entrepreneurial ecosystem and cultivating a culture of innovation among students and faculty. The ED Cell serves as a catalyst for entrepreneurship and innovation within HEIs, nurturing the next generation of entrepreneurs, fostering economic growth, and creating societal impact through job creation and innovation-driven ventures.

The ED Cell motivates students to pursue Entrepreneurship as their career. To motivate, support, and mentor students for the identification and development of their innovative ideas. To organize business plan competitions that involvement of industry. Its primary functions include:

Promoting Entrepreneurial Culture: The ED Cell works to instill an entrepreneurial mindset among students and faculty, encouraging them to identify opportunities, think creatively, and take calculated risks.

Skill Development: It provides training, workshops, and mentorship programs aimed at enhancing entrepreneurial skills such as idea generation, business planning, financial management, marketing, and networking.

Incubation Support: The ED Cell offers support to startup ventures emerging from within the institution, providing access to infrastructure, resources, and **mentorship** to help them develop and grow.

Networking and Collaboration: It facilitates connections between students, faculty, industry experts, investors, and other stakeholders to create opportunities for collaboration, knowledge exchange, and partnerships.

Access to Funding: The ED Cell assists aspiring entrepreneurs in accessing funding opportunities, including grants, loans, and investment capital, to finance their ventures.

Industry Interface: It fosters collaboration with industry partners to provide real-world insights, industry exposure, and opportunities for internships, projects, and mentorship.

Supporting Innovation: The ED Cell encourages research and innovation activities within the institution, promoting the commercialization of research outcomes and the development of technology-based startups.

Policy Advocacy: It advocates for policies and initiatives that support entrepreneurship and innovation at both institutional and governmental levels, contributing to the overall ecosystem development.

Go to Market

What is in a market analysis/ Market study?

Market analysis is a documented investigation of a market that helps companies plan their activities. It involves several components, including market research, industry analysis, competitor analysis, and SWOT analysis. It is a proactive analysis of market demand for a product or service. It looks at all of the factors involved in the market that influence the demand for that product or service. This includes price, location, competition, substitutes, and general economic activity. A market analysis is a thorough qualitative and quantitative assessment of the current market.

Why you should conduct market analysis?

It helps you understand the volume and value of the market, potential customer segments and their buying patterns, the position of your competition, and the overall economic environment, including barriers to entry, and industry regulations.

Once you have in-depth knowledge of your market, you'll be better positioned to develop products and services that your customers are going to love. it can be broken up into four simple elements as shown in **Figure 6.2.**

1. **Market research (Target Market):** Involves surveying consumers to gather customer data. Who are your actual customers? You'll detail how many of them are there, what their needs are, and describe their demographics. Include market size, market segmentation, demographics, location, trends, psychographics, and behavior.

2. **Industry analysis:** An industry analysis is a marketing process that provides statistics about the market potential of your business products and services. This section of your plan needs to have specific information about the current state of the industry, and its target markets. Industry analysis provides the general industry environment in which a company competes. You'll describe the

current state of your industry and where it is headed. Include key industry metrics such as size, trends, and projected growth.

3. **Competitor analysis**: This is a process of evaluating the strengths and weaknesses of your competitors to gain a strategic advantage in the market. It can help you identify opportunities and threats, and develop strategies to stay ahead of the competition. Describe your competitors' positioning, strengths, and weaknesses. Include direct and indirect competitors, entry barriers, and your unique selling proposal.

4. **SWOT analysis (Pricing and Forecast)**: A tool that helps companies identify their strengths, weaknesses, opportunities, and threats. The SWOT analysis process gives you smart insights and a strategic view of market conditions, new technologies, objectives, and even insights into the competition. It will help to determine how you position your company in the market, pricing and your forecast will show what portion of the market you hope to get.

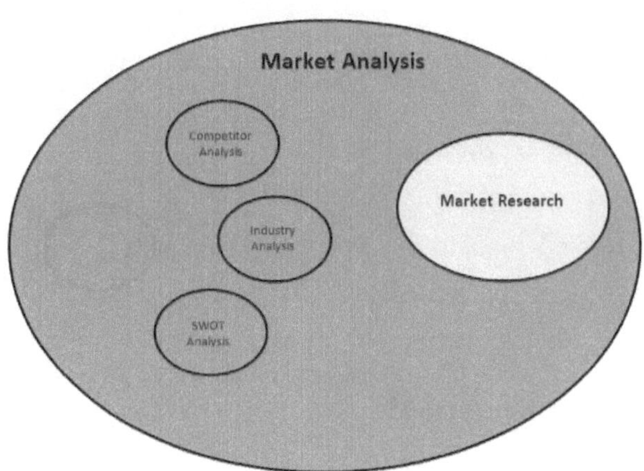

Figure 6.2. Market Analysis

Market Research

Market research is the subset of market analysis. It is the process of gathering information about your target market and customers to verify the success of a new product, help your team iterate on an existing product, or understand brand perception to ensure your team is effectively communicating your company's value.

Market research allows you to meet your buyers where they are. As our world (both digital and analog) becomes louder and demands more and more of our attention, this proves invaluable. By understanding your buyer's problems, pain points, and desired solutions, you can aptly craft your product or service to naturally appeal to them. Market research also provides insight into a wide variety of things that impact your bottom line, including:

- Identify target audience and current customers
- Which of your competitors your target audience looks to for information, options, or purchases?
- What's trending in your industry and the eyes of your buyer?
- Who makes up your market and what their challenges are?
- What influences purchases and conversions among your target audience
- Consumer attitudes about a particular topic, pain, product, or brand
- Whether there's demand for the business initiatives you're investing in?
- Unaddressed or underserved customer needs that can be flipped into a selling opportunity
- Attitudes about pricing for a particular product or service

What is Market Segmentation?

Market segmentation is a key part of market research and is used to identify profitable market segments that can be targeted with specific marketing strategies. Market segmentation seeks to identify targeted groups of consumers to tailor products and branding in a way that is attractive to the group. The key features of market segmentation are:

- Market segmentation allows a company to increase its overall efficiency by focusing limited resources on efforts that produce the best return on investment (ROI).
- Market segmentation seeks to identify targeted groups of consumers to tailor products and branding in a way that is attractive to the group.
- Markets can be segmented in several ways such as geographically, demographically, or behaviorally.
- Market segmentation helps companies minimize risk by figuring out which products are the most likely to earn a share of a target market and the best ways to market and deliver those products to the market.
- With risk minimized and clarity about the marketing and delivery of a product heightened, a company can then focus its resources on efforts likely to be the most profitable.
- Market segmentation can also increase a company's demographic reach and may help the company discover products or services they hadn't previously considered

Benefits of market segmentation

1. Increased resource efficiency
2. Strong brand image
3. Greater potential for brand loyalty
4. Strong market differentiation
5. Better-targeted digital advertising

Box 6.2. Incubation Centre in HEIs

The National Innovation and Startup Policy 2019 from the Ministry of HRD Government of India for students and faculty of Higher Education Institutions (HEIs) will enable the institutes to actively engage students, faculties, and staff in innovation and entrepreneurship-related activities. This framework will also facilitate the Ministry of Human Resource Development in bringing uniformity across HEIs in terms of Intellectual Property ownership management, technology licensing, and institutional startup policy, thus enabling the creation of a robust innovation and startup ecosystem across all HEIs.

The Incubation Centre plays a crucial role in nurturing startup ventures, promoting innovation, and contributing to the economic development of the region by fostering entrepreneurship within the HEIs ecosystem. The Incubation Centre within a Higher Education Institution (HEI) serves as a critical hub for fostering entrepreneurship and supporting the growth of startup ventures. Its key roles include:

Startup Support: The Incubation Centre provides comprehensive support to startup ventures, including access to infrastructure, office space, and shared facilities, enabling entrepreneurs to focus on developing their business ideas.

Mentorship and Guidance: It offers mentorship and guidance from experienced entrepreneurs, industry experts, and faculty members, helping startups navigate challenges, refine their business models, and make informed decisions.

Access to Resources: The Incubation Centre facilitates access to resources such as funding, market research, legal support, and technology infrastructure, enabling startups to overcome barriers and accelerate their growth.

Networking Opportunities: It creates opportunities for startups to network with peers, industry professionals, investors, and potential customers, fostering collaboration, partnerships, and knowledge exchange.

Training and Capacity Building: The Incubation Centre organizes workshops, training programs, and skill development initiatives aimed at enhancing the entrepreneurial capabilities of startup founders and their teams.

Validation: It provides validation to startups, helping them validate their business ideas, test their products or services, and refine their value propositions based on market feedback.

Access to Markets: The Incubation Centre facilitates access to markets and customers through market linkage programs, industry collaborations, and participation in trade fairs, exhibitions, and networking events.

Community Building: It fosters a vibrant entrepreneurial community within the HEI, bringing together startups, mentors, investors, and other stakeholders to share knowledge, experiences, and resources.

Financing and Funding Your Startup

Raising capital for a startup can be a challenge and a barrier to the eventual commencement and implementation of your business. Debt and equity are the two major sources of financing.

Debt Financing: When a company borrows money to be paid back at a future date with interest it is known as debt financing. It could be in the form of a secured as well as an unsecured loan. A firm takes up a loan to either finance a working capital or an acquisition.

Equity Financing: It deals with exchanging a portion of the ownership of the business for a financial investment in the business. The ownership stake resulting from an equity investment allows the investor to share in the company's profits. Equity involves a permanent investment in a company and is not repaid by the company at a later date.

What is Debt Financing vs. Equity Financing?

Both are financing methods used by the entities to raise capital for business requirements. However, equity financing is non-debt financing and leaves no obligations for the entity issuing the equity since it does not involve borrowing, unlike the other method. But sells a portion of ownership in the company, diluting ownership.

While sourcing for funds, you need to, first of all, identify how much you need to start or grow your business. Here are the various ways to finance your business.

1. **Bootstrapping/Personal Savings**: This is the most preferred source of funds for most businesses. It involves funding your startup using personal savings, credit cards, or revenue generated by the business itself. It gives you full control over your company but can limit growth potential if you have limited personal resources.

2. **Family and Friends (Love money):** This is the next most common source of funding after personal savings. This is the money you receive from wealthy family members or friends.

3. **Angel investors:** Angels are generally wealthy individuals or retired company executives who invest directly in small firms owned by others. They are often leaders in their field who not only contribute their experience and network of contacts but also their technical and/or management knowledge.

4. **Venture Capitalist**: Venture capitalists are groups of wealthy individuals, government-assisted sources, or major financial institutions who have a dedicated pool of capital and make it available for the expansion of businesses with great profit potential.

5. **Crowd Funding**: It is a form of fundraising where a business asks the public for a contribution, usually in exchange for equity in the company. There are various types of crowdfunding such as Equity, Debt, and Donation crowdfunding. Crowdfunding platforms like Kickstarter, Indiegogo, or GoFundMe allow startups to raise funds from a large number of individuals in exchange for rewards, pre-orders, or equity. It's a way to validate your idea and generate buzz, and it requires significant marketing effort.

6. **Grants and Subsidies:** Governments, non-profits, and corporations may offer grants, subsidies, or tax incentives to support startups, particularly in certain industries or for projects with social or environmental impact. These funding sources often come with specific eligibility criteria and requirements.

7. **Accelerators and Incubators:** Accelerator and incubator programs provide startups with funding, mentorship, resources, and networking opportunities in exchange for equity or a small fee. These programs typically last for a fixed period and culminate in a demo day where startups pitch to investors.

8. **Debt Financing:** Startups can also raise funds through debt financing, such as bank loans, lines of credit, or peer-to-peer lending platforms. While it doesn't involve giving up equity, it requires regular repayments with interest, which can strain cash flow, especially in the early stages.

9. **Initial Public Offerings (IPOs):** They are used when companies have profitable operations, management stability, and strong demand for their products or services. This generally doesn't happen until companies have been in business for several years. To get to this point, they usually will raise funds privately one or more times.

What the Investors look for while funding your startup?

As a startup founder, it's important to know what investors look for when they're considering investing in a startup. A great idea is just the beginning. You also need to have a solid plan for how to make your startup profitable. The most important elements that investors look for in startups are given below.

a. **A financially viable business model**

Investors require quantifiable financial projections that demonstrate the economic viability of your startup. They prefer to fund startups that have earned revenue or reached advanced development stages. A convincing business model, market knowledge, and clear marketing and financial plans are essential. Long-term plans are also necessary to show the depth of your vision.

b. **An authentic brand story**

Investors want to know if your startup has a story that will resonate with your target audience. You need to have strong branding backed up by a compelling story that conveys why you do what you do. This includes both the details of your business and your passion for it. A strong narrative can be just as important as financial data in convincing investors to support your startup.

c. **A strong and passionate team**

Investors care about the leadership and teamwork skills of a startup's founders when considering investments. A passionate team with complementary skills and good chemistry is essential for success.

d. **A dynamic market opportunity**

Investors consider market attractiveness before investing in a startup. A large and viable market with good revenue opportunities is preferred. Driving growth is important for a startup to scale and get investors' money's worth.

e. **A competitive edge**

Investors want to bet on something sustainable and profitable. Show them your startup's competitive advantage and what you are doing differently. Your business model will help you convince investors that you have a sustainable plan in place.

f. **A clear investment structure**

When seeking funding for your startup, it's important to consider the different types of capital available and create a solid financial structure. Determine whether your investors will be partners or shareholders and how involved they'll be in decision-making. Be prepared to negotiate and seek legal advice to ensure you maintain control over your startup.

g. **A shared vision**

Having a common goal with your investor is crucial for funding. Investors seek authenticity, enthusiasm, and drive-in founders. Establish your credibility and find an investor who's a good fit for your startup. Treat investors with thoughtfulness and give them something to believe in.

Building a Core Team for Your Start-Up

Building a team for a startup is a multifaceted endeavour that requires careful planning, strategic thinking, and a deep understanding of your business's needs. Here's a more elaborate and comprehensive guide:

1. **Craft Your Vision and Mission**: Start by defining your startup's vision and mission. What problem are you solving, and why does it matter? A clear and compelling vision will not only attract top talent but also align your team around a common purpose.
2. **Identify Key Roles and Responsibilities**: Determine the key functions and roles necessary to drive your startup forward. This might include positions such as co-founders, product manager, software engineer, marketing lead, sales representative, and operations manager.
3. **Assess Your Current Needs and Future Growth**: Consider both your immediate needs and your long-term growth trajectory. Your team composition may evolve as your startup progresses through different stages of development, from idea validation to product launch and beyond.
4. **Define Core Competencies and Skill Sets**: Outline the specific skills, expertise, and attributes required for each role. Beyond technical skills, consider factors such as industry knowledge, domain expertise, leadership qualities, and cultural fit.

5. **Recruitment Strategy**: Develop a recruitment strategy that encompasses a mix of channels, including job postings, networking events, referrals, and recruitment agencies. Leverage your professional network and industry connections to identify potential candidates who may not be actively seeking employment.

6. **Prioritize Diversity and Inclusion**: Building a diverse team not only fosters creativity and innovation but also reflects the diverse needs of your customer base. Actively seek out candidates from underrepresented backgrounds and create an inclusive work environment where all voices are valued.

7. **Evaluate Cultural Fit**: Cultural fit is crucial for startup success. Look for candidates who share your values, work ethic, and passion for the mission. Assess how well they align with your startup's culture and whether they will thrive in a fast-paced, dynamic environment.

8. **Compensation and Benefits**: While startups may not always match the salaries offered by larger companies, they can offer other incentives such as equity, flexible work arrangements, professional development opportunities, and a chance to make a significant impact.

9. **Invest in Onboarding and Training**: Develop a comprehensive onboarding program to help new hires acclimate to your startup's culture, processes, and expectations. Provide ongoing training and mentorship to support their professional growth and development.

10. **Promote Collaboration and Communication**: Foster a culture of collaboration, transparency, and open communication within your team. Encourage regular meetings, brainstorming sessions, and cross-functional collaboration to drive innovation and problem-solving.

11. **Provide Growth Opportunities**: Offer opportunities for career advancement and skill development. Emphasize the potential for employees to take on leadership roles, grow with the company, and make a meaningful impact on its success.

12. **Monitor Team Dynamics and Performance**: Continuously assess your team's dynamics, performance, and overall effectiveness. Solicit feedback from team members and address any issues or challenges that may arise proactively.

Box 6.3. The Growth Ladder of Startups: From Minicorns to Hectocorns

Startups are classified into stages based on their valuation, including Minicorns, Soonicorns, Unicorns, Decacorns, and Hectocorns. These categories represent the growth, scalability, and market influence of startups. The terms highlight significant milestones that startups reach as they advance in their entrepreneurial journey, showcasing their importance in the global economy.

These classifications illustrate the lifecycle of a startup as it increases in valuation, providing a structured approach to understanding how startups progress from potential-driven enterprises to industry-transforming giants. The valuation reflects market trust, growth potential, and industry impact. Each stage attracts different types of investors: early-stage investors for Minicorns, venture capitalists or private equity for Unicorns and Soonicorns, and institutional investors for Decacorns and Hectocorns.

Minicorns are startups valued at less than $1 billion that exhibit significant growth potential. These companies are generally in their early to mid-stages of development, attracting initial venture capital funding while establishing scalable business models. For instance, **Dunzo** in India and **Bolt** in Europe are promising minicorns that are focused on market expansion and innovation.

Soonicorns are startups that are nearing a $1 billion valuation and are close to achieving Unicorn status. These companies are typically in the late stages of funding, experiencing rapid growth, and attracting significant investor confidence. Examples of

Soonicorns in India include **Curefit** and **ShareChat,** both of which have strong market traction and impressive growth trajectories.

Unicorns are startups that have a valuation of $1 billion or more. They often lead their industries and disrupt traditional markets. Examples of unicorns include **Byju's** in the educational technology sector, **Zomat**o in food delivery, and **Razorpay** in financial technology (fintech). Unicorns represent successful business models with significant market penetration and global appeal.

Decacorns are startups valued at $10 billion or more, signifying a higher level of success and dominance in their industries. These companies have a strong global presence and often set trends in their respective fields. Notable examples include **SpaceX**, which is leading the way in space exploration; **Stripe**, which is transforming digital payments; and **ByteDance**, the parent company of **TikTok.**

Hectocorns, often referred to as **"super unicorns,"** are startups or companies valued at $100 billion or more. These are global giants that have typically evolved from startups into fully mature corporations. Examples of such companies include **Google** and **Facebook** during their early years, as well as **Tesla**, which continues to drive innovation in the automotive and energy sectors.

Constitution of the Unit

A business entity is an organization that's formed to conduct business. The type of entity determines how a business is taxed and its owner's or owners' exposure to liability. You choose a business entity when you start a business

A startup can be owned and organized in various forms. Every entrepreneur has to decide on the form of business organization. Business organization refers to all necessary arrangements required to conduct a business. Each form has its advantages and disadvantages.

The choice of the form of business is governed by several interrelated and independent factors such as the nature of the business, scale of operations, area of operation, liability, the degree of control desired by the promoter(s), the cost of the project, risk and return, and comparative tax liability.

The choice of the form of enterprise not only helps in the initial phase but also during the growth of the enterprise. To start an enterprise, the promoters have to decide on the constitution of the unit. The constitution of the unit has to be decided at the initial stages of the project and the necessary formalities should be completed. There are ten major types of business entities in India. They are:

1. Sole Proprietorship
2. Partnership
3. Limited Liability Partnership
4. Private Limited Companies
5. Public Limited Companies
6. One-Person Companies
7. Section - 8 Company
8. Joint Stock Company
9. Non-Government Organization (NGO)
10. Joint Hindu Family Business

1. Sole Proprietorship: A Sole Proprietorship is an enterprise that. is wholly controlled by one person. Many entrepreneurs start small businesses in their names and continue as sole proprietors. Such an establishment and its owner are not considered separate entities. There is no formal registration required to start a business in India under Sole Proprietorship. While it is easy to register this entity, the proprietor must bear responsibility for all liabilities.

2. Partnership: In a partnership firm, two or more people come together to work and earn profits. There is a partnership deed that specifies the invested interest of each partner and their profit-sharing ratios along with other terms of business functioning and operations. The partners are responsible for all liabilities and there is no limit to it. When it comes to the registration of a partnership it is not mandatory but suitable to get it registered.

3. Limited Liability Partnership: A Limited Liability Partnership is incorporated under the Limited Liability Partnership Act 2009. As opposed to partnership firms, partners in an LLP are not burdened with unlimited liabilities caused by the business. Their responsibility towards losses or debts is limited to investments made by them.

A limited liability partnership and its partners are considered separate legal entities. Further, no partner is liable on account of the independent actions of other partners, thus individual partners are safe and shielded from joint liabilities upon the commission of another partner's misconduct.

4. Private Limited Companies: As per Section 2(68) of the Companies Act 2013, A private company is defined as a company having a minimum paid-up share capital as may be prescribed, and which by its articles,

  i.   restricts the right to transfer its shares;
  ii. except in the case of One Person Company, limits the number of its members to two hundred;
  iii. prohibits any invitation to the public to subscribe for any securities of the company.

Most Startups and businesses in India with higher ambitions choose Private Limited Companies as a suitable business structure.

5. Public Limited Companies: As per Section 2(71) of the Companies Act, a public company means "a company which is not a private company". A public limited is formed by a minimum of 7 (seven) persons with a minimum paid-up capital.

The company may get listed on the stock exchange and thereafter shares of the same are traded openly. There are more legal restrictions on this type of establishment than a Private Limited Company.

6. One-Person Companies: As per Section 2(62) of the Companies Act 2013, "one-person company" means a company that has only one person as a member. This is a recent invention to facilitate entrepreneurs to own and manage companies alone.

All the shares can be owned by one person but there must be a nominee for the sole member to register this form of business. The introduction of this concept of a company under the legal system is believed to not only cater to economic growth but also create a good amount of employment opportunities.

7. Section 8 Company: A Section 8 Company or we may also call it a Non-profit Company. It can be incorporated under the provisions of the Companies Act, 2013. It has the status of a limited company without the addition to its name of the word "Limited" or "Private Limited". The Company shall use its profits or other income in promoting its objects only and prohibit the payment of any dividend to its members as well.

Section 8 companies shall enjoy all the privileges and be subject to all the obligations of limited companies. A firm may also be a member of a Section 8 company.

8. Joint Stock Company: A Joint Stock Company is a type of company where the capital is divided into a large number of shares, and the shareholders are the owners of the company. The ownership of the company is determined by the number of shares held by each shareholder. A Joint Stock Company is also known as a corporation under the provisions of the Companies Act, 2013.

9. Non-Government Organization (NGO): NGOs are organizations that are formed to manage different types of activities that aim to benefit society at large, especially for underprivileged people. NGOs can be in the form of Trust, registered under the Trust Act of 1882, Society to be registered under the Societies Registration Act, of 1860, or Section 8 Company to be registered under the Companies Act, of 2013.

10. Joint Hindu Family Business: The Joint Hindu Family (JHF) is a jointly-owned business and is governed by the Hindu Succession Act, of 1956. The joint Hindu family business came into existence as per the

Hindu inheritance laws of India. It is a distinct type of organization, which is unique to India for forming the JHF business there must be at least two members in the family and the family should have some ancestral property.

In this form of business organization, all members of an undivided Hindu family do business jointly under the control of the head of the family who is known as the Karta. The members of the family are known as "coparceners." There is no membership other than the members of the joint family. All co-parceners have equal shares in the profit of the business. The liability of the Karta is unlimited. The liability of each member of the joint Hindu family business is limited to the extent of their share in the business.

Micro Small and Medium Enterprises (MSMEs)

Definition of MSMEs

Effective from 1st July 2020, a new definition of MSMEs has been drawn based on their net turnover, and their net investments in plants, machinery, and other equipment required for the proper functioning of their business. The definition is applicable for both goods-based and service-based MSMEs as given in Table 6.1.

Table 6.1. Classification of MSMEs

Type of Units	Investment in Plant and Machinery INR	Annual Turnover INR
Micro Enterprises	Does not exceed 1 Crore	Does not exceed 5 Crore
Small Enterprises	Does not exceed 10 Crore	Does not exceed 50 Crore
Medium Enterprises	Does not exceed 50 Crore	Does not exceed 250 Crore

Source: https://msme.gov.in/know-about-msme

MSME Registration Process

The registration of MSMEs is not made mandatory by the Government of India. It is beneficial to get registered as it provides a lot of benefits in terms of taxation, credit facilities, subsidies, loans, and setting up of business. The registration of MSME can be undertaken online absolutely free of cost on the Udyam registration portal of the Government of India. The documents required for registration of MSMEs are:

1. Aadhar number.
2. PAN number.
3. Address of the business.
4. Bank account number.
5. The basic business activity.
6. National Industrial Classification (NIC) 2-digit code.
7. Investment details (Plant/equipment details)
8. Turnover details (as per the new MSME definition)

Government Schemes for Startups

GOI has announced 16 January as the National Startup Day to connect startup ecosystem stakeholders to encourage entrepreneurship (PIB, 2023). The government of India has launched several government schemes to support startups and foster innovation, aiming to provide financial assistance, mentorship, and infrastructure. These schemes help startups secure financial backing, benefit from mentorship, access markets, and drive innovation across sectors. Some notable schemes are furnished in **Table 6.2.**

Stand-Up India scheme was launched in 2016 and it aims to promote entrepreneurship at the grassroots level for economic empowerment and job creation (PIB, 2022). The objective of this scheme is to facilitate bank loans to at least one scheduled caste or scheduled tribe borrower and at least one woman borrower per bank branch to facilitate their participation in the economic growth of the nation

Table 6.2. Government Schemes for Startups

S.No.	Scheme	Overview	Key Features	Funding
1	**Startup India Initiative**	Provides a complete ecosystem for startup growth.	Tax exemptions, compliance simplification, and Startup India Hub for mentorship and networking	Fund of Funds for Startups (FFS) provides capital via SEBI-registered venture funds.
2	**Atal Innovation Mission (AIM)**	Encourages R&D and entrepreneurship through incubators and tinkering labs.	Atal Tinkering Labs in schools, Atal Incubation Centers	Grants for schools, institutions, and startups through incubators
3	**Credit Guarantee Scheme for Startups (CGSS)**	Reduces financial risk for lenders to help startups access loans.	Collateral-free credit guarantee of up to ₹10 crore per startup	Funding covers loans from eligible financial institutions
4	**Pradhan Mantri Mudra Yojana (PMMY)**	Supports micro and small enterprises with collateral-free loans.	Loans under three categories: Shishu, Kishor, and Tarun	Loans of up to ₹10 lakh with varying interest rates
5	**SIDBI Fund of Funds for Startups (FFS)**	Invests in Alternative Investment Funds (AIFs) that support startups.	Focus on sectors like social impact, agritech, and biotech	The initial corpus of ₹10,000 crore for co-funding with AIFs
6	**Support for International Patent Protection in Electronics & IT (SIP-EIT)**	Helps startups protect their innovations internationally.	Covers patent filing expenses in electronics and IT domains	Reimbursement of up to 50% of cost, or max ₹15 lakh per invention

S.No.	Scheme	Overview	Key Features	Funding
7	**NewGen Innovation and Entrepreneurship Development Centre (NewGen IEDC)**	Promotes innovation at institutional levels.	Establishes centers for idea generation and product development	Provides seed funding and infrastructure grants to institutions
8	**Digital India Initiative**	Empower startups in the tech and digital sector with resources and connectivity.	Incentives for digital platforms, cloud storage, and government tech resources	Grants, subsidies, and resources for digital and tech startups
9	**MSME Credit Guarantee Fund Trust (CGTMSE)**	Provides credit guarantees to Micro, Small, and Medium Enterprises (MSMEs)	Collateral-free credit to MSMEs, including startups	Covers credit facilities of up to ₹2 crore from financial institutions
10	**National Initiative for Developing and Harnessing Innovations (NIDHI)**	Supports startups through seed funding, incubation, and grants.	NIDHI PRAYAS centers, seed funding programs, and accelerator support	Seed funding, grants, and support through NIDHI's incubation centers and startup accelerator program

Finanace for Entrepreneurs

Introduction to Financial Statements

Every business—small or large—maintains books of accounts. Accounting is the system of recording financial transactions. Using this recorded data, the management/owners of the business try to understand if the business has made profits or incurred losses in a given period. They are also able to assess their financial standing at a particular point in time. Common terms used in Financial Statements are:

Assets: They are resources owned by a business to use for generating future profits. Assets may be tangible assets, non-tangible assets, current assets, or non-current assets.

Liabilities: These are obligations of a financial nature to be settled at a future date. Liabilities represent the amount of money that the business owes to the other parties. Liabilities may be current liabilities and non-current liabilities.

Income/Revenue: It is the money generated from normal business operations, calculated as the average sales price times the number of units sold. It is the top-line (or gross income) figure from which costs are subtracted to determine net income. Revenue is also known as sales on the income statement.

Expenses: They are the amount spent by the business. Expenses are of two types – Revenue Expenditure and Capital Expenditure

Revenue Expenditure: This represents expenditure incurred to earn revenue of the current period. The benefits of revenue expenses get exhausted in the year of the incurrence. For example, repairs, insurance, salary and wages to employees, travel, etc. The revenue expenditure results in a reduction in profit or surplus. It forms part of the income statement.

Capital Expenditure: This represents expenditure incurred to acquire a fixed asset that is intended to be used over the long term for earning profits therefrom, e.g., the amount paid to buy a computer for office use is a capital expenditure. At times expenditure may be incurred for enhancing the production capacity of the machine. This will also be a capital expenditure. Capital expenditure forms a part of the Balance Sheet.

Shareholders' Funds: It consists of equity share capital, reserves & surplus, retained profits of the year, and/or adjusted for any debit balance (loss) in the P&L a/c.

Profit: The excess of revenue income over expenses is called profit. It could be calculated for each transaction or the business as a whole.

Loss: The excess of expense over income is called loss. It could be calculated for each transaction or business as a whole.

Purpose and types of Financial Statements: Many users rely on financial statements as the major source of financial information. Therefore, financial statements should be prepared and presented by their requirement. Financial statements enable entrepreneurs to understand the health of the company.

Financial statements are a compilation of financial data, collected and classified systematically according to accounting principles, to assess the financial position of an enterprise as regards its profitability, operational efficiency, long- and short-term solvency, and growth potential. A complete set of financial statements normally consists of:

1. Income Statement (Profit and Loss Account)
2. Balance Sheet
3. Cash Flow Statement

Income Statement

A Profit and Loss Account (P&L) is a financial statement that summarizes a company's revenue, costs, and expenses over a specified period, usually a fiscal quarter or year. It shows the difference between a company's total revenue and total expenses, determining whether it made a profit or incurred a loss during the period. The P&L statement is an important tool for businesses to track their financial performance and make informed decisions. The salient features of a profit and loss account are:

- ✓ Prepared for a given period.
- ✓ Comparative position.
- ✓ Vertically drawn.
- ✓ Grouping on income and expenditure.
- ✓ Details in schedules and notes to the accounts.

    ✓ Appropriation of profit and transfer to the balance sheet.

    ✓ Signed by a person who prepared it and the auditors

The main purpose is to know how much profit or loss the entity has made during a particular year.

Balance Sheet

A Balance Sheet is a financial statement that shows a company's financial position at a specific point in time. It lists the company's assets, liabilities, and shareholders' equity.

Assets: This includes all the resources owned by a company that have monetary value, such as cash, investments, property, and inventory.

Liabilities: This includes all the obligations owed by the company, such as loans, bills payable, and taxes owed.

Shareholders' equity: This includes the capital contributed by the owners, as well as retained earnings.

The balance sheet provides a snapshot of a company's financial situation, including its ability to pay debts, its liquidity, and its overall net worth. The balance sheet equation:

Assets = Liabilities + Shareholders' Equity

Cash Flow Statement

A Cash Flow Statement is a financial statement that shows the inflows and outflows of cash over a specific period, usually a quarter or a year. It provides information on a company's ability to generate and use cash, which is important for its financial stability and growth. There are four key components of the Cash Flow Statement.

Operating activities: This section shows the cash generated from the company's main operations, such as sales and services.

Investing activities: This section shows the cash used or generated from investments, such as the purchase or sale of long-term assets.

Financing activities: This section shows the cash generated or used from financing activities, such as the issuance of stocks or bonds, and the repayment of loans.

Net increase/decrease in cash: This section shows the overall increase or decrease in cash during the period, and is calculated by adding the cash generated from operating activities, subtracting the cash used in investing activities, and adding/subtracting the cash generated/used in financing activities.

The Cash Flow Statement provides important information on a company's liquidity, solvency, and ability to generate and manage cash, which is critical for its financial health and success.

<u>**Exercise**</u>

Kalyani Limited was incorporated on January 1, 2022. Based on the following transaction during the period financial year (January 1, 2022, till December 31, 2022), construct a Profit & Loss Account and a Balance Sheet of the company. Through an issue of shares, the company raised INR 50 million. This money was received in the company's bank accounts.

The company also raised a loan of INR 100 million from financial institutions. The interest of INR11 million has accrued for the period ended December 31, 2022, but would be falling due for payment only later. With the money raised from the issue of shares and loans from financial institutions, the company has purchased machinery worth INR80 million. This machinery has been used immediately. The machinery depreciates with each passing year to the extent of 10% of its original value. The company recognizes depreciation to this extent.

The company has around 100 employees. The annual employee cost is INR 10 million and has been fully paid for the company incurs other administrative expenses totalling to INR 6 million. Out of these expenses equal to INR 1 million are yet to be paid by the company. During the year, the company purchased material worth INR 150 million. Out of this material worth INR 25 million is available in stock at the end of the year. The company has not paid for the entire material purchased. INR 30 million is yet to be paid to the suppliers.

The company has been able to notch up sales of Rs. 175 million. In addition, some dealers have already booked orders with the company and have paid an advance of Rs.5 million. At the same time, the company has not been able to recover the total amount due on sales. Despite, the best push given by the sales team, INR20 million is outstanding to be collected.

The tax rate applicable to the company is 40%. The company is currently enjoying an excellent liquidity position. But soon it is likely to embark on an expansion plan. The company has set aside in liquid investments a sum of Rs. 65 million which would be used. Use the data to construct a P&L account and a balance sheet.

Profit and Loss statement is provided in **Table 6.3**. The Balance Sheet is provided in **Table 6.4.**

Table 6.3. Profit & Loss Statement

Kalyani Limited			
P & L Statement for the Year 31.12.2022			
Expenses	**INR**	**Revenue**	**INR**
Purchases	150	Sales	175
Salary	10	Closing Stock	25
Other Administrative Expenses	6		
Depreciation	8		
Interest Expenses	11		
Provision for Taxation	6		
Net Profit	9		
Total	**200**		**200**

Table 6.4. Balance Sheet

Kalyani Limited			
Balance Sheet as of 31.12.2022			
Liabilities	**INR**	**Assets**	**INR**
Share Capital	50	Fixed Assets	80
Surplus in P&L Account	9	Less: Depreciation	8
Loan from Financial Institutions	100	Net fixed assets	72
Advance received from Customers	5	Investments	65
Creditors for Materials	30	Receivables from customers	20
Creditors for Expenses	1	Inventory	25
Interest accrued is not due	11	Balance in Bank Account	30
Provision for Taxation	6		
Total	**212**	**Total**	**212**

Cash Budgeting

Cash budgeting is the process of forecasting a company's expected cash inflows and outflows to make informed decisions about managing cash resources. This involves creating projections for both regular operating expenses (such as salaries and utilities) and one-time expenditures (such as capital investments). The goal of cash budgeting is to ensure that the company has enough cash on hand to meet its obligations and avoid a cash shortfall.

A cash budget is a company's estimation of cash inflows and outflows over a specific period, which can be weekly, monthly, quarterly, or annually. A company will use a cash budget to determine whether it has sufficient cash to continue operating over the given time frame.

Cash budgeting is a crucial aspect of financial management as it helps companies plan for and manage their short-term cash needs, improving their financial stability and allowing them to take advantage of growth opportunities. Cash receipts, cash payments, and short-term financing are three sections of the cash budget. The steps in cash budgeting include:

1. Identifying sources of cash inflows (such as sales, investments, loans)
2. Forecasting cash outflows (such as operating expenses, debt repayments, and capital expenditures)
3. Comparing cash inflows to outflows to determine the net cash flow
4. Adjust the budget as needed to ensure adequate cash resources.

Exercise

SKR a retail company has the following expected cash inflows and outflows for the next quarter. Calculate Net cash flow and comment on the answer.

Cash inflows:

- Sales revenue: Rs 200,000
- Loan proceeds: Rs 50,000

Cash outflows:

- Rent: Rs 20,000
- Employee salaries: Rs 50,000
- Utilities: RS 10,000
- Inventory purchases: Rs 80,000
- Loan repayments: Rs 30,000

Net cash flow = Cash inflows - Cash outflows

= Rs 200,000 + Rs 50,000 - (Rs 20,000 + Rs 50,000 + Rs 10,000 + Rs 80,000 + Rs 30,000)

= Rs 200,000 + RS 50,000 – Rs 190,000

= Rs 60,000

In this example, the retail company has a net positive cash flow of Rs 60,000, indicating that they will have adequate cash resources to meet their obligations and carry out planned expenditures in the next quarter. If the company were to find that their projected net cash flow was negative, they might need to revise their budget or look for additional sources of funding to ensure they have sufficient cash on hand.

Capital Budgeting

Capital budgeting is the process of evaluating and prioritizing potential investments or expenditures that an organization will make in fixed assets, such as buildings, machinery, or equipment.

The goal is to determine which investments will generate the highest returns and provide the best long-term value to the company. It involves forecasting future cash flows and discounting them to present value, taking into account the time value of money and the risks involved.

Planning the eventual returns on investments in machinery, real estate, and new technology are all examples of capital budgeting.

Types of Capital Budgeting

There are mainly two types of capital budgeting techniques.

1. **Non-Discounting Criteria:** Refers to methods of evaluating investment opportunities that don't consider the time value of money. Examples include PBP and ARR.
2. **Discounting Criteria:** Refers to methods of evaluating investment opportunities that take into account the time value of money, i.e., they consider the present value of future cash flows. Examples include NPV, IRR, and BCR.

Each method provides a different perspective on the potential value of an investment, and companies may use a combination of these techniques to make informed investment decisions.

a. **Payback Period (PBP):** Measures the time it takes for an investment to recoup its cost.

PBP = Initial Investment Cost / Annual Cash inflows

b. **Accounting Rate of Return (ARR):** measures the expected profitability of an investment by dividing the average annual profit by the average investment. It is calculated by dividing the average annual profit from the investment by the average investment cost.

ARR = Average Annual Profit / Average Investment Cost

c. **Net Present Value (NPV):** Calculates the present value of expected future cash flows, and compares it to the initial investment.

NPV = (Sum of Present Value of Future Cash Flows) - (Initial Investment Cost)

d. **Internal Rate of Return (IRR):** Determines the rate at which the NPV of an investment becomes zero, representing the break-even point for an investment. The internal rate of return by definition is the rate of return at which the net present value of a stream of payments/incomes is equal to zero. It is the discount rate that equates the present value of future cash flows with the initial investment.

$$0 = CF_0 + \frac{CF_1}{(1 + IRR)} + \frac{CF_2}{(1 + IRR)^2} + \frac{CF_3}{(1 + IRR)^3} + \ldots + \frac{CF_n}{(1 + IRR)^n}$$

Or

$$0 = NPV = \sum_{n=0}^{N} \frac{CF_n}{(1 + IRR)^n}$$

Where:
CF_0 = Initial Investment / Outlay
$CF_1, CF_2, CF_3 \ldots CF_n$ = Cash flows
n = Each Period
N = Holding Period
NPV = Net Present Value
IRR = Internal Rate of Return

e. **Benefit-Cost Ratio (BCR):** Compares the total benefits of an investment to its total costs. It is also called as Profitability Index.

BCR = PV of Benefit Expected from the Project / PV of the Cost of the Project.

PV= Present Value

BCR = Total Benefits / Total Costs.

Exercise

Alliance solar company is considering a new project that requires an investment of Rs 500,000. The project is expected to generate cash flows of Rs 100,000 in the first year, Rs 120,000 in the second year, Rs 150,000 in the third year, Rs 200,000 in the fourth year, and Rs 250,000 in the fifth year. Find out whether the project is a good investment opportunity.

BCR = Total Benefits / Total Costs

= (100,000 + 120,000 + 150,000 + 200,000 + 250,000) / 500,000 = 1.2

The BCR is equal to 1.2, meaning that for every rupee invested, the company will receive Rs 1.20 in benefits over the five years of the project. This indicates that the project is likely to be a good investment as the benefits outweigh the costs. The Rules for selecting each method are given in **Table 6.5** below.

Table 6.5. Types of Capital Budgeting

Techniques	Criteria	Accept	Reject
Payback Period (PBP)	Non-Discounting	PBP < Target Period	PBP > Target Period
Accounting Rate of Return (ARR)	Non-Discounting	ARR > Target Rate	ARR < Target Rate
Net Present Value (NPV)	Discounting	NPV > 0	NPV < 0
Internal Rate of Return (IRR)	Discounting	IRR > Cost of Capital	IRR < Cost of Capital
Benefit-Cost Ratio (BCR)	Discounting	BCR > 1	BCR < 1

Working Capital Management

Working capital is the money needed to fund the normal, day-to-day operations of the enterprise. It is needed for the smooth operation of an enterprise. The working capital cycle is the length of time between the company's outflow on raw materials, wages, and other expenditures and the inflow of cash from the sale of goods.

Working capital = Current assets – Current liabilities

Current assets are assets that are expected to be converted into cash within one year. Examples include cash, accounts receivable, inventory, short-term investments, and prepaid expenses.

Current liabilities are obligations that are due within one year. Examples include accounts payable, short-term loans, taxes payable, wages payable, interest payable, and unearned revenue.

Working capital is made up of the following three core components in the cycle:

1. Inventory and work in progress (work in progress generally applies to manufacturers)
2. Accounts payable (payments due to suppliers; creditor payments)
3. Accounts receivable (cash due from customers; debtor collection)

Working Capital Cycle

The working capital cycle is the time it takes for a company to convert its current assets into cash and then use that cash to pay off its current liabilities. It refers to the flow of a company's funds from the point of purchase of raw materials to the point of collection from its customers. The shorter the working capital cycle, the more efficiently a company is using its resources. The Working Capital Cycle is given in **Figure 6.3.**

The working capital cycle: Inventory Days + Receivable Days – Payable Days.

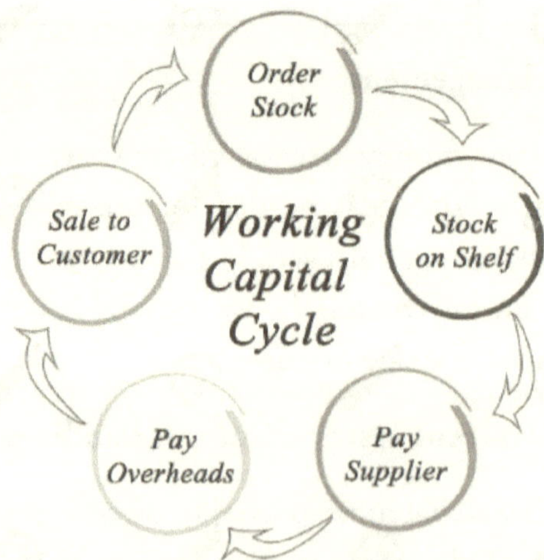

Figure 6.3. Working Capital Cycle

Working capital is calculated as the difference between current assets and current liabilities.

<u>Exercise:</u>

ABC company has the following Data. Calculate the working capital.

Current assets: Rs 500,000 (cash Rs 100,000, accounts receivable Rs 300,000, and inventory Rs 100,000)

Current liabilities: Rs 300,000 (accounts payable Rs 200,000 and short-term debt Rs 100,000)

Working capital = Current assets - Current liabilities

= Rs 500,000 – Rs 300,000

= Rs 200,000

Working capital management can bring several benefits to a company, including:

a. **Improved cash flow**: Effective management of working capital can help improve the company's cash flow by ensuring timely payments to suppliers, efficient collection of receivables, and reducing excess inventory.

b. **Increased profitability**: By managing working capital efficiently, a company can reduce the cost of funding its operations, leading to an increase in profitability.

c. **Reduced risk**: Efficient working capital management can help a company avoid cash flow shortages and reduce the risk of default on obligations.

d. **Increased competitiveness:** A company with good working capital management is better equipped to respond to market changes and take advantage of business opportunities, increasing its competitiveness.

e. **Improved credit ratings:** Companies with good working capital management are viewed as less risky by lenders and investors, which can lead to improved credit ratings and better borrowing terms.

Forecasting

Forecasting is the process of making predictions about future events or trends based on historical data and statistical analysis. This can be applied to a wide range of areas including finance, economics, sales, weather, and more. The accuracy of forecasts can vary and often depends on factors such as the availability of data, the quality of data, the method used for analysis, and the expertise of the forecaster. Forecasting methods can be broadly categorized into two groups: qualitative and quantitative.

Quantitative methods include:

- **Time series analysis**: using historical data to predict future trends
- **Regression analysis:** modeling the relationship between variables to make predictions
- **Econometrics**: using economic theory and statistical methods to make predictions about economic variables
- **ARIMA (Auto Regressive Integrated Moving Average):** a statistical model for time series data
- **Machine learning**: using algorithms to learn from data and make predictions

Qualitative methods include:

- **Expert judgment**: relying on the opinions and experience of experts to make predictions
- **Delphi method:** a group decision-making process that aggregates the opinions of experts to make a prediction
- **Market research:** gathering information through surveys and focus groups to inform predictions
- **Scenario analysis**: exploring possible future scenarios based on trends and events.

Purpose of Forecasting

The purpose of forecasting is to provide information and insights that can inform decision-making, planning, and resource allocation. Overall, the purpose of forecasting is to provide organizations with the information they need to make informed decisions, reduce uncertainty, and achieve their goals. Some of the key benefits of forecasting include:

- ✓ **Improved planning**: Forecasting can help organizations plan for future trends and events, such as sales, expenses, and resource requirements.
- ✓ **Better resource allocation:** By predicting future demand and supply trends, organizations can optimize their resource allocation and avoid overstocking or under-supplying.
- ✓ **Risk management:** Forecasting can help organizations identify potential risks and plan accordingly, reducing the impact of uncertainty on their operations.
- ✓ **Competitive advantage**: By having accurate and reliable forecasts, organizations can make informed decisions that give them a competitive advantage over their rivals.
- ✓ **Increased efficiency:** Forecasting can help organizations streamline their operations and reduce waste by better aligning resources with future demand.
- ✓ **Better decision-making**: Forecasting provides decision-makers with a basis for comparing and choosing between alternative courses of action.

Applications of forecasting include:

- **Financial forecasting:** projecting future sales, expenses, and profits for a company to inform budgeting and investment decisions.
- **Economic forecasting:** predicting future economic trends, such as inflation, gross domestic product (GDP), and employment, to inform government policy and business planning.
- **Sales forecasting:** estimating future demand for a product or service to inform production and inventory management.

- **Weather forecasting:** using historical data and current weather patterns to predict future weather conditions.
- **Political forecasting:** predicting the outcome of elections, policies, and events in the political arena.
- **Traffic forecasting:** estimating future traffic patterns to inform transportation planning and infrastructure development.
- **Energy demand forecasting:** predicting future energy consumption patterns to inform power generation and distribution planning.
- **Agricultural forecasting:** estimating future crop yields and food supplies to inform food security planning.

Box 6.4. Mentoring Program for Start-up

Starting a mentoring program for startups can be incredibly valuable for both mentors and mentees. Here's a guide on how to establish a mentoring program for startups:

Define Objectives: Determine the goals and objectives of your mentoring program. What do you hope to achieve? Common objectives include providing guidance, support, networking opportunities, and skill development for startup founders.

Identify Mentors: Recruit experienced entrepreneurs, industry professionals, investors, and experts who are willing to volunteer their time as mentors. Look for individuals with relevant experience and expertise in areas such as business development, marketing, finance, product development, and scaling startups.

Recruit Mentees: Reach out to startups housed in the incubation center of your institute and invite them to participate as mentees. Consider factors such as stage of development, industry focus, and specific areas where they need guidance.

Match Mentors and Mentees: Pair mentors and mentees based on compatibility, expertise, and the specific needs of the mentees.

Consider factors such as industry experience, business stage, and personality fit.

Establish Program Structure: Define the structure and format of your mentoring program. Will it be one-on-one mentoring, group mentoring, or a combination of both? Determine the frequency and duration of mentoring sessions, as well as the communication channels (e.g., in-person meetings, video calls, email).

Set Clear Expectations: Clarify the expectations and responsibilities of both mentors and mentees. Provide guidelines on topics to discuss, goals to set, and how to maintain confidentiality.

Provide Training and Resources: Offer training and resources for mentors to enhance their mentoring skills and provide guidance on best practices. Provide mentees with resources to help them make the most of the mentoring relationship, such as goal-setting templates, communication tips, and networking opportunities.

Facilitate Communication: Establish channels for mentors and mentees to communicate effectively, such as a mentoring platform, online forums, or dedicated Slack channels. Encourage regular check-ins and provide ongoing support and guidance as needed.

Monitor and Evaluate Progress: Track the progress of mentoring relationships and gather feedback from both mentors and mentees. Use this feedback to identify areas for improvement and make adjustments to the program as necessary.

Celebrate Successes: Recognize and celebrate the achievements and milestones of both mentors and mentees. This helps to reinforce the value of the mentoring program and fosters a sense of community and support.

By following these steps, you can establish a mentoring program that provides valuable support and guidance to startup founders, helping them navigate the challenges of entrepreneurship and achieve their goals.

Why Startups Fail

- ✓ **No Market Need**: The product doesn't solve a real problem or meet market demand.
- ✓ **Running Out of Cash**: Poor financial management or inability to secure funding.
- ✓ **Weak Business Model**: Lack of a clear revenue-generating strategy.
- ✓ **Strong Competition**: Inability to differentiate or compete in a crowded market.
- ✓ **Team Issues**: Inexperienced leadership or founder conflicts.
- ✓ **Poor Product**: Low-quality product or technical issues.
- ✓ **Ineffective Marketing**: Inadequate customer acquisition or costly marketing.
- ✓ **Regulatory Challenges**: Compliance issues or sudden regulatory changes.
- ✓ **Lack of Focus**: Trying to do too much or frequent changes in direction.
- ✓ **Failure to Pivot**: Not adapting based on feedback or changing market needs.

Business Strategy

Strategic thinking involves analyzing complex situations, anticipating future challenges, and developing innovative strategies to achieve long-term goals. It's about taking a holistic and forward-thinking approach to decision-making to create sustainable value and maintain a competitive edge.

A business strategy is a comprehensive plan outlining how a company aims to achieve its long-term goals and objectives. It involves defining the company's mission, vision, and values, analyzing its internal and external environments, setting specific goals, and determining the action plans needed to achieve those goals.

The importance of business strategy lies in several key aspects:

- **Direction and Focus:** A well-defined strategy provides clarity on the direction the company should take and ensures that all efforts are aligned toward common goals.
- **Competitive Advantage:** It helps identify unique selling propositions and competitive advantages that differentiate the company from its competitors.
- **Resource Allocation:** By prioritizing initiatives and allocating resources effectively, a business strategy ensures optimal use of resources, maximizing efficiency and profitability.
- **Risk Management:** Through thorough analysis of internal and external factors, a business strategy helps identify potential risks and provides mechanisms to mitigate them.
- **Adaptability:** A good strategy is flexible and adaptable, allowing the company to respond effectively to changes in the market environment.

Developing a business strategy involves several key steps:

- **Define the Mission, Vision, and Values:** Clearly articulate the purpose of the company, its long-term vision, and the core values that guide its actions.
- **Conduct PEST Analysis:** A Political, Economic, Social, and Technological (PEST) analysis is a strategic tool used by organizations to understand the external macro-environmental factors that can influence their operations and decision-making. The acronym PEST stands for Political, Economic, Social, and Technological factors.
- **Conduct Stakeholder Analysis:** Stakeholder analysis is the process of collecting information about any person that will be impacted by (or can impact) your project. The purpose of stakeholder analysis is to understand the needs, expectations, influence, and

impact of these stakeholders on the project's or organization's success. This analysis helps in developing effective strategies to engage and manage stakeholders to achieve desired outcomes.

- **Conduct a SWOT Analysis:** Evaluate the company's strengths, weaknesses, opportunities, and threats to identify internal capabilities and external factors that may impact the business. While PEST and SWOT analyses serve distinct purposes, they are interconnected in the strategic planning process, with PEST analysis providing the foundational understanding of the external environment that is then incorporated into the broader SWOT analysis to inform strategic decision-making.

- **Set Objectives and Goals:** Establish specific, measurable, achievable, relevant, and time-bound (SMART) objectives that align with the company's mission and vision.

- **Market Analysis:** Understand the industry landscape, market trends, customer needs, and competitor strategies to identify growth opportunities.

- **Develop Strategic Initiatives:** Based on the analysis, define key initiatives and action plans to achieve the set objectives and goals.

- **Allocate Resources:** Determine the resources required to implement the strategic initiatives effectively, including financial, human, and technological resources.

- **Monitor and Review:** Continuously monitor the progress of the strategy implementation, evaluate its effectiveness, and make adjustments as necessary to stay on track toward achieving the goals.

- **Communicate and Align:** Ensure that the strategy is effectively communicated throughout the organization and that all employees understand their roles in executing the strategy.

Growing Your Business

Growth is a necessary stimulant for most business firms. Growth is the precondition for the survival of a business firm. The reasons that drive business enterprises toward growth are given below:

- To obtain economies of scale.
- For exploiting business opportunities.
- For facing competition in the market by diversifying the product line.
- For protecting adverse business conditions.
- For making optimum utilization of resources.
- For Business Sustainability

Generally, the growth strategies adopted by enterprises can be classified as:

1. Organic growth and 2. Inorganic growth

1. Organic growth strategies

Organic growth refers to the growth of a business through internal processes, relying on its resources. Strategies for organic growth include: a. Business Expansion; b Diversification and c. Modernization

a. **Expansion**: Expansion strategy involves increasing market share, sales revenue, and profit of existing products/services. It's useful for firms with smaller market share and can be used for market penetration, development, and product development. HUL penetrated rural markets, Colgate introduced "Colgate Active Salt" and Cadbury expanded their market among elderly persons and children.

b. **Diversification:** Diversification is a strategy where companies expand their business by developing new products or services for their existing customer base, a similar market, or a different clientele entirely. Despite the potential challenges, it's an effective way to achieve stability and growth in the long term. Examples of diversification include LIC diversifying into mutual funds and McDonald's introducing the McCafé.

- **Horizontal** - Horizontal integration involves the addition of parallel new products to the existing product line. For example, seven small cement firms combined and formed Associated Cement Companies (ACC).

- **Concentric** - A company can use the strategy of concentric diversification when the reputation of the present product or service is high and can be used for new products or services. Therefore, when a firm diversifies into a business, that is related to its present business in terms of marketing, technology, or both, it is called concentric diversification. For example, Amul has added ice creams to its range of milk products. HDFC Bank provides mutual fund services to its customers.

- **Vertical** - Vertical integration involves adding new complementary products or services to the existing product line. It can be backward or forward. Backward integration moves towards the inputs of the present product, while forward integration involves selling the present products directly. For instance, Amazon.com became a book publisher as well as a bookseller, while Starbucks bought coffee farms in China. Companies like Bata, Bombay Dyeing, and Raymond's sell their fabrics through their retail outlets.

- **Conglomerate** - When a firm diversifies into a business, that is not related to its existing business both in terms of marketing and technology, it is called conglomerate diversification. Companies such as Reliance, HMT, ITC, and Godrej have grown mainly by conglomerate diversification.

c. Modernization: A firm may use a modernization strategy to achieve growth. A modernization strategy involves the upgradation of technology to increase production, improve quality, and reduce wastage and the cost of production. Modernization improves the productivity and efficiency of the firm. The growth is systematic and does not affect the normal functioning of the firm. For example, public-sector banks in India used digitalization as a modernization strategy in the year 2000.

Inorganic growth strategies

Inorganic growth of an enterprise refers to growth achieved through external means rather than relying solely on internal expansion. The inorganic growth strategies include Mergers and Acquisitions, Joint Ventures,

Strategic Alliances, Licensing Agreements, Private Equity Investments, and Strategic Partnerships.

a. Mergers and Acquisitions: Mergers and Acquisitions (M&A) refer to the consolidation of companies or assets through various forms of business combinations. M&A can take the form of mergers, acquisitions, consolidations, tender offers, purchase of assets, and other similar transactions. The primary objective of M&A is to create value for shareholders by combining complementary resources, such as complementary products, technologies, or customer bases.

Examples of M&A deals that have occurred include Reliance Industries Limited's acquisition of Future Retail; TATA Motors' acquisition of JLR (Jaguar Land Rover); Bharti Airtel's acquisition of Tata Teleservices; HDFC Bank's acquisition of Centurion Bank of Punjab; Wipro's acquisition of Alight Solutions.

b. Joint Ventures: Joint Ventures (JV) and Strategic Alliances are cooperative agreements between two or more companies to achieve common business goals. Joint Ventures involve the creation of a new separate entity where both parties share ownership, control, and profits. Example of Joint Venture: Maruti Suzuki India Ltd., is a famous example of a joint venture in the automobile industry in India.

c. Strategic Alliances: are fewer formal agreements between two or more companies, where they collaborate and share resources to achieve a specific objective without creating a new separate entity. Examples of Strategic Alliances: Reliance and BP; Hero MotoCorp and Honda; Tata Consultancy Services and Microsoft; Airtel and Amazon Web Services; HDFC Bank and American Express.

Both JVs and Strategic Alliances allow companies to pool their resources and expertise to pursue new market opportunities, reduce risks and costs, and access new technologies.

d. Licensing Agreements: Licensing arrangements involve a licensor granting the use of their intellectual property to a licensee in exchange for compensation. This allows companies to monetize their unused IP and expand their product offerings without incurring additional costs.

Examples of Licensing Arrangements include Coca-Cola and Hindustan Coca-Cola Beverages Pvt. Ltd.; IBM and Tata Consultancy Services; Microsoft and Wipro; Johnson & Johnson and Hinduja Group; Procter & Gamble and Britannia Industries.

e. Private Equity Investments: PE investments involve acquiring a stake in a privately held company by a PE firm or investors, who provide capital in exchange for ownership. The investment is made in growing companies with a clear growth strategy and a need for financing. PE investors bring expertise to help companies grow and succeed.

Examples of Private Equity Investments: KKR's investment in Jio Platforms (2020); Blackstone's investment in Embassy Office Parks (2019); Warburg Pincus' investment in Byju's (2017); Bain Capital's investment in Flipkart (2017); TPG Capital's investment in Power Grid Corporation of India (2016)

f. Strategic partnerships: are mutually beneficial relationships between two or more organizations that work together to achieve common goals. Examples of strategic partnerships from India include collaborations between companies in the same industry or different industries with complementary products or services. Some examples of strategic partnerships in India are:

- **Reliance Jio and Microsoft** - Jio and Microsoft entered into a strategic partnership to offer cloud solutions and other technology services to small and medium businesses in India.
- **Tata Motors and Jayem Automotives** - Tata Motors and Jayem Automotives formed a strategic partnership to develop high-performance electric vehicles for the Indian market.
- **Flipkart and Aditya Birla Group** - Flipkart and Aditya Birla Group entered into a strategic partnership to expand their online and offline retail presence in India.

- **Amazon and Future Retail** - Amazon and Future Retail entered into a strategic partnership to expand the reach of their retail businesses in India.
- **Airtel and Amazon Web Services (AWS)** - Airtel and AWS entered into a strategic partnership to offer cloud services to customers in India.

What is Franchising?

Franchising is a hybrid of organic and inorganic growth. It enables a company to expand its business without incurring the cost of traditional organic growth methods. A franchisor grants the right to use its trademark, products, and operating systems to another business in exchange for an initial fee and ongoing royalties. The franchisee operates the business using the franchisor's established systems and guidelines, while also benefiting from the franchisor's brand recognition and marketing efforts. Some examples of franchising are:

- KFC - KFC is a fast-food chain that has been operating in India through the franchising model since 1995.
- Subway - Subway is a sandwich chain that has been operating in India through the franchising model since 2001.
- Domino's Pizza - Domino's Pizza is a pizza chain that has been operating in India through the franchising model since 1996.
- McDonald's - McDonald's is a fast-food chain that has been operating in India through the franchising model since 1996.
- CCD (Café Coffee Day) - CCD is a coffee chain that has been operating in India through the franchising model since 1996.

Pros and Cons of Franchising

Pros of franchising:

a. Established brand recognition and reputation
b. Access to proven business models and systems
c. Increased market penetration and geographic expansion

d.   Shared marketing and advertising efforts

e.   Lower start-up costs compared to starting a business from scratch

Cons of franchising:

a.   Loss of control over brand standards and quality

b.   Dependence on franchisees for success

c.   Limited flexibility in business operations and decision-making

d.   Royalty and ongoing franchise fees

e.   Potential liability for franchisees' actions.

AI for Business

AI tools offer a wide range of applications for businesses across various industries, helping them improve efficiency, streamline and automate tasks, optimize workflows, and decision-making, market research, build websites, and logos, create personalized customer experience, customer service, and more. Here is some common AI tools used in business:

1.   **Chatbots**: AI-powered chatbots can handle customer inquiries, provide support, and even process orders, reducing the need for human intervention in customer service.

2.   **Predictive Analytics**: AI algorithms can analyze large datasets to predict future trends, customer behavior, and market dynamics, helping businesses make informed decisions and optimize their operations.

3.   **Natural Language Processing (NLP)**: NLP technology enables computers to understand, interpret, and generate human language, allowing businesses to automate tasks such as sentiment analysis, content generation, and language translation.

4.   **Recommendation Systems**: AI-driven recommendation engines analyze customer preferences and behavior to provide personalized recommendations for products, services, content, and more, enhancing the customer experience and increasing sales.

5.   **Virtual Assistants**: AI-powered virtual assistants like Siri, Google Assistant, and Alexa can perform tasks such as scheduling

appointments, setting reminders, and answering questions, improving productivity and efficiency for both individuals and businesses.

6. **Image and Video Recognition**: AI algorithms can analyze images and videos to recognize objects, faces, gestures, and patterns, enabling applications such as facial recognition, object detection, and visual search.

7. **Robotic Process Automation (RPA)**: RPA tools automate repetitive and rule-based tasks by mimicking human actions, freeing up employees to focus on more strategic and value-added activities.

8. **Machine Learning Platforms**: Machine learning platforms provide tools and frameworks for developing and deploying machine learning models, enabling businesses to extract insights from data, automate decision-making processes, and build intelligent applications.

9. **Speech Recognition**: AI-powered speech recognition technology converts spoken language into text, enabling applications such as virtual assistants, voice-controlled devices, and transcription services.

10. **Fraud Detection**: AI algorithms can analyze patterns and anomalies in financial transactions to detect fraudulent activities, helping businesses prevent financial losses and protect their assets.

Table 6.6 presents the top AI tools for businesses poised to make a significant impact on businesses throughout the year. From enhancing productivity to streamlining operations, these tools represent the forefront of innovation, empowering businesses to thrive in a dynamic marketplace.

When selecting AI tools for business, it's crucial to align them with specific business objectives while considering factors such as data availability and quality, technical requirements, customization options, accuracy, interpretability, scalability, cost, ethical considerations, and user experience. By carefully evaluating these factors, organizations can choose AI solutions that not only address their immediate needs but also support long-term growth and innovation while ensuring compliance with regulatory requirements and ethical standards.

Table 6.6. AI Tools to Run Your Business from A-Z

AI Tool	Application
ClickUp	Text generation, translation, answering queries, summarisation, documentation
ChatGPT	Question answering, language translation, text generation, competitor analysis
Dall-E 2	Artistic Creation, Product Design, marketing collateral, education and training
Bricabrac	web app development
Tome	Storytelling, generate presentations, outlines, text, images, pitching ideas
Second Brain	Writing companion, create superior articles, emails, tweets, messages
Jasper	Writing assistant, crafting engaging blog posts and articles, developing marketing content, addressing customer inquiries, Digital marketing
Plus	Streamline and automate reporting and analytics processes for businesses
FireFlies	Transcribing, summarizing, and analyzing meetings.
Speechify	AI-powered text-to-speech (TTS) solution designed to enhance your reading and listening efficiency.
Logo Maker	Generate logo
Jimdo	Website Builder
CoreML	Mobile app development
Speak	Market research
Pecan	Predictive analytics
Hotjar	Customer experience
Browse AI	Data extraction and monitoring
Gemini	Multimodal- generalize and seamlessly understand, operate across, and combine different types of information including text, code, audio, image, and video.

Source: Compiled from various sources

Key Takeaways

- To build a startup, you need to identify a business idea, convert it into an opportunity, create a POC by conducting a feasibility study, build a prototype, develop an MVP, create a lean business canvas model, analyze the market, fundraise, and build a core team.

- Feasibility Study analyses whether the proposed business ideas will succeed or fail. It determines the practicality by assessing the opportunities and threats of the proposed plan.

- There are different types of studies to check feasibility, such as technical feasibility, market feasibility, organizational feasibility, and financial feasibility, that help to build a lean canvas business model.

- The Lean Business Model Canvas is a framework for startups to articulate their business model, identify opportunities for improvement, and communicate their vision to stakeholders.

- The nine building blocks of the Lean Business Canvas model are Problem, Customer Segments, Unique Value Proposition (UVP), Solution, Channels, Revenue Streams, Key Metrics, Cost Structure, and Unfair Advantage.

- The important types of business models are e-commerce, subscription-based, freemium, marketplace, franchise, platform, on-demand, brick-and-mortar, razor and blade, and asset-light.

- Market analysis is important for businesses to make informed decisions about product development, marketing strategies, resource allocation, and overall business planning. It helps them understand the market, anticipate changes, and identify growth opportunities.

- Market analysis helps understand the volume and value of the market, potential customer segments and their buying patterns, the position of your competition, and the overall economic environment, including barriers to entry, and industry regulations.

- Raising capital for a startup can be a challenge and a barrier to the eventual commencement and implementation of your business. Debt and equity are the two major sources of financing.
- Bootstrapping, friends and family, angel Investors, venture capital, crowdfunding, accelerators and incubators, grants, and government Programs, Debt Financing, and IPO are various ways to finance a startup.
- Investors look for startups with growth potential, a strong value proposition, a capable team, and a clear path to success.
- To build a strong core team, look for individuals who complement your skills, share your vision, and are committed to helping your startup thrive. It requires patience, persistence, and a keen eye for talent.
- Pitching your business idea effectively is crucial for gaining support. Keep it focused, persuasive, and memorable.
- Entrepreneurs have to decide how to organize their startups. There are different forms of business organization, each with its pros and cons.
- There are ten major types of business entities in India. They are sole proprietorship, partnership, limited liability partnership (LLP), private limited company, public limited company, one-person company, section-8 company, joint stock company, non-government organizations (NGO), and joint Hindu family businesses.
- From 1st July 2020, new MSME definitions are based on net turnover and investments in equipment.
- Registering your business as an MSME in India is not mandatory but comes with several benefits such as tax exemptions, credit facilities, subsidies, and loans, and online registration is free of cost on the Udyam portal.
- The Government of India has launched several government schemes to support startups and foster innovation, aiming to provide financial assistance, mentorship, and infrastructure.

- A complete set of financial statements normally consists of an Income Statement (Profit and Loss Account), a Balance Sheet and a Cash Flow Statement

- Cash budgeting is the process of forecasting a company's expected cash inflows and outflows to make informed decisions about managing cash resources.

- Capital budgeting is the process of evaluating and prioritizing potential investments or expenditures that an organization will make in fixed assets, such as buildings, machinery, or equipment.

- There are mainly two types of capital budgeting techniques: Non discounting criteria (PBP and ARR) and discounting criteria (IRR, NPV, BCR).

- Working capital is the money needed for day-to-day operations. The working capital cycle is the time between a company's spending and cash inflow from sales.

- Forecasting involves predicting future trends based on historical data and analysis. There are two types of methods used: quantitative and qualitative.

- A business strategy is a plan that outlines how a company aims to achieve its long-term goals. It involves defining the mission, analyzing internal and external environments, setting specific goals, and determining the action plans needed to achieve those goals.

- The growth strategies adopted by the enterprise can be classified as organic growth and inorganic growth

- Organic growth refers to the growth of a business through internal processes, relying on its resources. Strategies for organic growth include: Business expansion, diversification and modernization

- Inorganic growth refers to external expansion strategies like Mergers and Acquisitions, Joint Ventures, Strategic Alliances, Licensing Agreements, Private Equity Investments, and Strategic Partnerships.

- Franchising is a business model where a company allows others to operate under its brand name and business model for a fee.

Franchisees get support while the franchisor expands its brand presence and revenue streams.

- AI tools can help businesses in various industries by improving efficiency, automating tasks, optimizing workflows, and assisting with decision-making, market research, website and logo creation, customer experience, and customer service.

Key Terms

Startup, Business Idea, POC, Feasibility Study, MVP, Lean Business Model Canvas, Business Models, e-commerce, Subscription-based, Freemium, Marketplace, Franchise platform, On-demand, Brick-and-mortar, Razor and Blade, Asset-light, Market Analysis, Capital Raising, Investors, Core Team, Pitching, Business Organization, Business Entities, Sole proprietorship, Partnership, Limited liability partnership (LLP), Private limited company, Public limited companies, One-person company, section-8 company, Joint stock company, Non-government organizations (NGO), Joint Hindu family businesses, MSME, Financial Statements, Balance Sheet, Profit and Loss Account, Cash Flow Statements, Cash Budgeting, Capital Budgeting, PBP, ARR, IRR, NPV, BCR, Working Capital Cycle, Forecasting, Business Strategy, Organic Growth, Inorganic Growth, Business Expansion, Diversification, Modernisation, Mergers and Acquisition, Joint Ventures, Strategic Alliances, Licensing Agreements, Private Equity Investments, Strategic Partnerships, Franchising, AI Tools.

Quiz – Multiple Choice Questions

1. Which tool is used to by startups summarize the key aspects of a business idea and its feasibility?

- a. Lean Business Model Canvas
- b. Cash Budgeting
- c. Capital Budgeting
- d. Franchising

2. **Which term refers to the various methods a company can use to generate revenue and profit?**

    a. Market Analysis
    b. Business Models
    c. Investors
    d. Core Team

3. **What is the process of evaluating the attractiveness of a market for a product or service?**

    a. Capital Raising
    b. Forecasting
    c. Market Analysis
    d. Working Capital

4. **What is the term for the process of obtaining funds from external sources to finance a business?**

    a. Pitching
    b. Business Organization
    c. Capital Raising
    d. Business Entities

5. **Which term refers to the individuals who are responsible for operations of a startup in the early stage?**

    a. Investors
    b. Core Team
    c. Business Strategy
    d. Organic Growth

6. **What is the term for the formal presentation of a business idea to potential investors?**

    a. Business Strategy
    b. Organic Growth

    c.   Pitching

    d.   Inorganic Growth

7. **Which term refers to the legal structure of a business, such as a corporation or partnership?**

    a.   Business Organization

    b.   Business Entities

    c.   MSME

    d.   Financial Statements

8. **Which term refers to small and medium-sized enterprises?**

    a.   Financial Statements

    b.   Cash Budgeting

    c.   MSME

    d.   Capital Budgeting

9. **What documents provide a summary of a company's financial position and performance?**

    a.   Market Analysis

    b.   Cash Budgeting

    c.   Financial Statements

    d.   Capital Budgeting

10. **What is the process of estimating the cash inflows and outflows of a business?**

    a.   Franchising

    b.   Cash Budgeting

    c.   Capital Budgeting

    d.   Working Capital

11. **What is the process of evaluating long-term investment decisions?**

    a.   Capital Raising

    b.   Forecasting

c. Capital Budgeting

d. Working Capital

12. Which term refers to the difference between current assets and current liabilities?

a. Forecasting

b. Business Strategy

c. Organic Growth

d. Working Capital

13. What is the process of predicting future trends and outcomes?

a. Organic Growth

b. Forecasting

c. Inorganic Growth

d. Franchising

14. Which term refers to growing a business using internal resources?

a. Inorganic Growth

b. Forecasting

c. Organic Growth

d. Franchising

15. What is the process of growing a business through mergers and acquisitions?

a. Organic Growth

b. Forecasting

c. Inorganic Growth

d. Franchising

16. What is the business strategy of expanding a business through licensing agreements?

a. Forecasting

b. Organic Growth

   c. Inorganic Growth

   d. Franchising

17. Which term refers to tools and technologies that simulate human intelligence?

   a. Business Strategy

   b. Organic Growth

   c. AI Tools

   d. Franchising

18. A plan that outlines how a company aims to achieve its long-term goals.

   a. Business Strategy

   b. Business Model

   c. AI Tools

   d. Forecasting

19. The money needed for day-to-day operations of a Business

   a. Working Capital

   b. Balance Sheet

   c. Forecasting

   d. Capital Budgeting

20. From 1st July 2020, new MSME definitions are based on

   a. Net turnover and investments in equipment.

   b. Net turnover

   c. Investment in plant and machinery

   d. None of the above

<u>ANSWERS</u>

   1. a

   2. b

   3. c

   4. c

5. b
6. c
7. b
8. c
9. c
10. b
11. a
12. d
13. b
14. c
15. c
16. d
17. c
18. a
19. a
20. a

Exercise 6.1

<u>From Idea to Startup: Building Your Entrepreneurial Venture</u>

<u>Objective:</u> The objective of this exercise is to guide participants through the process of transforming a business idea into a viable startup. By following structured steps, participants will develop essential skills in ideation, validation, business model creation, and pitching.

Duration: This exercise can be conducted over several sessions, depending on the depth of exploration and the level of engagement desired.

Materials Needed:

- Whiteboard or flipchart
- Markers
- Sticky notes
- Laptop or tablet with internet access (optional)
- Handouts or worksheets (optional)

Exercise Steps:

1. Ideation Session (1 session):

- Participants brainstorm business ideas individually for 10-15 minutes.
- Each participant presents their idea briefly (1-2 minutes) to the group.
- Group discussion: Participants provide feedback, ask clarifying questions, and offer suggestions for improvement.

2. Idea Validation (1 session):

- Using the Lean Startup methodology, participants identify assumptions underlying their business ideas.
- Participants conduct market research to validate or invalidate these assumptions.
- Group discussion: Participants share their findings and insights, and refine their ideas based on feedback.

3. Lean Business Model Canvas (1-2 sessions):

- Participants create a Lean Business Model Canvas for their startup idea, filling in each section with key elements such as customer segments, value proposition, channels, revenue streams, etc.
- The facilitator guides participants through each section, providing explanations and examples as needed.
- Group discussion: Participants share their canvases, receive feedback, and iterate on their models.

4. Pitch Preparation (1 session):

- Participants develop a concise pitch for their startup idea, focusing on capturing the attention of potential investors or partners.
- The facilitator guides the structuring the pitch, including elements such as problem statement, solution, market opportunity, business model, traction, and team.
- Participants practice delivering their pitches to the group and receive constructive feedback.

5. Mock Pitch Session (1 session):

- Participants present their pitches to a panel of "investors" (other participants or facilitators acting as investors).
- After each pitch, the panel provides feedback and asks questions to simulate a real investment pitch scenario.
- Participants incorporate feedback and refine their pitches based on the mock session.

6. Reflection and Next Steps (1 session):

- Participants reflect on their journey from idea to startup, highlighting key learnings, challenges, and successes.
- The facilitator leads a discussion on the next steps, including considerations for further development, potential pivots, or additional resources needed.

- Participants set actionable goals for moving forward with their startup ideas.

Optional Extensions:

- Invite guest speakers who are successful entrepreneurs or investors to share their insights and experiences.
- Incorporate team-based activities where participants work in groups to refine and develop their startup ideas collaboratively.
- Organize a pitch competition where participants present their final pitches to a panel of judges, with prizes awarded for the most promising ideas.

Exercise 6.2

Investment Decisions

You are considering investing in a manufacturing project that requires an initial investment in machinery and equipment. The project is expected to generate cash flows over five years. Additionally, you need to assess the impact of the project on working capital requirements.

Data:

Initial Investment (Year 0): ₹30,00,000

Estimated Annual Cash Flows (Years 1-5): ₹10,00,000

Discount Rate (Cost of Capital): 10%

Working Capital Requirements:

- Initial Working Capital: ₹5,00,000
- Annual Increase in Working Capital: ₹1,00,000

Tasks:

1. Calculate the Payback Period (PBP) for the project.
2. Determine the Accounting Rate of Return (ARR) for the project.
3. Calculate the Internal Rate of Return (IRR) for the project.

4. Calculate the Net Present Value (NPV) of the project.

5. Determine the Benefit-Cost Ratio (BCR) for the project.

Conclusion:

Based on the calculations, the project has a Payback Period of 3 years, an Accounting Rate of Return of approximately 13.33%, an Internal Rate of Return of approximately 15.89%, a Net Present Value of ₹7,97,128.98, and a Benefit-Cost Ratio of approximately 1.2657. These metrics suggest that the project is financially viable and could generate positive returns for the investor.

Activity 6.1

Strategic Planning for Your Business

When planning a project, it is important to learn about the internal and external factors that can affect the project. There is some excellent strategic planning Strategic planning is an ongoing process, not a one-time event. Regularly revisit and refine the strategic plan to ensure its relevance and effectiveness in guiding the company toward its long-term goals. Developing a strategic plan for a company involves several key steps and considerations. Here's a general framework you can follow:

1. Understand the Current State

Conduct a thorough analysis of the company's current situation, including political, environmental, social, and technological (PEST) analysis and also its strengths, weaknesses, opportunities, and threats (SWOT) analysis.

PEST analysis is a framework that helps ascertain aspects of various external factors (political, economic, sociological, and technological, or PEST) that can mean opportunities or threats for a business concern. The outcome such as opportunities and threats which are external factors of PEST analysis are used in SWOT analysis.

Political Factors	**Economic Factors**
Government type and stability	Stage of business cycle
Tax policy	Impact of globalisation
Changes in the political environment	Labour costs
Regulation and deregulation trends	Environmental policies
Levels of corruption	GDP, exchange rate and inflation
Social Factors	**Technological Factors**
Demography	Technology trends
Talent and Education	Research and development
Socio-cultural factor	Infrastructure
Religion and lifestyle	Access to technology
Job security	Impact of technology transfer

Here's a simple SWOT matrix template you can adapt to your specific needs:

Strengths	**Weaknesses**
1. What is our competitive advantage?	1. Where can we improve?
2. What resources do we have?	2. What products are underperforming?
3. What products are performing well?	3. Where are we lacking resources?
Opportunities	**Threats**
1. What new technology can we use?	1. What regulations are changing?
2. Can we expand our operations?	2. What are competitors doing?
3. What new segments can we test?	3. How are consumer trends changing?

Review financial performance, market position, customer feedback, employee capabilities, and other relevant factors.

2. Define Vision, Mission, and Values

- Clearly articulate the company's vision for the future, defining what it aspires to achieve in the long term.
- Develop a mission statement that succinctly communicates the company's purpose and how it adds value to customers, employees, and stakeholders.
- Establish core values that guide decision-making and behavior within the organization.

3. Set Strategic Objectives:

- Based on the analysis of the current state and the company's vision, establish specific, measurable, achievable, relevant, and time-bound (SMART) strategic objectives.
- These objectives should align with the company's vision and address key areas such as revenue growth, market expansion, innovation, operational efficiency, or customer satisfaction.

4. Identify Strategic Initiatives:

- Determine the strategic initiatives necessary to achieve the defined objectives.
- These initiatives may include expanding into new markets, developing new products or services, improving operational processes, enhancing customer service, or strengthening the brand.

5. Allocate Resources:

- Assess the resources (financial, human, technological, etc.) required to execute the strategic initiatives.
- Develop a resource allocation plan that ensures sufficient investment in priority areas while optimizing efficiency and effectiveness.

6. Develop Action Plans:

- Create detailed action plans for each strategic initiative, outlining specific tasks, responsibilities, timelines, and milestones.
- Ensure clarity and accountability among team members involved in executing the plans.

7. Monitor and Measure Progress:

- Establish key performance indicators (KPIs) to track progress toward strategic objectives.
- Implement regular performance monitoring and reporting mechanisms to assess the effectiveness of strategic initiatives.

- Identify any deviations from the plan and take corrective actions as necessary.

8. Adapt and Iterate:

- Continuously review and reassess the strategic plan in response to changes in the internal and external environment.
- Be open to adapting strategies and tactics based on new information, market dynamics, or emerging opportunities and threats.

9. Communicate and Engage:

- Communicate the strategic plan effectively to all stakeholders, including employees, customers, investors, and partners.
- Foster engagement and alignment by involving stakeholders in the strategic planning process and soliciting their input and feedback.

10. Cultivate a Strategic Culture:

- Foster a culture of strategic thinking and agility within the organization, where employees at all levels understand the company's strategic objectives and their role in achieving them.
- Encourage innovation, collaboration, and a willingness to challenge the status quo to drive continuous improvement and adaptation.

Situation 6.1

Go To Market

A new business opportunity has arisen to develop a wellness retreat centre in a rural area that offers a range of wellness activities and services. The retreat centre will provide a peaceful and rejuvenating environment for individuals seeking to improve their mental and physical health. The wellness retreat centre will offer a range of activities and services, including yoga, meditation, nutrition classes, spa treatments, and outdoor adventures. The retreat centre will differentiate itself by offering a unique blend of wellness activities and services in a peaceful, rural environment. Anand, Kiran, and Prakash the promoters of the wellness centre have approached Mr. Ashok Patnaik a management consultant to conduct a feasibility analysis.

Market Analysis:

Target Market: The target market for the wellness retreat center will be individuals looking for a break from their busy lives and seeking to improve their physical and mental health. This could include working professionals, families, and seniors.

Market Size: The wellness and health industry is growing rapidly and there is a large market for wellness retreat centers in rural areas.

Competition: There is some competition in the wellness retreat center market, but there is room for new entrants, especially in rural areas where there are fewer options. The retreat center will differentiate itself by offering a unique blend of wellness activities and services in a peaceful, rural environment.

Situation 6.2

Funding Your Start-up by an Angel

A start-up financed by an angel investor typically refers to a company that is just starting up and is backed by a wealthy individual or group of individuals. Remedi Inc. is a start-up founded by Gautam Singh and Naveen Kumar developing a mobile app for organizing and sharing personal photos. The founders have invested Rs 5,00,000 each as an initial investment. The amount invested by the founders was sufficient for product development and market research. During the market research, the promoters found that they had to add some more features to their product. Therefore, the founders are looking for initial funding of Rs 5,00,000 who are interested in their product, so that they can add some more features to the product and launch it in the market. Guide them?

Learning: The promoters of Remedi Inc. have to find an Angel investor to fund their Start-up. The promoters have pitched their venture to many angels and found Mr. Jagadeesh Patil, who was interested in their idea and provided an initial investment of Rs 5,00,000 for a 25% equity stake in the company. With the funding in place, the founders hired a team of developers and started building the app. They also hired a marketing team to create a buzz around the product.

Situation 6.3

Financing Your Startup

Ravi Shah and Neetu Singh are the founders of Ananya Technologies Pvt. Ltd., an IT startup The founders prepared a comprehensive business plan, financial projections, and a pitch deck to present to potential investors. Ravi and Neetu approached several venture capital firms that specialize in funding technology startups in India. After several meetings and presentations, Ravi received interest from a well-known venture capital firm based in India.

The venture capital firm conducted a thorough due diligence process to evaluate Ananya Technologies' potential for growth and profitability. This included reviewing the business plan, financial projections, market analysis, and management team. After a positive due diligence outcome, the venture capital firm entered into negotiations with Ravi to finalize the investment terms. They agreed on a Rs 5 million investment in exchange for a 20% equity stake in the company. The parties signed a term sheet and closed the deal by exchanging funds for equity.

Learning: The venture capital firm became a shareholder in Ananya Technologies and provided support and resources to help the company grow and achieve its goals. The investment allowed Ravi and Neetu to hire additional team members, increase marketing efforts, and further develop the technology. This is a hypothetical mini-case of venture financing in India, and the actual process can be much more complex and may vary based on the specific circumstances of each company and investor.

Situation 6.4

Grow Your Business

Rashmi Technologies a startup was founded by two software engineers Vinayak and Jagadish in Bangalore to provide innovative solutions for businesses in the region. The startup experienced rapid growth in its first few years and quickly became one of the leading players in its industry. However, as the market matured, the startup faced challenges in maintaining its growth:

- Competition: The market was becoming increasingly crowded, with several similar startups vying for market share.
- Access to finance: The startup struggled to secure funding to invest in research and development, marketing, and expanding operations.
- Hiring and retaining talent: The startup faced challenges in attracting and retaining top talent, as the competition for skilled workers was fierce in the tech industry.

To overcome these challenges, the startup developed a growth strategy that focused on expanding into new markets, leveraging technology, and cultivating partnerships. The startup entered into strategic partnerships with two established companies in complementary industries, which provided access to new customers and resources. The startup also invested in research and development to create innovative products that would give it a competitive advantage.

Additionally, the startup launched a talent development program that provided training and mentorship to employees, which helped to attract and retain top talent. The program also helped to cultivate a culture of innovation and collaboration, which supported the growth of the business.

Learning: This situation highlights the challenges that startups in India face as they try to maintain growth and succeed in a competitive market. The growth strategy developed by the startup demonstrates how startups can overcome these challenges by leveraging technology, forming partnerships, investing in talent development, and focusing on innovation.

Simulation Game 6.1

Cost-Benefit Analysis of Your Project

The State Government is planning for the implementation of a waste management project in an urban area. Given the following data, find out whether the project is viable.

Cost of the Project: The cost of waste collection and disposal is ₹75,00,000 per year, the cost of setting up waste recycling facilities is ₹3,75,00,000 and the cost of public education and outreach programs is ₹37,50,000 per year.

Benefits: The benefits from reduced environmental pollution and improved public health are estimated to be ₹1,12,50,000 per year, and the benefits from increased economic activity through waste recycling are estimated to be ₹37,50,000 per year.

The discounted present value of the costs and benefits would be calculated using a discount rate of 5%. The results would be as follows:

- The discounted present value of the cost of waste collection and disposal over 5 years is ₹3,49,19,906.
- The discounted present value of the cost of setting up waste recycling facilities is ₹3,38,67,432.
- The discounted present value of the cost of public education and outreach programs over 5 years is ₹1,62,68,292.
- The discounted present value of the benefits from reduced environmental pollution and improved public health over 5 years is ₹5,39,56,058.
- The discounted present value of the benefits from increased economic activity through waste recycling over 5 years is ₹1,62,68,292.

Learning: In this project, the total discounted present value of the benefits of the waste management program is ₹9,55,92,701, which exceeds the total discounted present value of the costs, which is ₹8,50,55,630. This suggests that the waste management project would be a viable and economically beneficial option for the urban area.

Simulation Game 6.2

Forecasting by Delphi Technique

Rivot Motors is designing, developing, and building ultra-long-range electric scooters. They are trying to bring a change to the fear of range anxiety among perspective consumers and no quick or super-fast recharging technology. The company is claiming their scooters can reach a range of 200 KM, but the cost of the same will still start at the same price as that of a petrol version, and will still be able to get refueled/recharged at a refueling station just like how a petrol vehicle is done currently. Rivot Motors is planning to develop electric cars. One of the founders Ajit Patil has consulted Mr. Venkatesh Patil an expert to forecast the demand for electric cars in India for the next five years. Mr. Venkatesh Patil has suggested Mr. Ajit Patil use the Delphi method of forecasting the demand for electric cars in India by following the steps mentioned below:

1. **Select the panel of experts:** The company could select a panel of experts in the automotive industry, such as automotive engineers, economists, and market researchers.

2. **Distribute the first questionnaire:** The first questionnaire could contain questions such as: "What do you think will be the demand for electric cars in the next 5 years?" and "What factors do you think will influence the demand for electric cars?"

3. **Collect and analyze the responses**: The responses from the experts could be collected and analyzed to identify any trends or patterns in their opinions. For example, if a majority of the experts believe that the demand for electric cars will increase significantly

due to increased government support and declining battery costs, this information can be used to revise the questionnaire.

4. **Redistribute the questionnaire**: Based on the analysis of the first round of responses, the questionnaire can be revised and redistributed to the experts for a second round of responses. For example, the revised questionnaire could contain more specific questions about the factors influencing demand and the expected growth rate of electric cars.

5. **Repeat the process**: The process of collecting and analyzing responses can be repeated as many times as needed until a consensus forecast is reached.

6. **Aggregate the responses:** Finally, the responses from the experts can be aggregated and used to arrive at a consensus forecast for the demand for electric cars in the next 5 years. The consensus forecast could be presented in the form of a graph or table, showing the expected growth rate of electric cars over the next 5 years.

Learning: This is just an example of how the Delphi method could be used for forecasting. The method can be adapted to a variety of different forecasting scenarios, as long as a panel of experts can be selected and a questionnaire can be developed to gather their opinions.

Role Play 6.1

<u>**Selecting a Business Model for a Startup**</u>

Participants

1. **Arun** - Founder and CEO of the EdTech startup
2. **Saroj** - Chief Operating Officer (COO)
3. **Manju** - Chief Financial Officer (CFO)
4. **Leela** - Chief Marketing Officer (CMO)
5. **Dravid** - Chief Technology Officer (CTO)

[The scene is set in an incubation center at the Rajaram University. Arum, Saroj, Manju, Leela, and Dravid are seated around a table, with a whiteboard at one end for brainstorming.]

Arun: Alright, team, today's agenda is crucial. We need to nail down our business model for the startup. As you all know, this decision will shape the trajectory of our company.

Saroj: Absolutely, Arun. We've done some preliminary research on various business models, but we need to evaluate them thoroughly before making a decision.

Manju: I agree. Our financial projections will heavily depend on the chosen business model. We need to ensure it is profitable, scalable, and sustainable in the long run.

Leela: From a marketing perspective, we also need to consider how each business model aligns with our target audience and branding strategy.

Dravid: And as the CTO, I'm concerned about the technological implications of each model. We need a model that complements our technological capabilities and can be easily integrated into our systems.

Arun: Alright, let's dive in. The first business model on our list is the subscription-based model. It offers recurring revenue but may require a significant upfront investment in customer acquisition.

Saroj: That could work well if we're providing a valuable and ongoing service to our customers. But we also need to ensure our churn rate is low to maintain a steady stream of revenue.

Manju: Agreed. Let's crunch some numbers and see how the subscription model stacks up against our cost projections.

[Manju starts writing financial projections on the whiteboard while the rest of the team discusses the pros and cons of the subscription model.]

Leela: Another option we've considered is the freemium model. It allows us to attract a large user base with a free version of our product and then upsell premium features.

Dravid: From a technological standpoint, we need to make sure our platform can support both the free and premium versions seamlessly. We also need to consider how we'll entice users to upgrade to the premium tier.

Arun: That's a good point. Freemium could be a great way to drive user adoption while still generating revenue. Let's explore that option further.

[The team continues to brainstorm and evaluate different business models, including pay-per-use, licensing, and advertising-based models. They weigh the pros and cons of each model in terms of revenue potential, scalability, customer acquisition, and technological feasibility.]

Saroj: After considering all our options, I think we've narrowed it down to two promising models: subscription-based and freemium. Both offer their own set of advantages, but we need to make a final decision.

Manju: Agreed. Let's revisit our financial projections and market research to see which model aligns best with our goals and resources.

[Arun takes a moment to review the whiteboard, considering the input from each team member.]

Arun: Alright, everyone, based on our discussions and analysis, I believe the freemium model aligns best with our vision and capabilities. It allows us to capture a wide audience while still generating revenue through premium features.

Leela: I'm on board with that decision. I think it offers the best balance of attracting users and monetizing our product effectively.

Dravid: From a technological standpoint, I'm confident we can implement the freemium model seamlessly into our platform.

Manju: And financially, it looks like the freemium model offers solid growth potential without overextending our resources.

Saroj: It's settled then. Let's move forward with the freemium model for our startup. I'll start drafting the implementation plan, and we can reconvene next week to discuss the next steps.

[The team nods in agreement, feeling confident in their decision as they prepare to embark on the next phase of their startup journey.]

Project 6.1

Academic Entrepreneurship Incubator

Overview: The Academic Entrepreneurship Incubator project aims to establish a platform within academic institutions to foster entrepreneurship among students, researchers, and faculty members. This initiative will provide resources, guidance, and support to individuals interested in commercializing their research findings or innovative ideas.

Objectives:

1. Create an environment conducive to entrepreneurship within the academic institution.
2. Support researchers and students in identifying commercialization opportunities for their intellectual property.
3. Provide mentorship and guidance from experienced entrepreneurs and industry professionals.
4. Facilitate networking opportunities with potential investors, industry partners, and mentors.
5. Offer access to funding resources and grants to support the development and commercialization of innovative ideas.
6. Develop entrepreneurship-focused curriculum and workshops to educate and train students and researchers.
7. Establish partnerships with local industries, startup incubators, and government agencies to leverage additional resources and support.

Project Components:

1. **Needs Assessment**: Conduct surveys and interviews to understand the current entrepreneurial ecosystem within the academic institution and identify the needs and challenges faced by potential entrepreneurs.

2. **Resource Development**: Develop a comprehensive set of resources including business plan templates, intellectual property protection guidelines, market research tools, and funding databases.

3. **Mentorship Program**: Recruit experienced entrepreneurs, industry experts, and alumni to serve as mentors and advisors for aspiring entrepreneurs. Organize networking events, workshops, and one-on-one mentorship sessions.

4. **Funding Opportunities**: Research and compile a list of funding opportunities including grants, fellowships, and competitions available for academic entrepreneurs. Guide writing grant proposals and navigating the funding application process.

5. **Curriculum Development**: Collaborate with academic departments to integrate entrepreneurship education into existing courses or develop standalone courses focused on topics such as innovation management, technology commercialization, and startup entrepreneurship.

6. **Incubation Space**: Establish a physical or virtual incubation space equipped with office facilities, meeting rooms, and prototyping labs where entrepreneurs can collaborate, brainstorm ideas, and work on their projects.

7. **Evaluation and Monitoring**: Implement mechanisms to track the progress and success of entrepreneurial ventures supported by the incubator. Collect feedback from participants to continuously improve and refine the program.

Expected Outcomes:

- Increased number of startups and spin-off companies launched by students and faculty members.

- Growth of an entrepreneurial culture within the academic institution.
- Enhanced collaboration between academia and industry leading to technology transfer and commercialization.
- Development of a pipeline of skilled entrepreneurs and innovators contributing to economic development and job creation.

By implementing the Academic Entrepreneurship Incubator project, academic institutions can empower their students and researchers to transform their ideas into successful ventures, thereby fostering innovation and driving economic impact.

Quick Case 6.1

"Smart Home Solutions: From Garage Startup to Indian Unicorn"

Abstract: This case study follows the journey of SmartHome Solutions, a tech startup based in Bangalore, India. Founded in 2015 by a group of young entrepreneurs, SmartHome Solutions disrupted the Indian market with its innovative home automation technology, ultimately achieving unicorn status. The study explores the challenges faced, strategies employed, and key milestones achieved by the company.

Introduction: The Indian startup ecosystem has witnessed remarkable growth in recent years, with several ventures achieving unicorn status. SmartHome Solutions emerged as a prominent player in this landscape, leveraging technology to address the burgeoning demand for smart home solutions in India.

Background: SmartHome Solutions was founded by four graduates from premier Indian Institutes of Technology (IITs) who shared a vision of making home automation accessible to the masses. Drawing inspiration from global trends and local market insights, they embarked on their entrepreneurial journey.

Idea Generation and Validation: The founders conducted extensive market research to validate the demand for smart home solutions in India.

They identified a growing trend of urbanization and increasing disposable income among the middle class, leading to a heightened interest in home automation. This insight formed the basis of their business idea.

Product Development and Launch: SmartHome Solutions developed its flagship product, "SmartLiving," a comprehensive home automation system designed to enhance convenience, security, and energy efficiency. The product underwent multiple iterations based on feedback from beta testers and early adopters before its official launch in 2016.

Initial Challenges and Pivot: Despite a promising start, SmartHome Solutions faced challenges such as funding constraints and market competition. In response, the founders pivoted towards a subscription-based model, offering tiered pricing plans with varying levels of features and services. This strategic shift enabled them to generate recurring revenue and enhance customer loyalty.

Scaling and Growth: SmartHome Solutions adopted a multi-pronged approach to scale its operations and expand its market reach. The company forged strategic partnerships with real estate developers, home builders, and retail chains to integrate SmartLiving into new construction projects and retail outlets. Additionally, targeted marketing campaigns were launched to raise brand awareness and acquire customers.

Achieving Unicorn Status: By 2020, SmartHome Solutions had established itself as a market leader in the home automation industry. Its innovative product offerings, coupled with aggressive expansion strategies, attracted significant interest from investors. In a Series D funding round led by prominent venture capital firms, SmartHome Solutions secured $100 million, propelling its valuation to over $1 billion and earning unicorn status.

Conclusion: The case of SmartHome Solutions illustrates the transformative journey of a startup from ideation to unicorn status in the Indian startup ecosystem. Through innovation, strategic pivots, and relentless execution, the founders navigated challenges and capitalized on opportunities, positioning the company as a trailblazer in the smart home industry.

Case Questions

1. What were the key market insights that drove the founders' decision to enter the smart home industry in India?
2. How did SmartHome Solutions validate the demand for its product, and what role did customer feedback play in shaping its development?
3. Discuss the implications of SmartHome Solutions' pivot towards a subscription-based model. How did this decision impact the company's revenue stream and customer engagement?
4. Evaluate the effectiveness of SmartHome Solutions' scaling strategies, including its partnerships and marketing initiatives, in driving growth and market expansion.
5. Analyze the significance of SmartHome Solutions achieving unicorn status. What are the opportunities and challenges associated with being a unicorn startup in the Indian market?

Discussion Questions

1. What factors should entrepreneurs consider when evaluating the feasibility of a business idea?
2. How does the concept of a Minimum Viable Product (MVP) contribute to the success of a startup?
3. Discuss the key components of the Lean Business Model Canvas and their significance in developing a startup.
4. What are the different types of business models commonly employed by e-commerce ventures, and how do they differ?
5. Compare and contrast subscription-based and freemium business models. What are their respective advantages and challenges?
6. How do marketplace platforms operate, and what strategies can they employ to achieve sustainable growth?

7. Explain the concept of an asset-light business model and provide examples of industries where it is commonly utilized.

8. What are the key steps involved in capital raising for startups, and what factors do investors consider when evaluating investment opportunities?

9. Discuss the importance of the core team in the success of a startup. What qualities should founders look for when building their team?

10. What are the different types of business entities available to entrepreneurs, and how do they differ in terms of liability, taxation, and governance?

11. Compare and contrast various methods of financial statement analysis, including balance sheets, profit and loss accounts, and cash flow statements.

12. Explain the concept of the working capital cycle and its significance in managing a company's liquidity and operational efficiency.

13. Discuss the importance of forecasting in business planning and decision-making. What are some common forecasting techniques?

14. Compare and contrast organic growth and inorganic growth strategies. When is each strategy most appropriate for a startup?

15. What are the key considerations when expanding a business through diversification or modernization initiatives?

16. Discuss the role of mergers and acquisitions, joint ventures, and strategic alliances in business expansion and market consolidation.

17. Explain the process of licensing agreements and how they can be utilized to monetize intellectual property assets.

18. What are the benefits and challenges associated with private equity investments for startups?

19. Discuss the role of strategic partnerships and franchising in expanding a business's reach and market presence.

20. How can AI tools and technologies be leveraged by startups to enhance efficiency, innovation, and competitiveness in today's market landscape?

References

1. Berk, J., & DeMarzo, P. (2016). Corporate Finance. Pearson Education.

2. Blank, S. G. (2013). The Lean Startup: How Today's Entrepreneurs Use Continuous Innovation to Create Radically Successful Businesses. Crown Business.

3. Brealey, R. A., Myers, S. C., & Allen, F. (2017). Principles of Corporate Finance. McGraw-Hill Education.

4. Brigham, E. F., & Ehrhardt, M. C. (2013). Financial Management: Theory & Practice. Cengage Learning.

5. Burns, P. (2016). Entrepreneurship and Small Business. Palgrave Macmillan.

6. Chandra, P. (2019). Projects: Planning, Analysis, Financing, Implementation, and Review. Tata McGraw-Hill Education.

7. Christensen, C. M. (2013). The Innovator's Dilemma: When New Technologies Cause Great Firms to Fail. Harvard Business Review Press.

8. Datar, S. M., & Rajan, M. V. (2019). Financial Management: Text, Problems and Cases. Vikas Publishing House.

9. Eisenmann, T. R. (2013). Managing Partner at Benchmark Capital and Faculty Co-Chair of the HBS Rock Center for Entrepreneurship. Harvard Business Review.

10. Gitman, L. J., & Zutter, C. J. (2014). Principles of Managerial Finance. Pearson Education.

11. Hoffman, R., & Yeh, C. (2018). Blitzscaling: The Lightning-Fast Path to Building Massively Valuable Companies. Currency.

12. Hsieh, T. (2010). Delivering Happiness: A Path to Profits, Passion, and Purpose. Grand Central Publishing.

13. Khandelwal, P. (2018). The Future of Finance: How Private Equity and Venture Capital will Shape the Global Economy. Penguin Random House India.

14. Osterwalder, A., & Pigneur, Y. (2010). Business Model Generation: A Handbook for Visionaries, Game Changers, and Challengers. John Wiley & Sons.

15. Palepu, K. G., Healy, P. M., & Peek, E. (2013). Business Analysis and Valuation: Using Financial Statements. Cengage Learning.

16. Porter, M. E. (2008). The Five Competitive Forces That Shape Strategy. Harvard Business Review, 86(1), 25–40.

17. Rajan, R. G., & Zingales, L. (1998). Financial Dependence and Growth. American Economic Review, 88(3), 559–586.

18. Ries, E. (2011). The Lean Startup: How Today's Entrepreneurs Use Continuous Innovation to Create Radically Successful Businesses. Crown Publishing Group.

19. Ross, S. A., Westerfield, R. W., & Jordan, B. D. (2016). Essentials of Corporate Finance. McGraw-Hill Education.

20. Van Horne, J. C., & Wachowicz, J. M. (2013). Fundamentals of Financial Management. Pearson Education.

WORKSHEETS